KEATS AND THE
MIRROR OF ART

Oxford University Press, Ely House, London W. 1

GLASGOW NEW YORK TORONTO MELBOURNE WELLINGTON
CAPE TOWN SALISBURY IBADAN NAIROBI LUSAKA ADDIS ABABA
BOMBAY CALCUTTA MADRAS KARACHI LAHORE DACCA
KUALA LUMPUR HONG KONG TOKYO

POUSSIN: The Realm of Flora

IAN JACK

Keats and the Mirror of Art

To live over people's lives is nothing unless
we live over their perceptions, live over the
growth, the change, the varying intensity of
the same—since it was *by* these things they
themselves lived

HENRY JAMES

OXFORD
AT THE CLARENDON PRESS
1967

15114

FOR
MARGARET DALZIEL
AND ALL MY
NEW ZEALAND FRIENDS

PREFACE

I BEGAN this book in 1957, as the result of a chance discovery. The interest taken in the project by Professor Mario Praz, the first person—apart from my wife—with whom I had an opportunity of discussing it, gave me the encouragement to continue. Soon, however, I found that what had been planned as an essay was going to turn into a book, and I was obliged to postpone further work until I had completed my more general study, *English Literature 1815–1832*. Not long after my return to Keats I was honoured by an invitation to deliver the de Carle Lectures for 1964 in the University of Otago, and chose 'Keats and the Visual Arts' as the title for the series. The dedication of this book is intended as a record of my gratitude to Dr. Margaret Dalziel and the other friends who made my visit to New Zealand so enjoyable. It is (to me) a pleasant coincidence that Mr. D. M. Davin, of the Clarendon Press, and Dr. J. B. Trapp, of the Warburg Institute, are also New Zealanders. On this as on other occasions Mr. Davin has done a great deal to make the business of publishing a book more human and less frustrating; while Dr. Trapp has been extraordinarily generous with his time and knowledge. When I reached the Warburg Institute, and found the word *MNHMOΣYNH* inscribed above the door, I realized that I might at last be on the way to a deeper understanding of Keats. But without the kindness and tolerance of Dr. Trapp and other art-historians I would not have dared to venture so far into unkown territory.

So many scholars have helped me at various times that I can thank only a few. Professor Jean Hagstrum and Professor Moelwyn Merchant encouraged me early in my work. Dr. Peter Murray, of the Courtauld Institute, introduced me to that astonishing storehouse, the Witt Library of reproductions; and he has constantly been at hand to answer my questions. On all matters relating to Poussin I have been able to rely on the authority of Sir Anthony Blunt. Professor Edmund Blunden has been particularly helpful in supplying missing references to the voluminous writings of Leigh Hunt. Mr. Derek Halfpenny aided my search for a Wedgwood original for the 'Grecian Urn'.

Miss Aileen Ward and Mr. Robert Gittings have allowed me to draw on their unrivalled knowledge of Keats's life and circumstances. Professor Willard Pope's edition of *The Diary of Benjamin Robert Haydon* has been constantly on my desk.

Mr. D. S. Bland, whose article on 'Poussin and English Literature' I read with the greatest interest, has answered several inquiries, as have Signora Vera Cacciatore, Professor Margaret Whinney, Dr. Fred J. Cummings, Dr. Alastair Fowler, and Mr. David Irwin. Mr. B. D. H. Miller has come to my assistance more than once. Dr. Donald Strong and Dr. A. F. Shore, of the British Museum, have helped me in my search for that elusive sphinx. Signora Mariaclotilde Magni, Dr. Calabri, and Professor Limentani have advised me about the frescoes from 'the Church at Milan' the name of which Keats so inconveniently forgot. The Master of St. Cross, Mr. R. N. Quirk, Mr. Peter Guy, and Mr. Thomas Schuller have been similarly helpful in the matter of the 'interresting picture of Albert Durers' that Keats reported seeing at Winchester. Other inquiries have been answered by Miss Sandra Raphael, Professor R. M. Cook, Brother Francis McCarthy, Mr. Thomas Balston, Professor Leon Edel, Mr. Cecil Gould, and Mr. Jack Gold. Mr. Croft-Murray and his staff in the Print Room of the British Museum have been most helpful. Mr. Roy Park read and criticized the chapter on Hazlitt. Not the least kindness was that of Mrs. Peggy Martin, who sold me her set of the *Galerie du Musée de France* at a nominal price—just when I needed it most.

So much has been written about Keats in the last decade or two that I have made no attempt to indicate every point of agreement or disagreement with other critics. I hope it will not be supposed that I am ignorant of all the essays and articles that find no place in my notes. I make no reference (for example) to the penetrating discussion of the 'Ode on a Grecian Urn' in *The Well-Wrought Urn* by Professor Cleanth Brooks. The notes are already too long: further references would merely have made the book unwieldy.

I am indebted to the Editor of the *Times Literary Supplement* for permission to reprint a short passage in Chapter VII. The text-illustration on page 110 is based on a photograph by Mr. Christopher Oxford of a letter in Keats House, Hampstead.

Acknowledgements for permission to reproduce the works of art in the other illustrations are recorded at the end of the List of Plates.

And finally I wish to thank my wife, whose advice and encouragement have been indispensable.

I. J.

Pembroke College, Cambridge
1 June 1966

CONTENTS

LIST OF PLATES

ACKNOWLEDGEMENTS

Plates XVI, XIX, and XXVI are reproduced by gracious permission of
Her Majesty the Queen. Plates IV and VI are by permission of Her Majesty
and the Keeper of the Victoria and Albert Museum. Acknowledgements
for the photographs on which the other Plates are based are due to the
following: Alinari (XXVII–XXVIII); The British Museum (Frontispiece,
I, VII–VIII, IX(*d*), XI–XII, XX–XXI, XXIX, XXXIII–XXXVI, XLI;
the Louvre (XXIV, XXXI, XXXVII, XL); the Warburg Institute
(V, XVII, XXV); the Courtauld Institute (X, XXXIX); the Victoria
and Albert Museum (IX(*a*) and IX(*b*)); the Athenaeum of Ohio (II); the
Fogg Museum of Art (IX(*c*)); Lord Ellesmere and the National Gallery
of Scotland (XIV); The National Gallery, London (XIII); Mr. Thomas
Balston (XXII); Southampton Art Gallery (XXIII); the Keats–Shelley
Memorial House, Rome (XXX); Professor Frederick Hartt and
Yale University Press (XXXVIII); The Pennsylvania Academy of the
Fine Arts (III).

It will be noticed that as a rule I have reproduced contemporary engravings rather than the original paintings, where the latter could not have
been available to Keats.

INTRODUCTION

A Question is the best beacon towards a little Speculation.
KEATS[1]

T H E origin of this book was my discovery that a key-passage in
'Sleep and Poetry', the early poem in which Keats outlined his
poetic ambitions, had been suggested by a painting of Poussin's.
I began to wonder whether there were many other passages in
his poetry which had a similar background; but when I turned
to the detailed studies by Amy Lowell, Middleton Murry, H. W.
Garrod, and C. L. Finney, I found hardly a reference to such a
possibility.[2] I know now that if I had pursued my inquiries into
slightly older books, or into articles in periodicals, I would have
come on some further information;[3] but instead I went straight
back to the evidence provided by Keats's friends and contemporaries. I found that most of them had been men who were
keenly interested in painting and sculpture, and that they had
frequently commented on the visual quality of his imagination.
It began to seem possible that an important part of the truth
about Keats had for some reason been forgotten. I remembered
the saying that stands at the top of this page, and decided to try to
answer for myself the question how deeply the poetry of Keats
was indebted for inspiration to the visual arts.

The fact that the 'Ode to a Nightingale' and the 'Ode on a
Grecian Urn' were both first published in a periodical called
Annals of the Fine Arts provided an excellent starting-point. It
did not take long to discover that this was the first quarterly ever
devoted to the visual arts in England, that it ran from 1816 to
1820—so spanning the whole of Keats's brief creative career—
and that his friend Haydon had not only been its chief contributor but also its editor in all but name. I began to realize that
there had been an extraordinary ferment of excitement about
painting and sculpture in England at this time. Three of the five
volumes of the *Annals* have a most significant epigraph from
Jonathan Richardson the Elder:

b

I am no prophet, nor the son of a prophet; but I will venture to predict, that if ever the ancient, great and beautiful taste in painting revives, it will be in England.[4]

Keats and his friends were disposed to believe that Richardson's observation was in fact prophetic. Benjamin West, the American who became President of the Royal Academy after the death of Sir Joshua Reynolds in 1791, summed the matter up in one of his *Discourses*:

In no age of the world have the arts been carried in any country to such a summit as they now hold among us, in so short a period as half a century . . . . If . . . the British School has risen so . . . speedily . . ., what should hinder her professors from becoming the most distinguished rivals of the fame acquired by the Greeks and Italians . . . ?[5]

Even those who attacked the Academy, like Haydon himself, agreed that its establishment in 1768 had marked the beginning of this revival, and hardly anyone dissented from the view that Reynolds had been the Moses who had led English painters towards their Promised Land. He was a major painter, closer to the 'grand style' of the Italian masters than the gifted Hogarth: his wide culture and his worldly success (epitomized by his friendship with Johnson and his acceptability at Court) had raised the status of the painter in England, much as Garrick had raised the status of the actor: while in his *Discourses* he had not only written a volume of advice for aspiring painters, but also provided a reasoned account of painting for those who wished to learn something about the visual arts and so increase the range of their general culture.

When a contributor to the *Annals* stated that 'we have done wonders . . . during the fifty years in which art has been revived in this country',[6] therefore, he was merely echoing a common belief. It does not matter that such a claim must seem to us today to be exaggerated; nor does it matter that the true successes of English art in this period lay in directions very different from that of Haydon's 'heroic painting'—in the work of men as various as Blake and Constable, Wilkie and Turner, Cotman and Bewick and Samuel Palmer. What does matter is that as Keats grew to manhood there was a feeling in the air that English art was poised on the threshold of a great new era.

Yet it was not of English artists that I was most often reminded, as I read and reread Keats's poetry, but rather of Titian, of Claude, and of Poussin. This raised a serious difficulty. It would clearly be absurd to claim that Keats had been influenced by a painting unless I could show that it was probable that either the original or a reproduction had been accessible to him. Since he did not travel abroad until he went to Italy to die, it seemed at first unlikely that his acquaintance with great pictures could have been as extensive as I was tempted to believe. But once again the *Annals* provided decisive evidence. From its pages I began to learn something of the remarkable circulation and celebrity of many of the world's greatest pictures at this time. I came to realize that the formation of the vast collection in the Louvre that was known as the 'Musée Napoléon' should be recognized as one of the most important events in the cultural history of modern Europe.[7] At the Peace of Amiens, in the spring of 1802, a great many English people made their way to Paris to see this extraordinary accumulation. Artists and writers were prominent among a host that included Charles James Fox, John Kemble, Benjamin West, Fuseli, Flaxman, Turner, Samuel Rogers, Maria Edgeworth, and Fanny Burney. Fortunately for us Hazlitt was one of the visitors, and it is he who described the Louvre most unforgettably:

I marched delighted through a quarter of a mile of the proudest efforts of the mind of man, a whole creation of genius, a universe of art! I ran the gauntlet of all the schools from the bottom to the top . . . . Reader, 'if thou has not seen the Louvre, thou art damned!'—for thou hast not seen the choicest remains of the works of art; or thou hast not seen all these together, with their mutually reflected glories . . . . Here, for four months together, I strolled and studied . . . . How often, thou tenantless mansion of godlike magnificence—how often has my heart since gone a pilgrimage to thee![8]

In his *Notes of a Journey through France and Italy* Hazlitt makes it clear that the Louvre haunted his thoughts for the rest of his life, from the moment of his first astonished visit:

There was one chamber of the brain (at least) which I had only to unlock and be master of boundless wealth—a treasure-house of pure thoughts and cherished recollections. Tyranny could not master, barbarism slunk from it; vice could not pollute, folly could not gainsay it. I had but to touch a certain spring, and lo! on the walls the divine grace of Guido appeared free from blemish—there were the golden hues of Titian, and Raphael's speaking faces, the splendour of Rubens, the gorgeous gloom of Rembrandt, the airy elegance of Vandyke, and

Claude's classic scenes lapped the senses in Elysium, and Poussin breathed the spirit of antiquity over them.[9]

Although the formation of the 'Musée Napoléon' was the greatest and most obvious result of the French Revolution in the realm of art, it was only one of its results. As a consequence of the rapacity of Napoleon the world's great paintings became a centre of excited attention. Many of the great collections were split up or dispersed: paintings were bought and sold, and travelled from one country to another, far more frequently than before. The attitude of the English collector and dealer was summed up by a certain William Buchanan, who wrote a book called *Memoirs of Painting, with a chronological history of The Importation of Pictures by the Great Masters into England since the French Revolution.* His motto is from Rousseau:

La chûte du trône de Constantin porta dans l'Italie les débris de l'ancienne Grèce; la France s'enrichit à son tour de ces précieuses dépouilles.[10]

While Buchanan could afford to draw a parallel between the dispersal of works of art in this period and the dispersal of classical manuscripts after the fall of Constantinople, it is hardly surprising that many practising painters were less conscious of excitement at the possibility of a pictorial Renaissance than of anxiety that English painting might be overlooked altogether in the wild rush to purchase the 'black masters'. In 1805, for example, we find Martin Arthur Shee complaining, in his *Rhymes on Art; or, The Remonstrance of a Painter,* that nowadays 'the painter gives way to the picture-dealer':

Our arts . . . have experienced the fate which was denounced against our liberties—they have been invaded from every port upon the continent,—overrun by a posse of picture-dealers . . . . The superior wealth of this country, and the almost incredible prices paid here for some celebrated collections, set in motion the trading tribes of Taste in every corner of Europe; a general rummage took place for our gratification. . . . He was more than an unlucky traveller who could not turn his tour to account, and pick up a Titian, or a Correggio on his road.[11]

Others, like Benjamin West, took a more favourable view of the process. He used to say that 'next to the merit of having painted a picture which should do honour to the art . . . was the credit of having brought from foreign countries works of the great masters'.[12] Nor was it only paintings that were brought to England: at no other time have our collections been enriched with such masterpieces of sculpture. As a writer in the *Annals* acknowledged in the year in which Keats wrote his Odes, 'the present English government has certainly done great things by the purchase of the Townley, the Elgin and the Phigaleian marbles'.[13]

What happened was not merely that a remarkable number of outstanding works of art were brought to England at this time: it was also that works of art were made available to a wider public than they had been in the past. In the eighteenth century (after all) England had been rich in the work of Claude and Poussin, Hogarth and Reynolds; but most of their paintings had remained in the 'cabinets' of private collectors, readily accessible only to their owners and their friends.[14] Unlike the establishment of the Louvre, the change in England was not the result of a social revolution. On the contrary, a number of enlightened aristocrats were prominent among the founders of the British Institution, the association which destroyed the monopoly of the Royal Academy and introduced an annual exhibition of paintings by the Old Masters at which Keats and his friends were to be frequent and enthusiastic visitors.[15] Some of the same men began to open their own collections to painters and other interested members of the general public. Among them were Thomas Hope, the Marquis of Stafford, and Sir John Leicester, whose gallery Keats visited one day in 1819.[16]

The opening of these private galleries to a wider public on certain days of the week was the beginning of the process that led to the establishment of the National Gallery in 1824,[17] but it is important to realize that in Keats's time a visit to the Stafford Titians (for example) was still felt to be something of a privilege. Before the Angerstein pictures became the property of the nation people did not visit them—as many do today— simply to escape for a few moments from the noise of the London traffic.[18] Visitors still had the sense that they were visiting works of genius (and of great value) which one particular man had chosen to collect because of their beauty and because he delighted in looking at them.

In spite of this new generosity on the part of the wealthy collectors, it remained almost as true as it had been in the previous century that the majority of the world's greatest paintings were to be found abroad. It does not follow, however, that they were completely unknown in this country. In the days before the invention of photography the art of the engraver made it possible for the masterpieces of painting to be known throughout the civilized world, and there can be little doubt that the practice of print-collecting grew greatly in popularity about the turn of the century. It became common to publish books of engravings of the pictures in particular collections. For this reason we can readily turn to reproductions of the principal works in the Stafford Gallery, the Leicester Gallery, the Angerstein Gallery —and above all the Musée Napoléon.[19]

Print-collecting may seem remote from poetry, but one has only to turn to the writings of Keats's friends to find that it did not seem so to them. Soon after coming on a dogmatic statement that the publication of Lessing's *Laokoon* in 1766 had put an end to the old idea that Poetry and Painting were Sister Arts, I was lucky enough to chance on a passage in Leigh Hunt's neglected book, *Imagination and Fancy*. It occurs in the section entitled 'A Gallery of Pictures from Spenser':

> It has been a whim of late years with some transcendental critics, in the excess of the reaction of what may be called spiritual poetry against material, to deny utterly the old family relationship between poetry and painting. They seem to think, that because Darwin absurdly pronounced nothing to be poetry which could not be painted, they had only to avail themselves of the spiritual superiority of the art of the poet, and assert the contrary extreme . . . . But to say . . . that the poet does not include the painter in his more visible creations, is to deprive him of half his privileges, nay, of half of his very poems. Thousands of images start out of the *canvass* of his pages to laugh at the assertion. Where did the great Italian painters get half of the most bodily details of their subjects but out of the poets? and what becomes of a thousand landscapes, portraits, colours, lights and shades, groupings, effects, intentional and artistical pictures, in the writings of all the poets inclusive, the greatest especially? [20]

So Leigh Hunt wrote in the year 1844. It was because critics a hundred years later were no less disposed to 'deny . . . the old family relationship between poetry and painting' that the discovery of so many 'pictures' in the poetry of Keats had come as such a surprise to me.

The arrangement of the following chapters needs little explanation. I begin by considering the views on the visual arts expressed by the members of Keats's inner circle of friends, and then proceed by way of his own letters to a study of his poetry, from the *Poems* of 1817 to *The Fall of Hyperion* and the 'Ode to Autumn'.

I

THE DILETTANTE: LEIGH HUNT

'Tis well you think me truly one of those,
Whose sense discerns the loveliness of things.
HUNT: 'To John Keats', 1818

'THE busy time has just gone by', Keats wrote on the 9th of October 1816, 'and I can now devote any time you may mention to the pleasure of seeing Mʳ Hunt—'t will be an Era in my existence.' For some months Leigh Hunt was to be Keats's guide to the world of nature and the world of books, to the delights of the visible universe and the enjoyments of the intellect. A better guide at such a time could hardly be imagined. As all Hunt's writings testify, he was a man with an extraordinary gift for enjoyment. He was aware of this himself, and refers more than once to 'that . . . tendency to reap pleasure from every object in creation'[1] which was his natural endowment. As he remarked in his *Autobiography*, he was

of a temperament easily solaced in mind, and as easily drowsed in body; quick to enjoy every object in creation, everything in nature and in art, every sight, every sound, every book, picture, and flower, and at the same time really qualified to do nothing, but . . . to preach the enjoyment of those objects in modes derived from his own particular nature and breeding.[2]

We have the best possible evidence that at first he 'preached' his enjoyment of pictures (among other things) to a willing audience as he talked with Keats. In 'Sleep and Poetry' it is clearly Hunt whom Keats has in mind when he says:

Thus I remember all the pleasant flow
Of words at opening a portfolio.

In some ways Keats and Leigh Hunt were very like each other. This makes it all the more interesting to notice that Hunt first learned about Greek mythology from the same sort of books as Keats. Hunt tells us that there were three books which he was

particularly fond of when he was at school, and which often got
him into trouble: Tooke's *Pantheon*,[3] Lemprière's *Classical Dictionary*, and Spence's *Polymetis*:

> Tooke was a prodigious favourite with us. I see before me, as
> vividly now as ever, his Mars and Apollo, his Venus and Aurora, which
> I was continually trying to copy; the Mars, coming on furiously in his
> car; Apollo, with his radiant head, in the midst of shades and fountains;
> Aurora with hers, a golden dawn; and Venus, very handsome, we
> thought, and not looking too modest in 'a slight cymar'. It is curious
> how completely the graces of the Pagan theology overcame with us
> the wise cautions and reproofs that were set against it in the pages
> of Mr. Tooke.[4]

The boys used to identify the pretty girls who lived about the
school 'with the picture of Venus in Tooke's *Pantheon*'.[5] The
habit of visualizing mythological beings remained with Hunt to
the end of his life. He tells us elsewhere in his *Autobiography*
that the *Parnaso Italiano*, a collection of the principal Italian
poets,

> aided Spenser himself in filling my English walks with visions of gods
> and nymphs—of enchantresses and magicians; for the reader might be
> surprised to know to what a literal extent such was the case. I suspect
> I had far more sights of 'Proteus coming from the sea', than Mr.
> Wordsworth himself.[6]

'Gods and nymphs—enchantresses and magicians': the value
to a poet of such imaginary creatures was a topic to which Hunt
returned time and again in his criticism. And to him no mythology
seemed so compelling as that of the Greeks:

> Every forest, to the mind's eye of a Greek, was haunted with
> superior intelligences. Every stream had it's presiding nymph, who
> was thanked for the draught of water. Every house had it's protecting
> gods, which had blessed the inmate's ancestors; and which would bless
> him also, if he cultivated the social affections: for the same word
> which expressed piety towards the Gods, expressed love towards
> relations and friends. . . . Imagine the feelings with which an ancient
> believer must have gone by the oracular oaks of Dodona, or the calm
> groves of the Eumenides, or the fountain where Proserpine vanished
> under ground with Pluto; or the Great Temple of the Mysteries at
> Eleusis; or the laurelled mountain Parnassus, on the side of which was
> the temple of Delphi, where Apollo was supposed to be present in
> person.[7]

The fact that Hunt could read Greek and Latin must have been one of the many things about him that Keats admired. Keats must have been all the more struck by the way in which a man who was able to frequent the writings of Homer and Virgil and Ovid whenever he pleased insisted on the importance of pictures to illustrate their poetry.

Hunt's background helps to account for this. All his life he had been closely associated with artists. Benjamin West was his uncle. When Hunt's parents were hard up during his boyhood they stayed with the Wests, whose house in Newman Street, with its gallery full of paintings and works of sculpture, made a deep impression on him:

> It runs a good way back from the street, crossing a small garden, and opening into loftier rooms on the other side of it. We remember how the world used to seem shut out from us, the moment the street door was closed, and we began stepping down those long carpeted aisles of pictures, with statues in the angles where they turned. . . . It was the statues that impressed us, still more than the pictures. It seemed as if Venus and Apollo waited our turning at the corners; and there they were,—always the same, placid and intuitive, more human and bodily than the paintings, yet too divine to be over-real. It is to that house . . . that we owe the greatest part of our love for what is Italian and belongs to the fine arts.[8]

It must have been from West that Hunt picked up much of his first information about the visual arts—about which he was to know a great deal, in an unsystematic way, by the time of his maturity. He tells us that West 'would talk of his art all day long, painting all the while'.[9] When Hunt recalled West's house, in later life, it was usually the sculpture that came to his mind first, with its 'tranquil, intent beauty':[10] as he finely remarks, 'there is a sort of presence in sculpture, more than in any other representations of art'.[11] But he was also impressed by many of the painter's own pictures, mentioning particularly, in his *Autobiography*, 'Death on the Pale Horse', 'The Deluge', 'The Scotch King hunting the Stag', 'Moses on Mount Sinai', a sketch of 'Christ healing the Sick', 'Sir Philip Sidney giving up the Water to the Dying Soldier', 'The Installation of the Knights of the Garter', and 'Ophelia before the King and Queen'. Hunt's mother 'was in the habit of stopping to look at some of the pictures . . . with a countenance quite awe-stricken', and used to point out to him 'the subjects relating to liberty and patriotism, and the domestic affections', such as 'Agrippina bringing home the ashes of Germanicus' and 'the Angel slaying the Army of Sennacherib'—'a bright figure lording it in the air, with a chaos of human beings below.'[12] Apart from West's own paintings, his house was full of drawings and prints. The parlour, a room which so delighted Hunt that in his own study he seems to have tried to recapture something of the same atmosphere, looked into a garden which 'had an Italian look':

> The room was hung with engravings and coloured prints. Among them was the Lion Hunt, from Rubens; the Hierarchy with the God-head, from Raphael . . .; and two screens by the fireside, containing prints (from Angelica Kauffmann, I think, but I am not sure that Mr. West himself was not the designer) of the Loves of Angelica and Medoro.[13]

By a strange chance Hunt found himself passing the house a short time after West's death in 1820, when the contents were being sold off. The door stood open, and he went in:

> There was the privileged study, which we used to enter between the Venus de Medicis and the Apollo of the Vatican. They were gone, like their mythology. Beauty and intellect were no longer waiting on each side of the door. . . . [In another room] huddled up in a corner, were the busts and statues which had given us a hundred thoughts.

He could not bring himself to look into the parlour, where he had grown up among 'the divine humanities of Raphael'.[14]

Much of this description of West's house comes from *The Indicator*. No one who dips into this or any other of the periodicals which form a running commentary on his life and opinions can be left in any doubt of Leigh Hunt's unflagging interest in the visual arts. His elder brother Robert had been apprenticed to an engraver, and although he was an artist 'utterly devoid of any natural talent',[15] throughout his life he continued to paint and to provide art-criticism for his brother's journals. *The Examiner*, which was described by a contemporary as 'this Sunday Paper, which pays more attention to art, and in a more spirited manner, than any other Political Journal',[16] printed a good deal of his work. Since *The Examiner* was generally of the *avant garde* in art, as in other matters, it is ironical that the most celebrated piece of art criticism which it contains should be an attack on 'Mr. Blake's Exhibition' by Robert Hunt in the issue for the 17th of September 1809. This article, in which Blake is described as 'an unfortunate lunatic, whose personal inoffensiveness secures him from confinement',[17] is of value only as a reminder that the Right has no exclusive claim to critical wrong-headedness. Blake's portrayal of Chaucer's pilgrims is contrasted with Stothard's 'admirable picture of the same subject . . ., from which an exquisite print is forthcoming from the hand of Schiavonetti', and he is counselled to study the 'hues, forms, and expressions of passion' in Haydon's 'Death of Dentatus'. Haydon's painting is often referred to, while he himself contributes on such subjects as the need for patronage of the arts by the Government and the Church, the Cartoons of Raphael, and the Elgin Marbles, to which 'divine things' (as he affirms) 'I owe every principle of Art I may possess'.[18] In his Diary he claims that this passage had a tremendous influence in the country as a whole—which we must doubt—and adds—which seems more likely—that it had a bad effect on his own chances of finding patronage. In 1817 he launches one of the bitter attacks on the Royal Academy that were later to become so familiar in the *Annals of the Fine Arts.*

Painting and sculpture were also among the 'Liberal Arts' dealt with in *The Reflector*, the quarterly magazine which Hunt edited and largely wrote from October 1810 to December 1811. In the Prospectus he suggests that whereas the drama in England 'is in it's second infancy with all the vices of a frivolous dotage', 'the *Fine Arts* . . . are in their first infancy and must be handled more tenderly'. He opposes Winckelmann's wholesale condemnation of English art and points out that 'his assertion has been disproved, in the best way, by the reputations of *Reynolds, Barry, Wilson,* and *West,* the Fathers of the English school of painting', insisting that 'every thing calls upon their successors to finish the structure'. This conviction that a great tomorrow was awaiting English painting was characteristic of the society in which Keats was soon to find himself: it is expressed in *The Reflector* in an essay 'On the Spirit proper for a Young Artist', which opens with the words: 'The arts are now rising into greater notice every day'.[19] A much longer piece, 'Remarks on the Past and Present State of the Arts in England', repeats that 'the subject is beginning to excite a general interest' and points out that there has been 'very little either good or distinterested [criticism] upon our Artists'—perhaps because such criticism as has been written has been the work of artists themselves and has been marked by an inevitable bias. Hunt presents himself as an amateur, keenly interested in the arts but without any claim to be an expert:

The writer . . . attempts to estimate [Art] in no other way than by the general standard of poetry, music, and other works of genius; that is to say, by its invention, it's harmonious agreement, and it's nature. . . . [This] may be of use . . . as a small help to persons of cultivated minds who would easily blend a love of painting and sculpture with that of the other liberal arts already established in this country.[20]

As Haydon noticed, Hunt 'relished and felt Art without knowing anything of its technicalities'.[21] Hunt's criticism—therefore—was of just the sort that was most likely to appeal to Keats. 'Criticism of this kind' (Hunt continues)

does not pretend to instruct the painter in the process of his art, to decide between the merits of strata and substrata, of oils and of my-gylphs,—or indeed to assume any tone of pictorial learning. It's whole endeavour is to try the artist upon the general principles of taste, and to interest the general taste in favour of the artist; to suggest to the one the best means of exciting a public feeling for art, and to prepare this feeling, as much as possible, by familiarizing people with the contemplation of art: in a word, to do what little it can towards giving painting and sculpture their due share in the social honours of poetry, and making them current in books, in discourse, and in general admiration.[22]

Hunt comments on a number of the principal living painters. He has some interesting remarks on Fuseli (on whom he often wrote elsewhere), saying that he possesses great powers, but is apt to give himself 'indolently up to a cheap and perishing eccentricity'. He particularly censures 'his appalling designs for Chalmers's Shakspeare, and for the octavo edition of Cowper,—a series of outrages upon the human form', accusing him of producing 'men with scarcely any body, their wrists sprained, fingers jerked out like an idiot's, and legs stretched to a horrible tension, as if seized with the agonies of sudden cramp', and 'huge affected women with skewers through their hair, and without a particle of anything feminine'.[23] Hunt praises English architecture, and the sculpture of Flaxman—though he remarks that Flaxman tends 'to carry his love of the antique to an excess'. Haydon and Hilton are singled out as 'the two most promising of our young students'—this being before Haydon (as already mentioned) became more prominent and began contributing to *The Examiner*. The second issue contains a long letter 'On the Connection and the mutual Assistance of the Arts and Sciences, and the Relation of Poetry to them all'. The writer insists on the kinship of Poetry and Painting, quotes the passage from Cicero which had served as one of the mottoes of Spence's *Polymetis*,[24] and explains the significance of Apollo and Mnemosyne and of the 'beautiful . . . device of Cupid and Psyche'.[25] Another article, 'On the Responsibility of Members of Academies of Arts, and in Vindication of the late Professor Barry from the Aspersions of the Edinburgh Review', takes the form of a dialogue between Crito and Academicus, the latter speaking throughout in a parody of the style of Samuel Johnson. In the third issue we find Lamb's celebrated essay 'On the Genius and Character of Hogarth' and an interesting letter from 'Philographicus', 'On the Talents of Frey and Piranesi, considered with reference to the State of Italian Engraving in the Century which preceded them'.

A later periodical, *The Indicator*, which appeared between October 1819 and March 1821, is of particular interest to us because of its evidence of what was in Hunt's mind just after the period of his closest association with Keats. It was here that Keats's sonnet, 'A Dream, after reading Dante's episode of Paulo and Francesca', was first published—suitably enough, as this must have been a passage that he had discussed with Leigh Hunt, if he did not first come on it in his company. Here, too, full and generous treatment was given to Keats's great volume of 1820, sixteen pages being devoted to criticism and extract. And here we find the eloquent apostrophe to Keats on his leaving England to seek for health in Italy—a remarkable passage which particularly mentions his skill in metaphor.[26]

The importance of prints to Leigh Hunt and his friends could not be more clearly explained in a hundred pages than it is by one italicized word in the second number. It is autumn:

Here we are . . . with our fire before us, and our books on each side. What shall we do? Shall we take out a *Life* of somebody, or a

Theocritus, or Dante, or Ariosto, or Montaigne, or Marcus Aurelius, or Horace, or Shakspeare who includes them all? Or shall we *read* an engraving from Poussin or Raphael?[27]

The italics are Hunt's own: here we are taken straight into the circle which meant so much to Keats for a brief, memorable period. It was by learning to '*read*' prints in this way (we may conjecture) that Keats began his real education in the visual arts. A later issue of *The Indicator* contains a description of a print-seller's shop:

Of all shops in the streets, a print-seller's pleases us most. We would rather pay a shilling to Mr. Colnaghi of Cockspur-street, or Mr. Molteno of Pall-mall, to look at his windows on one of their best furnished days, than we would for many an exhibition. We can see fine engravings there,—translations from Raphael and Titian, which are newer than hundreds of originals.[28]

Keats, too, was a frequenter of the print-sellers, no doubt sometimes in Hunt's company. The same is probably true also of the sculptors' shops, of which we hear in the next issue:

Many persons are not aware that there are show-rooms in these places, which are well worth getting a sight of by some small purchase. For the best artistical casts, the Italian shops, such as Papera's in Marylebone-street, Golden-square, are, we believe, the best . . . Shout in Holborn seems to deal chiefly in modern things; but he has a room up stairs, full of casts from the antique, large and small, that amounts to an exhibition. Of all the shop pleasures, that are 'not inelegant', an hour or two passed in a place of this kind is surely one of the most polite. Here are the gods and heroes of old . . . the paternal majesty of Jupiter, the force and decision of Minerva, the still more arresting gentleness of Venus, the budding compactness of Hebe, the breathing inspiration of Apollo. Here the Celestial Venus, naked in heart and body, ties up her locks, her drapery hanging upon her lower limbs. Here the Belvidere Apollo, breathing forth his triumphant disdain, follows with an earnest eye the shaft that has killed the serpent. Here the Graces, linked in an affectionate group, meet you in the naked sincerity of their innocence and generosity, their hands 'open as day', and two advancing for one receding. Here Hercules, like the building of a man, looks down from his propping club as if half disdaining even that repose. There Mercury, with his light limbs, seems just to touch the ground, ready to give a start with his foot and be off again. . . . The Vatican Apollo . . . leans upon the stump of a tree, the hand which hangs upon it holding a bit of his lyre, the other arm thrown up over his head, as if he felt the air upon his body and heard it singing through the strings. In a corner on another side, is the Couching Venus of John of Bologna, shrinking just before she steps into the bath.[29]

We know that Hunt bought some of the casts that he so admired. In his 'Letter to Maria Gisborne' Shelley says of him:

> . . . His room no doubt
> Is still adorned with many a cast from Shout,
> With graceful flowers tastefully placed about;
> And coronals of bay from ribbons hung,
> And brighter wreaths in neat disorder hung. (212–16)

'Sleep and Poetry' makes it clear that Leigh Hunt's room, with its pictures and its casts, meant a great deal to the imagination of the young Keats,[30] and when in a sonnet he mentions 'Sweet Sappho's cheek'[31] as an object of delightful contemplation he may well be remembering a cast belonging to his friend. Like his uncle, Benjamin West, Hunt collected drawings: on the 25th of July 1815 Haydon records that he 'spent the Evening with Hunt looking over some of his finest drawings by Raphael, Michel Angelo, &c.'[32] When Leigh Hunt and his brother were imprisoned for political reasons Haydon, knowing their love of the visual arts, sent them 'Port-folios of Prints'.[33] Hunt had a flair for describing pictures, and more particularly sculpture—as in his description (quoted above) of Hercules as being 'like the building of a man'. It must have been partly from Hunt that Keats learned how to bring his personifications and his figures from Greek mythology so startlingly alive.[34]

Hunt's poems contain almost as much evidence of his interest in art as do his periodical writings. Edmund Blunden has pointed out the remarkable number of Royal Academicians among the subscribers to his *juvenilia*: apart from his uncle himself, they include George Stubbs, Fuseli, Thomas Lawrence, Beechey, Copley, Cosway, Downman, Hoppner, Stothard, Westall, and Bartolozzi, who gave an engraving for the book. Those of them who turned the pages found an ode, 'The Progress of Painting', devoid of poetical merit yet indicative of the young poet's interest in painting. It contains references to Raphael, Michelangelo, Correggio, and 'Titian's glowing hand', as well as to Barry, Fuseli, T. Kirk, R. K. Porter, and 'Britain's fav'rite West'. Later in life Hunt was to address sonnets to a number of artists, including Haydon, 'Fit to be numbered in succession due' to Raphael and Michelangelo, and Stothard, whose work he compares to that of

> . . . those southern masters fine,
> Whose pictured shapes like their own souls appear
> Reflected many a way in waters clear.

He also wrote a sonnet on an engraving of a self-portrait of Raphael in his youth. In prison he wrote sonnets on Hampstead which contain more than one touch reminiscent of painting. In one of them, for example, he describes

> The cold sky whitening through the wiry trees

in winter time, using the word 'paint' of his own description; while another, which begins with the line

> A steeple issuing from a leafy rise,

is aptly described by Blunden as a 'sonnet in water-colours'.[35] Hunt's friends and reviewers all comment on the pictorial and painterly handling of his pen, Haydon (for example) mentioning 'the intense painting of the scenery'[36] in *The Story of Rimini*. One reason for the superiority of the descriptions in that poem to the dramatic passages is that in the former Hunt was guided by his knowledge of painting. In his *Autobiography* he remarks that *The Story of Rimini* 'was written in what . . . I may perhaps be allowed, after the fashion of painters, to call my "first manner" '; while in the preface to the first edition of the poem he had acknowledged (among other debts) that he had taken one image from William Gilpin's *Remarks on Forest Scenery, and other Woodland Views*, and another from Poussin: 'Part of the description of the nymphs, in the third canto [comes] from Poussin's exquisite picture of Polyphemus piping on the mountain.'[37] Many kinds of painting appealed to Hunt, not least that in which goddesses and nymphs are portrayed in a landscape,

> Their white backs glistening through the myrtles green.[38]

In such passages the affinity with Keats is obvious. The same amorous imagination is at work in *The Nymphs*, which has been well described as 'Hunt's parallel to Keats's *Endymion*'.[39] 'How are the Nymphs?', Keats asks Hunt on the 10th of May 1817; 'I

wager you have given several new turns to the old saying "Now
the Maid was fair and pleasant to look on".' In all such passages
Hunt's descriptive technique reminds us of his intimacy with the
pictorial arts. That 'southern insight into the beauties of colour'
which he claims as characteristic of *The Story of Rimini*, and
particularly of 'the procession which is described in the first
canto'[40]—that surely owes a great deal to painting, and in
particular (perhaps) to the example of Titian.

In two of his critical essays Hunt emphasizes the fact that
Poetry and Painting are Sister Arts by citing particular passages
from Spenser and discussing which of the great painters could
most fittingly have illustrated them. Although both essays appeared long after the death of Keats they simply sum up what
Hunt had often said in conversation, and there can be little
doubt that Keats heard Hunt discussing Spenser and other poets
from this point of view. In the first essay, which appeared with
the title 'A New Gallery of Pictures' in the *New Monthly Magazine* for June 1833, Hunt reminds us of the old lady to whom
Pope read passages from Spenser and who told him that he had
been showing her a 'gallery of pictures'.[41] Hunt claims that
Spenser is the most pictorial of English poets,

the painter of the poets . . . the poet for the painters. . . . He is in the
habit of soothing his senses and delighting his eyes by painting pictures
as truly to be called such, as any that came from the hands of Titian
and Raphael. It is easy to show that he took a painter's as well as
poet's delight in colour and form, lingering over his work for its
corporeal and visible sake, studying contrasts and attitudes, touching
and re-touching, and filling in the minutest parts; in short, writing as
if with a brush instead of a pen, and dipping with conscious eyes into
a luxurious palette. Spenser's muse is dressed in the garments of a
sister who is only less divine than herself; and the union of the two
produces an enchantment, never perhaps to be perfectly met with
elsewhere.

He intends to extract some of the most 'masterly poetical pictures' from Spenser's work and so to demonstrate

that he includes in his singular genius the powers of the greatest and
most opposite masters of the art, of the Titians in colouring and classical gusto, the Rembrandts in light and shade, the Michael Ange-
los in grandeur of form and purpose, the Rubenses in gorgeousness,
the Guidos in grace, the Raphaels and Correggios in expression, and

the Claudes and Poussins, and even the homely Dutch painters, in landscape. . . . His naked women are equal to Titian's, his dressed to Guido's, his old seers to Michael Angelo's, his matrons and his pure maidenhood to Raphael's, his bacchanals to Nicholas Poussin's.

After assigning 'The Den of Error' to Rembrandt, 'for its light and shade', and another passage to Cuyp, Hunt quotes three stanzas from Spenser's description of 'The House of Morpheus', concluding:

> And, more to lulle him in his slumber soft,
> A trickling streame from high rock tumbling downe,
> *And ever-drizzling raine upon the loft,*
> *Mixt with a murmuring wind, much like the sowne*
> *Of swarming bees,* did cast him in a swowne.
> No other noyse, nor people's troublous cries,
> As still are wont t'annoy the walled towne,
> Might there be heard: *but careless quiet lies*
> *Wrapt in eternall silence, far from enemies.*
>
> (I. i. 41: Hunt's italics)

Hunt describes this as 'a picture for Nicholas Poussin—classical, dark, solemn, imaginative'. The description of 'Una in the Solitude', two stanzas ending with the lines—

> From her fair head her fillet she undight,
> And laid her stole aside: *her angel face,*
> *As the great eye of heaven, shined bright,*
> *And made a sunshine in the shady place;*
> Did never mortal eye behold such heavenly grace (I. iii. 4)

—is assigned to Correggio. Hunt discusses whether, in the lines which he italicizes, 'the poet intend[s] us to have [a] literal notion of the light, or to feel only the lustre of the sentiment', and decides that the last line means that the light is 'made manifest as a kind of saintly grace'. Since this passage may have been in Keats's mind when he described Madeline in *The Eve of St. Agnes*, it is interesting to notice that it is one of those which Hunt quotes again in the more elaborate 'Gallery of Pictures from Spenser' which he published in his book, *Imagination and Fancy*, in 1844. There he speculates whether 'it would take Raphael and Correggio united to paint this, on account of the exquisite *chiaroscuro*', commenting that the italicized lines 'are one of the most favourite quotations from the *Faerie Queene*'.[42]

In his earlier essay Hunt next quotes *The Faerie Queene*, I. v. 28–32, with the description 'Night and the Witch Duessa take the Body of Sansfoy to the House of Pluto', and recommends Giulio Romano to paint this 'picture of the supernatural . . . wonderfully fine and ghastly'. This passage too reappears in *Imagination and Fancy*: its description of 'Wicked Beauty' may conceivably have been in Keats's mind as he wrote the transformation scene in *Lamia*.

Hunt's next quotation is a celebrated stanza from Canto vii. He heads it:

THE CREST AND THE ALMOND-TREE.—Titian or Claude.

> Upon the top of all his lofty crest,
> A bunch of heares, discoloured diversly,
> *With sprincled pearl and gold full richly drest,*
> *Did shake, and seem'd to dance for jollity;*
> *Like to an almond-tree ymounted high*
> *On top of green Selinis all alone,*
> *With blossoms brave bedecked daintily;*
> *Whose tender locks do tremble every one*
> *At everie little breath that under heaven is blown.* (I. vii. 32)

When he wrote *Imagination and Fancy* Hunt had come to agree with Coleridge that this description, 'however charming, is not fit for a picture'.[43] The next passage in the earlier article also reappears in 1844. It is entitled 'A Landscape with Lightning', and Rubens is named as its illustrator. 'The rapidity, turbulence, and magnificence of this scene', Hunt comments, 'would have excited the highest powers of Rubens. We see the middle of the picture lit up with lightning, which, at the same moment, is rending the towers on some lofty hill, and breaking the necks of the old woods.' Of the description of Charity at I. x. 30–31, Hunt remarks:

The dispassionate aspect, the exceeding chastity, the one predominating colour, the babes, the diadem, and the formality of the ivory chair with the pair of turtledoves by it, point out a sympathy of treatment which cannot be missed by the connoisseur. . . . This figure . . . is exactly in the style of Raphael's allegorical portraitures, such as those of Temperance, Fortitude, &c.

Another passage also chosen in both essays is the description of Aurora at I. xi. 51:

The joyous day 'gan early to appeare,
And fair Aurora from the dewy bed
Of aged Tithone 'gan herself to reare
With rosy cheeks, *for shame as blushing red:*
Her golden locks, for haste, were loosely shed
About her eares, when Una did her marke
Climbe to her chariot, *all with flowers spread,*
From heaven high to chace the cheerless darke;
With merry note her loud salutes the mounting larke.

'This is a complete Titianesque painting', Hunt observes in his earlier essay. 'The chariot with the flowers would have admirably suited him; the sleeping, bearded, old man; the shame-faced goddess, whose blush mingles with her hair; and the lark beneath all, mounting up in the coolness of the nether atmosphere, ecstatic with the joy of another day. We see the picture before us, as if it were in the National Gallery.' This is the only passage decisively allotted to a different painter in the later essay, where the commentary reads as follows:

Character, Young and Genial Beauty, contrasted with Age,—the accessories full of the mixed warmth and chillness of morning: Painter, Guido.[44]

Spenser's description of Belphoebe, of which Hunt quotes four stanzas but we have room for only one, must have made a deep appeal to Keats:

Her yellow locks, crisped like golden wyre,
About her shoulders weren loosely shed;
And, when the winde amongst them did inspire,
They waved like a penon wyde dispred,
And low behind her backe were scattered:
And whether art it were or heedless hap,
As through the flouring forest rash she fled,
In her rude hairs sweet flowers themselves did lap,
And flourishing fresh leaves and blossoms did enwrap.

(ii. iii. 30)

'Her lily-white silken dress, sprinkled with golden points, and skirted with a golden fringe; her rosy-budding beauty; her locks of gold, and careless crown of flowers caught by her head as she went through the forest, would have taxed all the delicacy and richness of [Titian's] colouring', Hunt remarks. 'Can anything be more evident than the *pictorial* delight which Spenser took in drawing and colouring these pictures? Does he not dip his pen into a palette instead of an inkstand; look at each bit of colour as he takes it up with the relishing eye of an artist, and linger and brood over it as he lays it on?' The description of 'Furor bound by Sir Guyon' at II. iv. 15 first reminds Hunt of 'some quaint old fiery sketch of Giulio Romano', but he decides that Michelangelo would be its ideal illustrator; while 'The Cave of Mammon' (II. vii. 26–30) is predictably assigned to Rembrandt. 'The Black Garden', at II. vii. 52–53, moves Hunt to particular admiration:

Here is an unique piece of colour for a painter! The black, observe, is not entire black, but partly dark green, and tinged with poppy colour —a beautiful mixture; and we may suppose that the silver seat is itself partly shaded, and that the golden apples cast a further addition of colour among the flowers—an evening sunshine. It is the garden in which Proserpine used to take her melancholy recreation.

The garden should be painted by Titian, the figure of Proserpine by Michelangelo.

At III. vi. 17–19 Hunt points out 'a picture so completely in the style of Titian that one might have fancied him to have written it':

VENUS AND DIANA

Shortly unto the wastefull woods she came,
Whereas she found the goddess with her crew,
After late chace of their embrewed game,
Sitting beside a fountain in a rew;
Some of them washing with the liquid dew
From off their dainty limbs the dusty sweat
And soyle which did deform their lively hue;
Others lay shaded from the scorching heat;
The rest upon her person gave attendance great.

She, having hung upon a bough on high
Her bow and painted quiver, *had unlaste*
Her silver buskins from her nimble thigh,
And her *lanck loins* ungirt, and breasts unbraste;
After her heat the *breathing* cold to taste:
Her golden locks, that late in tresses bright
Embreaded were *for hindering of her haste*,
Now loose about her shoulders hung undight,
And were with sweet ambrosia all besprinckled light.

> Soon as she Venus saw behinde her back,
> She was ashamed to be so loose surprized,
> And woxe half wroth against her damsels slacke
> That had not her thereof before avized,
> But suffred her so carelessly disguized
> Be overtaken: *soon her garments loose*
> *Upgathering, in her bosome she compriz'd*
> *Well as she might, and to the goddess rose,*
> *Whiles all her nymphs did like a girlond her enclose.*

Hunt points out that Spenser has enriched the Ovidian original and comments that one may imagine the nymphs 'snatching up as well as they can their green and otherwise coloured garments, and crouching round their mistress, whose tall figure and severe beauty of countenance would admirably set off the smiling approach of the Goddess of Beauty'. In *Imagination and Fancy* he emphasizes the 'Contrast of Impassioned and Unimpassioned Beauty' in these stanzas, wonders whether 'Annibal Caracci would not better suit the demand for personal expression in this instance', but concludes (as Keats would have concluded) that 'the recollection of Titian's famous Bath of Diana is forced upon us'.[45]

Of Spenser's description of 'Proteus and Florimel' at III. viii. 35, Hunt comments: 'Another picture for the Caracci, or Raphael, or Giulio Romano. . . . The painter of the "Triumph of Galatea" [Raphael] would have hit to a nicety this picture of rugged, bearded manliness, kissing frightened beauty.' After some discussion, 'The Party at Table' (III. ix. 27–30) is allotted to Ludovico Caracci. But III. x. 44–45 is a passage of more relevance to Keats:

HELLENORE AMONG THE SATYRS—Nicholas Poussin

> . . . Close creeping as he might,
> He in a bush did hide his fearful head;
> The jolly Satyrs, full of fresh delight,
> Come dauncing forth, and with them nimbly led
> Faire Hellenore with girlands all bespredd,
> Whom their May-Lady they had newly made.
> She, proud of that new honour which they redd,
> And of their lovely fellowship full glad,
> Daunced lively, *and her face did with a laurel shade.*

The silly man that in the thicket lay
Saw all this goodly sport, and grievèd sore;
Yet durst he not against it do or say,
But did his heart with bitter thought *engore*,
To see the unkindness of his Hellenore.
All day they daunced with great lustyhed,
And with their hornèd feet the green grass wore,
The whiles their goats upon the brouzes fed,
Till drooping Phoebus 'gan to hide his golden head.

'Luxurious Abandonment to Mirth' is the description of these stanzas in *Imagination and Fancy*.[46] The last two quotations in the earlier essay are IV. v. 32–33, which Hunt describes as 'a Dutch painting in the style of the late Mr. Crabbe', and 'the celebrated vision of the shepherd piping to

A hundred naked maidens, lily white,
All ranged in a ring, and dancing in delight',

from the tenth Canto of Book VI. In the earlier essay he observes that 'the landscape in which the poet has put them would have been worthy of Claude'. In *Imagination and Fancy* Hunt quotes the whole of stanzas 10 to 14, with the title 'The Nymphs and Graces Dancing to a Shepherd's Pipe; or, Apotheosis of a Poet's Mistress' and the comment:

Character, Nakedness without Impudency; Multitudinous and Innocent Delight; Exaltation of the principal Person from Circumstances rather than her own Ideality.[47]

The ideal painter is Albano.

Like most prolific journalists, Hunt was apt to repeat himself over the years. But the fact that the 'Gallery of Pictures from Spenser' in *Imagination and Fancy* is simply a fuller and more elaborate essay on the same subject as his earlier article in the *New Monthly Magazine*, is of great importance as evidence of his lifelong belief in the relationship between poetry and painting. The opening sentences of this section of the book have already been quoted in the Introduction to the present study. Hunt then goes on to speculate once more that if Spenser 'had not been a great poet, he would have been a great painter', and makes the slightly absurd suggestion that if Spenser had been a painter 'England would have possessed, and in the person of one man, her Claude, her Annibal Caracci, her Correggio, her Titian, her Rembrandt, perhaps even her Raphael'.

The numerous passages which are cited in both of Hunt's essays are of particular interest because they are obviously favourite quotations which he is likely to have discussed with Keats. But several of the further passages first 'taken from the walls' of Spenser's gallery in 1844 also demand our attention. The first is Spenser's description of Hope (iii. xii. 13), which may well have interested the poet who was to be so notably successful in his own personifications of Joy and of Autumn. Hunt describes its 'character' as 'Sweetness without Devotedness; Painter, Correggio'. The description of 'Cupid usurping the Throne of Jupiter' (iii. xi. 35) is said to exhibit 'Potency in Weakness', and is assigned to Raphael. The 'Marriage Procession of the Thames and Medway' is a passage that must have appealed to Keats:

> First came great Neptune with his three-forked mace,
> That rules the seas and makes them rise or fall;
> *His dewy locks did drop with brine apace,*
> *Under his diadem imperial:*
> *And by his side his queen, with coronal,*
> *Fair Amphitrite, most divinely fair,*
> *Whose ivory shoulders weren covered all,*
> *As with a robe, with her own silver hair,*
> And deck'd with pearls which the Indian seas for her prepare.
>
> These marchèd far afore the other crew,
> And all the way before them as they went
> Triton his trumpet shrill before him blew,
> For goodly triumph and great jolliment,
> *That made the rocks to roar as they were rent.*   (iv. xi. 11–12)

'Character'—Hunt comments—'Genial Strength, Grace, and Luxury; Painter, Raphael'. Two passages about Maia are of significance because of Keats's fragmentary 'Ode to Maia, Written on May Day, 1818'. The first comes from *Prothalamion*:

JUPITER AND MAIA: Character, Young and Innocent but Conscious and Sensuous Beauty; Painter, Correggio.

> Behold how goodly fair my love does lie
>   *In proud humility!*
> Like unto Maia, when as Jove her took
> In Tempè, *lying on the flowery grass,*
> *'Twixt sleep and wake, after she weary was*
> *With bathing in the Acidalian brook.*

The second is from *The Faerie Queene*:

M A Y: Character, Budding Beauty in male and female; Animal Passion; Luminous Vernal colouring; Painter, Titian.

> Then came *fair May, the fairest maid* on ground,
> Deck'd all with dainties of her season's pride,
> *And throwing flowers out of her lap around:*
> Upon two brethren's shoulders she did ride,
> The Twins of Leda; which, on either side,
> Supported her *like to their sovereign queen.*
> *Lord! how all creatures laugh'd when her they spied,*
> *And leap'd and danc'd as they had ravish'd been;*
> *And Cupid's self about her flŭttĕr'd all in green.* (VII. vii. 34)

As Hunt remarks, 'Raphael would have delighted (but Titian's colours would be required) in the lovely and liberal uniformity of this picture,—the young goddess May supported aloft; the two brethren on each side; animals and flowers below; birds in the air, and Cupid streaming overhead in his green mantle. . . .'

A passage which may remind us of Keats's 'Ode to Psyche' is II. viii. 5: I give only the last stanza:

AN ANGEL, WITH A PILGRIM AND A FAINTING KNIGHT: Character, Active Superhuman Beauty, with the finest colouring and contrast; Painter, Titian.

> Beside his head there sat a fair young man,
> Of wondrous beauty and of freshest years,
> Whose tender bud to blossom new began,
> And flourish fair above his equal peers;
> *His snowy front, curlèd with golden hairs,*
> Like Phoebus' face adorn'd with sunny rays,
> Divinely shone; *and two sharp wingèd shears,*
> *Deckèd with diverse plumes, like painted jays,*
> Were deckèd at his back *to cut his airy ways.*

'The superhuman beauty of this angel should be Raphael's, yet the picture, as a whole, demands Titian. . . . As to the angel's body, no one could have painted it like him. . . . See a picture of Venus blinding Cupid, beautifully engraved by Sir Robert Strange, in which the Cupid has variegated wings.' Hunt then cites from *Epithalamion* the description of the bride at the altar —'Character, Flushed yet Lady-like Beauty, with ecstatic Angels regarding her; Painter, Guido'—and the passage about 'A

Nymph Bathing' from *The Faerie Queene*, ii. xii. 67–68—assigning her 'Ecstasy of Conscious and Luxurious Beauty' to Guido, and commenting that the last three lines are 'perhaps . . . the loveliest thing of the kind, mixing the sensual with the graceful, that ever was painted'—

> *Withal she laughèd, and she blush'd withal,*
> *That blushing to her laughter gave more grace,*
> *And laughter to her blushing.*

The 'character' of Spenser's Cave of Despair (i. ix. 33–36) is 'Savage and Forlorn Scenery, occupied by Squalid Misery; Painter, Salvator Rosa': the passage may well have been at the back of Keats's mind as he wrote the rejected opening stanza of his 'Ode to Melancholy' and even (perhaps) the description of Saturn at the beginning of *Hyperion*. The last passage that need be quoted is also Keatsian:

LANDSCAPE, WITH DAMSELS CONVEYING A WOUNDED SQUIRE ON HIS HORSE: Character, Select Southern Elegance, with an intimation of fine Architecture; Painter, Claude. (Yet 'mighty' woods hardly belong to him.)

> Into that forest far they thence him led,
> Where was their dwelling, in a pleasant glade
> With mountains round about environèd;
> And mighty woods which did the valley shade
> And like a stately theatre it made,
> Spreading itself into a spacious plain;
> And in the midst a little river play'd
> Amongst the pumy stones, which seem'd to plain
> With gentle murmur, that his course they did restrain.
>
>   (iii. v. 39)

The description of 'A fair pavilion, scarcely to be seen' in this 'dainty place', this 'earthly paradise', which we find in the following stanza, is very much in the spirit of Keats's *Poems* of 1817.

If I have seemed to dwell at inordinate length on two essays written long after the death of Keats, it is because I believe them to be of conclusive importance. These essays give us vital information about the 'long talk of poetry and painting'[48] which often kept Keats and his friends so long from their beds: 'making wings for the night', in Keats's phrase.[49] Such was the background, and such the inspiration, of the most revealing of all his early poems, 'Sleep and Poetry'. It is interesting to notice that a number of the passages which Keats marked in the volume of Spenser which he gave to his brother George correspond to passages assigned to particular painters by Leigh Hunt, while others are also remarkable for their pictorial quality.[50] Keats may well have heard Hunt lighting on some of the phrases which he was later to use in his articles—pointing out that 'looking through the leaves of Spenser is like turning over a portfolio of prints from the old masters' or insisting that 'his pages glow . . . like those of some gorgeous missal'.[51] In his essays Hunt refrains from discussing the Bower of Bliss, remarking that he would not know where to begin or end, and fearing that extracts 'might seem too particular and luxurious':[52] but in the company of his friends he would not have been deterred on either count. The 'Imitation of Spenser' in the *Poems* of 1817 is probably the earliest piece of poetry by Keats to survive, and in it he is obviously remembering the Bower of Bliss and attempting to paint in words in the most obvious sense.

Not quite in the most obvious sense, however: that was reserved for Hunt. In *The Keepsake* for 1828 he wrote as follows:

Did anybody ever think of painting a picture in writing? I mean literally so, marking the localities as in a map.

The other evening I sat in a landscape that would have enchanted Cuyp.

Scene—a broken heath, with hills in the distance. The immediate picture stood thus, the top and the bottom of it being nearly on a level in the perspective:

Trees in a sunset, at no great distance from the foreground.
A group of cattle under them, party-coloured,
principally red, standing on a small landing place;
the Sun coming upon them through the trees.

A rising ground   A rising ground
Broken ground
with trees.   with trees.

Another landing place, nearly on a level
with the cows, the spectator sitting and looking at them.

The Sun came warm and serious on the glowing red of the cattle, as if recognising their evening hues; and every thing appeared full of that quiet spirit of consciousness, with which Nature seems rewarded at the close of its day labours.[53]

Of course there was something a little obvious about Leigh Hunt himself. Keats—at least—came to think so, complaining that he expatiated and explained too much, spoiling things in the process: 'It is a great Pity that People should by associating themselves with the finest things, spoil them', he wrote to Haydon on the 21st of March 1818. '—Hunt has damned Hampstead and Masks and Sonnets and italian tales. . . .' At the end of the following year he wrote to George and Georgiana:

[Hunt] understands many a beautiful thing; but then, instead of giving other minds credit for the same degree of perception as he himself possesses—he begins an explanation in such a curious manner that our taste and self-love is offended continually. Hunt does one harm by making fine things petty and beautiful things hateful— Through him I am indifferent to Mozart, I care not for white Busts— and many a glorious thing when associated with him becomes a nothing —This . . . perplexes one in the standard of Beauty. ii. 11 (17 Dec. 1818.)

Long before this Keats had turned away to other friends and other guides. Yet Hunt had given Keats a great deal, and it is partly because of him that so many pages of Keats's poems, like so many of Spenser's, may fitly be described as 'walls glowing with life and colour'.[54] 'I suspect that if Spenser's history were better known', Hunt was to write in *Imagination and Fancy*, 'we should find that he was a passionate student of pictures, a haunter of the collections of his friends Essex and Leicester.'[55] We know enough about the history of Keats himself, that 'jealous honourer' of Spenser, to say that he too was a 'passionate student of pictures', and it is clear that one of the influences which helped to make him so was that of his early friend, Leigh Hunt.

II

THE PAINTER:
BENJAMIN ROBERT HAYDON

I have lived to see the triumph and the glory of these divine
productions! [the Elgin Marbles]. I have lived to see them
purchased by an English Parliament, and contributed by my
efforts towards influencing their purchase! I have lived to see
the nobility and the people of my own country, crowd to look
at and study the expressions of Raphael, and the graces of the
Elgin Marbles; all feeling for which they were totally denied!
and I shall yet live to see the triumph of English art, and the
fame and glory of English artists!

HAYDON in *Annals of the Fine Arts*, iv. 58–59

I T is easy to laugh at Haydon. He might have been born to
provide a subject for Max Beerbohm. 'This week has really
been a week of great delight', he wrote in his Diary on the
29th of April 1815. 'Never have I had such irresistible, perpetual, & continued urgings of future greatness. I have been like a
man with air balloons under his arm pits and ether in his
soul.'[1] 'What fire, what magic!' he could comment on his own
day's painting: 'I bow and am grateful.' 'The truest thing you
ever said of mortal', he once wrote to Keats, 'was that I had a
touch of Alexander in me!—I have, I know it, and the World
shall know it.'[2] He must be one of the few men who have ever
seriously considered putting up a brass plate in their own honour.
When in later life he revisited the room where he had painted
the picture which he considered his masterpiece, he was greatly
inclined to immortalize the house with a plaque reading: 'Here
Haydon painted his Solomon, 1813.' From time to time he seems
to have realized that enthusiasm was getting the better of him.
He explains how it came about that he proved 'unmanageable'
on one occasion by confessing that 'the idea of being a Luther or
John Knox in art got the better of my reason'.[3] But in fact a
jubilant sense of belonging to the immortals was his ordinary
state of mind: it is summed up by an exclamation in one of his
letters:

What a race the young Haydons would have been with the blood of Michael Angelo mingled with mine![4]

So little did he doubt the importance of his life and opinions that he recorded them in more than a million words contained in twenty-six vellum-bound folios—leaving instructions to his executors that they should be published in full: 'The style, the individuality of Richardson. . . . I wish not curtailed by an Editor.'[5] In the face of egotism on this scale the English are apt to feel embarrassed and resentful. If Haydon had been a great genius we would have had to accept it, however unwillingly: as he was not, we are inclined to consign him with relief to the uses of comedy.

Yet that would be unjust. Although Haydon was not a genius he was a remarkable and highly talented man, and it so happened that Keats met him when he seemed well on his way to the top of Fortune's wheel. 'This was the most glorious period of Haydon's life', as a writer in the *Annals of the Fine Arts* was later to comment. 'Haydon now, by general acknowledgement, was at the head of his art.'[6] Although the second statement was a gross exaggeration, of no other point in Haydon's life could such a statement be made at all. But in the winter of 1816–17 it would have taken a shrewd prophet to foretell that it was the young poet who was destined to be immortal, while the painter would be remembered only as a diarist and as the friend of men greater than himself. It is not surprising that Keats was as excited at the prospect of getting to know Haydon as he had been at the prospect of meeting Leigh Hunt: 'I will be as punctual as the Bee to the Clover'—he wrote to Cowden Clarke—'Very glad am I at the thoughts of seeing so soon this glorious Haydon and all his Creation.'[7] His first letter to Haydon was written three weeks later, and shows that Keats had in no way been disappointed:

My dear Sir—

Last Evening wrought me up, and I cannot forbear sending you the following—Your's unfeignedly John Keats—   (i. 117)

'The following' was the sonnet 'Great Spirits now on Earth are sojourning', with its enthusiastic references to Wordsworth, Leigh Hunt, and Haydon himself,

> . . . whose stedfastness would never take
> A Meaner Sound than Raphael's Whispering,

and its prophecy that by the work of such men the world will be renewed and given 'another heart And other pulses'.[8] Haydon took to Keats no less whole-heartedly than Keats had taken to Haydon. 'Keats is the only man I ever met with', he was soon to write in his Diary, 'who is conscious of a high call and is resolved to sacrifice his life to attain it, except Wordsworth, but Keats is more of my own age.'[9] He therefore acknowledged the sonnet enthusiastically, suggesting an alteration which Keats hastened to adopt, and mentioning that he would forward the poem to Wordsworth. A few weeks later Keats addressed to Haydon his two sonnets on the Elgin Marbles, and received a reply including the words: 'You filled me with fury for an hour, and with admiration for ever . . . God bless you.'[10] How close to each other the two men felt themselves to be at this time can best be shown by quoting the greater part of Haydon's next letter:

> Consider this letter a sacred secret—Often have I sat by my fire after a day's effort, as the dusk approached, and a gauzey veil seemed dimming all things—and mused on what I had done and with a burning glow on what I would do till filled with fury I have seen the faces of the mighty dead crowd into my room, and I have sunk down & prayed the great Spirit that I might be worthy to accompany those immortal beings in their immortal glories, and then I have seen each smile as it passed over me, and each shake his hand in awful encouragement— My dear Keats, the Friends who surrounded me, were sensible to what talent I had,—but no one reflected my enthusiasm with that burning ripeness of soul, my heart yearned for sympathy,—believe me from my Soul in you I have found one,—you add fire, when I am exhausted, & excite fury afresh—I offer my heart & intellect & experience . . . I have read your Sleep & Poetry—it is a flash of lightening that will sound men from their occupations, and keep them trembling for the crash of thunder that *will* follow—
> God bless you let our hearts be buried in each other
>
> > B R Haydon
>
> . . . I confide these feelings to your honor   (i. 124–5)

It is not surprising that 'Sleep and Poetry' made a deep impression on Haydon: few even of the poems of Keats contain so many references to painting. And while we read Haydon's letter with a sense of retrospective irony, to Keats it must have appeared in a very different light. He must have been proud to receive such a letter from such a man, a painter nine years his senior whom Fame seemed already to have taken by the shoulder. One of his letters opens with Berowne's speech from *Love's Labour's Lost*:

> Let Fame, which all hunt after in their Lives,
> Live register'd upon our brazen tombs . . .

and adds the comment: 'To think that I have no right to couple myself with you in this speech would be death to me.' The same letter ends with the valediction:

> So now in the Name of Shakespeare Raphael and all our Saints
> I commend you to the care of heaven!   (i. 145)

Ten months later, referring to the imminent appearance of *Endymion*, Keats playfully transposes it with the name of one of Haydon's first ambitious paintings: 'How does the Work go on? I should like to bring out my Dentatus at the time your Epic makes its appearance.'[11]

It is not surprising that Keats's talented publisher, John Taylor, should have suggested that Haydon should provide an illustration for *Endymion*, proposing (if he would) to publish the poem in quarto. Keats accordingly called on Haydon:

> He said he would do anything I liked, but said he would rather paint a finished picture, from it, which he seems eager to do; this in a year or two will be a glorious thing for us. . . . The next day [I] received a letter from him, proposing to make, as he says, with all his might, a finished chalk sketch of my head, to be engraved in the first style & put at the head of my Poem, saying at the same time he had never done the thing for any human being, & that it must have considerable effect.   (i. 213)

Keats quite agreed that Haydon should take his time—

> so much so that it would be as well to wait for a choice out of *Hyperion* —when that Poem is done there will be a wide range for you—in Endymion I think you may have many bits of the deep and sentimental cast—the nature of *Hyperion* will lead me to treat it in a more naked and grecian Manner . . . .   (i. 207)

The heroic *Hyperion* would be more congenial to Haydon than the sentimental *Endymion*. In the event Haydon did nothing, but the proposal had a strange aftermath. Ten years after the death of Keats Haydon dreamed about him:

I thought he appeared to me & said, 'Haydon, you promised to make a drawing of my head before I died, & you did not do it. Paint me now.' I awoke & saw him as distinctly as if it was his spirit. I am convinced such an impression on common minds would have been mistaken for a ghost. I lay awake for hours dwelling on his remembrance. Dear Keats! I will paint thee—worthily & poetically.[12]

At this point Haydon sketched Keats's profile in his Diary, but he did no more. Instead he continued to devote himself to his lifelong ambition of creating a worthy school of heroic painting in England.

A few months before his twenty-first birthday Haydon had knelt down, brush in hand, and prayed to God

to grant me energy to create a new era in art, and to rouse the people and patrons to a just estimate of the moral value of historical painting.[13]

All his friends knew of his ambition. On the 23rd of December 1818, for example, he wrote to Keats:

My great object is the public encouragement of historical painting and the glory of England, in high Art, to ensure these I would lay my head on the block this instant.   (i. 416)

It is one thing to be possessed by such an ambition if you are Raphael, another if you are Haydon. Here, as so often, it seems Haydon's fate to be a sort of parody of Renaissance Man, not Michelangelo but MacFlecknoe. Yet his ambition was of the most honourable kind—and the most orthodox. Modern critics of art are apt to be disconcerted by the theory of historical painting: they might find guidance in the Renaissance theory of epic poetry. Like an epic poem, an historical painting in the fullest sense must deal with a great action in a style of fitting grandeur. Its religious or moral scope and the profundity of its significance to human life will elevate it above all other kinds of painting, as an epic is raised above all other kinds of poetry. The terms in which Reynolds describes historical painting—a traditional misnomer, as he points out: it would be better to call it heroic painting—are close to those used by Imlac in *Rasselas* when he is explaining the business of the poet, while Imlac's words (in their turn) may owe something to Jonathan Richardson's account of historical painting in his *Essays on the Theory of Painting*.[14] As Reynolds emphasizes, the historical painter is not to concern himself with detailed truth to fact: 'Agesilaus was low, lame, and of a mean appearance: none of these defects ought to appear in a piece of which he is the hero.'[15] Like the epic poet, the historical painter should

raise the whole species and give them all imaginable beauty and grace. . . . Every several character, whether it be good or bad, amiable or detestable, must be stronger and more perfect. . . . A brave man . . . must be imagined more brave. . . . A villain must be conceived to have something more diabolical than is to be found amongst us.[16]

Since the subject of an historical painting should be of universal significance, the range of possibilities is strictly limited. Scripture, classical history, and mythology are the principal storehouses from which the painter may take his choice. When Haydon, like Milton before him, made a list of eligible subjects at the outset of his career, such subjects were very prominent: 'Adam reconciling Eve after her Dream', 'Joseph and Mary resting on the Road to Egypt', 'Samson pulling down the Philistines', 'The Spirit of Caesar appearing to Brutus', 'Antigone and her Mother and murdered Brother'. The importance attached to the choice of subject had consequences which are apt to disconcert the modern critic. A successful painting of a great subject must be regarded as a work of a higher kind than an equally successful painting of a 'mean' subject. So it happened that when Constable called on the President of the Royal Academy after his election, Sir Thomas Lawrence

did not conceal from his visitor that he considered him peculiarly fortunate in being chosen an Academician at a time when there were historical painters of great merit on the list of candidates. . . . The president, who attached great importance to subject, and considered high art to be inseparable from historical art . . . thought the painter of, what he considered, the humblest class of landscape was as much surprised at the honour just conferred on him, as he was himself.[17]

Lawrence was being traditional in his critical theory, just as Haydon was when he objected to Payne Knight's ranking of the paintings of Rembrandt with the masterpieces of historical art: 'You praise the pictures of Rembrandt, Sir', he wrote in the *Annals*, 'as all men praise such pictures who know they are in a lower rank, in spite of their wishes.'[18] While this view persisted it was inevitable that such a painter as David Wilkie, with his great gift for familiar painting, should also have attempted the more dignified 'historical painting'; yet no one today is likely to consider his 'Defence of Saragossa' as comparable in merit to 'The Blind Fiddler' or 'The Penny Wedding'. Haydon himself now seems of more account as the painter of 'Punch' and 'The Mock Election' than as the creator of 'Christ's Triumphant Entry into Jerusalem' and 'The Judgment of Solomon'. If he knew this, he would suppose that critics of art had gone mad.

Keats was by no means the only writer in Haydon's circle of friends. Writing of a period three years or so before he met Keats, Haydon tells us that 'the usual companions of [his] relaxation' included Hazlitt, Leigh Hunt and his brother, Charles Lamb, Thomas Barnes of *The Times*, and the ill-fated John Scott, who was to be editor of *The London Magazine* during its memorable years. 'In our meetings Hazlitt's croaking, Leigh Hunt's wit and Lamb's quaint incomprehensibilities made up rare scenes. Lamb stuttered his quaintness in snatches, like the fool in Lear, and with equal beauty; and Wilkie would chime in with his "Dear, dear".'[19] 'The daily contests with Hazlitt', he remarks elsewhere, 'with Leigh Hunt and with Wilkie, tended certainly to do my mind a great deal of good, for we all thought conclusively and differently on all subjects.'[20] A favourite topic of Haydon's on such occasions was the merits of the various poets, and the connexion between poetry and painting: in another place he tells us how at such meetings 'long talk of poetry and painting . . . opened our hearts'.[21] There was no affectation about his interest in literature. In 1826, when his perennial consumption of the purse obliged him to pawn his lay figures and his studies from the Elgin Marbles, he could not bring himself to pawn his favourite books:

I looked at Vasari, at Lanzi, at Homer, at Tasso, at Shakespeare, but my heart beat firm. The back of a Book containing the Works of celebrated Geniuses is enough to fill the mind, if you know the contents well, with crowds of associations. I kept them. I may do without a lay figure for a time, but not without old Homer. . . . The truth is, I am fonder of books than any thing else on Earth.[22]

He was in the habit of reading a passage of poetry to put him in the right mood to begin the day's painting. 'At this time', he writes of the year 1810, 'I devoted a great deal of time to Homer, Virgil, Dante and Æschylus, to tune my mind to make a fine picture of Macbeth.'[23] His literary taste is indicated by his proposal that he should be buried with Shakespeare on his heart, Homer, in his right hand, Ariosto in his left, Dante under his head, Tasso at his feet, Keats also in a position of honour, and Corneille, that 'heartless tirade-maker', in the reverse.[24] It was Haydon's copy of Chapman's *Homer* that inspired Keats's famous sonnet. His Diary is full of quotations, right up to the last tragic lines from *King Lear*. He never tired of pointing Keats to the model of Shakespeare:

> Go on, dont despair, collect in[cidents], study characters, read Shakespeare and trust in Providence.   (i. 135)

It was to Haydon that Keats wrote the passage that served Middleton Murry as a final quotation for his brilliant and sometimes misleading book, *Keats and Shakespeare*:

> I remember your saying that you had notions of a good Genius presiding over you—I have of late had the same thought. for things which [I] do half at Random are afterwards confirmed by my judgment in a dozen features of Propriety—Is it too daring to Fancy Shakspeare this Presider?   (i. 141–2)

I believe that Haydon's unwavering belief in epic painting helps to explain his censorious remark that Keats 'had no decision of character, had no object on which to direct his great powers':

> One day he was full of an epic Poem! another, epic poems were splendid impositions on the world! & never for two days did he know his own intentions.[25]

It is a strange reflection that while Keats had many doubts about the possibility of writing an epic poem in the nineteenth century, Haydon had no doubt of his own ability to produce a masterpiece of historical painting.

Haydon's whole career may be regarded as an ironical comment on his own belief that 'a man who has a fixed purpose to which he devotes his powers is invulnerable'. Just after recording that view in his Diary, he set down an account of an experience which gave rise to a rumour greatly to his disadvantage:

> I can to this day recollect a poor creature who saw her son dashed to pieces by a horse, near Temple Bar. Nothing could exceed her dreadful suffering. Her nose and cheeks became a settled purple, a burning tear hung fixed, without dropping, in her eyelid, her livid lips shook with agony, while she screamed and groaned with agitated hoarseness on

her dear boy. I was passing an hour afterwards: I heard her dreadful screams, which had now become incessant, till they died away from exhaustion into convulsive sighs. My heart beats at the recollection. I put her expression into the mother in Solomon.[26]

No doubt an inaccurate account of this incident lies behind a passage in the *London Magazine* for 1821:

> I was told the other day of a living artist who, when a child was run over by a cart before its own loved home, and the bankrupt mother stood rigid as stone, staring with maniac agony on her crushed darling, calmly and deliberately gazed on her 'to study the expression', as he called it!! I care not to know his name. My friend assured me, on his honour, that he did not belong to the Academy (I never imagined that he did); but let me take this opportunity to assure him that, as a man, I hold him in the most sovereign contempt, not to say detestation![27]

It is just the sort of story that would naturally have attached itself to Haydon. One notices that whereas, in his own account of the matter, he passed the scene an hour after the accident, and felt deep pity (he was naturally a compassionate man), the *London Magazine* writer describes him as present at the death of the child. Perhaps the strangest feature of the whole affair is that the writer of the article appears to have been Thomas Griffiths Wainewright, whose art criticism will be examined in Chapter V below, but who is better known as a forger and a murderer.

As an historical painter Haydon failed; but he did not fail in his other great enterprise, his championing of the authenticity and the unique value of the Elgin Marbles. The Marbles arrived in England in several shiploads between 1803 and 1812. At first there could be no question of a public display, but permission was granted to suitable people who wished to examine the sculptures, and it was with one of these privileged persons, his friend David Wilkie, that Haydon first came into the presence of the masterpieces that were to haunt his mind and govern his imagination for the remainder of his life. His career had reached a critical moment. He was labouring on his 'Death of Dentatus', as he tells us in his *Autobiography*, and could not decide between the evidence of his own eyes and the practice of the ancient sculptors:

> In my model I saw the back vary according to the action of the arms. In the antique these variations were not so apparent. Was

nature or the antique wrong? Why did not the difference of shape from difference of action appear so palpably in the antique as in nature? This puzzled me to death. If I copied what I saw in life, Fuseli said: 'This is too much like life'. If I copied the marble, Wilkie said: 'That looks as if you had painted from stone'.[28]

Then he came to the pent-house where the Marbles were temporarily stored:

The first thing I fixed my eyes on was the wrist of a figure in one of the female groups, in which were visible, though in a feminine form, the radius and ulna. I was astonished, for I had never seen them hinted at in any female wrist in the antique. I darted my eye to the elbow, and saw the outer condyle visibly affecting the shape as in nature. I saw that the arm was in repose and the soft parts in relaxation. That combination of nature and idea which I had felt was so much wanting for high art was here displayed to midday conviction.[29]

It was as great a discovery for Haydon as it had been for a writer of the previous century to find that Homer and Nature were the same. He felt that he had been right in his strivings from boyhood onwards:

Now was I mad for buying Albinus without a penny to pay for it? Now was I mad for lying on the floor hours together, copying its figures? I felt the future, I foretold that they would prove themselves the finest things on earth, that they would overturn the false beau-ideal, where nature was nothing, and would establish the true beau-ideal, of which nature alone is the basis.

I shall never forget the horses' heads—the feet in the metopes! I felt as if a divine truth had blazed inwardly upon my mind and I knew that they would at last rouse the art of Europe from its slumber in the darkness.[30]

The lesson that Haydon learned from the Elgin Marbles was to be summed up by Keats in the most-discussed line (perhaps) in the whole of the English poetry, a line that presents fewer problems if we remember its background in the theory of art, and particularly if we remember the art of sculpture as we read the familiar words:

Beauty is truth, truth beauty.

The terms in which Haydon repeatedly writes of his first experience of the Marbles remind us irresistibly of descriptions of religious conversion. 'All the varieties of action, all the great

I. A. ARCHER: The Temporary Elgin Room in 1819

(The figure at the extreme left, behind the Ilyssus, is Haydon. West is seated in the left foreground, with his left hand extended. The Theseus or Dionysus may be seen above the horse's head.)

truths of nature, flashed on his mind like a revelation from Heaven', as a writer in the *Annals* was to sum the matter up. 'He
felt instantly they would overturn every thing hitherto looked
up to as authority.'[31] It was a rediscovery, a renaissance:

> I drew at the marbles ten, fourteen, and fifteen hours at a time;
> staying often till twelve at night, holding a candle and my board in
> one hand and drawing with the other ... I ... pondered on the change
> of empires and thought that I had been contemplating what Socrates
> looked at and Plato saw.[32]

The imaginative effect of the Marbles was particularly great at
night. After a while Haydon used to bribe the porter at Burlington House, where they were moved to a temporary shed in 1811,
to allow him to come at night, with a lantern:

> As the light streamed across the room and died away into obscurity,
> there was something solemn and awful in the grand forms and heads
> and trunks and fragments of mighty temples and columns that lay
> scattered about in sublime insensibility—the remains, the only actual
> remains, of a mighty people. The grand back of the Theseus would
> come towering close to my eye and his broad shadow spread over the
> place a depth of mystery and awe.[33]

It is not to be supposed that the authenticity and merit of the
Marbles were at once universally acknowledged. Lord Elgin had
expected this to happen, but he, as Haydon comments, 'little
knew the political state of art'.[34] Established authorities and in-
stitutions for the promotion of arts and sciences are seldom swift
to welcome novelty, even novelty that has more than 2,000 years
of history behind it. Both the authenticity and the merit of the
sculptures were disputed—the two being usually considered different aspects of the same question. There was the further question of the morality of Elgin's action. Byron, whose lack of taste
in the fine arts contrasts sharply with the understanding shown
by Hazlitt, Leigh Hunt, and Keats, attacked Elgin and disputed
both the merit and the authenticity of the works:

> Let ABERDEEN and ELGIN still pursue
> The shade of fame through regions of Virtù;
> Waste useless thousands on their Phidian freaks,
> Misshapen monuments and maimed antiques;
> And make their grand saloons a general mart
> For all the mutilated blocks of art.[35]

'Lord Elgin', he wrote in his note on these lines, 'would fain persuade us that all the figures, with and without noses, in his stoneshop, are the work of Phidias! "Credat Judaeus!" ' While Byron played his part in popularizing the mistaken view, however, he would hardly have ventured to lead the way. The opposition to the Marbles was led by Richard Payne Knight, a well-known collector and connoisseur who had written a didactic poem called *The Landscape* and *An Analytical Inquiry into the Principles of Taste*. It is fitting that most people now remember Knight only as one of Peacock's satiric butts and for his celebrated remark, directed at Lord Elgin over the dinner table 'in a loud voice':

> You have lost your labour, my Lord Elgin; your marbles are over-rated; they are not Greek, they are Roman of the time of Hadrian.[36]

It is one of the celebrated *bêtises* of criticism, a remark that must often have made subsequent 'connoisseurs' pause and refrain from judgement.

While an admirably full account of Elgin's purchase of the Marbles and of the protracted negotiations which followed their arrival in England was published half a century ago,[37] less attention has been paid to the theoretical basis of the debate among the art critics of the time. The reactions of critics to a new fact are always interesting—the different attitudes they adopt as they survey the canvas, the poem, or the revolutionary musical score. When the novelty is of great age, and the required re-valuation retrospective, the struggle is greater, the entertainment and enlightenment to be derived by the observer correspondingly enhanced. What was at issue on this occasion was not merely the verdict to be pronounced on a new candidate for fame, but the validity of the critical principles on which the judges had based all their previous decisions. It was a test-case that might have been invented for the precise purpose of demonstrating what was still vital in the neo-classical approach, and what had fossilized with the years. An intelligent study of the whole affair would throw a great deal of light on the development of art criticism between the time of Reynolds and the time of Ruskin.[38]

It is difficult to estimate the importance of Haydon's passionate championship of the Marbles. While Haydon himself was not called upon to give evidence before the Select Committee, evidence in favour of the purchase was given by the President of the Royal Academy, Benjamin West, by Thomas Lawrence (who was destined to succeed him), and by the sculptors Nollekens, Flaxman, Westmacott, Chantrey, and Rossi, as well as by collectors and enthusiasts including Lord Aberdeen, Scott's friend J. B. S. Morritt, and Alexander Day. It seems likely that things would have taken the same course even if Haydon had never said or written a word. But what concerns us is Keats's view of the matter, and there can be little doubt that he regarded Haydon as the man who, after Lord Elgin himself, deserved the credit for persuading the nation to purchase the treasure. Keats says as much in the first of the two, disappointing, sonnets on the Marbles that he addressed to Haydon:

> For when men star'd at what was most divine
>   With browless idiotism—o'erwise phlegm—
> Thou hadst beheld the Hesperean shine
>   Of their star in the East, and gone to worship them.

It is worth quoting from Haydon's once-celebrated letter 'On the Judgment of Connoisseurs being preferred to that of Professional Men', a letter which was published in both *The Examiner* and *The Champion* in 1816:

It is this union of nature with ideal beauty,—the probabilities and accidents of bone, flesh, and tendon, from extension, flexion, compression, gravitation, action, or repose, that rank at once the Elgin Marbles above all other works of art in the world. The finest form that man ever imagined, or God ever created, must have been formed on these eternal principles. The Elgin Marbles will as completely overthrow the old antique, as ever one system of philosophy overthrew another more enlightened. Were the Elgin Marbles lost, there would be as great a gap in art as there would in philosophy if Newton had never existed. Let him that doubts it study them as I have done, for eight hours daily, and he will doubt it no longer. They have thrown into light principles which would only have been discovered by the inspiration of successive geniuses—if ever at all—because we had, what the Greeks had not, an antique and a system to mislead us, and misplaced veneration, and early habits to root out. In painting, on the same principles, they will completely annihilate that strange system, that colour, and light, and shadow, though a consequence of the nature of things, are incompatible with the expression of a refined passion and beautiful fancy, or a terrible conception by the imitation of natural objects; as if they were not more likely to detract from the intellect in either by being execrable, than by being consistent with the subject or expression displayed.[39]

To Payne Knight's remark that the Marbles are the work of the assistants of Pheidias, Haydon rejoins:

> I should wish to ask the most unskilful observer that ever looked at one of the friezes, or at a horse's leg, or a rider's arm, or even a horse's ear, in it,—what he thinks of such a modest assertion! Does Mr Knight remember that divine form in a metope, grappling a Centaur by the throat, and heaving up his chest, and drawing in his breast, preparing to annihilate his enemy:—or the one, in all the loosened relaxation of death under the Centaur's legs, who prances in triumph;—or the other, who presses forward, while he dashes back his opponent with tendinous vigour, as if lightning flashed through his frame?[40]

Haydon took Keats to see the Marbles on the 1st or 2nd of March 1817,[41] and he must have heard endless talk on the subject in Haydon's painting room. This was a favourite meeting-place for Haydon's friends, and we have Haydon's own word for it that Keats visited it 'at all times, and at all times was welcome'.[42] He was no doubt attracted by the same things that drew Hazlitt to Northcote's studio: a complete absence of stiffness and formality, an unfailing welcome, and 'endless topics of discourse'. 'Many men of genius were wont to meet' there, as Monckton Milnes points out, 'and, sitting before some picture on which he was engaged, [they would] criticise, argue, defend, attack, and quote their favourite writers. Keats used to call it "Making us wings for the night".'[43] There is no better account of the conversation there than in Haydon's own description of a memorable dinner party at the end of 1817:

> On December 28th the immortal dinner came off in my painting-room, with Jerusalem [Plate II] towering up behind us as a background. Wordsworth was in fine cue, and we had a glorious set-to—on Homer, Shakespeare, Milton and Virgil. Lamb got exceedingly merry and exquisitely witty; and his fun in the midst of Wordsworth's solemn intonations of oratory was like the sarcasm and wit of the fool in the intervals of Lear's passion.[44]

This was the occasion on which Lamb addressed Wordsworth as 'you old lake poet, you rascally poet' and asked him why he had called Voltaire dull, as well as berating Haydon for putting New-

11. HAYDON: Christ's Triumphal Entry into Jerusalem

'On December 28th the immortal dinner came off in my painting-room, with Jerusalem towering up behind us as a background.' ('The arrow points to the head of Keats: Wordsworth is immediately below him.)

ton into the painting—'a fellow who believed nothing unless
it was as clear as the three sides of a triangle'. Lamb and Keats
agreed that Newton 'had destroyed all the poetry of the rainbow
by reducing it to the prismatic colours' and led the company in a
toast—'Newton's health and confusion to mathematics'. No
doubt Keats remembered this conversation when he came to
write *Lamia*:

> . . . Do not all charms fly
> At the mere touch of cold philosophy?
> There was an awful rainbow once in heaven:
> We know her woof, her texture; she is given
> In the dull catalogue of common things.
> Philosophy will clip an Angel's wings,
> Conquer all mysteries by rule and line,
> Empty the haunted air, and gnomed mine—
> Unweave a rainbow, as it erewhile made
> The tender-person'd Lamia melt into a shade.
>
> (ii. 229–38)

'It was a night worthy of the Elizabethan age', Haydon commented, 'and my solemn Jerusalem flashing up by the flame of
the fire, with Christ hanging over us like a vision, all made up a
picture which will long glow upon

> "that inward eye
> Which is the bliss of solitude".'

There was one moment during the evening at which it would
have been particularly interesting to have looked over Keats's
shoulder. The comptroller of stamps who had so incongruously
imposed himself on the company said something more than
usually foolish—the remark which compelled Lamb to ask if he
might examine his 'phrenological development'. Haydon tells us
that Keats tried to disguise his amusement by 'put[ting] his
head into my books'. As it happens, we know what many of these
books were, for we can turn for information to the auctioneer's
catalogue of his *Paintings, Engravings and Books of Prints* as
they were sold on the 11th and 12th of June 1823, as a result of
one of his periodical bankruptcies. He owned a considerable
number of classical books and translations: a Folio Shakespeare
and the works of such standard English authors as Spenser, Milton, Jeremy Taylor (6 volumes), Burton, Johnson, and Boswell:
the principal periodical essayists and novelists of the eighteenth

century: the historical writings of Gibbon, Hume, Robertson, and Burnet: Adam Smith's *Theory of Moral Sentiments*, 'Scott's Visits to Paris', 'Aikin on Song Writing', 'Eustace's classical tour through Italy', 'Letters on England', and 'Pinkerton's Scotland'[45]: a considerable number of French and Italian books, including Rousseau's letters, a three-volume edition of Montesquieu, Ariosto's *Orlando Furioso*, a Petrarch, and two editions of Dante, one in four volumes. As one would expect, he owned a number of books by Wordsworth, Hazlitt, and Lamb, as well as long runs of *The Champion* and *The Examiner*. 'Chapman's Omer' also occurs in the list—a more intelligible misprint than many in this villainous piece of printing. Among his books on the fine arts we find the works of Barry and Mengs, *The Artist* by Prince Hoare, Northcote's *Life of Sir Joshua Reynolds*, a *Life of Poussin*, the lectures of Opie and Landseer, Belzoni's 'Researches', and 'Winkerman on Painting'.[46] He obviously kept his Vasari and his Lanzi, as he was to do again three years later, and one can hardly doubt that he also retained the huge folio of Albinus on Anatomy, for which as a boy he had paid fifty shillings that he did not possess. He may have been equally unwilling to part with his copy of 'John Bell on the Bones', with the engravings which he was for ever setting his pupils to copy. It is equally hard to imagine him parting with his copy of the *Discourses* of Sir Joshua Reynolds—a book which had had a decisive effect on his whole life:

> It placed so much reliance on honest industry, it expressed so strong a conviction that all men were equal and that application made the difference, that I fired up at once. I took [it] home and read [it] through before breakfast the next morning. The thing was done. I felt my destiny fixed. The spark which had for years lain struggling to blaze, now burst out for ever.[47]

It is possible that the books mattered less to Keats than the prints which were a feature of the room. Haydon's father was a bookseller in Plymouth, and an advertisement which he published during the painter's infancy proclaimed that he had recently collected from the leading London print-shops

> The most beautiful and elegant variety of ENGLISH and FOREIGN ENGRAVINGS ever seen in the West of England, from the following great masters, viz. Guido, Rembrandt, L. de Vinci, Raphael, S. Rosa,

Claude, Sir J. Reynolds, Bunbury, Cipriani, Gainsborough, Cosway, &c.[48]

Although Haydon did not like having engravings made of his own paintings—a fact to which he later attributed the oblivion which overtook his 'Solomon'—he depended heavily on prints for his knowledge of the work of the great Italian painters and sculptors, since he travelled very little.[49] We happen to know that the most successful historical painting of his career was inspired by a print which he saw in the British Museum. It told the story of Lazarus, but was 'in such a state that a place was left vacant where the head of Lazarus ought to be. My imagination filled the vacancy and I trembled at my terrific conception of the head.'[50] The result was his 'Raising of Lazarus', now in the Tate Gallery. We know as a fact that looking at books of prints made a powerful appeal to the imagination of Keats. In Chapter VI I shall discuss the identity of one such book, which he came on in Haydon's painting-room and which gave him 'a greater treat' than anything outside Shakespeare. We know from the auctioneer's catalogue that Haydon owned some hundreds of prints, many of them engravings after the work of Raphael, Giulio Romano, Michelangelo, Rubens, Titian, Claude, Poussin, Salvator Rosa, Dürer, Rembrandt, Wilkie, and Reynolds.[51] He also possessed quite a number of volumes of 'Books of Prints', including 'Prints from the Vatican, after Raphael', 'Lewis's scenery on the River Dart', and 'a volume of views in Rome' by Piranesi.

Keats must also have been familiar with many of Haydon's own sketches, and with some of the copies of Raphael's Cartoons drawn by pupils under his supervision. One of the achievements on which Haydon valued himself was his success in having two of the Cartoons—'The Miraculous Draught of Fishes' and 'Paul Preaching at Athens'—moved from Hampton Court to the British Gallery, so that he and his pupils might study and copy them at their leisure.[52] When Keats began to appreciate the Cartoons he felt that he was making some progress as a student of the visual arts.

On his visits to Haydon Keats must often have seen the numerous casts which he used as models and inspiration for the figures in his paintings. Haydon tells us how one night in 1809, full of his 'Macbeth':

I awoke and found myself standing in my cast-room, where I must have been a long time, half dead with cold, bewildered and staring at the head of Niobe. . . . The clock struck three and I became conscious I had been walking in my sleep.[53]

No doubt Haydon still possessed the first casts he had ever bought, the Apollo and the Discobolus, as well as 'the Laocoon's head, with some arms, hands and feet', which he purchased on his very first day in London.[54] He probably had one or two of Shout's admired casts—perhaps his reproduction of Canova's 'Hebe'.[55] He had a fine cast of a negro called Wilson, who was lucky to escape with his life when the cast was made.[56] But pride of place among his reproductions of sculpture went to his casts from the Elgin Marbles, notably the Theseus and the Ilyssus. He valued himself on having been the first man to make casts from the Parthenon frieze, and the year after the 'immortal dinner' he sent casts of the Marbles to the Imperial Academy of Arts in Russia and received in return a number of casts of works in Russia, notably 'the beautiful bust of Achilles'.[57]

And then there were Haydon's own paintings. As he had a passion for working on a canvas almost as large as his painting-room,[58] only one was likely to be there at a time; but we know from the letters that Keats saw four of his paintings—'The Death of Dentatus' (1808–9), 'The Judgment of Solomon' (1812–14), 'Christ's Triumphal Entry into Jerusalem' (1814–20), and 'The Raising of Lazarus' (1820–3). He must also have heard of 'Joseph and Mary resting on the Road to Egypt' (1806–7), 'Macbeth' (1809–11), and 'Romeo leaving Juliet at the Break of Day' (1810). At first, at least, there is no doubt that Keats greatly admired Haydon's work. In a neglected fragment of verse, the 'Castle Builder', Keats describes his ideal study, 'rich and sombre', furnished with

> A tambour-frame, with Venus sleeping there,
> All finish'd but some ringlets of her hair,

a skull to serve as a *memento mori*, a large mirror with the warning words 'Mene, Mene, Tekel-Upharsin' inscribed on it, ebony couches, and some self-consciously un-Grecian pottery:

> Greek busts and statuary have ever been
> Held, by the finest spirits, fitter far
> Than vase grotesque and Siamesian jar;

Therefore 'tis sure a want of Attic taste
That I should rather love a Gothic waste
Of eyesight on cinque-coloured potter's clay,
Than on the marble fairness of old Greece.

What about paintings? Keats answers explicitly:

My pictures all Salvator's, save a few
Of Titian's portraiture, and one, tho' new,
Of Haydon's in its fresh magnificence.

It is interesting to compare the taste exhibited in Keats's Castle
in Spain with that shown in Beckford's Fonthill and in later
imaginary studies. As one would expect, Keats is much closer to
Leigh Hunt and Wainewright than to Poe, whose pictures were
to be by Clarkson Stanfield and Chapman, and to be accompanied by 'three or four female heads . . . in the manner of Sully'.[59]
The 'Castle Builder' is undated, but there seems little reason to
dispute the usual conjecture that it was written early in 1818.[60]
As Keats's understanding of painting developed he is likely to
have become less impressed by Salvator Rosa. The fact that
Keats only wants one Haydon is not, as Amy Lowell supposed,
evidence of a diminished admiration, but rather a sign that even
in his dreams Keats could not imagine himself the owner of a
room large enough to contain two of his friend's enormous can-
vasses.

There is a particularly interesting allusion to Haydon and
heroic painting in a letter written in April 1818, the very time
at which Keats seems likely to have composed the 'Castle
Builder'. It refers to 'Christ's Triumphal Entry into Jerusalem':

I am nearer myself to hear your Christ is being tinted into immortality—Believe me Haydon your picture is a part of myself—I
have ever been too sensible of the labyrinthian path to eminence in
Art (judging from Poetry) ever to think I understood the emphasis
of Painting. The innumerable compositions and decompositions which
take place between the intellect and its thousand materials before it
arrives at that trembling delicate and snail-horn perception of Beauty—
I know not you[r] many havens of intenseness—nor ever can know
them[61]—but for this I hope [nought] you atchieve is lost upon me: for
when a Schoolboy the abstract Idea I had of an heroic painting—was
what I cannot describe, I saw it somewhat sideways large prominent
round and colour'd with magnificence—somewhat like the feel I have
of Anthony and Cleopatra. Or of Alcibiades, leaning on his Crimson

Couch in his Galley, his broad shoulders imperceptibly heaving with the Sea—What passage in Shakspeare is finer than this

'See how the surly Warwick mans the Wall'.   (i. 264–5)

That passage was written by a man with a powerfully visual imagination.

Haydon noticed this characteristic right away, and was always urging Keats to nourish his imagination on paintings, works of sculpture, faces and attitudes, and above all on the scenes of external nature. As one reads his letters to Keats one is reminded of Reynolds urging the young painter to 'lay . . . in proper materials, at all times, and in all places'. 'I cannot help imagining'—Reynolds goes on—'that I see a promising young painter, equally vigilant, whether at home, or abroad, in the streets, or in the fields. Every object that presents itself, is to him a lesson. He regards all Nature with a view to his profession; and combines her beauties, or corrects her defects.'[62] In the same spirit Haydon wrote to Keats in March 1818:

> Surely you will not leave Devonshire without going to Plymouth the country round which is most exquisite. . . . Stay till the Summer, and then bask in its deep blue summer Sky, and lush grass, & tawny banks, and silver bubbling rivers—you must not leave Devonshire without seeing some of its Scenery rocky, mossy, craggy with roaring rivers & as clear as crystal—it will do your mind good. (i. 257–8)

For the sake of his brother Tom, Keats had to leave Devonshire, but he assured Haydon that he was soon going on a walking tour in the north, 'to make a sort of Prologue to the sort of life I intend to pursue' and to get himself 'an accumulation of stupendous recollections'.[63] A few weeks later Haydon wrote that he was longing to hear an account of this tour, adding significantly:

> If it has done as much good to the *inside* as the outside of your head you will feel the effects of it as long as you live.   (i. 372)

When Keats came back from his northern tour, to which we shall return in Chapter VI, he found that Haydon and Hunt were on bad terms, one reason for this no doubt being that Hunt 'walks up and down [Haydon's] painting room criticising every head most unmercifully'.[64] On the whole Keats seems to have inclined to Haydon's side of the matter, but this is not the place for a detailed biographical investigation. What is relevant is a passage about Haydon in a letter to Bailey written on the 22nd of November 1817:

> To a Man of your nature, such a Letter as Haydon's must have been extremely cutting—What occasions the greater part of the World's Quarrels? simply this, two Minds meet and do not understand each other time enough to praevent any shock or surprise at the conduct of either party—As soon as I had known Haydon three days I had got enough of his character not to have been surprised at such a Letter as he has hurt you with. Nor when I knew it was it a principle with me to drop his acquaintance although with you it would have been an imperious feeling. I wish you knew all I think about Genius and the Heart. . . . Men of Genius are great as certain ethereal Chemicals operating on the Mass of neutral intellect—but they have not any individuality, any determined Character.[65]

Keats had no doubt that Haydon was a Man of Genius. A year or eighteen months after their first meeting we notice that such terminations as 'Yours eternally' tend to give way to 'Your affectionate friend', and this may well reflect a modification in the first passionate enthusiasm Haydon had aroused in Keats. It is possible to read a passage written on the 11th of January 1818 as a bid to consolidate matters on a less emotional basis—

> Your friendship for me is now getting into its teens—and I feel the past—

but we find that Keats continues very emphatically:

> Also every day older I get—the greater is my idea of your atchievements in Art: and I am convinced that there are three things to rejoice at in this Age—The Excursion Your Pictures, and Hazlitt's depth of Taste.

A letter to George and Tom Keats begun two days later shows that Keats was 'quite perplexed in a world of doubts and fancies'. He tells them that he considers Bailey '. . . one of the noblest men alive at the present day' and goes on:

> In a note to Haydon about a week ago, (which I wrote with a full sense of what he had done, and how he had never manifested any little mean drawback in his value of me) I said if there were three things superior in the modern world, they were 'the Excursion', 'Haydon's pictures' & 'Hazlitts depth of Taste' So I do believe.

It is clear that Keats's high estimation of Haydon's painting at this point was not an empty compliment. At the end of the year—on the 22nd of December—Keats told Haydon that he had been thinking of 'Christ's Triumphal Entry into Jerusalem' 'not only now but for this year and a half'. It is important to notice that this deep interest in Haydon's painting survived all the misunderstandings and hard feelings occasioned by Keats's loan to Haydon and his subsequent attempts to get it back. On the 20th of September 1819 we find him writing:

> I shall perhaps still be acquainted with him, but for friendship that is at an end.   (ii. 208)

Yet on the 3rd of October, just a fortnight later, Keats wrote to Haydon as follows:

> I have no quarrel, I assure you, of so weighty a nature, with the world, on my own account as I have on yours. . . . I have no cause to complain because I am certain any thing really fine will in these days be felt. . . . [You would be famous] now if the operation of painting was as universal as that of writing—It is not. . . . That [more] has not been done is a disgrace to the country. I know very little of Painting, yet your pictures follow me into the Country—when I am tired with reading I often think them over and as often condemn the spirit of modern Connoisseurs Upon the whole indeed you have no complaint to make being able to say what so few Men can 'I have succeeded'.

The following month Keats told George and his wife that 'Our Set still continue [to] separate as we get older, each follows with more precision the bent of his own Mind'.[66] It is clear that he was beginning (in some moods, at least) to find Haydon something of a bore: 'You said in one of your Letters that there was nothing but Haydon and Co in mine', he wrote to America on the 13th of January 1820: 'There can be nothing of him in this for I never see him or Co.'[67] Later in the same letter he complains that if he goes to Haydon's he hears nothing but 'worn out discourses of poetry and painting'.[68]

That Keats's opinion of Haydon's painting declined at this time there is no firm evidence. It is true that 'Haydon's great picture' figures in a list of boring things in a sonnet which makes an odd companion-piece to the lists of delights that are so common in Keats's early poetry. The probable date of the sonnet is early 1820,[69] but it is worth noticing that other sources of boredom include 'The voice of Mr. Coleridge' and 'Wordsworth's Sonnet On Dover'. If Keats sometimes felt that he had heard enough on the subject of 'Christ's Entry', it is hardly surprising: Haydon had been at work on it for more than two years before Keats met him: he had been at work on it, and talking endlessly about it, ever since. On the other hand, we know that Keats went to the private view on Saturday the 25th of March, at a time when his doctor had forbidden him 'the slightest exertion',[70] and it is hardly likely that he went only for the pleasure of looking at his own head, in the crowd in the background of the picture. What exactly Keats thought of the completed painting we do not know, but Haydon had no doubt that he was enthusiastic. 'The room was full', he wrote in an ebullient account of the exhibition in his *Autobiography*. 'Keats and Hazlitt were up in a corner really rejoicing.'[71]

III

'ANNALS OF THE FINE ARTS'

To receive the approbation of such men [as Haydon] is our
greatest ambition and reward.   *Annals of the Fine Arts*, iii. 167

THROUGHOUT his life Haydon wrote a great deal about art.
Before Keats met him *The Examiner* had been his main outlet,
but between 1816 and 1820 he wrote almost exclusively in the
Annals of the Fine Arts, and since four of Keats's poems were
first published in this review—poems which included the 'Ode
to the Nightingale' (as it was first called) and the 'Ode On a
Grecian Urn'—some account of it is now in place. If we wish to
understand something of 'the political state of art' at this time
(in Haydon's phrase), there is no better way than to turn over
the pages of this scarce and neglected periodical.

From the first the *Annals* was a publication with a mission, a
combative and controversial affair. To see what it stood for we
have only to look at the dedications to the five volumes which
appeared. The first is dedicated

To the Select Committee of the Honourable the House of Commons,
who by duly estimating the value and recommending the purchase of
the Elgin Marbles to the British Legislature, have created an Epoch
in the History of their Country.

The second is dedicated

To the Directors of the British Institution for Promoting the Fine
Arts in the United Kingdom; in acknowledgment of their Services to
the Cause of Legitimate Art, by the Exhibition of the Cartoons of
Raffaelle.

The third is dedicated to the Earl of Elgin,

In Respect and Admiration of his Energy and Perseverance in
Rescuing the Splendid Remains of Grecian Genius from the Hands
of Barbarians.

The fourth is dedicated to Sir J. Fleming Leicester,

One of the first Patrons, who had the Sense to despise the Prejudices against his Countrymen, and the Courage to form a Gallery of their Works.

The fifth volume is dedicated

To the Royal Academy of London, in Respect for its recent Symptoms of Improvement, and in hopes of its continued Reformation, till it be restored to the original Intention of its august Founder, George the Third, namely, the Cultivation of Historical Painting.

The subject of the final dedication must have come as a surprise to regular readers, though its terms reveal clearly enough the attitude to the Academy of the editor and his contributors. The editor was the architect James Elmes, an old friend of Haydon's. In the very first number he republished Haydon's attack on the Academy from *The Examiner*—with dramatic effect, if Haydon's own account of the matter is to be credited:

The Art was soon in an uproar, and the quarterly appearance of the *Annals* was watched for with the same sort of anxiety as a shell in the air during a siege. 'Here it comes; now for it'. . . . Every weapon of attack was resorted to—ridicule, sarcasm, allegory and insinuation— with such success that a member said: 'By and by a man will be afraid to become an Academician.' Once when Wilkie was with me, and an Academician came in, Wilkie seeing the *Annals* on the table said, in absolute horror, 'Just take away that publication'.[1]

As the writer of the preface to the third volume makes clear, the Academy was held to have failed in its duty of encouraging the highest form of painting, historical painting:

The Annals have now reached the third volume, in spite of the opposing influence of the Royal Academy. . . . We think . . . the encouragement of historical painting, ought to be the first object in any great nation that wishes to encourage art. . . . The foundation of the Royal Academy was laid with the best intentions, but time has filled it with a preponderance of portrait painters, who have sacrificed the interests of the art . . . to their own private emolument.

Elmes and his colleagues felt passionately about this because they were convinced that there was now a real opportunity for High Art to flourish. 'The progress of the arts in this country has been by no means rapid', as one contributor put it, 'yet it has been sure and certain, as the growth of public opinion.'[2] Reynolds and others had pointed the way: the public was ready to be guided: what was needed was a courageous lead and the wise direction of patronage. 'The voice of Genius cries aloud for employment. . . . The voice of High Art cries aloud for employment.'[3] The British Institution was doing its best, but the British Academy, from whom the lead should have come, was doing nothing—or less than nothing. At times it is 'a mere club of portrait painters',[4] a collection of indolent men deficient in imagination and interested only in the high fees available to those who are prepared to flatter the faces of the rich. At other times it takes on a more sinister aspect and becomes a 'stumbling block and coiled snake', a malevolent body of artists 'who would willingly see high Art sink, and secretly give her a stab while sinking'.[5]

A typical issue of the *Annals* consists of two or three articles on such subjects as the comparative greatness of Raphael and Michelangelo, the history of historical painting, the need for a National Gallery, some aspect of art in classical times, some opportunity for the public patronage of painters, sculptors, or architects; accounts of recent exhibitions; reviews of recent books, pamphlets, and lectures on the fine arts and related subjects; a satirical piece attacking the Academy; something about the Elgin Marbles; perhaps a technical note on methods of manufacturing paint; items of news about painters and sculptors; and two or three poems. A few of the articles were reprinted from elsewhere: Hazlitt's essay 'On the Character of Sir Joshua Reynolds', for example, had already been published in *The Champion*.[6] Among the contributions which may have caught the eye of Keats are a long essay on 'The Arts among the Ancients', an article on James Barry (probably by Haydon), a survey of the history of English painting by George Stanley, and two articles by Michael William Sharp on the methods of expressing emotion by the use of gesture, with notes on Supplication, Prayer, Grief, Admiration, Applause, Indignation, Reproach, Despair, Indolence, Melancholy, Pleasure, Resignation, Protection, Reproof, Command, etc., and a discussion of how a figure in painting or sculpture may Triumph, Entreat Silence, Swear, Give Suffrage, express Repulsion or Defiance, Beg, or indicate Bounty or Friendship.[7] Whether or not Keats noticed Sharp's contributions, his skill in vivid personification and in what he was later to term 'stationing' clearly owes something to the discussions he must often have heard among his painter friends. How should Joy be personified, for example? Here is Keats's answer:

> And Joy, whose hand is ever at his lips
> Bidding adieu.

An analogous article deals with 'Attributes and Allegory, for the Use of Painters, Sculptors and Architects, selected from Spence, Millin, Ripa, and other Authorities'.[8] The accounts of exhibitions are of particular interest because they mention a great many pictures that Keats may have seen. The most important exhibitions in this period were the British Institution's exhibition of the Flemish painters, including Rubens, Rembrandt, Vandyke and others, in 1815, and that of the Italian, French, and Spanish masters the following year—an exhibition which included work by Raphael, Titian, Poussin, and Claude. The exhibition which Keats visited in February 1818 is noticed in the eighth issue.[9] There are also accounts of the Dulwich Gallery, with its numerous Poussins and Claudes, and of the private collections of Sir George Beaumont, the Duke of Bedford, and Thomas Hope.[10] The Lansdowne Marbles are described in detail. Occasionally there are lists of the works of individual artists: there is a list of the paintings of Josiah Boydell, for example, and another of the sculpture of Canova—who had visited England in 1815 and delighted Haydon by sharing his enthusiasm for the Elgin Marbles.[11] Publications reviewed include such catalogues as 'A Description of the Collection of Ancient Marbles in the British Museum, with Engravings', and E. J. Burrow's brief account of the Elgin Marbles. Other reviews deal with Haydon's letter 'On the Judgment of Connoisseurs being preferred to that of Professional Men', the notorious 'Catalogue Raisonnée'[12] of the pictures shown by the Academy in 1816 (about which Hazlitt wrote with such eloquent scorn), the Memoirs of Visconti, the great authority on art, William Carey's pamphlet on West's 'Death on the Pale Horse', and the 'Abstract of the Select Committee's Report on the Elgin Marbles'.

Among the lectures noticed are those of the Royal Academy's Professor of Anatomy, Anthony Carlisle, whose favourite topic appears to have been 'the indelicacy and indecency of anatomical studies and demonstrations in the lecture room'. When he brought himself to exhibit 'the naked figure, cloathed only where delicacy required it should be cloathed', the *Annals* hailed it as a sign of progress and enlightenment.[13] The editor's own lectures on architecture are noticed, while Hazlitt's discussion of Hogarth in his *Lectures on the English Comic Writers* is excerpted at length, as are his remarks on David Wilkie. The discovery of a new Hogarth, featuring portraits of Pope and some of the Dunces who assailed him, is recorded in the sixteenth issue. Throughout a good deal of attention is paid to prints, which were of great importance before the invention of photography, at a time when many connoisseurs never went abroad at all and even painters had sometimes to be content with one memorable visit to Italy. 'There is this advantage possessed by the poet over the painter', as a contributor pointed out in the fifteenth issue, 'in studying the works of the great masters of his art, he can readily and cheaply obtain possession of those works, and at any time indulge his mind with a reference to them. Not so the painter.'[14] Elmes and his colleagues accused the Academicians of giving engravers less than their due, and in the *Annals* we find engravers listed in the 'Annual Directory of British Artists' and their work noticed from time to time. In the fifteenth issue, for example, there is a list of the engravings of Raffaelle Morghen.

Elmes was a great admirer of Haydon's, and encouraged him to contribute as often as he could. Haydon was not unwilling. As he wrote in his *Autobiography*,

Thinking to help my views of founding a school, and to put the editor in the right road of sound Art, I flung some of my best writing into it, and upheld through its pages the necessity of public encouragement. . . . Elmes encouraged me, of course, and I was too ready to listen to him. Elmes was a man of considerable talent, of great good-nature, and a thorough admirer of mine. He had been the very first to notice and criticise my early works . . . I cared nothing for his peculiarities. I hated the Academy, and was very glad of the use of a publication where I had unlimited control.[15]

Haydon's eyes were frequently too sore to allow him to paint, and on these occasions he was in the habit of dictating to Elmes or whatever other amanuensis was available. He loved controversy. His initiation occurred in *The Examiner* in 1811, where he wrote enthusiastically and at length, bringing in the experience he had gained in the process of dissecting a lion and his views on 'the intellectuality or non-intellectuality of negroes'. Nothing could be more characteristic than his reason for welcoming the opportunity with such avidity:

I was animated by a desire to write in early life, because Reynolds, having deferred composition till late in life, was accused of not writing his own lectures.[16]

And so he became the principal contributor to the *Annals*, the 'Letters on Subjects connected with the Fine Arts' and the satirical 'Visions of Somniator' (in which the principal Academicians are attacked) being merely the most prominent amongst his numerous anonymous and pseudonymous contributions. One of his favourite subjects was the Cartoons of Raphael. 'The exhibition of the Cartoons', he wrote in the ninth issue,

has struck a blow and elicited a spark, which will never die; and if there be any who don't admire them, let them be a little diffident of their own judgment, and not doubt the judgment of all the greatest artists since they were painted. Perhaps if all their beauties were proved to such men, it might appear extraordinary that every body had not the power to see and execute beauties, the chief excellence of which was *their truth*   (iii. 258)

—a passage which forms an appropriate comment on one of the letters of Keats.[17] In another of his articles on the Cartoons we find Haydon quoting Keats, though without giving his name.[18] Elmes admired Haydon's criticism of Raphael so deeply that he tells his readers that he is anxious to have 'all that Mr Haydon has written upon the Cartoons embodied in our work'.[19]

Apart from his own contributions, references to Haydon are so numerous that one might almost suspect Elmes of a subtle scheme to turn his readers against 'that extraordinary young artist'. 'Haydon's picture advances to a conclusion', readers are assured in No. iv. 'He is complained of by more than one correspondent as slow. Gentlemen, wait, and your complaints will vanish.' 'Did Raffaelle at twenty put forth a more powerful picture than Dentatus?', 'Veritas' asks in No. vi. 'I have no hesitation in saying, No! and that in the essential qualities of heroic form, the figure of Dentatus alone will bear comparison with any figure Raffaelle ever executed in the heroic style.' 'May

success attend his future labours' is a characteristic wish expressed in No. xi. In the sixteenth issue twenty pages are devoted
to 'Christ's Triumphal Entry into Jerusalem', and the article
includes a verbatim reprint of Haydon's own pamphlet on the
picture. We are never left in any uncertainty about the Master's
progress, while his pupils, busily at work drawing from the
Elgin Marbles or copying the Cartoons *at full size* (a point that
is always emphasized), keep reappearing throughout the *Annals*
like a Chorus of Industrious Apprentices. No praise, it would
appear, was too fulsome for Haydon's acceptance, if not also for
his own invention. While we must accept his assurance, upon
his 'word of honour', that he was not the author of the letters by
'The Ghost of James Barry', it is clear that the author was (to
say the least of it) very much in his confidence; while in one of his
own 'Visions of Somniator' he makes the spirit of Michelangelo
send him his best wishes, with the assurance that he will 'succeed
in all his noble views and plans'. The general tone of the allusions
to Haydon is epitomized by a remark in the seventh issue:

I read with great pleasure Veritas's spirited comparison between
Raffaelle and Haydon, in which I think he has done great good to
modern art, and deserves the thanks of every living artist. (ii. 475)

'Mr Haydon shall ever have our support, as the Editor of the
Annals',[20] Elmes once remarked, the shaky syntax suggesting
an uncertainty about the identity of the editor which many readers must have shared. In the ninth issue Elmes acknowledges
a restiveness on the part of his subscribers:

We have been several times accused of having mentioned Haydon's
name . . . oftener than that of other artists. To this we answer, that we
have mentioned it oftener than other artists, and shall continue so to
do, while he stands the most prominent in the art. . . . He does more for
the good of the art, and is every where to be found standing up for its
advancement and its high interests.   (iii. 332)

Later the protests became more and more numerous. 'For the
four years, and upwards, that our work has been established',
Elmes wrote in the sixteenth issue,

. . . have we run a perpetual gauntlet for asserting the right of Haydon
to the title of an historical painter of the highest order. Letters anonymous, imploring and threatening, with and without caricatures;
friends and acquaintances, and people with whom we were only on

speaking terms; artists with shrugs of shoulders, critics with expressions of regret, and actors with squeezes of condolence at our infatuation, blindness and ignorance, have been . . . shaking their [heads].

(v. 128)

If in previous issues there had been any attempt at discretion in this matter, it is abandoned altogether at the end. 'Our triumph is now complete.'[21] In 'A Vision of Futurity' in the last issue of all 'Somnambulus' finds himself looking at monuments in St. Paul's: when he comes to Haydon's he bows 'involuntarily' in tribute to the genius of that greatest of painters.'[22] In this same issue readers are presented with an engraving of Haydon and with a thirty-four page memoir which is clearly based on material provided by himself.

In the preface to this final volume the editor congratulates himself on having in a great measure accomplished the objects which he has had in view:

The Academy is palpably in a state of progressive reformation. Young men of talent and vigour begin to be regularly admitted members at the different elections. We have successfully defended the British Institution from the infamous attacks made upon its members by the Catalogue Raisonné; seen Haydon triumphantly established upon the rock of public opinion, and the feeling for historical painting evidently becoming the paramount feeling of the country for art. If the Government could but be induced to lend some aid to second the efforts of the painters, our most sanguine expectations of the success of British genius would be realized.

But Elmes, as even Haydon came to see later, was deficient in judgement, 'extremely thoughtless, full of imagination, always scheming and very likely to bring himself and his friends into scrapes'.[23] No doubt the Academy deserved to be attacked, but the way in which Elmes and his contributors laid about them was hardly likely to lead to the 'reformation' of such a body, and there can be little doubt that his well-known association with the *Annals* played its part in bringing about the final overthrow of Haydon's fortunes.

The most important feature of the *Annals*, from our point of view, is the emphasis laid by its contributors on the close affinity between the visual arts and literature. The first volume opens with a reprint of Sidmouth's Oxford Prize Essay 'On the Affinity between Painting and Writing'. The author insists that in ancient times 'the analogy between the two arts was universally felt and allowed; their rules and principles were in many respects the same; and the same expressions equally characterised the similar and congenial productions of both'. That is why 'the Treatise of Horace on one art is illustrated by frequent allusions to the other; and a variety of images and descriptions interspersed in the Latin Poets are so animated and picturesque, as to admit a well-grounded conjecture, that they were taken from Paintings universally known and admired.' Sidmouth refers to Spence's *Polymetis*, the obvious authority, mentions the debt to poetry of a number of particular painters, and quotes the remark of Simonides that 'a Picture is a silent Poem, and a Poem a speaking Picture'. He particularly emphasizes the analogy between Landscape Painting and Pastoral Poetry:

> Both are conversant in rural scenes; both require a particular turn of mind for what is romantic and picturesque; and both must closely study and imitate nature. Claude Lorrain and Titian are in the one, what Theocritus and Virgil are in the other; and the same grotesque wildness equally characterizes the scenes of Theocritus, and of Salvator Rosa. Both become more interesting by the introduction of human figures, without which, even the Arcadia of Poussin, and the happiest descriptions of the Sicilian poet, would lose their effect.

One reason for the insistence on the relationship between poetry and painting throughout the *Annals* becomes clear when we consider Sidmouth's (perfectly orthodox) parallel between Historical Painting and Epic Poetry. Elmes and his associates wanted to explain to a public which knew more of poetry than of painting that the primacy of Historical Painting was as evident as that of Epic Poetry. So Raphael is described as 'the Virgil of Epic Painting'.[24] 'Poetry and Painting require the same minds', as Haydon remarks in one of his articles, 'the means only are different: language and versification are the means of the one, and form, colour, and light and shadow, the means of the other'.[25] 'We want a higher standard raised', another contributor proclaims, 'and history, poetry, grandeur, more cultivated and studied by the British School. We wish Miltons and Shakespeares of painting, not Cowleys or Moores, however pretty and entertaining soever they may be.'[26] Artists should be highly educated men, capable of intelligent reading and shrewd criticism: 'Rubens, Raphael, Michael Angelo, and Phidias, were as capable of deciding upon the two arts, clearly and impartially, as Tasso, Virgil, Milton, or Homer.'[27]

Reynolds had insisted that 'every man whose business is description ought to be tolerantly conversant with the poets, in some language or other; that he may imbibe a poetical spirit, and enlarge his stock of ideas'.[28] As one glances through the *Annals* one notices that a great many of the modern paintings referred to are based on passages from the poets. Indeed Haydon felt it necessary to warn painters against excessive reliance on the Sister Art: they should follow the example of Raphael, who contented himself with a brief though inspiring text from the Bible, instead of basing a whole picture on a passage of literary description:

> Poets should only be called in as assistants: Painters should be ever jealous of doing nothing but realizing the conceptions of Poets: they should shew, by every subject they paint, that nature has given them the same fertility of imagination and powers of creation, the same power of exciting sympathies by the characters and the passions they display. (iii. 249–50)

Shakespeare, Milton, and Thomson, are the poets in whose work the painters of the time most frequently found subject-matter and inspiration. In 1817, for example, the subject proposed for a prize offered by the British Institution was 'Samson Agonistes'. The prominence of Thomson is particularly striking. The motto of the first volume is from *Liberty*—

> O Greece! thou sapient nurse of finer arts
> Which to bright science blooming fancy bore!
> Be this thy praise, that thou, and thou alone,
> In these hast led the way, in these excelled (ii. 252–5)

—and in the first number we also find an 'Analysis of the Poem called "LIBERTY" ', possibly by Haydon, with copious extracts. 'What a description for the pencil of West or Haydon, or the chissel of Flaxman!' the writer exclaims of the figure of Liberty herself.[29] The ubiquitous emphasis on the 'refined taste of Thomson in art'[30] is worth remembering, when we turn to the poetry of Keats.

A number of poems on painting are referred to, among them

Hayley's *Poetical Epistle*, Pollinger Robinson's *The Beauties of Painting*, Martin Archer Shee's *Rhymes on Art*, a poem by a certain Bramston (probably James Bramston's *The Man of Taste*) and an unpublished poem by an unnamed author called *Vicissitudes of Art* from which two separate lines are quoted:

> The silver-footed Hebe ever young,

and

> Crowning with purple nectar Juno's cup.[31]

The majority of the poems printed at the end of most issues deal with the fine arts. These include Wordsworth's sonnet to Haydon, 'High is our calling, Friend!' and his sonnet 'Upon the Sight of a Beautiful Picture'.[32] The latter is one of a number of poems inspired by particular works of art. We find (for example) an Italian poem on Michelangelo's 'Notte' in the Medici Chapel in Florence, accompanied by a translation by Anna Seward:

> Night's marble figure, stranger, which you see
> Recline with so much grace and majesty.

Milman's Oxford Prize Poem on 'The Belvidere Apollo' is re-printed, with its fine line:

> And the cold marble leapt to life a god.

Southey's comic poem, 'The Painter of Florence', is also re-printed, as well as Lamb's poems on Leonardo's 'Virgin of the Rocks' and Haydon's 'Christ's Entry into Jerusalem' (the latter in both Latin and English). There is an acceptable epigram on the Elgin Marble controversy:

> While DAY believes them 'bove all price
> KNIGHT thinks a small sum would suffice;
> Thus still we find that Day and Knight
> Differ as *darkness* does from *light*.

A sonnet, 'descriptive of a Painting of Nicolo Poussin', is of particular interest, because of Keats's affinity to that painter:

> Here—on a rock that shot up, bare and gray
> Sate piping, the vast giant Polypheme.—

The woods below seem'd ringing with his theme,
And the blue, motionless waters far away
Look'd listening.—Here, his staff beside him lay
Huge as a forest pine.—A sunny gleam
Had touch'd the leaves, while dark in front a stream,
Such as the fauns love, babbling told its way,
And still its talk a Naiad's urn supplied;
And on its margin fringed with rushes green,
A group of beauteous figures might be seen
Reclining.—Such painters of Italy
Figure or feign at will, but none beside.
—It was a summer scene of pure tranquillity.[33]

The two sonnets by Keats addressed to Haydon on the Elgin Marbles appeared under his name in the eighth issue. The 'Ode to the Nightingale' appeared in the thirteenth, and the Ode 'On a Grecian Urn' in the fifteenth, each being signed only by a dagger. The fact that the latter was immediately followed by a 'Sonnet to Michel Agnolo' by 'B[arry] C[ornwall]', from his recent volume of *Dramatic Scenes*, constitutes one of the great anti-climaxes of literary history. Yet the juxtaposition of Keats's poem and that, with its penultimate line,

Painting, and Sculpture, and wing'd Poetry,

at least serves to remind us that in his choice of a subject for this famous poem Keats was following the fashion of the time.[34]

IV

THE CRITIC: WILLIAM HAZLITT

> Every object becomes lustrous from the light thrown back
> upon it by the mirror of art: and by the aid of the pencil we may
> be said to touch and handle the objects of sight. The air-wove
> visions that hover on the verge of existence have a bodily
> presence given them on the canvas: the form of beauty is
> changed into a substance: the dream and the glory of the
> universe is made 'palpable to feeling as to sight'.
>
> 'On the Pleasure of Painting'[1]

Keats seems to have met Hazlitt soon after he met Leigh
Hunt and Haydon, during the eventful winter months of
1816–17. The two men never became intimate friends—Hazlitt
was a difficult man to know, and perhaps too good a critic to
give the early poems of Keats that unqualified praise which can
be more valuable to a young writer of genius than a balanced
assessment—yet Hazlitt came to exert a very deep influence on
Keats's conception of poetry. I have already quoted Keats's
reference to 'Hazlitt's depth of Taste' as one of the 'three things
to rejoice at in this Age'. It occurs in a letter written at the
beginning of 1818, and underlines the fact that Hazlitt succeeded
Leigh Hunt as Keats's principal guide in matters of taste.
Keats's profound respect for Hazlitt is one of the instances of
his astonishing critical shrewdness. His interest in Hazlitt
extended even to the least readable of his books, the *Essay on
the Principles of Human Action*, which was almost the only book
on philosophy to be found in Keats's collection after his death.
On the 27th of April 1818 he told John Hamilton Reynolds that
he was planning to learn Greek 'and very likely Italian—and in
other ways prepare myself to ask Hazlitt in about a years time
the best metaphysical road I can take'. His underlined and
annotated copy of *Characters of Shakespear's Plays* still survives,
and we know with what admiration he read *The Round Table*.
Hazlitt shares with Burton the honour of being one of the only
two prose writers from whom Keats ever quoted extensively:
he transcribed a long passage from *A Letter to William Gifford*,

Esq., drawing attention to 'the manner in which this is managed: the force and innate power with which it yeasts and works up itself', adding that it 'is in a style of genius—He hath a demon as he himself says of Lord Byron'.[2] Keats often heard Hazlitt talking: we find him echoing one or two of Hazlitt's favourite turns of speech in his letters. Whereas he made no attempt to hear Coleridge lecture, he was an attentive and enthusiastic member of the audience at Hazlitt's *Lectures on the English Poets*. The illness and death of Tom made it impossible for him to attend the *Lectures on the English Comic Writers*, but one day Keats called on Hazlitt and carried off a manuscript copy, from which we find him quoting in a letter to George and his sister-in-law in America.[3]

It is therefore an important fact that Hazlitt had begun life as an artist, and became a very distinguished critic of painting. In reacting against Leigh Hunt Keats might well have reacted against the kind of poetry that is nourished by the work of great painters and sculptors. Fortunately he found in Hazlitt a mentor who understood painting, as well as literature, more profoundly than did Hunt, a new guide whose critical expositions, so far from irritating him, aroused his passionate enthusiasm.

'Till I was twenty', Hazlitt once wrote, 'I thought there was nothing in the world but books; but when I began to paint I found there were two things, both difficult to do and worth doing.'[4] Painting was in the family. His elder brother John was a miniaturist who had studied under Sir Joshua Reynolds. There survives a delightful letter from the nine-year-old William to his elder brother, asking him what pictures he is hoping to exhibit and describing the writer's own activities:

I am a busybody, and do many silly things: I drew eyes and noses till about a fortnight ago. I have drawn a little boy since, a man's face, and a little boy's front face, taken from a bust. Next Monday I shall begin to read Ovid's Metamorphoses and Eutropius. I shall like to know all the Latin and Greek I can. I want to learn how to measure the stars. I shall not, I suppose, paint the worse for knowing everything else.[5]

The first ambition of Hazlitt's that we know of was to become a painter, no doubt in emulation of his brother; and later, when he realized that he could not with a good conscience become a clergyman, he turned back to the idea of painting as a career. At first he was unenthusiastic, because literature had come to

mean much more to him than painting; but then in 1799 he
visited an exhibition of the work of the Italian masters, and the
effect on him was dramatic:

> I was staggered when I saw the works there collected, and looked at
> them with wondering and with longing eyes. A mist passed away from
> my sight: the scales fell off. A new sense came upon me, a new heaven
> and a new earth stood before me.... We had all heard of the names of
> Titian, Raphael, Guido, Domenichino, the Caracci—but to see them face
> to face, to be in the same room with their deathless productions, was
> like breaking some mighty spell—was almost an effect of necromancy!
> From that time I lived in a world of pictures.   (viii. 14)

From this time onwards, he tells us, 'speeches in parliament' and
the affairs of every day seemed trivial, 'compared with those
mighty works and dreaded names that spoke to me in the eternal
silence of thought'. Although he was not destined to become a
major painter, he soon became extremely competent. The portrait of his father which he describes in the essay 'On the Pleasure
of Painting' was hung in the Royal Academy Exhibition of 1802,
and several of his other portraits had a similar success, notably
that of Lamb as a Venetian Senator—a picture that has often
been reproduced.

In 1802 Hazlitt was one of the many Englishmen who
hastened over to France, thrown open again by the Peace of
Amiens. He describes his first visit to the Louvre in the seventh
of the *Lectures on the English Comic Writers*, as a coda to his
discussion of Hogarth:

> There was her [Art's] treasure, and there the inventory of all she
> had. There she had gathered together her pomp, and there was her
> shrine, and there her votaries came and worshipped as in a temple. The
> crown she wore was brighter than that of kings. Where the struggles
> for human liberty had been, there were the triumphs of human genius.
> For there, in the Louvre, were the precious monuments of art:—There
> 'stood the statue that enchants the world;' there was Apollo, the Lao-
> coon, the Dying Gladiator, the head of the Antinous, Diana with her
> Fawn, the Muses and the Graces in a ring, and all the glories of the
> antique world:—
>
> > 'There was old Proteus coming from the sea,
> > And wreathed Triton blew his winding horn.'
>
> There, too, were the two St. Jeromes, Correggio's, and Domeni-
> chino's; there was Raphael's Transfiguration; the St. Mark of

Tintoret; Paul Veronese's Marriage of Cana; the Deluge of Poussin; and Titian's St. Peter Martyr. It was there that I learned to become an enthusiast of the lasting works of the great painters, and of their names no less magnificent; . . . whom, having once seen, we always remember, and who teach us to see all things through them; without whom life would be to begin again, and the earth barren; of Raphael, who lifted the human form half way to heaven; of Titian, who painted the mind in the face, and unfolded the soul of things to the eye; of Rubens, around whose pencil gorgeous shapes thronged numberless, startling us by the novel accidents of form and colour, putting the spirit of motion into the universe, and weaving a gay fantastic round and Bacchanalian dance with nature; of Rembrandt, too, who 'smoothed the raven down of darkness till it smiled', and tinged it with a light like streaks of burning ore: of these, and more than these, of whom the world was scarce worthy, and for the loss of whom nothing could console me—not even the works of Hogarth![6]   (vi. 148–9)

The latter part of this passage had first appeared in *The Round Table*, so that Keats may well have read it more than once; while much of it was repeated again, after Keats's death, in *Notes of a Journey through France and Italy*, in the description of Hazlitt's favourite 'chamber of the brain'.[7] It is no wonder that Hazlitt repeated himself: as he wrote on another occasion, when Poussin was his theme, 'it is hard that we should not be allowed to dwell as often as we please on what delights us', and it may well be that his first visit to the Louvre delighted him more, and did more to form his personality than anything else that ever happened to him.

During that winter in Paris, Hazlitt tells us, he spent five or six hours a day at his easel in the Louvre, on the four days in the week 'in which one is allowed to, or at least able to, do anything'.[8] A Mr. Railton of Liverpool had commissioned him to make five copies for him, while he had also

promised Northcote to copy Titian's portrait of Hippolito de Medici for him. He had a print of it lying on the floor one morning when I called on him, and was saying that it was one of the finest pictures in the whole world . . . .[9]

In another letter Hazlitt gives us an account of two further projects, and makes it clear with what intensity he worked:

I have begun to copy one of Titian's portraits. . . . I made a very complete sketch of the head in about three hours, and have been working upon it longer this morning; I hope to finish it this week. . . . There are great numbers of people in the rooms (most of them English) every day, and I was afraid at first that this would confuse and hinder me; but I found on beginning to copy that I was too occupied in my work to attend much to, or to care at all about, what was passing around me. . . . I intend to occupy the vacant days of the week in making duplicates of the copies which I do here, and in doing a picture of myself, in the same view as that of the Hippolito de Medici.[10]

He was deeply impressed by some of the great landscapes at the Louvre, and mentions that he would like to 'do a copy of a most divine landscape by Rubens . . .; but it will take at least a fortnight to do it, most probably three weeks'.[11] He was painting at extraordinary speed:

I have been working upon the portrait of Titian's Mistress, as it is called, these two last days. I intend to complete this the beginning of next week, if possible. . . . If I succeed in this, which I am pretty confident of doing, I shall have done eight of my pictures in eight weeks, from the time I came here. . . . I intend to give an hour a day to copying a Holy Family, by Raphael, one of the most beautiful things in the world. Of this, and The Death of Clorinda [by Lodovic Lana], I shall probably be able to get prints taken in London, as this is frequently done; as my copies certainly contain all that is wanted for a print, which has nothing to do with colouring . . . .[12]

He believed that he was best at a 'sort of rapid sketching', and that after the first hour or two he 'generally made [his] pictures worse and worse, the more pains [he] took with them'.[13]

He even began to enjoy a modest degree of success as a portrait painter. In the following year Coleridge recommended him to the attention of Thomas Wedgwood as being 'a thinking, observant, original man, of great power as a Painter of Character Portraits, & far more in the manner of the old Painters, than any living Artist'—though with the interesting reservation that 'the Object must be *before* him he has no imaginative memory'.[14] Hazlitt painted Coleridge himself about this time, Southey reading aloud to the sitter all the while, with metaphysical argument between painter and subject interrupted only during the actual progress of the painting. The result was generally considered a satisfactory piece of work, unlike Hazlitt's portrait of Wordsworth, which a friend—surely Charles Lamb?— considered so dismal that he broke out: 'At the gallows—deeply

affected by his deserved fate—yet determined to die like a man'.[15]
When Lamb wrote a mock-obituary of Hazlitt in 1808 he wrote
of him (we notice) primarily as a deceased painter, addressing
the credulous reader of the *Morning Post* in the following words:

> Last night Mr. H., a portrait painter in Southampton Buildings,
> put an end to his existence in a shocking manner. It is supposed that
> he must have committed his purpose with a pallet-knife, as the edges
> of the cicatrice, or wound, were found besmeared with a yellow con-
> sistence, but the knife could not be found.[16]

Hazlitt acknowledged that it was as hard to say 'whether he
ought to be considered as an author or a portrait-painter' as it
was to decide whether he should be classed as a gentleman or
'a low fellow'.

What influenced Keats was not Hazlitt's own painting, but
the enthusiasm for art and discrimination in everything relating to
painting that was as evident in his conversation as in his critical
writings. His enthusiasm was that of a practitioner. 'Hazlitt is
a man who can do great good to the Art', Haydon wrote in his
Diary in 1816. 'He practised Painting long enough to know it;
and he carries into Literature a stock which no literary man ever
did before him.'[17] Hazlitt himself attributed his tepid interest in
sculpture—always excepting the Elgin Marbles—to the fact
that he had never attempted this art himself. With painting it
was very different:

> Statuary does not affect me like painting. I am not, I allow, a fair
> judge, having paid a great deal more attention to the one than to the
> other. Nor did I ever think of the first as a profession; and it is that
> perhaps which adds the sting to our love of excellence, the hope of
> attaining it ourselves in any particular walk. We strain our faculties
> to the utmost to conceive of what is most exquisite in any art to which
> we devote ourselves, and are doubly sensitive to it when we see it
> attained. . . . We come to the contemplation of truth and beauty with
> the passionate feeling of lovers. . . . No wonder that the youthful
> student dwells with delight and rapture on the finished works of art,
> when they are to his heated fancy the pledge and foretaste of im-
> mortality; when at every successful stroke of imitation he is ready to
> cry out with Correggio—'I also am a painter!'   (x. 162–3)

Hazlitt was particularly fond of the conversation of painters.
This becomes clear as one reads his *Conversations of James
Northcote, Esq., R.A.* It is not one of his most brilliant books,

yet nothing that he ever wrote tells us more about his own character, or shows him in a more amiable light. Like Hazlitt's brother, Northcote had been a pupil of Reynolds, and he also remembered the other great men of that age, Goldsmith, Burke, and Samuel Johnson. Northcote's anecdotes had their appeal for Hazlitt, but the great thing about Northcote was that he was not a mere literary man. Whereas Godwin (for example) could tell Hazlitt only what he himself already knew, or knew where to find in a book, Northcote, 'as an artist', had 'been pushed into an intercourse with the world as well as an observation of nature; and combine[d] a sufficient knowledge of general subjects with living illustrations of them.'[18] And besides, there was something about the atmosphere of a studio that appealed to the Bohemian in Hazlitt, and disposed him for talk. This is amusingly illustrated by the disappointment which he felt when he called on Northcote one day and found him not in his studio:

He was downstairs in the parlour, and talked much as usual: but the difference of the accompaniments, the sitting down, the preparations for tea, the carpet and furniture, and a fat little lap-dog interfered with old associations and took something from the charm of his conversation.

It was when Northcote was in his studio (as a passage already quoted makes clear) that Hazlitt delighted to visit him:

I know that I can get there what I get nowhere else—a welcome, as if one was expected to drop in just at that moment, a total absence of all respect of persons and of airs of self-consequence, endless topics of discourse, refined thoughts, made more striking by ease and simplicity of manner—the husk, the shell of humanity is left at the door, and the spirit, mellowed by time, resides within!   (xii. 85–86)

It is not only in *The Conversations of Northcote* that we find evidence of Hazlitt's artistic taste. He wrote a great deal about painting, particularly in *Sketches of the Principal Picture-Galleries in England* and *Notes of a Journey through France and Italy*. Much further art-criticism is to be found in occasional essays and reviews, or occurs by way of digression or illustration in his literary criticism. Many of the most interesting passages—like the three books just mentioned—were written after the death of Keats; but in calling the roll of Hazlitt's favourite painters I shall quote indiscriminately from his earlier and later writings, since he seems to have expressed very much the same views in the years when Keats knew him as he did later.

I have already quoted Hazlitt's description of the effect that the Orleans Gallery had on him, when he first saw it:[19] it was an effect that was never to wear off:

My first initiation in the mysteries of the art was at the Orleans Gallery: it was there I formed my taste, such as it is; so that I am irreclaimably of the old school in painting. (viii. 14)

At any point in his writings he is always liable to recall one of the 'visions of our youth, in the Orleans Collection,—where we used to go and look at it by the hour together, till our hearts thrilled with its beauty, and our eyes were filled with tears'.[20] What impressed him above all was the Titians, so that it is appropriate that we should find him referring to 'Titian's golden hue' in a letter to his wife that throws a great deal of light on his taste in art:

Both parcels of prints came safe, & I need hardly say that I was glad to see them. . . . The catalogue [of a recent sale] did not tempt me so much as I expected. There were a parcel of Metzus & Terburghs & boors smoking & ladies at harpsichords, which seemed to take up as much room as the St. Cecilia, the Pan & St. George, the Danae, & the Ariadne in Naxos. Did Lamb go to the sale, & what is the report of the pictures? But I have got my complete set of Cartoons, 'here I sit with my doxies surrounded', & so never mind. I just took out my little copy of Rembrandt to look at, & was so pleased with it. . . . With respect to my painting, I go on something like Satan, through moist & dry, sometimes glazing & sometimes scumbling, as it happens, now on the wrong side of the canvas & now on the right, but still persuading myself that I have at last found out the true secret of Titian's golden hue & the oleaginous touches of Claude Lorraine. I have got in a pretty good background. . . . I have been painting all day, & all day yesterday, & all the day before . . . .[21]

In 1806 Lamb had written to Hazlitt about the possible loss of 'a parcel containing besides a book, &c, a rare print, which I take to be a Titian' and humorously reproaching Hazlitt for remaining in Shropshire 'when so many fine pictures are a-going, a-going every day in London':

And there are you, perverting Nature in lying landscapes, filched from old rusty Titians such as I can scrape up here to send you, with an additament from Shropshire Nature thrown in to make the whole look unnatural.[22]

Lamb tells Hazlitt that there are Claudes and Titians at Angerstein's 'that will cure [him] of restless, fidgetty passions for a
week after'. There is even a passage in which Hazlitt oddly
ascribes his abandonment of painting to the impossibility of
finding Titianesque subjects in England:

> When I was young, I made one or two studies of strong contrasts of
> light and shade in the manner of Rembrandt with great care and (as
> it was thought) with some success. But after I had once copied some of
> Titian's portraits in the Louvre, my ambition took a higher flight.
> Nothing would serve my turn but heads like Titian—Titian expres-
> sions, Titian complexions, Titian dresses; and as I could not find these
> where I was, after one or two abortive attempts to engraft Italian art
> on English nature, I flung away my pencil in disgust and despair.
>   (xvii. 139)

Those who praised his portrait of Lamb for its Titianesque air
were therefore appreciating a quality that Hazlitt was passionately anxious to achieve. He wrote about Titian repeatedly, and
it is not surprising that he gave Northcote a good deal of assistance with his *Life of Titian*.

Hazlitt had also a particular enthusiasm for Raphael's Cartoons, about which (as we have seen) Haydon was apt to write
as if they had been his personal discovery. It was a set of these
Cartoons that Hazlitt had by him in Shropshire: he was to write
about them with high eloquence in *The Round Table*, a book
which Keats knew well:

> It is many years ago since we first saw the prints of the Cartoons hung
> round the parlour of a little inn on the great north road. . . . We had
> heard of [their] fame . . ., but this was the first time that we had ever
> been admitted face to face into the presence of those divine works.
> 'How were we then uplifted!' Prophets and Apostles stood before us,
> and the Saviour of the Christian world, with his attributes of faith and
> power; miracles were working on the walls; the hand of Raphael was
> there, and as his pencil traced the lines, we saw godlike spirits and
> lofty shapes descend and walk visibly the earth, but as if their thoughts
> still lifted them above the earth.   (iv. 144–5)

Like his interest in Raphael, Keats's interest in Hogarth, an
artist whom one might not (at first blush) have expected to
appeal to him, probably owed a good deal to the constant advocacy of Hazlitt, who is for ever returning to Hogarth's work
and puzzling away at the problem of how low subject-matter

can create high art. To remember Keats's admiration for Hogarth is a useful corrective to too narrow a view of his temperament and taste. But much more important—because more evident as an influence on his own poetry—was his love of Claude, whose reputation as a landscape painter reached its zenith in the eighteenth century, and about whom Hazlitt wrote with enthusiasm and understanding:

> Claude Lorraine pours the spirit of air over all objects, and new-creates them of light and sun-shine. In several of his master-pieces . . . the vessels, the trees, the temples and middle distances glimmer between air and solid substance, and seem moulded of a new element in nature. No words can do justice to their softness, their precision, their sparkling effect.   (x. 108)

That was written after the death of Keats, but there is no doubt that Hazlitt often talked about Claude, and we know that one of his friends insisted one evening that the story of Cupid and Psyche 'opens with a pastoral landscape equal to Claude',[23] so making the sort of connexion between poetry and painting that was characteristic of this circle. Those of Hazlitt's writings which were available to Keats are full of references to Claude. Although Hazlitt realized that Claude was hardly one of the world's supreme painters, he had (like Sir Joshua Reynolds) the highest admiration for him. 'However inferior the style of his best landscape may be', as he once wrote, 'there is something in the execution that redeems all defects. In taste and grace nothing can ever go beyond them. He might be called, if not the perfect, the faultless painter. Sir Joshua Reynolds used to say, that there would be another Raphael, before there was another Claude.'[24] Hazlitt particularly loved Claude's 'Enchanted Castle'. In his fine essay 'On the Ignorance of the Learned', where he describes the 'mere scholar', the man for whom the world of the senses has no existence, it is part of his indictment that such a being

> knows nothing of pictures;—'of the colouring of Titian, the grace of Raphael, the purity of Domenichino, the *corregiescity* of Corregio, the learning of Poussin, the airs of Guido, the taste of the Caracci, or the grand contour of Michael Angelo,'—of all those glories of the Italian and miracles of the Flemish school, which have filled the eyes of mankind with delight, and to the study and imitation of which thousands have in vain devoted their lives. These are to him as if they had never been, a mere dead letter, a bye-word; and no wonder: for he neither

sees nor understands their prototypes in nature. A print of Rubens's Watering-place, or Claude's Enchanted Castle, may be hanging on the walls of his room for months without his once perceiving them; and if you point them out to him, he will turn away from them.[25]

Keats was the opposite of such a man. It could never be said of him, as of the 'mere scholar', that 'the language of nature, or of art (which is another nature), is one that he does not understand'; and it is interesting to notice that while the beauty of many paintings left its impress on his poetry, Claude's 'Enchanted Castle' is the one picture that he mentions by name in a poem. I shall return to it in Chapter VII.

As we have already seen, Keats furnished his ideal room with 'a few' portraits by Titian, one painting of Haydon's, and (apparently) a great many Salvator Rosa's. His is a reputation that has worn less well than Claude's. During the later eighteenth century he had a tremendous vogue. Hazlitt admired him, but with reservations. In his *Sketches of the Principal Picture-Galleries in England* he describes one of Salvator's landscapes:

> It is one of his very best—rough, grotesque, wild—Pan has struck it with his hoof—the trees, the rocks, the fore-ground, are of a piece, and the figures are subordinate to the landscape. The same dull sky lowers upon the scene, and the bleak air chills the crisp surface of the water. It is a consolation to us to meet with a fine Salvator. His is one of the great names in art, and it is among our sources of regret that we cannot always admire his works as we would do, from our respect to his reputation and our love of the man . . . We cannot . . . fancy . . . him so great a painter as some others.   (x. 24)

In his *Notes of a Journey through France and Italy* Hazlitt draws the conclusion that 'Salvator was a great landscape-painter; but both he and Lady Morgan [in her biography] have been guilty of a great piece of *egotism* in supposing that he was any thing more', and severely criticizes two of his attempts at heroic painting.[26]

When he writes about Poussin Hazlitt has no such reservations. He tells us that when he returned to the Louvre in 1824 the Poussins were the first pictures that he looked for:

> At the sight of the first, which I distinctly recollected (a fine green landscape, with stately ruins,) the tears came into my eyes, and I passed an hour or two in that state of luxurious enjoyment, which is

the highest privilege of the mind of man, and which perhaps makes him amends for many sorrows.   (x. 108)

He continues by describing Poussin's landscapes as 'more properly pictures of time than of place':

They have a fine *moral* perspective, not inferior to Claude's aërial one. They carry the imagination back two or four thousand years at least, and bury it in the remote twilight of history. There is an opaqueness and solemnity in his colouring, assimilating with the tone of long-past events: his buildings are stiff with age; his implements of husbandry are such as would belong to the first rude stages of civilization; his harvests are such (as in the Ruth and Boaz[27]) as would yield to no modern sickle; his grapes . . . are a load to modern shoulders; there is a simplicity and undistinguishing breadth in his figures; and over all, the hand of time has drawn its veil.

Hazlitt himself (we notice) seems to have sensed the affinity between Poussin and Keats, if we are to judge from the fact that he used a line of Keats—

And blind Orion hungry for the morn[28]

—as the motto for his essay 'On a Landscape of Nicolas Poussin' in *Table-Talk*. This essay is so relevant to my subject that I must quote from it at length:

This great and learned man might be said to see nature through the glass of time: he alone has a right to be considered as the painter of classical antiquity. Sir Joshua has done him justice in this respect. He could give to the scenery of his heroic fables that unimpaired look of original nature, full, solid, large, luxuriant, teeming with life and power; or deck it with all the pomp of art, with temples and towers, and mythologic groves. . . . With a laborious and mighty grasp, he put nature into the mould of the ideal and antique; and was among painters (more than any one else) what Milton was among poets. There is in both something of the same pedantry, the same stiffness, the same elevation, the same grandeur, the same mixture of art and nature, the same richness of borrowed materials, the same unity of character. . . . He who can show the world in its first naked glory, with the hues of fancy spread over it, or in its high and palmy state, with the gravity of history stamped on the proud monuments of vanished empire,—who, by his 'so potent art,' can recal time past, transport us to distant places, and join the regions of imagination (a new conquest) to those of reality,—who teaches us not only what nature is, but what she has been, and is capable of being,—he who does this, and does it with simplicity, with truth, and grandeur, is lord of nature and her powers; and his mind is universal, and his art the master-art! . . . Poussin was, of all painters, the most poetical. He was the painter of ideas. No one ever told a story half so well; nor so well knew what was capable of being told by the pencil. He seized on, and struck off with grace and precision, just that point of view which would be likely to catch the reader's fancy. . . . His Giants sitting on the tops of craggy mountains, as huge themselves, and playing idly on their Pan's-pipes, seem to have been seated there these three thousand years, and to know the beginning and the end of their own story. . . . Even inanimate and dumb things speak a language of their own.   (viii. 169–71)

Hazlitt goes on to praise a specific painting of Poussin's, the 'Cephalus and Aurora' exhibited by the British Institution in 1816:

There was a picture of Aurora in the British Gallery a year or two ago. It was a suffusion of golden light. The Goddess wore her saffron-coloured robes, and appeared just risen from the gloomy bed of old Tithonus. Her very steeds, milk-white, were tinged with the yellow dawn. It was a personification of the morning.

It will have become apparent that many of the most eloquent passages in Hazlitt's writings are on the subject of painting. He felt the splendour of Titian or Poussin as a challenge, and only feared that he might not be able to rise to the occasion. So we find him ending his account of the pictures at Hampton Court with the remark:

We should be sorry indeed to have profaned them by description or criticism

—and concluding his account of two other collections with the words:

We have endeavoured to do justice to both, but we confess we have fallen very short even of our own hopes and expectations.

In fact his *Sketches* contain some of the most splendid tributes to great painting ever written, and since Keats must on occasion have heard him 'descanting' in conversation in just this way, I hope that I may be forgiven if I quote one further passage to exemplify this:

A fine gallery of pictures is a sort of illustration of Berkeley's Theory of Matter and Spirit. It is like a palace of thought—another universe, built of air, of shadows, of colours. Every thing seems 'palpable to feeling as to sight'. Substances turn to shadows by the painter's arch-chemic touch; shadows harden into substances. 'The eye is made the fool of the other senses, or else worth all the rest.' The material is in some sense embodied in the immaterial, or, at least, we see all things in a sort of intellectual mirror. The world of art is an enchanting deception. We discover distance in a glazed surface; a province is contained in a foot of canvass; a thin evanescent tint gives the form and pressure of rocks and trees; an inert shape has life and motion in it. Time stands still, and the dead re-appear, by means of this 'so potent art!' (x. 19)

Quite apart from his art-criticism, Hazlitt makes constant references to the visual arts in his writings on literature. This is strikingly illustrated by the fact that he devoted a whole lecture in the series *On the English Comic Writers* to 'Hogarth and the Grand and Familiar Style of Painting'. In his *Lectures on the English Poets*, which we know Keats to have attended, allusions to painting are ubiquitous. 'I went last tuesday, an hour too late, to Hazlitt's Lecture on poetry', he wrote on the 23rd of January 1818, '[and] got there just as they were coming out, when all these pounced upon me. Hazlitt, John Hunt & son, Wells, Bewick, all the Landseers, Bob Harris, Rox of the Burrough Aye & more.' On the 21st of February he wrote that he had become a regular attender, adding that he was 'very disappointed at his treatment of Chatterton'. No doubt he told Hazlitt so, for he began his next lecture by saying that he was sorry that he had 'given dissatisfaction to some persons, with whom I would willingly agree on all such matters', though he held firm to his point that it was foolish to praise Chatterton for the work which he might conceivably have produced if he had lived longer. Passages in these lectures which may have influenced Keats are not hard to find. In his fourth lecture, for example, Hazlitt remarked that 'a translation of some of the . . . serious tales in Boccaccio . . . if executed with taste and spirit, could not fail to succeed in the present day'. It is true that the plan of Keats and his friend John Hamilton Reynolds to write a number of poems based on the *Decameron* had originally been inspired by Leigh Hunt; but since then, as we have seen, Keats had come to feel that 'italian tales' were among the things that Hunt had cheapened by his advocacy of them, and it seems likely that

Hazlitt's encouragement was responsible for his turning back to Boccaccio, and perhaps also for his choice of the story of Isabella. Although the general question of the influence of these lectures on Keats is outside my scope, it is worth emphasizing that this series seems to be the only course of lectures on English poetry that is known to have had an important influence on a major poet.

It is remarkable how frequently Hazlitt refers to the visual arts in these lectures, whether for the purpose of indicating a parallel, marking a contrast, or simply finding a vivid metaphor or simile. He remarks that 'the strokes of [Chaucer's] pencil always tell' and singles out as his 'characteristic excellence . . . what might be termed *gusto*'. 'The colours with which he paints seem yet wet and breathing', he says of Thomson's *Seasons*; while he calls Crabbe 'his own landscape-painter, and engraver too', and describes his poems as examples of '*still life*'. In Byron he censures 'the everlasting repetition of one subject, the same dark ground of fiction, with the darker colours of the poet's mind spread over it'. He constantly refers to poems as pictures, and to poets as engaged in painting with words. In another critic this might be a figure of speech of little significance, but in Hazlitt it is not. He is for ever comparing the poets with particular painters: Poussin, Claude, Rubens, Raphael, Titian, Rembrandt. In his first lecture he deals with the old question of 'the comparative merits of painting and poetry', like a hundred critics of the eighteenth century:

Painting gives the object itself; poetry what it implies. . . . But it may be asked then, Is there anything better than Claude Lorraine's landscapes, than Titian's portraits, than Raphael's cartoons, or the Greek statues?

Not for the only time, he here plays down the importance of Greek sculpture:

The Greek statues are little else than specious forms. They are marble to the touch and to the heart. They have not an informing principle within them. In their faultless excellence they appear sufficient to themselves. By their beauty they are raised above the frailties of passion or suffering. By their beauty they are deified. But they are not objects of religious faith to us, and their forms are a reproach to common humanity. They seem to have no sympathy with us, and not to want our admiration.

It would be curious to have the comment of Keats on this passage.

Hazlitt's lectures must have played their part in helping to give Hunt the idea for his Spenser Gallery: perhaps it was from Hazlitt, as much as from Hunt, that Keats learned to read Spenser with a painter's eye. It is particularly interesting to find Hazlitt comparing the allegory of *The Faerie Queene* with the allegory in Poussin's paintings:

Some people will say . . . that they cannot understand it on account of the allegory. . . . This is very idle. . . . It might as well be pretended that, we cannot see Poussin's pictures for the allegory, as that the allegory prevents us from understanding Spenser.

Hazlitt's enthusiasm for Poussin and Claude is evident everywhere. In discussing pastoral, for example, he compares the *Arcadia* unfavourably with Poussin's celebrated painting 'Les Bergers d'Arcadie'.[29] The English climate is not an eternal spring, he remarks, and similarly 'we have no pastoral-writers equal to Theocritus, nor any Landscapes like those of Claude Lorraine'.

There is a particulary interesting passage in the fourth lecture in which Hazlitt quotes the following lines from Dryden's 'Ode on St. Cecilia'—

> The jolly god in triumph comes,
> Sound the trumpets, beat the drums;
> Flush'd with a purple grace,
> He shews his honest face

—and comments that this 'does not answer, as it ought, to our idea of the God, returning from the conquest of India, with satyrs and wild beasts, that he had tamed, following in his train; crowned with vine leaves, and riding in a chariot drawn by leopards—such as we have seen him painted by Titian or Rubens!' Hazlitt goes on to comment that 'lyrical poetry, of all others, bears the nearest resemblance to painting: it deals in hieroglyphics and passing figures, which depend for effect, not on the working out, but on the selection. It is the dance and pantomime of poetry.' The lectures also contain a number of references to 'the Grecian mythology', including a passage taken almost *verbatim* from an essay first published in the *Examiner* in 1814:

If we have once enjoyed the cool shade of a tree, and been lulled into a deep repose by the sound of a brook running at its foot, we are sure that wherever we can find a shady stream, we can enjoy the same pleasure again; so that when we imagine these objects, we can easily form a mystic personification of the friendly power that inhabits them, Dryad or Naiad, offering its cool fountain or its tempting shade. Hence the origin of the Grecian mythology.[30]

These sentences from *The Examiner* are strikingly close to a passage in 'I stood tiptoe' and must be associated with Book IV of *The Excursion* as among the formative influences on Keats's conception of Greek mythology.

In his partly satirical account of the Lake Poets Hazlitt points out that in their work 'all was to be natural and new', and that this involved the banishment of 'the whole heathen mythology':

A classical allusion was considered as a piece of antiquated foppery; capital letters were no more allowed in print, than letters-patent of nobility were permitted in real life.

A modern poet of this school, Hazlitt continues, is a great hater:

He hates prose; he hates all poetry but his own; he hates the dialogues in Shakespeare; he hates music, dancing, and painting; he hates Rubens, he hates Rembrandt; he hates Raphael, he hates Titian; he hates Vandyke; he hates the antique; he hates the Apollo Belvidere; he hates the Venus of Medicis.

Such a narrowness of taste was foreign to Hazlitt's genius. He knew that the delight felt by an understanding spectator as he studies the work of the great painters can be a spur to creative effort as well as 'a cure (for the time at least) for low-thoughted cares and uneasy passions':

We are abstracted to another sphere: we breathe empyrean air; we enter into the minds of Raphael, of Titian, of Poussin, of the Caracci, and look at nature with their eyes; we live in time past, and seem identified with the permanent forms of things. The business of the world at large, and even its pleasures, appear like a vanity and an impertinence . . . when compared with the solitude, the silence, the speaking looks, the unfading forms [in their great paintings]. . . . Here is the mind's true home. The contemplation of truth and beauty is the proper object for which we were created, which calls forth the most intense desires of the soul, and of which it never tires.   (x. 7–8)

The masterpieces of art deepen our understanding of the universe, and teach us to find more in the visible world than we would otherwise see:

Every object becomes lustrous from the light thrown back upon it by the mirror of art; and by the aid of the pencil we may be said to touch and handle the objects of sight. The air-wove visions that hover on the verge of existence have a bodily presence given them on the canvas: the form of beauty is changed into a substance: the dream and the glory of the universe is made 'palpable to feeling as to sight' . . . .

(viii. 7)

So it is that the painter 'learns to look at nature with different eyes . . ., understands the texture and meaning of the visible universe, and "sees into the life of things" . . . by . . . the improved exercise of his faculties, and an intimate sympathy with nature'.[31] Keats was not a painter, but he loved painting, and his poetry would not be what it is if he had not learned—partly from Hazlitt—to see nature with the creative eye of a lover of art.

V

THE REST OF 'OUR SET'—
AND A MURDERER

Whoever has been much in the way of visiting museums, and
of seeing collections of paintings . . . must have seen some pictures of the great masters, worthy of being seen and remembered; and even a copy, or engraving, if well executed, may
convey something like the enthusiasm of the original: it is true,
the light is only reflected, the heat is only reflected; yet real
is that light, and that warmth real.

Poetics, by GEORGE DYER, 1812[1]

LEIGH HUNT, Benjamin Robert Haydon, William Hazlitt:
Keats was fortunate to be introduced to the world of painting and
sculpture by three such men. Hunt was a dilettante in the most
honourable sense of the word, a man unusually endowed with
the faculty of enjoyment and the gift of communicating his enjoyment to others. Haydon was not a great painter, but he believed
that he was: the obsessive intensity with which he devoted himself to his art, and to leading the life of a genius, had a profound effect on Keats when he was at his most impressionable.
From Haydon's conversation he heard constantly of the labour
and concentration required of an artist and gained a deeper
understanding of the importance of technique in the continual
striving towards perfection. And then in Hazlitt Keats met the
only major English critic who has written as perceptively and
as eloquently of painting as he has of literature.

It is surprising how many of Keats's other friends were also
keenly interested in the visual arts. 'From a few Words of yours
when last I saw you', he wrote in one of his earliest letters, to
Charles Cowden Clarke, 'I have no doubt but that you have
something in your Portfolio which I should by rights see—I will
put you in Mind of it.'[2] Most members of Keats's circle had
portfolios of prints and drawings, and were in the habit of discussing poetry and painting as Sister Arts. John Hamilton
Reynolds wrote several poems inspired by particular paintings.
Charles Dilke was a great admirer of Fuseli: later in his life he

became a notable collector of Blake's drawings. Lamb wrote a poem 'On the Celebrated Picture by Lionardo da Vinci, Called The Virgin of the Rocks', and took a lively interest in prints. In his essay, 'Christ's Hospital Five and Thirty Years Ago', he remembers himself as a schoolboy with nothing to do, 'shivering at cold windows of print-shops, to extract a little amusement'; while in another essay he refers to 'the wary connoisseur in prints' who 'never fails to consult the *quis sculpsit* in the corner, before he pronounces some rare piece to be a Vivares, or a Woollet'.[3] Horace Smith shared Goethe's view that drawing was the most moral of all occupations, while in the 1820's he was to write enthusiastically about sculpture in *The London Magazine*. The survival of a single letter proves that Keats knew William Mayor well enough to urge him to spend a night at Wentworth Place:[4] Mayor was a pupil of Haydon's who became well known as a collector and art-dealer. John Landseer, the painter and engraver who was the father of Charles, Thomas, and (Sir) Edwin Landseer, was among those present at Haydon's 'immortal dinner'. Another minor figure in the world of art whom we find Keats meeting was Archibald Archer, who called on him one day towards the end of 1818 because he 'wanted some information, by my means, from Hunt and Haydon':[5] he was a regular exhibitor at the Royal Academy: in a later letter Keats censures him for jilting Caroline Mathew. Keats knew and liked much better William Bewick, another pupil of Haydon's who was also a passionate admirer of the Elgin Marbles. Bewick—who was no relation of the great Thomas Bewick—shared Haydon's taste for literary subjects: his painting entitled 'Una in the Forest' was exhibited at Spring Gardens in 1820. In 1818 Haydon told Keats that he and Bewick were 'the only men I ever liked with all my heart'.[6] We hear of Keats meeting him on one occasion at the Leicester Gallery, and on another at dinner at Haydon's when Hazlitt was also present. On the 20th of January 1818 Bewick was one of the friends who 'pounced' on Keats when he arrived at a lecture of Hazlitt's 'an hour too late':[7] later that year Keats sends Hazlitt and Bewick his regards, in a letter to Haydon.

Keats was also on friendly terms with Peter De Wint, best known as a painter in water-colours, and William Hilton, the historical painter, who were brothers-in-law and who lived at 10 Percy Street, Rathbone Place. One day in March 1819 Keats called at Taylor's and found that he and Hilton 'had set out to dine with me': accordingly he followed them back, later accompanying them part of their way home, after an agreeable evening topped off with a cigar.[8] Later in the year we hear of Keats dining with Hilton and Woodhouse at Taylor's. In his letters to Taylor he was in the habit of sending his remembrances to 'Percy Street', and it is clear that he took a lively interest in the painting that was done there. 'Prythee Remember me to Percy Street', he wrote to Taylor on the 21st of June 1818:

—Tell Hilton that one gratification on my return will bee to find him engaged in a History Piece to his content—and Tell Dewint I shall become a disputant on the Landscape.

It is clear that Keats's interest and affection were reciprocated, for both of the painters contributed to a fund to help meet his expenses in Italy. Hilton executed a well-known chalk drawing of Keats, as well as the disappointing portrait commissioned by Woodhouse and now in the National Gallery.

Keats had two other friends whose interest in the arts is of particular importance to us: Charles Brown and Joseph Severn.

Since Brown was Keats's most intimate associate for about two years, as well as his collaborator in *Otho the Great*, the fact that he was interested in painting confirms the impression that Keats found artistic people congenial. As a young man in St. Petersburg Brown must have seen something of the paintings there, and he himself (as his son recorded) 'was a very fair artist, with his pencil, and with water-colors':[9] a claim that is substantiated by his well-known pencil drawing of Keats.[10] Brown and Keats first met in 1817, and in June of the following year they set out on a walking tour to Scotland.

The letters which Keats wrote on this tour will be considered in the next chapter, but some mention must be made here of the account of it which Brown wrote and later published in a provincial newspaper.[11] Although it is not an outstanding piece of writing, it is of interest because Brown makes it clear that 'beauty and sublimity of nature' were the objects of their journey and gives one or two vivid glimpses of Keats, as in his description of the poet's first sight of Lake Windermere:

Hitherto, Keats had witnessed nothing superior to Devonshire; but, beautiful as that is, he was now tempted to speak of it with indifference.

At the first turn from the road, before descending to the hamlet of Bowness, we both simultaneously came to a full stop. The lake lay before us. His bright eyes darted on a mountain-peak, beneath which was gently floating on a silver cloud; thence to a very small island, adorned with the foliage of trees, that lay beneath us, and surrounded by water of a glorious hue, when he exclaimed—'How can I believe in that?—surely it cannot be!'   (i. 425–6)

Occasionally Brown's descriptions are well composed:

That craggy mountain at the head of Windermere increased in grandeur as we proceeded. . . . At every third step, something new, some change came upon us. A chasm was more distinctly seen; the woods on the opposite side seemed, now and then, to separate as if to display the torrent they had concealed; a new effect of light and shade was shown by some travelling cloud, shrouding midway a mountain, while its head was dazzling in the sun. . . . Here are the beautiful and the sublime in unison.   (i. 427–8)

Near Dundrennan the two men saw a striking scene:

With the town not far before us, we were enchanted with the view; the winding bay—the wood-covered hills—the blue mountains beyond them—the island at the mouth of the bay—the sea on each side of it, and in the distance—the extraordinary fertility of the valley, and the surrounding country—all formed a scene that even Keats confessed to be equal and similar to the best parts of his favourite Devon.   (i. 439)

Keats had to break short his holiday to nurse his brother, but when Tom died he moved into Brown's part of the large double house called Wentworth Place. 'The Art of Poetry is not sufficient for us', Keats wrote to Dilke on the 31st of July 1819:

and if we get on in that as well as we do in painting we shall by next winter crush the Reviews and the royal Academy. Indeed if Brown would take a little of my advice he could not fail to be first pallet of his day. But odd as it may appear, he says plainly that he cannot see any force in my plea for putting Skies in the back ground—and leaving indian ink out of an ash tree—The other day he was sketching Shanklin Church and as I saw how the business was going on, I challenged him to a trial of Skill—he lent me Pencil and Paper—we keep the Sketches to contend for the Prize at the Gallerry—I will not say whose I think best—but really I do not think Brown's done to the top of the Art.

By an odd chance we know that Brown's enthusiasm for Hogarth gave Keats a nightmare during the following year.[12]

An interesting sidelight on Brown's activities as a collector of prints is provided by a letter he wrote in Italy two years after the death of Keats:

> While in Rome I shall buy all the good engravings I can lay my hands on for my modicum of money. They are to be picked up here and there. . . . I have just purchased a book containing 191 large and small of Wierotter's engravings for £3. 15/-. . . . They are the most beautiful landscapes, and bits of landscape, you can conceive. . . . Are Piranesi's works still much sought after? I must buy some,—they are glorious prints, full of poetry and lies. The modern style of engraving in Italy is as hard as the copper; the artists might copy Ben West tolerably, but their copies of Raphael &c are intolerable,—they have no idea of an indefinite line, and, vain fools! they insist on making some cursed alterations in light or shade, or something they cannot understand. You will be surprised to hear that Italian painters make no use of their fine old masters. . . . In professed copies from Titian or Raphael they lay on their positive blues & reds, while the originals are entirely painted in mixed colours, and tell you the originals are *faded*,—this is incomprehensible. It is needless to say they have a poor opinion of English art, which certainly emulates the old masters.[13]

Another letter written on the same journey is of interest because it gives us a hint of the sort of conversation Brown and Keats had had five years before, on their northern tour. It is an imaginary conversation 'upon the difference of scenery in Italy and England':

> A Scotchman would not thank you for intersecting with hedge-rows the beautiful plain round Perth, [observes the one traveller] which has been truly likened to an Italian landscape; nor would any sort of enclosure be suitable to the character of this scenery. Observe the graceful composition of outline, its gentle undulations, so varied, so harmonious, and its well-wooded hills, backed by the lofty Apennines. Every thing here bears the stamp of classic ground,—ground trod by Fauns and Dryads. In England the character of the landscape is totally different; it has the look of comfort and home-feeling, and boasts of its Robin Goodfellow and his train of household fairies.

He appeals to his companion to 'compare the landscapes of Claude and Poussin with those of Gainsborough and Morland'; and when he objects to that, asks him to 'look at the works of

Turner, and tell me which are the superior ones,—those of real English scenery, or those where he has profited by his visit to Italy'. His opponent sees the force of this argument, but tries to counter with a reference to 'our romantic lakes and mountains in Cumberland and Westmoreland'.[14]

These Italian letters do not contain much criticism of works of art, though the Cathedral at Sienna stimulates some perceptive comments. Brown notes that here

the spirit of decoration is carried to so high a pitch, that in the insides of the marble basins for the holy water, there are sundry sorts of carved fishes, with eels wriggling up the sides. One of these basins rests on an antique tripod, with bas-reliefs of heathen deities,—and those who think it worth while, may take advantage of the allegory.

His opinion of the marble floor is less censorious: 'There are designs of the utmost style, spirit, and power of drawing; and the effect is produced by no more than a black outline on inlaid marble, of white and one or two shades of grey.' In the library he was impressed by the frescoes, and disposed to believe the tradition that some of them had been designed by Raphael: 'I was astonished at their freshness of colour', he adds, 'especially in the one ascribed to Raphael; it looks as if his hand had not quitted it longer ago than yesterday,—it makes him our contemporary.'[15]

Keats knew Joseph Severn before he knew Brown. Severn was the son of a musician, and had been apprenticed at an early age to an engraver called William Bond. Under his direction he spent seven or eight years copying famous works of art, but as respite from this drudgery he also managed to attend classes in painting at the Royal Academy. Keats and Severn probably met between the late autumn of 1815 and the spring of the following year. Severn later looked back on this meeting as a turning-point in his intellectual development:

A new world was opened to me, and I was raised from the mechanical drudgery of my art to the hope of brighter and more elevated courses.[16]

By 1817 the two men were close friends, if we can judge by the fact that Keats inscribed a copy of his *Poems* to Severn 'with all his Heart'; but it is clear that their meeting meant more to Severn than it did to Keats. Although Severn was the senior by almost two years, he did not have the personality to make a deep impression on Keats, nor was he the intellectual equal of the brilliant circle of men among whom Keats already found himself by the end of 1816.

Soon after he met Keats we find Severn making good progress in the Antique Class of the Royal Academy and so attracting the notice of Fuseli (who was Keeper at the time) and of other good judges. We hear of him drawing the Laocoon and the statue of the fighting gladiators. His first attempt in oils was a figure-study of Hermia and Helena in *A Midsummer Night's Dream*, which he read at the suggestion of Keats. But his great attempt was a painting on the subject set for the History prize by the Academy: Una seizing the dagger from the despairing Red Cross Night. Severn had already heard Keats talking enthusiastically about Spenser: now he found that his friend could repeat without the book part of the passage prescribed by the Academicians. On the 15th of November 1819 Keats wrote to Severn about his painting and made the same sort of transposition of painting and poem that we have already seen in a letter to Haydon:

> I have not been able to figure your manner of executing the Cave of despair, therefore it will be at any rate a novelty and surprise to me. . . . I shall call upon you some morning shortly . . . when we will proceed to the Academy. I think you must be suited with a good painting light in your Bay window. I wish you to return the Compliment by going with me to see a Poem I have hung up for the Prize in the Lecture Room of the surry Institution. I have many Rivals the most threatning are An Ode to Lord Castlereagh, and a new series of Hymns for the New, new Jerusalem Chapel—You had best put me into your Cave of despair.

It is interesting to notice that this passage was to be one of those in Leigh Hunt's 'Gallery of Pictures from Spenser' in *Imagination and Fancy*—where it is assigned to Salvator Rosa. Keats liked the painting, as did the judges, for it was awarded the first Gold Medal to have been given for twelve years.[17]

The success, the 'solid pudding' (as he himself put it) which Severn now expected, did not make its appearance: 'All I got was such an amount of ugly envy that I was obliged to forsake the Royal Academy.'[18] Sharp tells us that the friendship of Keats was particularly important for Severn at this time. Severn was greatly struck by Keats's powers of observation, and always remembered how Keats would watch the movement of the wind across fields of barley or oats and say that it reminded him of an 'inland sea'.

It is difficult to estimate the influence of the one man on the other in any detail, because Severn had a most inaccurate memory. At times his inaccuracy seems to have infected his biographer. Sharp tells us, for example, that 'Keats often journey[ed] to London expressly to see Severn and to go with him to the National Gallery, the Sculpture galleries of the British Museum, and elsewhere'.[19] Since the National Gallery did not come into existence until 1824, we can only conjecture that Sharp is referring to the Angerstein Collection. There is no reason to doubt Sharp's statement that Keats 'was always glad to learn anything he could about the technique of painting' from Severn, though there seems to be no corroboration for the assertion that 'it was through those lessons that he came to see how greatly his much-admired friend Haydon had over-estimated his powers'.[20] Sharp is on stronger ground when he tells us that it was Keats who first awakened Severn's mind to the beauty and the significance of Greek mythology. Severn acknowledged this when he found himself in Rome after the death of his friend:

Rome, the *real* Rome would never have become a joy to me—not, at any rate, for a very long time, and even then with difficulty and at best obscurely—had it not been for Keats's talks with me about the Greek spirit,—the Religion of the Beautiful, the Religion of Joy, as he used to call it. All that was finest in sculpture—and, as I came to see directly or indirectly, all that was finest too in painting, in *everything*— was due to that supreme influence. 'I never cease to wonder at all that incarnate Delight', Keats remarked to me once: nor do I either, now that in inferior measure I too see something of what he saw.[21]

'Keats made me in love with the real living Spirit of the past', Severn told a friend on another occasion. 'He was the first to point out to me how essentially modern that Spirit is: "It's an immortal youth", he would say, "just as there is no *Now* or *Then* for the Holy Ghost".'[22]

There is the ring of truth in the tradition that Keats once described Severn as 'the most astonishingly suggestive innocent'[23] he had ever met (a man would hardly invent such a description of himself), and everything seems to point to the general truth of the following passage in Sharp's biography:

Every time he went with Severn to the Sculpture Galleries, or to Picture Exhibitions, [Keats] learned something or gained some suggestive hint. One day, early in their friendship, for example, the young artist waxed so enthusiastic about Titian's 'Bacchus' that a visit was specially made to the National Gallery. Keats was deeply impressed, and soon after read to his friend the now famous description of Bacchus and his crew in 'Endymion'. He went again and again to see the Elgin marbles, and would sit for an hour or more at a time beside them rapt in revery. On one such occasion Severn came upon the young poet, with eyes shining so brightly and face so lit up by some visionary rapture, that he stole quietly away without intrusion.[24]

Since Severn had a gift for describing pictures in a way that made Keats want to see them, it seems worth while to quote a passage from an imaginary letter from Galileo to Milton which he wrote in 1848. It is introduced by a passage that also has its relevance to Keats:

We are at last emerging from these ugly, whitewashed puritanical blights, which have pressed down upon us as a nation; ... A ... murky cloud of Puritanism and Sectarianism, or by whatever name the thing be best called, is always striving to manufacture a besom wherewith to sweep away all the rainbow-glories of the imagination, all that innocent sunshine of life, wherein we love to recreate new brightened ways for our tired wandering feet, such as we see so readily as children when we do not place tyrannic bonds upon our imagination.[25]

There speaks the man who had heard Keats discoursing on the Greek 'Religion of Joy'. Here is the description of the painting:

There is a new fresco picture, by Guido, at the Rospigliosi Palace, which seems to me, as it seems to everybody, the most lovely work ever done. It represents Aurora flying onward, dispelling the night and its vapours of gloom. She gaily throws about her numerous flowers, which seem to collect the dew as they fall towards the grateful earth. She is a beautiful and graceful figure in ample flying folds of saffron windings, which do not conceal her feet, with which the earth is to be blessed.

She looks round on the ample light and radiant power of Apollo, who in his never-resting car guides his bounding Steeds, who seem to splash about the light he breathes on all sides; but more particularly he seems to inspire the gentle hand-in-handed Hours who so gratefully encircle his car, that he seems almost upheld by them. There is no end of their varied attitudes: some are turned from you like the hours you lose, some look cheerfully and catch your eye like the moments you profit by and enjoy, but they all go tripping on to show you the moral that Time never stops. All this golden light would be overpowering were it not that Guido has given one little touch of contrast, for down below on the right-hand side, deep under Aurora, you see the fresh blue mysterious sea, dark and lovely in its nature, yet about to be impressed with the moving light which has already begun to tinge its shore. . . . Carlo Maratti pointed out to me that Guido, in the happy composition of the Hours, had availed himself of an antique bas-relief at the Villa Borghese, which may also have given to him the idea of the picture; but if so, like a great genius, he has made the adaptation beautiful to our eyes by the marvellous way he has set it. In the marble I should not have been struck so much with the three figures hand in hand, but when they are made to represent the hours about the car of Apollo, then it is that the beauty comes out.[26]

The 'hand-in-handed Hours' on the bas-relief have an affinity with the vase that inspired the 'Ode on Indolence'.

Brown and Severn were among the closest and most devoted of Keats's friends. I now want to glance at the writing of a man whom Keats seems never to have met. Since crime has always appealed to a wider public than art, it is hardly surprising that Thomas Griffiths Wainewright is now remembered only as a forger and a murderer; but in the early 1820's he enjoyed a brief vogue as a critic of art. Since his essays did not begin to appear in the *London Magazine* until January 1820, there is no question of his having influenced the poetry of Keats; but they deserve our attention because they express a taste remarkably close to that of Keats and his friends.

Wainewright's grandfather, Ralph Griffiths, had been well known as the editor of the *Monthly Review*—in which office he was succeeded by Wainewright's father. Wainewright's mother, who died in giving him birth, was a highly intellectual woman whose interest in the philosophy of Locke was particularly mentioned in her obituary. The young Wainewright was therefore brought up in a cultivated environment, and since such men as Lawrence, Flaxman, Stothard, Westall, and Fuseli were among his father's visitors, it is easy to understand why he turned towards painting as a career. At the age of nineteen he was apprenticed to Thomas Phillips, the fashionable portrait-painter; while he was working for him he painted a portrait of Byron which is now lost.[27] After a year in the army, which seems to have done him little good, he returned to civilian life and to his former pursuits. At times he suffered from melancholia, and he probably wrote two articles entitled 'Memoirs of a Hypochondriac' which appeared in the *London Magazine* in obvious imitation of de Quincey's *Confessions of an English Opium-Eater*.[28] One of the many curious features of his life is his avowal that about the year 1815 'the writings of Wordsworth did much towards calming the confusing whirl necessarily incident to sudden mutations':[29] a strange anticipation of the experience of John Stuart Mill a decade later. Wainewright's taste in literature was often excellent, and he had a particular admiration for Keats, passages from whose poems he more than once compared to specific paintings.[30]

Oscar Wilde was fascinated by Wainewright, and was neither the first nor the last critic to see a close relationship between certain features of Wainewright's taste and the strange cruelty of his criminal career. Yet if Wainewright's taste was perverted, then the taste of a number of his contemporaries—including Leigh Hunt, Lamb, and perhaps Keats himself—comes perilously near to suspicion. Perhaps it is best to regard his essays as representing a vulgarization of the taste of the *London Magazine* group; but the vulgarization is more a matter of style and presentation than of critical opinion. What particularly concerns us is his insistence on the importance of prints and print-collecting to anyone interested in the visual arts.

The tone and object of Wainewright's essays are indicated by some of the titles he gave them—'Sentimentalities on the Fine Arts', 'Dogmas for Dilettanti', 'The Academy of Taste for Grown Gentlemen, or The Infant Connoisseur's Go-Cart'.[31] The facetious style has proved an effective deterrent to modern readers; but the aim of the essays is perfectly serious, being simply 'the correction of taste'. Wainewright is never tired of drawing parallels between poetry and the fine arts:

Our critics seem hardly aware of the intimate connexion, or rather of the identity, of the primal seeds of poetry and painting; nor that any true advancement in the serious study of one art co-generates a proportionate perfection in the other. If a man who did not feel Michel Angelo, should talk of his *gusto* for Milton, depend upon it he deceives one of two persons—you or himself: so likewise *vice versâ*. The moment you entered Elia's room, you could swear to his selection of authors by

his selection of framed prints—Leonardos and early Raffaëllos; and
it is impossible to read Barry Cornwall without a conviction that his
cored loves were Correggio, Parmegiano, and Bolognian Giulio . . .;
Michel, Leonardo, Rembrandt coming in only by way of relief: Rubens
rejected altogether.[32]

Often he quotes Reynolds:

Judgment in painting, as well as in poetry, 'is an acquired talent
which can only be produced by deep thought, and a long continued
intercourse with the best models of composition'. This unanswerable
truth should temper the rashness of decision, and suggest, 'that if
painting be a subject on which much time has not been bestowed, the
judgment *may* be erroneous, and in many cases *must* be so.' The proceedings and notions of people who regard poetry and painting as
matters of amusement are immaterial; but those who wish to form
their taste, and elevate their imagination, must begin by submitting
themselves humbly to the acknowledged masters, imputing all want
of relish to their own immature or distorted vision, and taking especial
care never to *risque* a criticism, until fully satisfied that they enter into,
and comprehend, the principles and aim of the object of their study.
This will ask some pains.[33]

'Some pains' Wainewright himself had clearly devoted to the
study of the fine arts. Yet when he set up as a critic he seems
never to have been abroad. One has only to turn over a few pages
of his essays to notice the frequency of his references to prints.
Talking of Rubens, for example, he points out that 'the famous
"Garden of love" ' is 'known by the splendid and somewhat
scarce print by Bolswert',[34] while he refers a little later to 'that
sublime vision of a dissolving world, Poussin's Deluge', adding
that he believes it to be 'tolerably well known by means of
Laurent's clever print'.[35] In his discussion of his favourite, Giulio
Romano, Wainewright observes:

The pictures occasionally exhibited in England as the works of this
master will certainly not bear me out in the following observations on
his style; . . . but if you will turn over the folios of Messrs. Woodburn,
Molteno, and Colnaghi, I think we shall not materially disagree.[36]

It soon becomes evident that the area of Wainewright's own
expertise—painter though he was—was not painting itself but
print-collecting. He accurately describes himself as 'not *picture*,
but *print-learned*'.[37]

In this matter Wainewright merely carried to an extreme a

common habit which must be taken into account by anyone who wishes to study the criticism of art before the present century. It is true that the best critics have always insisted on the need to see the paintings themselves, and have condemned the tendency to judge them from prints or photographs. This insistence can no more be gainsaid than the insistence of classical scholars that Homer should be read in Greek. Yet when one examines the inspiration which has been derived from the great masterpieces of painting or of poetry, one often finds that it has been a translation or its visual equivalent—a print or a photograph—that has played the vital role. Usually, of course, the parallel between translations and prints is inexact. Whereas many writers have derived inspiration from Greek literature, like Keats himself, without being able to read a single poem or play in the original language, most of them have been able to see a few great paintings. Wainewright and Keats both had access to a considerable number of great paintings in London collections. Yet it remains true that it was as often, or oftener, prints that he saw in Colnaghi's window, or in the houses of his friends, that caught the eye of Keats and helped to fill his poems with beauty caught from the conceptions of Titian, Poussin, and Claude Lorrain.

Wainewright sets out to help his readers to form collections of prints for themselves. He acknowledges that difficulties lie in their way:

Obstacles arise to the general diffusion, as in Italy, of the grand gusto, from different circumstances. One is, that several of the finest pictures have never been engraved at all, or so inadequately as to mislead rather than satisfy—another is, the extreme rarity and high price of many of the most desirable prints.[38]

He goes on to complain of the

want of a well-selected, roughly-priced catalogue of the *most faithful engravings from the most characteristic inventions of the most prominent masters,*

and to point out that for lack of such a manual,

Fuseli's admirable and indispensable second lecture loses much of its utility to the student in a practical point of view, who cannot be much enlightened by critiques on works which he never saw; but let it be placed before him accompanied by a proper set of illustrations, and he will acquire, in six days, as good a view of the generic features of the different schools as I have been able to do in six years.

He accordingly proposes to attempt 'a little essay towards this desirable object, to be continued . . . by small parcels through some succeeding numbers of the LONDON MAGAZINE', and in fact, in a characteristically sporadic and whimsical manner, he makes the attempt. In this same article he lists prints of seven of Tintoretto's paintings, including 'The Origin of the Galaxy' (The Origin of the Milky Way) and varying in price from a guinea to five shillings. The position with Caravaggio, as he points out, is much less favourable, since so many of his pictures have been destroyed that

we are obliged to glean our knowledge of their merit from the prints of Cherubino Alberti . . ., the small etchings of Gallestruzzi; and, what is still worse, from the exaggerations of Goltzius and Sanredam, and the wiry meagreness of that impudently-unfaithful mannerist, Sante-Bartoli.[39]

In his next contribution Wainewright gives a list of prints from Giulio Romano, including 'The Death of Procris', 'Hylas', 'The Hours leading out the horses of the Sun', 'The Dance of Apollo and the Muses', and 'Venus withholding Adonis from the Chase'. Giulio was a particular enthusiasm of Wainewright's, and he insisted that whereas

Poussin is vulgarly considered the most eminent [painter] in Grecian fable: the visitors to Mantua know otherwise, and that the agility, untrammelled motions, vigour, and earnestness of Giulio's actors shew a far deeper penetration into the spirit of the traditional days,—of the age of the demi-gods, than the painted statuary of the Frenchman.[40]

If you cannot get to Mantua, the next best thing is to look through the relevant portfolio in a print-shop. Wainewright shared Hazlitt's view that 'a capital print-shop (Molteno's or Colnaghi's) is a point to aim at in a morning's walk—a relief and satisfaction in the motley confusion, the littleness, the vulgarity of common life'.[41] It may be because the editor of the London Magazine, John Scott, was a son-in-law of Colnaghi's that his is the print-shop most often mentioned; but in fact it seems to have been the shop most in favour with Keats and his circle. Wainewright assures the inexperienced collector that he will find what he wants if he calls '(using *our* name) at Messrs. Colnaghi's or Molteno's for a portfolio of Cherubino Alberti or Polidoro'.[42] There is an amusing description of Wainewright fighting his way into an unnamed print-seller's (clearly Colnaghi's) which reminds one—like so many passages in Wainewright's articles—of the passion for collecting gramophone recordings at the present day. As he plunged 'recklessly amidst that assemblage of amateur Chimney Sweepers, and cognoscenti Bakers' Boys, which usually blockades the windows' his object is to ascertain 'the actual advancement made in Taste' as a result of his own excellent articles:

> We hoped much from the effects of this our warning to all Amateurs . . . to concentrate their forces, and, unfurling the banners of Michael Angelo, Raffaëllo, and Titian, to oppose, even unto the death, the onward march of that barbarous horde of Vandals and Pictorial *Radicals*, who now sweep broadly along, like a rising spring-tide, bearing down the meek lank head of the Italian muse.[43]

This he proposes to do

> by inquiring whether some of those thick massive piles or bales, containing the noblest inventions of the old masters, which have slumbered so deeply within the dark arches of Messrs. ——'s cellars and warehouses, ever since their first arrival from Italy, or France,—lying in state, hung with rotten cobweb valances and fringes, richly powdered with dust, and smoke-blacks,—whether they had not 'burst their bands of sleep asunder'

as the result of his eloquent advocacy. Would that 'honoured Tree of *high Romance* . . .', blasted by the scathing frown of Cromwell and the Puritans', but now slowly recovering, flourish triumphantly once again? When, however, he picks his way through the usual crowd of beauty and fashion inside the shop he hears no talk of the great Italians, but only inquiries for the latest print of the Princess Charlotte, 'some pictures of stage coaches', and 'a new portrait of that dear man, Lord S——'.

It is curious how many details about Colnaghi's shop one can pick up from these essays. We hear of a print of Correggio's 'Descent from the Cross', for example, hanging 'neglected in a dark corner of Colnaghi's little inner room': we hear of the barking of his dog as the shop door opens, and of the 'extra strong tables' provided for the huge portfolios of prints. In one of his essays Wainewright humorously describes a reader of his 'Dogmas' who has caught the true collector's fever:

His course is constrained to Colnaghi's: modestly and coyly at first doth he inquire for a *single* subject from Correggio or Giulio, and the panting shopman hurls on the extra strong table *whole elephantine portfolios!!* teeming with Volpatos, Müllers, Longhis, &c. If he resists, he is more than mortal. Alas! he does not. He buys prints, one, two and three! throws down the amount with desperation, refuses all offers of porterage, dashes home by the shortest ways, views with unmixed delight his acquisitions for two minutes, and then regrets the absence of 'those other two, which indeed were quite companions'.[44]

Nothing can stop him: 'his fingers spread over the slippery lock' of Colnaghi's shop once more; 'the fatal door opens; and under the white flame of gas his ruin is accomplished'. Since the author of these sentences seems to have become a murderer for no other reason than to provide himself with such luxuries of a cultivated existence as paintings and prints, his evidence on this point may be taken as decisive.

VI

THE EVIDENCE OF THE LETTERS

> Pictures are a set of chosen images, a stream of pleasant
> thoughts passing through the mind. It is a luxury to have the
> walls of our rooms hung round with them; and no less so to
> have such a gallery in the mind. . . . They are the bright con-
> summate essences of things.
>
> HAZLITT, 'On a Landscape of Nicolas Poussin'

> A Man is Taught to See as well as to Dance, and the Beauties
> of Nature open themselves to our Sight by little and little, after
> a long Practice in the Art of Seeing.
>
> JONATHAN RICHARDSON, *An Essay on the Theory of Painting*,
> 1715, (p. 203)

THE letters of Keats contain a great deal of further evidence of
his interest in the fine arts. We know, for example, that he
visited the British Gallery (or Institution) in February 1818,
and saw there 'some nice things by Stark and Bathsheba by
Wilkie which is condemned', as well as Washington Allston's
'Uriel in the Sun', which he 'could not bear'.[1] We know that he
accompanied Leigh Hunt to Sir John Leicester's Gallery early
in April of the following year, where he met 'Northcote—
Hilton—Bewick and many more of great and Little note'.[2] One
day a few weeks earlier he had written to his brother and sister-
in-law in America describing some of his recent activities:

> On Monday we [Brown and himself] had to dinner Severn &
> Cawthorn the Bookseller & print virtuoso; in the evening Severn went
> home to paint & we other three went to the play to see Sheild's new
> tragedy ycleped Evadné—In the morning Severn & I took a turn round
> the Museum, There is a Sphinx there of a giant size, & most volup-
> tuous Egyptian expression, I had not seen it before.   (ii. 67–68)

James Cawthorn was a printer and bookseller who also sold
prints.[3] The phrase 'print virtuoso' itself tells us a good deal
about the milieu in which Keats lived: it is hard to imagine
anyone using such a phrase today. The giant sphinx has proved
unexpectedly difficult to identify, but whatever it was it probably

helped to inspire the lines in 'The Fall of Hyperion' in which Keats describes

> An Image, huge of feature as a cloud,
> At level of whose feet an altar slept.[4]

Another vivid reference which is hard to track down now occurs in a letter to Haydon written in Winchester on the 3rd of October 1819:

> At St Cross there is an interresting Picture of Albert Durers—who living in such warlike times perhaps was forced to paint in his Gauntlets—so we must make all allowances. (ii. 221)

Since Keats's description is hardly applicable to the only valuable painting that remains at St. Cross today—a triptych of the Virgin and Child with saints, often attributed to Mabuse—it seems possible that he saw a painting which was removed after the great Chancery case of 1850.[5] There were very few authentic paintings of Dürer's in England at that time, but almost any painting of a generally 'Dutch' sort was liable to be attributed to the German master.

Keats was interested in portrait-painting, and was indeed something of a physiognomist himself. 'There is a famous exhibition in Pall Mall of the old english portraits by Vandyck and Holbein, Sir Peter Lely and the great Sir Godfrey', he wrote to Brown in June 1820. Among the unpleasant countenances that he singles out for mention are those of James I,

> whose appearance would disgrace a 'Society for the suppression of women;' so very squalid, and subdued to nothing he looks. Then, there is old Lord Burleigh, the high priest of economy, the political save-all, who has the appearance of a Pharisee just rebuffed by a gospel bonmot. Then, there is George the second, very like an unintellectual Voltaire, troubled with the gout and a bad temper. Then, there is young Devereux, the favourite, with every appearance of as slang a boxer as any in the court; his face is cast in the mould of blackguardism with jockey-plaster. (ii. 299)

On another occasion we catch a glimpse of Keats passing the window of Colnaghi's and seeing 'a profil Portraict of Sands the destroyer of Kotzebue'. 'His very look must interest every one in his favour'—he comments—

> I suppose they have represented him in his college dress—He seems to

me like a young Abelard—A fine Mouth, cheek bones (and this is no joke) full of sentiment; a fine unvulgar nose and plump temples.

(ii. 195)

In a humorous letter to Jane Reynolds Keats complains that if she goes on 'at this rate'—

I shall always have you in my imagination side by side with Bailey's Picture of Jeremy Taylor who always looks as if he were going to hit me a rap with a Book he holds in a very threatning position. My head is always in imminent danger   (i. 156)

—no doubt a reference to a print of Jeremy Taylor (like that often found in early editions of his *Works*) which Bailey had displayed on his wall.[6] A much more obscure reference to a print in a book which Keats himself owned, the *Universal Family Bible*, was pointed out by Livingston Lowes more than thirty years ago: I quote the passage in the notes.[7] A letter to Fanny Brawne contains an overt reference to a work of sculpture. Writing of *Otho the Great*, Keats remarks: 'The Lover is madder than I am —I am nothing to him—he has a figure like the Statue of Maleager and double distilled fire in his heart.'[8] Here Keats is probably remembering some reproduction of the famous statue which belonged to the Picchini in Rome: it shows Meleager as a powerful and complacent warrior, with a markedly unintellectual countenance, posing beside the head of the Caledonian boar. In another highly visual passage we find Keats joking in a way that reminds us of his artist friends:

Writing has this disadvantage of speaking, one cannot write a wink, or a nod, or a grin, or a purse of the Lips, or a *smile*. . . . But in all the most lively . . . parts of my Letter you must not fail to imagine me as the epic poets say—now here, now there, now with one foot pointed at the ceiling, now with another—now with my pen on my ear, now with my elbow in my mouth—O my friends you loose the action—and attitude is every thing as Fusili said when he took up his leg like a Musket to shoot a Swallow just darting behind his shoulder. And yet does not the word mum! go for ones finger beside the nose—I hope it does. I have to make use of the word Mum! before I tell you that Severn has got a little Baby—all his own let us hope—He told Brown he had given up painting and had turn'd modeller. I hope sincerely tis not a party concern; that no Mr —— or **** is the real *Pinxit* and Severn the poor *Sculpsit* to this work of art—You know he has long studied in the Life-Academy.[9]   (ii. 205)

Such passages are of interest because they remind us that Keats was a man who mixed a great deal with artists, a man for whom the world of the eye was a vivid reality. But there are also one or two passages of greater importance in which it becomes evident how significant a part the sister-art of painting played in the development of Keats's beliefs about poetry. In a rather obscure passage in one of his long letters to America, for example, he describes himself as 'young writing at random—straining at particles of light in the midst of a great darkness—without knowing the bearing of any one assertion of any one opinion', and goes on:

Yet may I not in this be free from sin? May there not be superior beings amused with any graceful, though instinctive attitude my mind may fall into, as I am entertained with the alertness of a Stoat or the anxiety of a Deer? Though a quarrel in the streets is a thing to be hated, the energies displayed in it are fine; the commonest Man shows a grace in his quarrel—By a superior being our reasonings may take the same tone—though erroneous they may be fine—This is the very thing in which consists poetry; and if so it is not so fine a thing as philosophy—For the same reason that an eagle is not so fine a thing as a truth. (ii. 80–81)

A similar train of thought may be found in the earlier letter in which Keats tells his brothers that he has been to see West's painting, 'Death on the Pale Horse' (Plate III), and comments:

It is a wonderful picture, when West's age is considered; But there is nothing to be intense upon; no women one feels mad to kiss; no face swelling into reality. The excellence of every Art is its intensity, capable of making all disagreeables evaporate, from their being in close relationship with Beauty & Truth—Examine King Lear & you will find this examplified throughout; but in this picture we have unpleasantness without any momentous depth of speculation excited, in which to bury its repulsiveness. (i. 192)

This melodramatic yet powerful painting, which has been described by a recent critic as pointing forwards to Delacroix rather than backwards to David,[10] created something of a sensation. The public admired the bold design and the striking colouring of the picture, while West's friends also sympathized with an old man whose wife had died and whose ambitious plan for a Chapel of Revealed Religion had come to nothing. In a newspaper advertisement the picture was hailed as a victory for England comparable to Waterloo, the figure of Death being described as 'animated almost to ignition with inextinguishable rage'.[11] William Carey, soon to be assailed in the *Annals of the Fine Arts* as 'one of the greatest pests in English Art',[12] wrote a *Critical Description* of the painting, which was also the subject of an anonymous poem.[13] Provoked by this exaggerated praise Hazlitt attacked the picture in the *Edinburgh Magazine* later in the year, accusing West of composing his own panegyric and also of failing to understand the conditions of his art:

The only way in which the painter of genius can represent the force of moral truth, is by translating it into an artificial language of his own, —by substituting hieroglyphics for words, and presenting the closest and most striking affinities his fancy and observation can suggest between the general idea and the visible illustration of it. Here we think Mr. West has failed. The artist has represented Death riding over his prostrate victims in all the rage of impotent despair. He is in a great splutter, and seems making a last effort to frighten his foes by an explosion of red-hot thunderbolts, and a pompous display of his allegorical paraphernalia. He has not the calm, still, majestic form of Death, killing by a look,—withering by a touch. His presence does not make the still air cold.[14]

It is hardly surprising that writers in the *Annals of the Fine Arts* were tepid in their praise. 'Mr. West is an eminent artist, but not a great one', one contributor wrote; while another—if both articles are not the work of Haydon himself—wrote that, by the standard of West's own best work, 'Death on the Pale Horse' was 'a complete failure', though 'a wonderful production for an octogenarian painter'.[15] In his criticism of this painting, therefore, Keats is in close agreement with his friends. The criterion invoked in 'no women one feels mad to kiss' is thoroughly Haydonesque, while 'intensity' was also a favourite term of Haydon's.[16] What is even more important, however, is that Keats's discussion of this painting reminds us how easily he passed from one art to another—reminds us also that his speculations about Beauty and Truth derive from his speculations about the visual arts as well as from his thinking about poetry itself.

The same reflection strikes us as we read a famous passage from a letter written in December 1818:

III. WEST: Death on the Pale Horse

'It is a wonderful picture . . . . But there is nothing to be intense upon; no women one feels mad to kiss; no face swelling into reality.'

IV(*a*). RAPHAEL: Christ's Charge to St. Peter

IV(*b*). RAPHAEL: The Miraculous Draught of Fishes

'A year ago I could not understand in the slightest degree Raphael's cartoons—now I begin to read them a little—and how did I learn to do so? By seeing something done in quite an opposite spirit—'

V. GUIDO RENI: The Virgin adored by the Patron Saints of Bologna

*'I mean a picture of Guido's in which all the Saints . . . had each of them both in countenance
and gesture all the canting, solemn melo dramatic mawkishness of Mackenzie's father
Nicholas.'*

VI. RAPHAEL: The Healing of the Lame Man at the Beautiful Gate of the Temple

'*Beauty is truth, truth beauty*.'

On my word I have thought so little that I have not one opinion upon any thing except in matters of taste—I never can feel certain of any truth but from a clear perception of its Beauty—and I find myself very young minded even in that perceptive power—which I hope will encrease—A year ago I could not understand in the slightest degree Raphael's cartoons—now I begin to read them a little—and how did I learn to do so? By seeing something done in quite an opposite spirit— I mean a picture of Guido's in which all the Saints, instead of that heroic simplicity and unaffected grandeur which they inherit from Raphael, had each of them both in countenance and gesture all the canting, solemn melo dramatic mawkishness of Mackenzie's father Nicholas. (ii. 19)

Since to most people Raphael is the least immediately striking of the supremely great painters, it is interesting that Keats should write of him in such a way. It shows (once again) how apt a pupil he was. As we have already seen, Haydon regarded himself as something of an expert on Raphael, and the editors of the *Annals of the Fine Arts* once reprinted a critique of his with the words 'we wish to have all that Mr Haydon has written upon the Cartoons embodied in our work'.[17] It was at Haydon's instance, indeed, and against the will of West and most of the other Academicians, that certain of the Cartoons were loaned to the British Institution each year between 1816 and 1818, for studying and copying. 'Up came the Miraculous Draught of Fishes and Paul at Athens', Haydon wrote in his *Autobiography*, under the year 1816:

I moved in directly, and drew full-size all the heads and the figure of Paul. My pupils came in after me, and we all set to work and made such studies and cartoons as had never been seen in England before. The excitement was tremendous. Bewicke, Harvey, C. and T. Landseer and Chatfield had all fine heads, and the way in which they stood up and manfully drew attracted the attention and wonder of all.[18]

Plates IVa and VI illustrate the Cartoons exhibited at the British Institution in 1818, 'Christ's Charge to St. Peter' and 'The Healing of the Lame Man at the Beautiful Gate of the Temple'. In another characteristic passage we again find Haydon using the Cartoons as a touchstone of artistic perception:

Good heavens! how taste among all classes of the English nation has advanced within these few years. We remember ourselves, when the Cartoons were looked upon as dusty lumber and an Academician, whom we could mention, asked us, when they were first exhibited, with great naiveté, 'Now what the devil is there in these Cartoons?'[19]

Another contributor wrote in a later issue:'The exhibition of such works as the Cartoons, for the express purpose of improving the public taste, is quite unexampled in the country.'[20] Whatever effect it may have had on the public taste, the exhibition seems to have helped John Keats in his meditations on about the relationship of Beauty and Truth.

The same letter contains a number of further parallels between literature and painting. Uncertain how far the interests of his brother and sister-in-law have changed as a result of their emigration to America, Keats asks them:

> With what sensation do you read Fielding?—and do not Hogarth's pictures seem an old thing to you? (ii. 18)

There follows a reference to the development of his literary taste which leads on to the passage about Raphael and Guido quoted on the previous page. 'Mrs Tighe and Beattie once delighted me—now I see through them and can find nothing in them.' The letter continues with a reference which is of great importance:

> When I was last at Haydon's I looked over a Book of Prints taken from the fresco of the Church at Milan the name of which I forget—in it are comprised Specimens of the first and second age of art in Italy—I do not think I ever had a greater treat out of Shakspeare—Full of Romance and the most tender feeling—magnificence of draperies beyond any I ever saw not excepting Raphael's—But Grotesque to a curious pitch—yet still making up a fine whole—even finer to me than more accomplish'd works—as there was left so much room for Imagination. (ii. 19)

Unfortunately no such book of prints has been discovered. Sir Sidney Colvin, who as Keeper of Prints at the British Museum was an expert in this field, states categorically that 'there are no such engravings',[21] and he appears to be right. It is true that the Chiesa del Monastero Maggiore contains paintings which could be described as 'Grotesque', as well as frescoes by Bernardino Luini which are characterized by a classical purity and elegance; but I have been unable to find any volume of engravings from these frescoes which could have been available to Keats.

VII. BENOZZO GOZZOLI: Vintage

'When I was last at Haydon's I looked over a Book of Prints . . . I do not think I ever had a greater treat out
of Shakspeare—Full of Romance and the most tender feeling—'

VIII. ORCAGNA: The Triumph of Death (detail)

'magnificence of draperies beyond any I ever saw not excepting Raphael's—But Grotesque to a curious pitch.'

Colvin concludes that Keats must have been confusing Milan and Pisa, and that the reference is in fact to a famous collection of prints published in Florence in 1812, *Pitture al Fresco del Campo Santo di Pisa intagliate da Carlo Lasinio*.[22] This is an enormous folio volume containing brilliant engravings of the frescoes by Giotto, Orcagna, Benozzo Gozzoli, and others.[23] The engravings are too large and detailed to be reproduced successfully in a book of this size, but Plates VII and VIII may serve to give some impression of the beauty of Lasinio's work. 'Romance and . . . tender feeling', 'magnificence of draperies' and the 'Grotesque' are all present in abundance. These are prints which create a visual world that one can step into, a realm of the imagination that so impressed Goethe that he refers to them at the end of the Second Part of *Faust*; while it was a copy of the same book that led Rossetti and his friends to study the painters before Raphael with a fresh enthusiasm.[24] One new piece of evidence now lends support to Colvin's hypothesis: a 'very fine' book of prints from the Campo Santo di Pisa is listed as item 79 in the catalogue of Haydon's effects sold by auction in 1823. It seems very likely that this volume, which was bought by an unknown purchaser for £2. 15s.,[25] was the book which had given Keats 'a greater treat' than he had ever had 'out of Shakespeare'.

Keats had an exceptionally active visual imagination. If we did not know this from his poems, we would know it from his letters. In April 1819, for example, he described a recent dream in a letter to George and Georgiana:

The fifth canto of Dante pleases me more and more—it is that one in which he meets with Paulo and Franchesca—I had passed many days in rather a low state of mind and in the midst of them I dreamt of being in that region of Hell. The dream was one of the most delightful enjoyments I ever had in my life—I floated about the whirling atmosphere as it is described with a beautiful figure to whose lips mine were joined as it seem'd for an age—and in the midst of all this cold and darkness I was warm—even flowery tree tops sprung up and we rested on them sometimes with the lightness of a cloud till the wind blew us away again—I tried a Sonnet upon it—there were fourteen lines but nothing of what I felt in it—o that I could dream it every night. (ii. 91)

It is possible that Keats's dream may have been influenced by

Flaxman's illustration of the passage, which was published in 1807 (although the illustrations were not printed with Cary's text until much later). But the important thing to notice is that the same passage that appealed to so many illustrators—including Fuseli, Blake, and D. G. Rossetti—also made a powerful appeal to Keats, and that the visual quality of Dante's lines inspired a dream so vivid that he strove to recapture it in a sonnet describing 'that second circle of sad hell',

> Where in the gust, the whirlwind and the flaw
> Of Rain and hailstones lovers need not tell
> Their sorrows—Pale were the sweet lips I saw
> Pale were the lips I kiss'd and fair the form
> I floated with about that melancholy storm.[26]

On the 14th of February the following year he referred to a dream of a very different sort, in a letter telling a friend that Charles Brown 'has left the inventive and taken to the imitative art—he is doing his forte which is copying Hogarth's heads. He has just made a purchace of the methodist meeting picture,[27] which gave me a horrid dream a few nights ago.' On the 4th of March we hear that 'Brown has been mightily progressing with his Hogarth. A damn'd melancholy picture it is, and during the first week of my illness it gave me a psalm singing nightmare, that made me almost faint away in my sleep. I know I am better, for I can bear the Picture.'

As well as collecting prints, many of Keats's friends collected 'Tassie's gems', a series of inexpensive reproductions of classical and neo-classical originals much in vogue at this time. The habit is more significant than might at first appear. From the Renaissance onwards the importance of studying ancient coins and medals had been well understood. The discovery of Pompeii in the middle of the eighteenth century gave a further stimulus to a branch of study already recommended by Spence and many others, and in his Sixth Discourse we find Sir Joshua Reynolds including cameos and coins among the all-important 'relicks' of ancient art:

All the inventions and thoughts of the Antients, whether conveyed to us in statues, bas-reliefs, intaglios, cameos, or coins, are to be sought after and carefully studied: the genius that hovers over these venerable relicks, may be called the father of modern art.[28]

Those who could not aspire to collect ancient coins for themselves could still form a modest collection of Mr. Tassie's glass-paste reproductions, which were most skilfully reproduced:

On looking at your seal [Keats wrote to his sister Fanny on the 13th of March 1819] I cannot tell whether it is done or not with a Tassi—it seems to me to be paste—As I went through Leicester Square lately I was going to call and buy you some, but not knowing but you might have some I would not run the chance of buying duplicates—Tell me if you have any or if you would like any—and whether you would rather have motto ones like that with which I seal this letter; or heads of great men such as Shakspeare, Milton &c—or fancy pieces of Art; such as Fame, Adonis &c—those gentry you read of at the end of the English Dictionary.

Keats often sealed his own letters with a head of Shakespeare, but the seal that he refers to here shows a lyre surrounded by the words 'Qui me néglige me désole' (Plate IXd). This seal had a strange history: Aileen Ward has suggested that it may well have been presented to Keats by Fanny Brawne, and it seems to have given him the idea for the device that he wished to be engraved on his tombstone—a Greek lyre with four of its eight strings broken.[29] We do not know which sort of seals Fanny asked for, but if they were 'motto ones' this would merely have confirmed Haydon in his opinion of the English character:

The English have more sentiment than taste, and more intense feeling for moral duty than for either. Put a head of Granville Sharpe by the side of a beautiful Mercury, there is no doubt which they would select—they have no notion of the abstract beauty of things independently of moral associations. A sentiment is more comprehensible to their understandings than the abstracted beauty of a Venus or a piece of drapery—they see Tassie's seals with sentiments go by thousands, while antique gems of the most exquisite art lie dirty & unsought for. A wretched Cupid with a wretched bow with a wretched heart, in the wretched stone, they mind not, provided there is written—'one amidst a thousand'.[30]

The Indicator for the 17th of November 1819 contains an interesting note about 'busts, vases, and other casts in plaister' which goes on to recommend Tassie's gems:

Impressions from ancient gems are now also to be had with singular cheapness, in consequence of an invention of Mr. Tassie's, of Leicester-square. He has found out a composition, which enables him to procure in a few days, for three-and-sixpence, an impression exactly resembling that of any gem you may select. This you may either have set for your watch-chain, or keep in your desk or pocket; for the composition is very hard, and does not easily wear or chip off, even at the edges . . . Mr. Tassie's collection of antiques appears to be very extensive. You may have your choice among all the gods and graces of the ancient world,—Jupiters, Apollos, Venuses, the Graces, the Muses, Lyres, Loves, Festivals, Pastorals, Patriots, Poets, and Philosophers.

'Very extensive' indeed: the two large volumes comprising

A Descriptive Catalogue of a General Collection of Ancient and Modern Engraved Gems, Cameos as well as Intaglios, taken from the Most Celebrated Cabinets in Europe; and cast in Coloured Pastes, White Enamel, and Sulphur, by James Tassie, modeller; arranged and described by R. E. Raspe

and published in 1791, list no fewer than 15,800 gems. The introduction is given both in French and in English, while the long subscribers' list includes such various eminences as the King of Sweden, Richard Payne Knight, and James Boswell, Esq. The prices are extremely low: 4*d.* for waxed impressions (only 3*d.* if you bought the whole set), 1*s.* 6*d.* to 2*s.* 6*d.* for seal and ring size replicas, 5*s.* to 21*s.* for larger replicas, 5*s.* and upwards for appliqués, and anything up to 42*s.* for cameos. When Shelley asked Peacock to buy him '£2's worth of Tassi's gems . . .', the prettiest according to your taste', therefore, the result may have been quite a pleasant little collection.[31] A collection of Tassie's gems, like a collection of prints, was obligatory for any one with any pretensions to connoisseurship. In one of the descriptions of a sybaritic study characteristic of the period[32] Wainewright begins by listing a number of prints and engravings ('a pair of shears, thirteen inches long' and 'a ream of tinted paper' being necessary concomitants), continues by recommending some of the finest casts of urns and sculptured figures, and concludes as follows:

But pleasures require intermission and variation: therefore it is necessary to convert that chiffoniere into a little store closet for Tassie's cameos and intaglios (or rather a selection out of his immense catalogue). Suppose you put in the following as nest eggs—they are among the finest, both in scientific drawing, harmony of composition, grace of outline (in which they stand unrivalled from the restoration of art in Italy downwards), and masterly workmanship. To appreciate these qualities, attention must be directed to throwing them into a forcible and appropriate chiaroscuro, and the general rule is, that the light should stream over the surface obliquely from the top: the gentlest projections are thus brought up, while the back-ground remains in a tender demi-tint.[33]

As a number of Wainewright's recommendations are of reproductions likely to have been familiar to Keats, I cite them here, with the relevant numbers in Tassie's catalogue:

The sublime head of Jupiter Ægiochus. . . . The fragment (but a nose, mouth and chin) of Apollo (2773). The large, high-breasted Minerva (1647), or rather Aspasia flattered with her attributes, a gem of unsurpassable refinement. The exquisite Diomedes with the Palladium (*to be studied with a magnifier*). Hercules (*Theseus*) with the Marathonian Bull. The Hercules and Iole of the Palais Pitti. Female crouching, with a laver (6266). The grand Front of Serapis, or Pluto. *The dancing Bacchus* (4290), justly deemed by Mr. Cumberland the *ne plus ultra* of Greek art. The portentous Sphinx (51), still and minacious as a growing storm-cloud. Heracles destroying the blood-feasting cranes of Stympalus. . . Philoctetes, left lonely in rude sea-girt Lemnos, wasted with lean disease. . . . Dark-haired Sappho . . . placed on an elevated seat, and supported partly by one slender arm, while the other glowing palm is held forth reproachfully to the deceitful Phaon. . . . Let Mr. Tassie also receive your instructions to cast the following beauties. The fragmental sitting Venus and Cupid, with two cornucopiæ. The voluptous kneeling Leda (1199). . . . The misnomed naked Psyche, her back nearly turned to us, looking up at a rock (engraved by Moses, as Diana and Actaeon). Greek warrior, completely armed, cowering behind his shield (7471). 'The Nymph of beauteous ankles, Amphitrite, Daughter of Doris many-tressed,'

—Whose haunt
Is midst the waters of the sterile main.—

Next, the Nereid (2600) skimming the briny green with buoyant limbs.—Another Nymph of deep-flowing ocean (2599). The Moon, Jove's daughter, in her chariot, drawn by two ramping horses, with manes of curled flames. . . . The sitting Clio, examining a scroll, her lyre near her on a pedestal, most delicate workmanship. The Egyptian Lioness (36) a terrific idea. The Sleeping Hermaphrodite, fanned by Cupids . . . (2516). A rich fragment. (Love reining in two Tigers yoked to a car, of which only the fore wheel remains, 6731). A bearded warrior and two high-bred horses, a matchless gem. Venus putting off her sandal (6230). The bust of Adrian's favourite, the Boy Antinous: the massy hair arranged with the utmost science and feeling (11701). The noted Minerva of the Florence Gallery (1536), wearing the

Ægis as a breast-plate. . . . The finely-shaped but singular *Amor drawing his bow*, engraved by Millin (6625). The precious cameo of Achilles beguiling the wearisome hours of his voluntary idleness with the sounds of his phorminx, agreeable to the description of Homer....[34]

Wainewright has constantly in mind the light thrown on literature by these reproductions. After recommending the Achilles cameo, for example, he first quotes Homer in Greek and then (rejecting Cowper's translation as 'flat and wrong') quotes from 'Mr. Lamb's fine old favourite, Chapman'. Commenting on the head of Sappho earlier in his list, Wainewright observes: 'No drapery hides her smooth shoulders and body; but over her knees a gauzy peplon spreads in folds transparent as a stream, and sinuous as its waves', and quotes part of Spenser's description of the Witch Acrasia.[35] It is also interesting to notice that Wainewright recommends, 'as a sort of supplement to the cast' and cameos, 'Sir W. Hamilton's second collection of vases, edited by Tischbein . . . in four volumes folio; each containing about 62 plates... illustrative of the Bacchic and Eleusinian mysteries'.

One of Keats's poems was almost certainly inspired by a Tassie reproduction, the sonnet 'On a Leander Gem which Miss Reynolds, my kind Friend, gave me'. Tassie's catalogue contains a number of Leanders: the most probable source for the poem is reproduced in Plate IXb. The sestet describes the exhausted swimmer:

> 'Tis young Leander toiling to his death.
> Nigh swooning, he doth purse his weary lips
> For Hero's cheek, and smiles against her smile.
> O horrid dream! see how his body dips
> Dead-heavy; arms and shoulders gleam awhile:
> He's gone: up bubbles all his amorous breath![36]

Many of the other gems must have appealed deeply to Keats, and some of them may have left their traces in his poetry. No fewer than twenty-two—Nos. 7177–98—portray Cupid and Psyche embracing. No. 2162 shows Endymion asleep, while in 2163 Diana is shown flying towards Endymion (Plate IXa). A number of the gems portray Bacchic processions. A complete set —in sulphur, as Wainewright recommended—may still be found in the Victoria and Albert Museum. It is fascinating to look through them: one has constantly the sense of coming on designs that would have appealed to Keats, and a note of Wood-

c. Head of Shakespeare

a. Diana and Endymion
b. Leander

d. Broken lyre with the motto: 'Qui me néglige me désole'.

IX. Tassie's Gems

house's bears out this impression: 'I believe it was once Keats's intention to write a series of sonnets and short poems on some of Tassie's gems.'[37]

Apart from giving pleasure in itself, art widens and deepens our perceptions, so that we become aware of aspects of our surroundings of which we have been unaware. It is not only in his manifest interest in the visual arts themselves that the influence of Keats's artistic friends may be traced: it can also be seen in his ever-growing appreciation of what Browning's Fra Lippo Lippi calls

> The shapes of things, their colours, light and shades,
> Changes, surprises . . .

It is as true of painting as of poetry 'that it makes every thing every place interesting—The palatine venice and the abbotine Winchester are equally interesting'[38] when they are looked at with the eye of the imagination.

As early as November 1816 we find Keats telling Severn that he 'particularly want[s] to look into some beautiful Scenery—for poetical purposes'.[39] 'Now that Haydon has pointed out how necessary it is that I sho[d] be alone to improve myself . . . I shall soon be out of Town', he wrote in March of the following year,[40] before leaving for the Isle of Wight, which gave him his first experience of true country scenery. In March 1818 he set off for Haydon's native Devonshire. On the 14th he wrote to Reynolds from Teignmouth, warningly:

> I am going among Scenery whence I intend to tip you the Damosel Radcliffe—I'll cavern you, and grotto you, and waterfall you, and wood you, and water you, and immense-rock you, and tremendous sound you, and solitude you. Ill make a lodgment on your glacis by a row of Pines, and storm your covered way with bramble Bushes . . . .

Keats had to leave Devonshire sooner than he wished. Telling Haydon that he intended to return there one day he also announces (in a passage already quoted in part) that he plans within a month

> to put my knapsack at my back and make a pedestrian tour through the North of England, and part of Scotland—to make a sort of Prologue to the Life I intend to pursue—that is to write, to study and to see all Europe at the lowest expence. I will clamber through the Clouds and

exist. I will get such an accumulation of stupendous recollolections
[*sic*] that as I walk through the suburbs of London I may not see them.

(i. 264)

I have already quoted Haydon's hope that the northern tour
would do as much good to the inside of Keats's head as to the
outside. Keats is similarly explicit about the reason for the
journey:

> I should not have consented to myself these four Months tramping
> in the highlands but that I thought it would give me more experience,
> rub off more Prejudice, use [me] to more hardship, identify finer
> scenes load me with grander Mountains, and strengthen more my
> reach in Poetry, than would stopping at home among Books even
> though I should reach Homer.   (i. 342)

When one recalls how eager Keats was to learn Greek in order
to 'reach Homer' one sees the great importance he attached to
the journey. On his way to Liverpool he visited a former col-
league of his at Guy's Hospital and told him that he 'had no
intention of practising in the Medical profession, but was still
devoted to Poetry'.[41] Keats was now a dedicated poet, a poet
whose gaze was fixed on an austerer territory than 'the realm
Of Flora and old Pan'. He had visited the Isle of Wight as the
author of *Endymion, A Poetic Romance*: now as he travelled
northwards he travelled as the poet of *Hyperion*, a poet whose
mind was becoming the stage for an action of an epic magnitude.
Whereas—as Leigh Hunt was to point out—Keats '*luxuriated*
in the Isle of Wight', he looked at 'the lakes and mountains of
the north . . . with an *epic* eye'.[42] Cary's translation of Dante was
the only book he took with him, while the English epic poets
Spenser and Milton were frequent subjects in his conversation
with Brown. It was because of his own preoccupations that he
was surprised that the mountains of Arran 'did not beckon Burns
to some grand attempt at Epic'.[43] The visit to Wordsworth was
an inevitable part of the whole expedition: he was the one living
poet whom Keats considered of potentially epic calibre. It is not
surprising that he was deeply disappointed when he found that
Wordsworth was away from home, canvassing for Lord Lowther.

Brown seems from the first to have thought of publishing an
account of the tour—as, in the end, he did. The same possibility
no doubt occurred to Keats. There is a playful reference, in a
letter to America written from the foot of Helvellyn, to Keats's

desire to appear in the best light in the 'many folio volumes' of
his correspondence which are destined one day to be published.[44]
In any event, there are some admirable descriptions in the letters
which show how profound an effect the mountain scenery had on
Keats—mountain scenery that he was now encountering for the
first time. Writing to Tom, for example, he remarks that the
views they have had of Windermere

> are of the most noble tenderness—they can never fade away—they
> make one forget the divisions of life; age, youth, poverty and riches;
> and refine one's sensual vision into a sort of north star which can never
> cease to be open lidded and stedfast over the wonders of the great
> Power. . . . I have an amazing partiality for mountains in the clouds.
> There is nothing in Devon like this.   (i. 299–300)

He was struck by the way in which 'the most beautiful and rich
view of Winander mere and the surrounding Mountains' 'burst
upon [them]',[45] and deeply moved by the view of the lake from
Wordsworth's study window—so moved that a 'Window opening on Winander mere' is one of the features in his description
of the perfect earthly felicity that he felt it his duty to resist.[46]

There is a vivid particularity in Keats's description of the
Ambleside waterfall:

> We . . . missed the direct path, and after wandering a little, found
> it out by the noise—for, mark you, it is buried in trees, in the
> bottom of the valley—the stream itself is interesting throughout with
> 'mazy error over pendant shades.' Milton meant a smooth river—this
> is buffetting all the way on a rocky bed ever various—but the waterfall
> itself, which I came suddenly upon, gave me a pleasant twinge. First
> we stood a little below the head about half way down the first fall,
> buried deep in trees, and saw it streaming down two more descents
> to the depth of near fifty feet—then we went on a jut of rock nearly
> level with the second fall-head, where the first fall was above us, and
> the third below our feet still—at the same time we saw that the water
> was divided by a sort of cataract island on whose other side burst out
> a glorious stream—then the thunder and the freshness.   (i. 300)

This description of what Keats calls the first waterfall he has
ever seen is reminiscent of a painting: he is looking at nature
with eyes trained by their study of works of art:

> At the same time the different falls have as different characters; the
> first darting down the slate-rock like an arrow; the second spreading
> out like a fan—the third dashed into a mist—and the one on the other

side of the rock a sort of mixture of all these. We afterwards moved away a space, and saw nearly the whole more mild, streaming silverly through the trees. What astonishes me more than any thing is the tone, the coloring, the slate, the stone, the moss, the rock-weed; or, if I may so say, the intellect, the countenance of such places. The space, the magnitude of mountains and waterfalls are well imagined before one sees them; but this countenance or intellectual tone must surpass every imagination and defy any remembrance.   (i. 300–1)

The next sentences are highly significant:

I shall learn poetry here and shall henceforth write more than ever, for the abstract endeavor of being able to add a mite to that mass of beauty which is harvested from these grand materials, by the finest spirits, and put into etherial existence for the relish of one's fellows. I cannot think with Hazlitt that these scenes make man appear little. I never forgot my stature so completely—I live in the eye; and my imagination, surpassed, is at rest.

It is evident that 'the finest spirits' include painters as well as poets, while the words 'I live in the eye' would serve admirably as a motto for this whole study.

It was not only on his northern tour that Keats 'lived in the eye'. 'Let my eyes be fed or I'll never go out to dinner any where', he wrote to George and his sister in January 1819;[47] while a similar attitude is evident in his description of Jane Cox, a few months earlier:

She is not a Cleopatra; but she is at least a Charmian. She has a rich eastern look; she has fine eyes and fine manners. When she comes into a room she makes an impression the same as the Beauty of a Leopardess . . . I always find myself more at ease with such a woman; the picture before me always gives me a life and animation which I cannot possibly feel with any thing inferiour—I am at such times too much occupied in admiring to be awkward or on a tremble. I forget myself entirely because I live in her.   (i. 395)

It is an easy transition from such passages to the second stanza of the 'Ode on Melancholy':

> Then glut thy sorrow on a morning rose,
>   Or on the rainbow of the salt sand-wave,
>   Or on the wealth of globed peonies;
> Or if thy mistress some rich anger shows,
>   Emprison her soft hand, and let her rave,
>   And feed deep, deep upon her peerless eyes.

Much as he admired the bare feet of the country girls, however, it was not to study men and women that Keats had gone on
his northern journey. 'We are mere creatures of Rivers, Lakes,
& mountains', as he wrote to Tom, complaining that they had
no opportunity of 'becoming learned in village affairs'.[48] They
traversed much of the territory described in two of William
Gilpin's popular books of *Observations relative chiefly to Picturesque Beauty*,[49] and we notice that the features and scenes that
Keats singles out for description are usually those of the most
approvedly 'picturesque' sort—mountains, lochs, waterfalls,
'prospects'. Keats is sure to have glanced into one or two of his
books, with their careful, rather pedestrian descriptions, and
their charming illustrations. One of the most celebrated views
was, of course, that of Derwentwater. 'The Approach to derwent
water is rich and magnificent beyond any means of conception',
he wrote on the 28th of June; 'the Mountains all round sublime
and graceful and rich in colour—Woods and wooded Islands
here and there—at the same time in the distance among Mountains of another aspect we see Bassenthwaite.' The view from
the top of Skiddaw had interested Keats before he started on his
northern tour, for in *Endymion* he uses it in a simile to express
the 'stress of vision' with which Endymion and the Indian
Maiden on their winged steeds search for Sleep 'as one would
look' for eels in a river,

> Or from old Skiddaw's top, when fog conceals
> His rugged forehead in a mantle pale,
> With an eye-guess towards some pleasant vale
> Descry a favourite hamlet faint and far.   (iv. 394–7)

Lodore waterfall rather disappointed them, being much smaller
than they had expected,[50] but Keats was delighted by the trees
that grew round it—

> There is no great body of water, but the accompaniment is delightful;
> for it ooses out from a cleft in perpendicular Rocks, all fledged with Ash
> & other beautiful trees. It is a strange thing how they got there (i. 306)

—a sight which may have given him an idea for the last stanza
of the 'Ode to Psyche':

> Far, far around shall those dark-cluster'd trees
> Fledge the wild-ridged mountains steep by steep.

Just after this, on their way to Penrith, they made a short detour 'to see the Druid temple'—which afforded Keats an image for the Second Book of *Hyperion*.[51]

Often we see Keats deliberately storing impressions—'sensations'—in his memory, for later use:

> When we left Cairn our Road lay half way up the sides of a green mountainous shore, full of Clefts of verdure and eternally varying— sometimes up sometimes down, and over little Bridges going across green chasms of moss rock and trees—winding about every where. After two or three Miles of this we turned suddenly into a magnificent glen finely wooded in Parts—seven Miles long—with a Mountain Stream winding down the Midst—full of cottages in the most happy Situations—the sides of the Hills covered with sheep—the effect of cattle lowing I never had so finely—At the end we had a gradual ascent and got among the tops of the Mountains whence In a little time I descried in the Sea Ailsa Rock 940 feet high—it was 15 Miles distant and seemed close upon us—The effect of ailsa with the peculiar perspective of the Sea in connection with the ground we stood on, and the misty rain then falling gave me a complete Idea of a deluge—Ailsa struck me very suddenly—really I was a little alarmed.   (i. 329)

It is fitting that this passage should be followed by the sonnet 'To Ailsa Rock'. Perhaps it is not too fanciful to compare the occasional poems which Keats wrote on this journey to the sketches which a painter makes as he travels about, to refresh his memory later. Keats is always looking round him to find views and images that will be of use to him in his poetry. In the following passage we find him giving marks (as it were) to the various features of the scene he is describing:

> The Banks of the Clyde are extremely beautiful—the north End of Loch Lomond grand in excess—the entrance at the lower end to the narrow part from a little distance is precious good—the Evening was beautiful nothing could surpass our fortune in the weather—yet was I worldly enough to wish for a fleet of chivalry Barges with Trumpets and Banners just to die away before me into that blue place among the mountains—I must give you an outline as well as I can

Not[a] B[ene] the Water was a fine Blue silverd and the Mountains
a dark purple the Sun setting aslant behind them—meantime the head
of ben Lomond was covered with a rich Pink Cloud.   (i. 334)

Here Keats is converting a Scottish view into a landscape of the
imagination, just as Richard Wilson (for example) had painted
Woburn Abbey as if it were to be found in the timeless Italy of
poets and painters. He is viewing Scottish scenery through an
imaginary Claude-glass, and providing it with 'chivalry-barges'
—as Claude had done with the scenery that he painted, and as
Turner had done more recently: a 'worldly' proceeding that
might have disgusted Wordsworth.

Keats's description of the walk towards Loch Awe is similarly
that of a man who knows a good deal about landscape painting:

The Approach to Loch Awe was very solemn towards nightfall—the
first glance was a streak of water deep in the Bases of large black
Mountains—We had come along a complete mountain road, where if
one listened there was not a sound but that of Mountain Streams We
walked 20 Miles by the side of Loch Awe—every ten steps creating a
new and beautiful picture—sometimes through little wood—there are
two islands on the Lake each with a beautiful ruin—one of them rich
in ivy. . . . Yesterday our walk was of this description—the near Hills
were not very lofty but many of their Steeps beautifully wooded—the
distant Mountains in the Hebrides very grand the Saltwater Lakes
coming up between Crags and Islands fulltided and scarcely ruffled—
sometimes appearing as one large Lake, sometimes as three distinct
ones in different directions—At one point we saw afar off a rocky
opening into the main Sea—We have also seen an Eagle or two. They
move about without the least motion of Wings when in an indolent fit.
                                                            (i. 338)

Fingal's Cave inspired the lines 'Not Aladdin magian', in which
Keats characteristically invents a sea-god whom he calls Lycidas
but who bears more resemblance to Neptune. As has often been
noticed, the scene remained in his memory and contributed a
detail to *Hyperion*: 'I am puzzled how to give you an Idea of
Staffa', Keats observes. 'It can only be represented by a first rate
drawing—

One may compare the surface of the Island to a roof—this roof is
supported by grand pillars of basalt standing together as thick as honey
combs The finest thing is Fingal's Cave—it is entirely a hollowing out
of Basalt Pillars. Suppose now the Giants who rebelled against Jove
had taken a whole Mass of black Columns and bound them together

like bunches of matches—and then with immense Axes had made a cavern in the body of these columns—of course the roof and floor must be composed of the broken ends of the Columns—such is fingal's Cave except that the Sea has done the work of excavations and is continually dashing there—so that we walk along the sides of the cave on the pillars which are left as if for convenient Stairs—the roof is arched somewhat gothic wise and the length of some of the entire side pillars is 50 feet—About the island you might seat an army of Men each on a pillar—The length of the Cave is 120 feet and from its extremity the view into the sea through the large Arch at the entrance—the colour of the colums is a sort of black with a lurking gloom of purple therin—For solemnity and grandeur it far surpasses the finest Cathedrall. . . . As we approached in the boat there was such a fine swell of the sea that the pillars appeared rising immediately out of the crystal—But it is impossible to describe it.'   (i. 348–9)

The last passages that demand quotation are descriptions of the upper reaches of Ben Nevis:

The whole immense head of the Mountain is composed of large loose stones—thousands of acres—Before we had got half way up we passed large patches of snow and near the top there is a chasm some hundred feet deep completely glutted with it—Talking of chasms they are the finest wonder of the whole—they appear great rents in the very heart of the mountain though they are not, being at the side of it, but other huge crags arising round it give the appearance to Nevis of a shattered heart or Core in itself—These chasms are 1500 feet in depth and are the most tremendous places I have ever seen—they turn one giddy if you choose to give way to it—We tumbled in large stones and set the echoes at work in fine style. Sometimes these chasms are tolerably clear, sometimes there is a misty cloud which seems to steam up and sometimes they are entirely smothered with clouds.   (i. 353)

Like Turner, Keats is particularly interested in the effect of light and mist on scenery:

After a little time the Mist cleared away but still there were large Clouds about attracted by old Ben to a certain distance so as to form as it appeard large dome curtains which kept sailing about, opening and shutting at intervals here and there and everrywhere; so that although we did not see one vast wide extent of prospect all round we saw something perhaps finer—these cloud-veils opening with a dissolving motion and showing us the mountainous region beneath as through a loop hole—these cloudy loop holes ever varrying and discovering fresh prospect east, west north and South—Then it was misty again and again it was fair—then puff came a cold breeze of wind and bared

a craggy chap we had not yet seen though in close neighbourhood—
Every now and then we had over head blue Sky clear and the sun
pretty warm. I do not know whether I can give you an Idea of the
prospect from a large Mountain top . . . .   (i. 353)

In describing the flat top of the mountain Keats has a fine phrase
when he describes 'the sudden leap of the eye from the extremity
of what appears a plain into so vast a distance'.

Yet in spite of its grandeur the scenery of Scotland did not
answer to Keats's deepest desires. It is revealing to find him
praising places in Scotland that have 'a little of Devon' about
them, as he does in his description of the country round Kirk-
cudbright.[52] He makes the same comparison when he describes
his first view of Ayr:

The Sight was as rich as possible—I had no conception that the
native place of Burns was so beautiful—the Idea I had was more
desolate, his rigs of Barley seemed always to me but a few strips of
Green on a cold hill—O prejudice! it was rich as Devon—I endeavour'd to drink in the Prospect, that I might spin it out to you as
the silkworm makes silk from Mulbery leaves—I cannot recollect it—
Besides all the Beauty, there were the Mountains of Annan Isle, black
and huge over the Sea—We came down upon every thing suddenly. . . .
First we stood upon the Bridge across the Doon; surrounded by every
Phantasy of Green in tree, Meadow, and Hill,—the Stream of the
Doon, as a Farmer told us, is covered with trees from head to foot—
you know those beautiful heaths so fresh against the weather of a
summers evening—there was one stretching along behind the trees.
                                                          (i. 323–4)

But richness is hardly the characteristic feature of the Scottish
landscape, as Keats acknowledges in his sonnet 'On visiting the
Tomb of Burns':

> The Town, the churchyard, and the setting sun,
> The clouds, the trees, the rounded hills all seem,
> Though beautiful, cold—strange—as in a dream . . . .

Keats could not help sinning against Burns's 'native skies', in
this way, as he puts it at the end of the sonnet. 'I know not how
it is,' he comments in the letter which accompanied the sonnet,
'the Clouds, the sky, the Houses, all seem anti Grecian & anti
Charlemagnish.'[53] As will be seen in the next chapter, Keats was
in the habit of contrasting the Greeks, with their 'religion of
joy', with the austerities which he associated with Christianity;

and the Church of Scotland struck him as a more austere version of the Church of England. Ireland came as a relief. 'The dialect on the neighbouring shores of Scotland and Ireland is much the same', he wrote to Tom on the 7th of July:

> Yet I can perceive a great difference in the nations from the Chambermaid at this nate Inn kept by Mr Kelly—She is fair, kind and ready to laugh, because she is out of the horrible dominion of the Scotch kirk—A Scotch Girl stands in terrible awe of the Elders—poor little Susannas—They will scarcely laugh—they are greatly to be pitied and the kirk is greatly to be damn'd. These kirkmen have . . . made Men, Women, Old Men Young Men old Women, young women boys, girls and infants all careful—so that they are formed into regular Phalanges of savers and gainers. . . . These kirkmen have done Scotland harm—they have banished puns and laughing and kissing . . . . Poor unfortunate fellow [Burns]—his disposition was southern . . . .
>
> (i. 319–20)

Keats understands Burns because he understands himself.

The other anomalous note in the letters from Scotland is an ambivalent attitude to the Picturesque itself—or at least to the description of the Picturesque. 'Descriptions are bad at all times', Keats writes near the beginning of the 'journal' of his northern tour—though he adds in the next breath that he must describe the places he has seen, so that Tom may share the pleasure of his journey without the attendant fatigue.[54] Writing to George and Georgiana from Winchester fifteen months later Keats echoes this remark: he apologizes for sending them 'this dull specimen of description', and adds: 'For myself I hate descriptions.'[55] It was partly that he realized the sheer difficulty of describing scenery satisfactorily in the medium of words—and so we find him listing

> Mountains, Rivers Lakes, dells, glens, Rocks, and Clouds,
> With beautiful enchanting, gothic picturesque fine, delightful,
> enchanting, Grand, sublime,   (i. 322)

and inviting Reynolds to rearrange the words for himself. But it was also partly because his deepest interest (after all) was in human life. As early as his visit to Devonshire we find him remarking that 'Scenery is fine—but human nature is finer',[56] and the observation might stand as an epigraph to all the descriptive passages in his letters, brilliant as they often are. 'There was as fine a row of boys & girls as you ever saw', he wrote to Tom from Keswick, 'some beautiful faces, & one exquisite mouth.... This is what I like better than scenery.'[57] Although he acknowledges that 'the first Mountains I saw... weighed very solemnly upon me', he soon finds that he has 'been among wilds and Mountains too much to break out much about their Grandeur. ... The effect is wearing away.'[58] There is self-satire in his tone when he tells Mrs. Wylie that he has been '*werry* romantic indeed, among these Mountains & Lakes'—as a result of which he has caught a cold.[59] In April 1819 he tells his sister that he intends to stay in town during the summer, 'chiefly for the sake of books', adding: 'besides my Scotch journey gave me a doze of the Picturesque with which I ought to be content for some time'.[60] In fact he went to the Isle of Wight towards the end of June, and we soon find him describing 'the parties about here who come hunting after the picturesque like beagles. It is astonishing how they raven down scenery like children do sweetmeats.'[61] Describing a walk he has taken, a few days later, he goes on:

> But I have been so many finer walks, with a back ground of lake and mountain instedd of the sea, that I am not much touch'd with it, though I credit it for all the Surprise I should have felt if it had taken my cockney maidenhead—But I may call myself an old Stager in the picturesque, and unless it be something very large and overpowering I cannot receive any extraordinary relish.   (ii. 135)

Soon he is telling Fanny Brawne that he is 'getting a great dislike of the picturesque'—though in her company it would be another matter:

> You would delight very greatly in the walks about here, the Cliffs, woods, hills, sands, rocks &c about here. They are however not so fine but I shall give them a hearty good bye to exchange them for my Cathedrall—Yet again I am not so tired of Scenery as to hate Switzerland—We might spend a pleasant Year at Berne or Zurich—if it should please Venus to hear my 'Beseech thee to hear us O Goddess'.
>   (ii. 137–8)

There is nothing surprising about all this. It is the natural reaction of a man who has been hearing a little too much about the Picturesque, and whose health has suffered as a result of his pursuit of it. It is also a reminder of the sort of poet Keats was, and in particular of the sort of poet he aspired to become. As

Woodhouse pointed out to John Taylor, 'There are gradations in Poetry & in Poets', and Keats was not a 'purely descriptive' poet, the sort of poet who confines himself 'to external nature & visible objects'.[62] We notice that the poetical sketches which occur in the letters written during his journey are practically all about people; while the whole body of his letters contains ample evidence of his perceptive interest in human nature. When Pope looked back on his own early poetry he said that in it 'pure Description held the place of Sense'; while in another passage he claimed in his own defence

> That not in Fancy's Maze he wander'd long,
> But stoop'd to Truth, and moraliz'd his Song.[63]

We may be reminded of these remarks by Keats's reference to 'The Eve of St. Agnes' in a letter to Taylor:

I have been endeavouring to persuade myself to untether Fancy and let her manage for herself—I and myself cannot agree about this at all. Wonders are no wonders to me. I am more at home amongst Men and women. I would rather read Chaucer than Ariosto—The little dramatic skill I may as yet have however badly it might show in a Drama would I think be sufficient for a Poem—I wish to diffuse the colouring of St Agnes eve throughout a Poem in which Character and Sentiment would be the figures to such drapery.   (ii. 234)

So Keats wrote in November 1819, when his creative career had almost reached its end. We must now go back to its extraordinary beginning, and to the *Poems* of 1817.

VII

'VISTAS OF BEAUTY':
THE *POEMS* OF 1817

Keats's rich fancy of Satyrs & Fauns & doves & white clouds,
wound up the stream of conversation.

HAYDON[1]

W H E N we open the *Poems* of 1817 we find ourselves in the
presence of a young medical student who is trying to escape
from the banalities of his everyday existence. One of his fellow-
students was later to recall how Keats, 'in a room, . . . was
always at the window, peering into space'.[2] It is the same in his
poetry: he is eager to escape from the noise and smell of his
everyday life, to construct for himself another world more free
and more beautiful than that of Guy's Hospital and the lecture
theatre. To understand this volume we must forget our distrust
of 'escapism' and accept the fact that Keats is looking through the
window in order to find another world on the other side.

Above all Keats is seeking a religion which will nourish his
imagination. As he writes in the dedicatory sonnet:

> Glory and loveliness have passed away;
>> For if we wander out in early morn,
>> No wreathed incense do we see upborne
> Into the east, to meet the smiling day:
> No crowd of nymphs soft voic'd and young, and gay,
>> In woven baskets bringing ears of corn,
>> Roses, and pinks, and violets, to adorn
> The shrine of Flora in her early May.

To see the sort of scene that Keats had in mind we have only to
look at Poussin's 'The Triumph of Flora' (Plate X). This is
one of the most exuberant of Poussin's works, painted at a time
when he was deeply impressed by the *colore* of the great
Venetians and particularly of the fine Titian Bacchanal now in
the Prado.[3] It is very likely that one of Keats's friends had a
print of this delightful picture of Poussin's.

The attitude expressed in the dedicatory sonnet may well remind us of a later poet who was also profoundly influenced by painting. 'I am very religious,' Yeats wrote in his *Autobiographies*, 'and deprived by Huxley and Tyndall, whom I detested, of the simple-minded religion of my childhood, I had made a new religion, almost an infallible Church of poetic tradition, of a fardel of stories, and of personages, and of emotions, inseparable from their first expression, passed on from generation to generation by poets and painters with some help from philosophers and theologians.'[4] With Keats it was not that rationalists had undermined his faith in a beautiful traditional religion, but rather that his own mind and senses rebelled against the lack of beauty in the religion with which he grew up. At the outset of his career, Christianity presented itself to him as something drab and hostile to the free play of the emotions and the imagination. This becomes evident if we compare the lines just quoted with the sonnet 'Written in Disgust of Vulgar Superstition' about the same time:

> The church bells toll a melancholy round,
>   Calling the people to some other prayers,
>   Some other gloominess, more dreadful cares,
> More hearkening to the sermon's horrid sound.
> Surely the mind of man is closely bound
>   In some black spell; seeing that each one tears
>   Himself from fireside joys, and Lydian airs,
> And converse high of those with glory crown'd.
> Still, still they toll, and I should feel a damp—
>   A chill as from a tomb, did I not know
> That they are dying like an outburnt lamp;
>   That 'tis their sighing, wailing ere they go
>   Into oblivion;—that fresh flowers will grow,
> And many glories of immortal stamp.

The key-words of the one are 'melancholy', 'gloominess', 'dreadful cares', and 'black spell': of the other, 'glory and loveliness' and 'the smiling day'. On the one hand we have the tolling of the church bells, the 'horrid sound' of the sermon, the damp of a tomb and the image of the outburnt lamp: on the other, the soft young voices of the nymphs and the incense that curls upwards as they bring gifts of corn and flowers with which to decorate the shrine of Flora. It is clear that Keats is not rebelling against all religion: on the contrary, both passages

X. POUSSIN: The Triumph of Flora

No crowd of nymphs soft voic'd and young, and gay,
In woven baskets bringing ears of corn,
Roses, and pinks, and violets, to adorn
The shrine of Flora in her early May.

describe professedly religious rites. He is rebelling against what seems to him a religion of death, and turning towards a religion of life. It is the same attitude that inspired Schiller's 'The Gods of Greece', as well as much in Novalis and Hölderlin and other German poets of their time.[5] It is possible that Keats came on a translation of some German poem written in this spirit; but to hear such views he had no need to do more than talk to Leigh Hunt, as we are reminded by an entry in Haydon's Diary made at this very time, on the 5th of November 1816:

Leigh Hunt says he prefers infinitely the beauties of Pagan Mythology to the gloomy repentance of the Christians.   (ii. 68)

Severn tells us that Keats used to talk to him 'about the Greek spirit,—the Religion of the Beautiful, the Religion of Joy, as he used to call it', and taught him about the 'incarnate Delight' of Greek sculpture.[6] Keats yearned for a religion of joy. It seemed to him a heavy misfortune, both as a man and as a poet, to have been born at a time

> . . . when under pleasant trees
> Pan is no longer sought.

As we look back we can see how a number of influences combined to direct Keats's imagination towards the mythology of Greece. One of the most important was his reading of *The Faerie Queene*. 'In Spenser's fairy land', Brown tells us in his brief *Life of John Keats*, 'he was enchanted, breathed in a new world, and became another being.'[7] *The Faerie Queene* made it inevitable that Keats should associate poetry with classical mythology, as with fairy land: it is interesting to notice how many of the myths to which he was later to turn—such as the story of Cupid and Psyche, and the story of Endymion—occur in Spenser's poem. And of course Keats's classical reading, in which he was guided by mythographers who were as exciting to him as the cartographers had been to men like Marlowe and Donne, had already introduced him to a realm in which he could breathe a larger air than that of his daily surroundings.[8] Sir Joshua Reynolds had claimed that 'the great events of Greek and Roman fable and history' were familiar and interesting 'to all Europe' by 'early education, and the usual course of reading, . . . without being degraded by the vulgarism of ordinary life'.[9] For Keats at this time it may well have been one of the attractions of classical mythology that it excluded the *profanum vulgus*. Goethe tells us that as a young man in Frankfurt he obtained casts of the head of the Laocoon, the daughters of Niobe, and other famous works of sculpture, and regarded them 'as a sort of esoteric antidote whenever the weak, the false, the mannered threatened to get power over me'.[10] At this early point there was still a good deal that was false and mannered in the style of Keats, but already one of the attractions of classical mythology may have been the sense it gave him of being an initiate. It was a language understood by people who cared for the arts—people like Leigh Hunt and Haydon—but which remained largely obscure to the outside world. What is more, the profound philosophical basis of mythology was the subject of a passage in *The Excursion*, a poem which appeared in 1814, when Keats was standing poised on the threshold of poetry. In Book IV the Sage discourses as follows:

> In that fair clime, the lonely herdsman, stretched
> On the soft grass through half a summer's day,
> With music lulled his indolent repose:
> And, in some fit of weariness, if he,
> When his own breath was silent, chanced to hear
> A distant strain, far sweeter than the sounds
> Which his poor skill could make, his fancy fetched,
> Even from the blazing chariot of the sun,
> A beardless Youth, who touched a golden lute,
> And filled the illumined groves with ravishment.
> The nightly hunter, lifting a bright eye
> Up towards the crescent moon, with grateful heart
> Called on the lovely wanderer who bestowed
> That timely light, to share his joyous sport:
> And hence, a beaming Goddess with her Nymphs,
> Across the lawn and through the darksome grove,
> Not unaccompanied with tuneful notes
> By echo multiplied from rock or cave,
> Swept in the storm of chase; as moon and stars
> Glance rapidly along the clouded heaven,
> When winds are blowing strong.   (iv. 851–71)

So Wordsworth describes the origin of Apollo and Cynthia, and that of the naiads, the oreads, the satyrs, and of Pan himself. From the first the passage attracted attention. Hazlitt quoted it in his review in *The Examiner*, describing it as 'one of a succession of splendid passages equally enriched with philosophy

and poetry, tracing the fictions of Eastern mythology to the
immediate intercourse of the imagination with Nature, and to
the habitual propensity of the human mind to endow the outward forms of being with life and conscious motion'.[11] Hazlitt
reprinted the review in *The Round Table*, and we notice that
when he discusses 'the origin of the Grecian myth' this passage
from *The Excursion* is never far from his mind. It is not surprising that it made a deep impression on Keats. On one occasion he
discussed it with Benjamin Bailey, and 'said this description of
Apollo should have ended at the "golden lute", & have left it to
the imagination to complete the picture'.[12] The problem of
portraying Apollo was to occupy Keats's mind a good deal, a
year or two later.

The first poem in the volume of 1817, 'I stood tip-toe', which
was entitled 'Endymion' until Keats decided to write a long poem
on that subject, contains a passage on the origin of mythology
which is very much in the spirit of *The Excursion*. Keats refers to
the myth of Cupid and Psyche, which had been a favourite with
painters from Raphael onwards, and which was to provide the
subject for the first of his mature Odes:

> So felt he, who first told, how Psyche went
> On the smooth wind to realms of wonderment;
> What Psyche felt, and Love, when their full lips
> First touch'd.   (141–4)

A passage a few lines later in the poem is highly visual in its
effect:

> So did he feel, who pull'd the boughs aside,
> That we might look into a forest wide,
> To catch a glimpse of Fawns, and Dryades
> Coming with softest rustle through the trees;
> And garlands woven of flowers wild, and sweet,
> Upheld on ivory wrists, or sporting feet:
> Telling us how fair, trembling Syrinx fled
> Arcadian Pan, with such a fearful dread.   (151–8)

It is clear that inspiration from painting has fused with literary
recollections in these lines, though it is impossible to be definite
about the particular painting in question: perhaps Keats is
remembering a 'Bacchanal' as well as a 'Pan and Syrinx'.[13] The
use of a figure pulling aside a bough is a common device to

'frame' a picture: often (for example) a satyr is pulling aside a branch to watch the play of nymphs and fauns.

The next lines in the same poem also deal with a subject treated by numerous painters:

> What first inspired a bard of old to sing
> Narcissus pining o'er the untainted spring?
> In some delicious ramble, he had found
> A little space, with boughs all woven round;
> And in the midst of all, a clearer pool
> Than e'er reflected in its pleasant cool
> The blue sky here, and there, serenely peeping
> Through tendril wreaths fantastically creeping.
> And on the bank a lonely flower he spied,
> A meek and forlorn flower, with naught of pride,
> Drooping its beauty o'er the watery clearness,
> To woo its own sad image into nearness:
> Deaf to light Zephyrus it would not move;
> But still would seem to droop, to pine, to love.
> So while the Poet stood in this sweet spot,
> Some fainter gleamings o'er his fancy shot;
> Nor was it long ere he had told the tale
> Of young Narcissus, and sad Echo's bale. (163–80)

The 'bard' is, of course, Ovid, who told the story in Book III of the *Metamorphoses*;[14] but the scene which Keats describes has often been painted, and as it happens we can identify a painting which may well have been in his mind. Claude's 'Landscape with Narcissus and Echo' is known to have been painted for an English patron, perhaps for Peter Lely.[15] In Keats's day it belonged to Sir George Beaumont: he gave it to the National Gallery, where it now hangs, in 1825. It is possible that Keats saw the original, almost inevitable that he should have seen a print, so that this painting of Claude's can confidently be named as one of the sources of the passage. It is a painting that he may well have heard discussed: in John Landseer's *Catalogue of . . . Pictures . . . in the National Gallery*, the work of a man whom Keats met, which has the opening lines of *Endymion* as its motto, there is a long and enthusiastic appreciation of the picture, with quotations from Milton and Gray.[16]

Near the end of the poem we come on two lines which suggest some memory of a museum or art gallery—

XI. CLAUDE: Landscape with Narcissus and Echo

What first inspired a bard of old to sing
Narcissus pining o'er the untainted spring?
In some delicious ramble, he had found
A little space, with boughs all woven round . . .

> Or young Apollo on the pedestal

and

> As Venus looking sideways in alarm.[16b]

Curiously enough, one can make a plausible guess at the figures which suggested these lines. Lot 193 in the *Catalogue of a Valuable Collection of Paintings, Engravings and Books of Prints* belonging to Haydon and sold on the 11th and 12th of June 1823 is described as 'A statue of Apollo and pedestal', while one of the several casts of Venus is Lot 212, 'A Venus De Medicis'. Goethe describes the effect on his imagination of the 'forest of statues' that he found in the Hall of Antiquities in Mannheim.[17] Soon Keats was to see the Elgin Marbles, with memorable effects; but before he saw these he saw the 'forest of statues' in Haydon's cast room, and these lines are early evidence of the effect of these still presences on a young man with an exceptionally quick eye for postures and attitudes. The lines just before the conclusion of the poem are also highly visual:

> And springing up, they met the wond'ring sight
> Of their dear friends, nigh foolish with delight;
> Who feel their arms, and breasts, and kiss and stare,
> And on their placid foreheads part the hair.
> Young men, and maidens at each other gaz'd
> With hands held back, and motionless, amaz'd
> To see the brightness in each other's eyes;
> And so they stood, fill'd with a sweet surprise,
> Until their tongues were loos'd in poesy.   (227–35)

It is hard to avoid the hypothesis that this description of one of the wonders which took place on the marriage-night of Cynthia and Endymion owes a debt to some picture of a miracle; but I have been unable to identify the picture that was in Keats's mind.[18]

The visual element in the inspiration of the second poem in the volume is proclaimed in its opening lines:

> Lo! I must tell a tale of chivalry;
> For large white plumes are dancing in mine eye.
> Not like the formal crest of latter days:
> But bending in a thousand graceful ways;
> So graceful, that it seems no mortal hand,
> Or e'en the touch of Archimago's wand,
> Could charm them into such an attitude.

                .   .   .   .   .   .

> Lo! I must tell a tale of chivalry;
> For while I muse, the lance points slantingly
> Athwart the morning air.

This may have been inspired by an illustration in a book, or perhaps by a print of Rubens's 'Tourney at the Castle': a painting which was later to be a favourite of the Pre-Raphaelites, as were Keats's poems themselves. In such passages we notice that Keats almost always associates the medieval with Spenser. At the outset of his poetic career medieval Spenserian themes vied with Greek for his allegiance:

> . . . How shall I
> Revive the dying tones of minstrelsy,
> Which linger yet about lone gothic arches,
> In dark green ivy, and among wild larches?

It is significant that these lines come from a 'Specimen of an Induction to a Poem' which was never to be written. 'Calidore', another medieval essay, also remains a fragment. As things turned out 'The Eve of St. Agnes' was to be the only major poem of Keats's which is at all medieval—apart from 'La Belle Dame sans Merci' and the fragmentary 'The Eve of Saint Mark'—just as it was to be the only major poem written in Spenserian stanzas.

In two other poems we see Keats composing a poetic landscape. The first describes the 'sweet spot of earth' that Calidore delights in:

> . . . The bowery shore
> Went off in gentle windings to the hoar
> And light blue mountains . . .
> The lonely turret, shatter'd, and outworn,
> Stands venerably proud; too proud to mourn
> Its long lost grandeur: fir trees grow around,
> Aye dropping their hard fruit upon the ground.
> The little chapel with the cross above
> Upholding wreaths of ivy; the white dove,
> That on the window spreads his feathers light,
> And seems from purple clouds to wing its flight.
> Green tufted islands casting their soft shades
> Across the lake; sequester'd leafy glades,
> That through the dimness of their twilight show
> Large dock leaves, spiral foxgloves, or the glow

> Of the wild cat's eyes, or the silvery stems
> Of delicate birch trees, or long grass which hems
> A little brook.   (26–28, 38–52)

These lines could well have been written as a commentary on a landscape painting by Claude: they are in the spirit of what a critic once called 'the grand quiescence of Claude'.[19] The particularity with which the flowers and trees are indicated exemplifies a quality which Haydon particularly admired in his favourite painters of the seventeenth century. In one of the 'Visions' in the *Annals of the Fine Arts* he makes the ghost of Michelangelo assure Turner that he is 'the greatest genius living in landscape' but ask him why he does not 'define the limbs of [his] trees . . . and vary the character of [his] plants and grass, as Poussin, and Salvator, and Claude, varied them?'[20] In the epistle 'To George Felton Mathew' the description of the setting in which Keats would like to write his poetry is also carefully organized:

> Where oaks, that erst the Druid knew, are growing,
> And flowers, the glory of one day, are blowing;
> Where the dark-leav'd laburnum's drooping clusters
> Reflect athwart the stream their yellow lustres,
> And intertwined the cassia's arms unite,
> With its own drooping buds, but very white;
> Where on one side are covert branches hung,
> 'Mong which the nightingales have always sung
> In leafy quiet: where to pry, aloof,
> Atween the pillars of the sylvan roof,
> Would be to find where violet beds were nestling,
> And where the bee with cowslip bells was wrestling.
> There must be too a ruin dark, and gloomy,
> To say "joy not too much in all that's bloomy".   (39–52)

No one acquainted with the poetry of the later eighteenth century will be surprised to find that there 'must be' a ruin in such a picture (as there is a turret in the previous passage). A month after the publication of this volume we find Keats describing Carisbrooke Castle and lamenting that he has 'not seen many specimens of Ruins'.[21] Sir Joshua Reynolds had emphasized the value of a ruin in a painting, on account of the ideas that it calls up in our minds:

As we have naturally a veneration for antiquity, whatever building brings to our remembrance ancient customs and manners, such as the Castles of the Barons of ancient Chivalry, is sure to give this delight. Hence it is that *towers and battlements* are so often selected by the Painter and the Poet, to make a part of the composition of their Ideal Landscape.[22]

A note refers the reader to 'L'Allegro', which Keats clearly remembered as he wrote several of the poems in this volume.

Since the verse epistle is an informal type of composition which often affords more direct evidence of what a poet is think-ing than a more highly finished poem, it is not surprising that two of the other epistles throw light on the sort of picture that often caught Keats's eye at this time. One of the epistles is addressed to his brother George:

> It has been said, dear George, and true I hold it,
> (For knightly Spenser to Libertas told it,)
> That when a Poet is in such a trance,
> In air he sees white coursers paw, and prance,
> Bestridden of gay knights, in gay apparel,
> Who at each other tilt in playful quarrel,
> And what we, ignorantly, sheet-lightning call,
> Is the swift opening of their wide portal,
> When the bright warder blows his trumpet clear,
> Whose tones reach naught on earth but Poet's ear.
> When these enchanted portals open wide,
> And through the light the horsemen swiftly glide,
> The Poet's eye can reach those golden halls,
> And view the glory of their festivals:
> Their ladies fair, that in the distance seem
> Fit for the silv'ring of a seraph's dream;
> Their rich brimm'd goblets, that incessant run
> Like the bright spots that move about the sun;
> And, when upheld, the wine from each bright jar
> Pours with the lustre of a falling star.
> Yet further off, are dimly seen their bowers,
> Of which, no mortal eye can reach the flowers.   (23–44)

'Libertas' is Leigh Hunt, and the poetic trance is also described in 'Sleep and Poetry' and elsewhere. Once again it is clear how much pictures mattered to Keats's imagination. Not that he is describing any one painting here: the passage is eclectic in its sources, drawing on reminiscences of Hunt's talk of Spenser, memories of *The Faerie Queene* itself, and the beauty of such

paintings as (perhaps) Bellini's 'Feast of the Gods' and a
Poussin Bacchanal, to create a vivid image of the 'glory and
loveliness' of which a young poet may dream.[23] The 'enchanted
portals' here anticipate the 'magic casements' of the 'Ode to a
Nightingale'.

The other verse epistle was written in March 1818. John
Hamilton Reynolds, to whom it is addressed, was ill, and Keats
wrote a letter to help him to pass the time. He tells him how
as he lay in bed the previous night

> There came before my eyes that wonted thread
> Of Shapes, and Shadows and Remembrances,
> That every other minute vex and please.

He goes on to describe the 'Things all disjointed' that drift
through one's mind as one waits for sleep. Ernest de Sélincourt was for once far from the mark when he wrote of the'mean-
ingless caprice' of these opening lines:[24] Keats is describing the
images that present themselves on the threshold of sleep and
become the material of our dreams and nightmares, and we
notice the sharply visual quality of his imagery—

> Two witch's eyes above a Cherub's mouth,
> Voltaire with casque and shield and Habergeon,
> And Alexander with his night-cap on.

Keats is writing as the contemporary of Coleridge and of Fuseli,
of whose 'Nightmare' we may well be reminded. But it is no
nightmare that Keats intends to describe, to entertain his friend,
but a poetic vision suggested by a favourite picture. 'You know,
I am sure, Claude's Enchanted Castle', he wrote in the covering
note, 'and I wish you may be pleased with my remembrance of
it':[25]

> You know the Enchanted Castle it doth stand
> Upon a Rock on the Border of a Lake
> Nested in Trees, which all do seem to shake
> From some old Magic like Urganda's sword.
> O Phoebus that I had thy sacred word
> To shew this Castle in fair dreaming wise
> Unto my friend, while sick and ill he lies.
>   You know it well enough, where it doth seem
> A mossy place, a Merlin's Hall, a dream.
> You know the clear Lake, and the little Isles,
> The Mountains blue, and cold near neighbour rills—

> All which elsewhere are but half animate
> Here do they look alive to love and hate;
> To smiles and frowns; they seem a lifted mound
> Above some giant, pulsing underground.

After a paragraph in which he gives a purely fanciful account
of the castle's history, Keats goes on:

> The doors all look as if they oped themselves,
> The windows as if latch'd by fays & elves—
> And from them comes a silver flash of light
> As from the Westward of a Summer's night . . .
>   See what is coming from the distance dim!
> A golden galley all in silken trim!
> Three rows of oars are lightening moment-whiles
> Into the verdurous bosoms of those Isles.
> Towards the Shade under the Castle Wall
> It comes in silence—now tis hidden all.
> The clarion sounds; and from a postern gate[26]
> An echo of sweet music doth create
> A fear in the poor herdsman who doth bring
> His beasts to trouble the enchanted spring:
> He tells of the sweet music and the spot
> To all his friends, and they believe him not.

Keats continues:

> O that our dreamings all of sleep or wake
> Would all their colours from the Sunset take:
> From something of material sublime,
> Rather than shadow our own Soul's daytime
> In the dark void of Night.[27]

Partly because it is so unpolished—Keats did not print the poem
—this passage tells us a great deal about his mind and his
associative processes.

It is not clear whether Keats realized that this painting
illustrates the story of Cupid and Psyche as told in *The Golden
Ass* of Apuleius—the story to which he was to turn for the
subject of the first of his mature Odes. He does not use the
more correct title, 'Landscape with Psyche and the Palace of
Amor', but rather the title which dates from Woollett's famous
engraving of 1782 (Plate XII).[28]

This picture is often mentioned by diarists and memoir-
writers of the time. On the 27th of April 1810 William Wells
told Joseph Farington that he 'had purchased the picture by

XII. CLAUDE: The Enchanted Castle

'You know, I am sure, Claude's Enchanted Castle, and I wish you may be pleased with my remembrance of it.'

Claude called "The Inchanted Castle" from Mr. Buchanan, the Picture dealer for £1000,—& that He shd. now cease from purchasing'.[29] We have already seen Hazlitt using this work as a criterion of taste:[30] he wrote of it more than once, and no doubt talked about it frequently. In *The Champion* for the 4th of December 1814, for example, he writes of the 'Enchanted Castle, with that one simple figure in the foreground,—

"Sole sitting by the shores of old romance"',

and insists that from nothing but 'an eye always intent on nature, and brooding over "beauty, rendered still more beautiful" by the exquisite feeling with which it was contemplated' could Claude have borrowed 'his verdant landscapes and his azure skies, the bare sight of which wafts the imagination to Arcadian scenes, "thrice happy fields, and groves, and flowery vales", breathing perpetual youth and freshness'.[31] The painting was exhibited at the British Institution in 1819. Whether Keats could have seen it before he wrote the verse-epistle in March of the previous year is uncertain, but his reference to 'a silver flash of light' is authentic—as Röthlisberger observes, 'the silvery light expresses the magic character of a divine scene'— and this suggests that if Keats did not see the painting, he heard a description of it from someone who had.

In any case, Keats does not set out to give a precise description of the picture. His 'golden galley all in silken trim' is not the little boat that can just be descried in the print, but an addition suggested to his imagination by other paintings of Claude's. Just as he was to be 'worldly enough to wish for a fleet of chivalry Barges with Trumpets and Banners' in Loch Lomond four months later,[32] so now Keats imagines a galley approaching the castle that overlooks the lake. Elaborate ships are common in Claude's paintings, and it is worth noticing that three of the five Claudes in the Angerstein Collection had galleys as a prominent part of their composition. One of these, 'Seaport with the Embarcation of St. Ursula', was a particular favourite of Hazlitt's. 'The water is exquisite', he wrote, 'and the sails of the vessels glittering in the morning sun, and the blue flags placed against the trees, which seem like an opening into the sky behind—so sparkling is the effect of this ambiguity in colouring—are in Claude's most perfect manner.'[33] This painting has probably contributed something to the passage, while Keats may also be remembering Claude's 'Landscape with the Father of Psyche sacrificing at the Milesian Temple of Apollo' (Plate XXXV) and perhaps his 'Landscape with the Landing of Æneas in Latium'.[34]

This passage is of central importance to anyone interested in the influence of the visual arts on the imagination of Keats. Nothing could be more revealing than the fact that he takes it for granted that to describe one of his favourite pictures will be an acceptable way of amusing an invalid: nothing more revealing than the wish that our dreams would form themselves from the beautiful things that we see, rather than from the vexations of our everyday lives: nothing more revealing than the way in which Keats here starts with a specific painting but moves away from it almost at once in the direction of inventive fantasy. If he had not named 'The Enchanted Castle' it is unlikely that anyone would have identified it as the source of his inspiration. Starting from this picture, what Keats does is to provide us with a set of informal variations on two themes of Claude. This is a pattern that we will find recurring in his later poetry.

The last and longest poem in the volume of 1817, 'Sleep and Poetry', throws a great deal of light on the nature of Keats's poetic ambitions. It also makes it clear how great a debt he owed to the Sister Art of Painting. He wrote the poem after a sleepless night spent on a couch in Leigh Hunt's study. Among the 'delights' of the day he particularly recalls

> . . . forms of elegance
> Stooping their shoulders o'er a horse's prance,
> Careless, and grand—fingers soft and round
> Parting luxuriant curls;—and the swift bound
> Of Bacchus from his chariot, when his eye
> Made Ariadne's cheek look blushingly.
> Thus I remember all the pleasant flow
> Of words at opening a portfolio.   (331–8)

The first reference may be to Vandyke, or to the painting by Rubens already referred to: the second can only be to a print of Titian's 'Bacchus and Ariadne'. This masterpiece, which is now in the National Gallery, was exhibited at the British Institution in 1816. As Buchanan observes in his *Memoirs of Painting*, 'no picture by Titian has ever come to this country which has enjoyed,

XIII. TITIAN: Bacchus and Ariadne

. . . The swift bound
Of Bacchus from his chariot, when his eye
Made Ariadne's cheek look blushingly.

since the period of its being painted, a greater reputation'.[35] Reynolds praised 'the harmony of colouring' in this work in his Eighth Discourse,[36] and when Lawrence saw it in 1807 he was delighted:

Lawrence called in the even'g in raptures on having seen a picture by Titian at Buchannan's in Oxendon St. [Farington wrote in his Diary]—the subject Bacchus & Ariadne. He described it to be the finest piece of colouring that He had ever beheld for splendour, force, & freshness. He said the Titians at the Marquiss of Staffords could not be mentioned with it. The colours of it Blue, Green, red and yellow. The landscape part being pushed to the extremity of colour in depth & feelings. In one corner Titian seems after He had otherways finished the picture, to have dashed a piece of bright yellow drapery, on which is a golden Vase, & this part alone by its effect proves it from the hand of Titian.[37]

It was much studied by Haydon, Hazlitt—who wrote of its 'prodigious *gusto* of colouring'—and other members of Keats's circle.[38] In a passage quoted elsewhere, Severn tells us that it inspired the description of Bacchus in *Endymion*.[39] To understand Keats's frequent references to Bacchus, it is essential to realize that they are to the beautiful young god portrayed in this painting, and not to the more familiar belly god. Wordsworth was probably remembering Titian's picture when he censured Dryden for his vulgar description of Bacchus in 'Alexander's Feast'. Hazlitt comments in *The Spirit of the Age* that when you heard Wordsworth speaking on the subject you could imagine 'that you saw Titian's picture of the meeting of *Bacchus and Ariadne*—so classic were his conceptions, so glowing his style'.[40] It is in fact one of the most classical of Titian's works: one can trace affinities to classical reliefs, to the Elgin Marbles, and to the paintings of Poussin. We should remember Titian when we read the line in the 'Ode to a Nightingale':

> Not charioted by Bacchus and his pards.

Although Keats refers to a print in 'Sleep and Poetry', it seems probable that he also saw the original at the British Institution. The fact that several of Titian's greatest paintings were to be seen in London in his lifetime is not the least important circumstance in the biography of Keats. When he wrote of

> Some Titian colours touch'd into real life[41]

he had a glowing image of actuality in his mind's eye.

Leigh Hunt was the high-priest of the Religion of Joy of which Keats was at this time a humble acolyte. This becomes very clear as we read the following passage:

> It was a poet's house who keeps the keys
> Of Pleasure's temple. Round about were hung
> The glorious features of the bards who sung
> In other ages—cold and sacred busts
> Smiled at each other. Happy he who trusts
> To clear Futurity his darling fame!
> Then there were fauns and satyrs taking aim
> At swelling apples with a frisky leap
> And reaching fingers, 'mid a luscious heap
> Of vine leaves. Then there rose to view a fane
> Of liny marble, and thereto a train
> Of nymphs approaching fairly o'er the sward:
> One, loveliest, holding her white hand toward
> The dazzling sun-rise: two sisters sweet
> Bending their graceful figures till they meet
> Over the trippings of a little child:
> And some are hearing, eagerly, the wild
> Thrilling liquidity of dewy piping.   (354–71)

No more circumstantial evidence could be desired of the fact that Leigh Hunt's study, with its busts of poets[42] and its prints in portfolios and on the walls, was the most exciting (because probably the first) picture gallery that Keats ever visited. There he often spent an evening 'growing wings for the night', hearing stimulating talk of the things that mattered to him most—poetry, painting, and the liberation of mankind from the tyranny of superstition and the tyranny of convention. He was in precisely the receptive mood in which fresh ideas, and fresh visual images, would make the deepest impression on his mind. The 'fauns and satyrs' must have been suggested by some 'Bacchanal' that I have failed to identify, while the more detailed description of the nymphs approaching a marble temple appears to be a composite from more than one original: a number of Claudes portray processions of this kind—his 'Landscape with Bacchus at the Palace of the Dead Staphylus', for example (Plate XXXVI), and his 'View of Delphi with a Procession',[43]—while Poussin's 'Triumph of Flora' (Plate X) has a fine procession of nymphs, one of whom (not two) is looking down at the 'trippings' of two little children. This religious procession is one of the archetypal images in all Keats's poetry, one of the essential clues to the labyrinth of his imaginative life.[44]

About the paintings referred to in the next passage of this poem there can be little uncertainty:

> See, in another picture, nymphs are wiping
> Cherishingly Diana's timorous limbs;—
> A fold of lawny mantle dabbling swims
> At the bath's edge, and keeps a gentle motion
> With the subsiding crystal.   (372–6)

There are many pictures of Diana, but there can be little doubt that the pictures in the forefront of Keats's mind were Titian's famous companion-pieces, 'Diana and Actaeon' (Plate XIV) and 'Diana discovering the Incontinence of Callisto'.

They are just the sort of paintings to appeal to a young poet with an eye for colour and attitude who is in love with the mythology of the Greeks. They belong to the category of Titian's work which he called 'poesie': a Venetian type of painting, associated with the name of Giorgione, which took its subject-matter from Ovid as interpreted by Boccaccio and other mythographers of the Renaissance. Historians of art distinguish sharply between the Ferrarese 'poesie' (which include the 'Bacchus and Ariadne') and those which Titian painted as an old man for the King of Spain. Waterhouse points out, for example, that between the two series

> Europe had undergone a transformation of spirit. Up to the sack of Rome in 1527 it was possible for artists and their patrons to value joyousness as the prevailing mood of artistic creation. It is this infectious quality of joy which marks the spirit in which the High Renaissance regarded antiquity. . . . Between [the Ferrarese paintings] and the Spanish series the menace of the Reformation had threatened Italy and the Counter-Reformation had begun its numbing work on the creative imagination. Briefly the mood of the Ferrara series is joyous, that of the Spanish series tragic.[45]

It was only because the King of Spain was such a dominating figure in the Catholic world that Titian was at liberty to dwell so uninhibitedly on the beauty of the nude in this new world of strict Church-censorship of the arts. Keats must have been aware of the tragic overtones of the paintings, for they were a frequent subject of conversation in his circle. A writer in the *Annals of the Fine Arts* tells us that during the whole of Haydon's preparatory studies for 'The Death of Dentatus', 'he had not ceased to study the pictures at the Marquess of Stafford's, and to prepare his mind for the study of painting. The *Diana and Actaeon* and the *Four Ages* by Titian, were pictures on which he used to dwell for hours'.[46] That was in 1807 and 1808. Fifteen years later Haydon was still studying the same pictures: on the 26th of December 1823 he wrote in his Diary:

> Went to Lord Stafford's for an hour & saw the Acteon on the ground. It is painted on a rough canvas with a great body of colour in the centre of the limb, and diminished each side to the contour. Nothing can be so soft, & sweet, & mellow.

The 'Diana and Actaeon' and the 'Diana and Callisto' were among the first great paintings that Hazlitt ever saw. In *The Picture Galleries of England* he apostrophizes the latter work and reflects that he first saw it on the same wall twenty-five years before. In these two paintings he finds 'a charm . . . which no words can convey':

> It is the charm thrown over each by the greatest genius for colouring that the world ever saw. . . . Either one or the other (whichever we turn to, and we can never be satisfied with looking at either—so rich a scene do they unfold, so serene a harmony do they infuse into the soul) is like a divine piece of music, or rises 'like an exhalation of rich distilled perfumes'. . . . With all this prodigality of genius, there is the greatest severity and discipline of art. The figures seem grouped for the effect of colour—the most striking contrasts are struck out, and then a third object, a piece of drapery, an uplifted arm, a bow and arrows, a straggling weed, is introduced to make an intermediate tint, or carry on the harmony . . . .[47]

Keats could not have read that passage, but it is certain that he knew an earlier sentence of Hazlitt's on the same subject, since it was first published in *The Examiner* and then reprinted in *The Round Table*: 'The effect of colour in Titian's Bath of Diana, at the Marquis of Stafford's, is perhaps the finest in the world, made up of the richest contrasts, blended together by the most masterly gradations.'[48] It would be remarkable if Keats never managed to see these paintings, having heard so much about

XIV. TITIAN: Diana and Actaeon

*See, in another picture, nymphs are wiping
Cherishingly Diana's timorous limbs.*

them: when he wrote 'Sleep and Poetry', however, he may have known only the print which he describes in Leigh Hunt's study. He looked at it so intently that he was able to distil the voluptuous beauty of the painting into four and a half lines of memorable verse.

It is not surprising that a poet so interested in the visual arts should have remembered them when he made an attempt to describe poetry. First Keats takes an image reminiscent of the story of Danae—

> . . . A drainless shower
> Of light is poesy

—and then he goes on:

> . . . 'tis the supreme of power;
> 'Tis might half slumb'ring on its own right arm.

As de Sélincourt remarked, the last line is 'characteristic of Keats's power of presenting in his poetry the effects of sculpture', and Woodhouse annotated it with the words 'Elgin Marbles'.[49] The Dionysus from the East Pediment is the only figure from the Parthenon frieze that seems to bear much resemblance to Keats's line. A more likely source is surely Michelangelo's Adam on the ceiling of the Sistine Chapel. In this great image of the first man touched into life by the hand of God the Father, Michelangelo has portrayed all the power, and all the latent desire for beauty, of all men who will ever live.

That must remain conjectural, but there is little room for doubt about the painting which throws the most important light of all on 'Sleep and Poetry'. The allusion occurs early in the poem:

> O for ten years, that I may overwhelm
> Myself in poesy; so I may do the deed
> That my own soul has to itself decreed.
> Then will I pass the countries that I see
> In long perspective, and continually
> Taste their pure fountains. First the realm I'll pass
> Of Flora, and old Pan: sleep in the grass,
> Feed upon apples red, and strawberries,
> And choose each pleasure that my fancy sees;
> Catch the white-handed nymphs in shady places,
> To woo sweet kisses from averted faces,—

> Play with their fingers, touch their shoulders white
> Into a pretty shrinking with a bite
> As hard as lips can make it: till agreed,
> A lovely tale of human life we'll read.
> And one will teach a tame dove how it best
> May fan the cool air gently o'er my rest;
> Another, bending o'er her nimble tread,
> Will set a green robe floating round her head,
> And still will dance with ever varied ease,
> Smiling upon the flowers and the trees:
> Another will entice me on, and on
> Through almond blossoms and rich cinnamon;
> Till in the bosom of a leafy world
> We rest in silence, like two gems upcurl'd
> In the recesses of a pearly shell.   (96–121)

Keats must first have come on the Realm of Flora in Ovid, or in some guidebook of mythology such as Spence's *Polymetis*. 'Ovid gives us a delightful description of the garden of Flora', Spence observes in his chapter on 'The Deities of the Earth'; 'with the Horæ gathering flowers in it, and the Graces composing garlands of them'.[50] He goes on:

I wish I had any antient picture, to answer this description; and think it might afford a very pretty subject for any painter now.

In fact Poussin's noble interpretation of the scene had been painted more than a century before, and there can be no doubt that a print of this painting was the main inspiration of Keats's lines.

It is true that more than one picture must have been in Keats's mind. The last three lines, with their description of two lovers reposing in the shell which is the symbol of Venus, certainly do not derive from 'The Realm of Flora'; while Poussin's 'Bacchanalian Revel before a Term of Pan', which was exhibited by the British Institution in 1816, probably contributes one or two details. But the following lines remove all possible doubt about the main source of inspiration:

> And can I ever bid these joys farewell?
> Yes, I must pass them for a nobler life,
> Where I may find the agonies, the strife
> Of human hearts: for lo! I see afar,
> O'er-sailing the blue cragginess, a car
> And steeds with streamy manes—the charioteer

Looks out upon the winds with glorious fear:
And now the numerous tramplings quiver lightly
Along a huge cloud's ridge; and now with sprightly
Wheel downward come they into fresher skies,
Tipt round with silver from the sun's bright eyes.

(122–32)

The most curious commentary on this passage is provided by Amy Lowell:

Keats realizes that to be a great poet he must find 'the agonies, the strife of human hearts', but he has so little idea of how this is to be done that all he can think of is to conjure up a fairy-tale of a charioteer whirling over a world of mysterious visions, the most concrete of which is 'a wreath of girls'.[51]

On the contrary, Keats has found a perfect image for what he wants to express, and Poussin's painting has helped him to find it.

The subject of the painting was suggested by the passage in the *Fasti* where Ovid apostrophizes Flora and describes the origin of the flowers in her garden. On the left of the painting, in which details from the *Metamorphoses* are also introduced, we see a statue of Pan, Ajax committing suicide, Clytia gazing at the sun, and Narcissus admiring himself in the water, with Echo beside him. In the centre Flora dances. At the right Hyacinthus and Adonis stand near each other, while Crocus and Smilax repose beside them. Such is the origin of the different kinds of flowers. The charioteer is Apollo, god of the sun. The painting is characteristic of Poussin in giving particular pleasure to those who know how to 'read' it, while remaining a thing of beauty even to the uninstructed spectator. He is painting what is at once the garden of nature and a land of heart's desire, a walled 'pleasaunce' from which all earthly cares are for ever excluded. While it is probable that Keats would have understood the allusion to the *Fasti*, it is on the other aspect of the garden that he concentrates, the aspect that led Spence to describe the garden of Flora as 'the paradise in the Roman mythology'. Keats follows Poussin, but he follows him freely and without constraint. He is only interested in the walled garden, the nymphs, Flora, and Apollo with his steeds and his chariot. His dancing figure is obviously suggested by Poussin's Flora, but is not an exact transcription. He is remembering a figure with a scarf blowing above her head, a frequent motif in Renaissance art, as well as Poussin's Flora. While Apollo in 'The Realm of Flora' is primarily if not exclusively the god of the sun, in 'Sleep and Poetry' he is the god of poetry, who is directing Keats away from the enchanted garden and towards the world of men and of suffering.

Which of the available prints Keats knew we have no means of telling. At least one of them moralizes the picture in a manner that takes us part of the way towards Keats's own interpretation. This is the print by Jean Moyreau, which has the following verses under the picture:

> Ces dons si précieux, si chers a tant de Cœurs,
> La fragile Beauté, la Bravoure inhumaine;
> Sans la vertu, ne sont que d'inutiles Fleurs,
> Qu'à leur naissance, un vent abbat, dessèche, entraîne:
> Tels, la Fable, en ces Traits, nous a representé,
> Tous ceux de qui les Jours ont terni la Mémoire;
> Pendant qu'elle a sçu rendre a l'Immortalité,
> Tout mortel Amoureux d'une solide Gloire.[52]

While this poetaster draws a moralist's moral from the picture, Keats draws a poet's moral. The best gloss on his interpretation of the painting is to be found in one of his annotations on Milton:

He had an exquisite passion for what is properly, in the sense of ease and pleasure, poetical Luxury; and with that it appears to me he would fain have been content, if he could, so doing, have preserved his self-respect and feel of duty performed; but there was working in him as it were that same sort of thing as operates in the great world to the end of a Prophecy's being accomplish'd: therefore he devoted himself rather to the ardours than the pleasures of Song. . . . Had he not broken through the clouds which envelope so deliciously the Elysian field of verse, and committed himself to the Extreme, we should never have seen Satan as described—

> 'But his face
> Deep scars of thunder had entrench'd,' &c.[53]

Here Keats is interpreting Milton in terms of his own experience. 'I have been hovering for some time between an exquisite sense of the luxurious and a love for Philosophy', he wrote to Taylor on the 24th of April 1818. '—were I calculated for the former I should be glad—but as I am not I shall turn all my soul to the latter.' If Keats had not, like Milton, 'broken through the clouds which envelope so deliciously the Elysian field of verse' and followed Apollo on his adventurous course, we should never have seen Saturn

> Deep in the shady sadness of a vale.

It is revealing that Poussin is the painter who inspired this central passage in 'Sleep and Poetry'. Wainewright's remark that 'Poussin is vulgarly considered the most eminent [of painters] in Grecian fable'[54] is a characteristic piece of adolescent posing. All reputable critics acknowledged Poussin's eminence as the interpreter of Greek mythology. Sir Joshua Reynolds had pointed out that to paint such a subject as the children of Niobe 'requires a mind thrown back two thousand years, and as it were naturalised in antiquity, like that of Nicholas Poussin'.[55] 'Poussin lived and conversed with the ancient statues so long', Reynolds wrote in his Fifth Discourse,

> that he may be said to have been better acquainted with them, than with the people who were about him. I have often thought that he carried his veneration for them so far as to wish to give his works the air of Ancient Paintings. . . . Like Polidoro he studied the ancients so much, that he acquired a habit of thinking in their way, and seemed to know perfectly the actions and gestures they would use on every occasion. . . . The favourite subjects of Poussin were Ancient Fables; and no painter was ever better qualified to paint such subjects, not only from his being eminently skilled in the knowledge of the ceremonies, customs and habits of the Ancients, but from his being so well acquainted with the different characters which those who invented them gave to their allegorical figures. . . . If Poussin in imitation of the Ancients represents Apollo driving his chariot out of the sea by way of representing the Sun rising, if he personifies Lakes and Rivers, it is nowise offensive in him; but seems perfectly of a piece with the general air of the picture.[56]

Poussin's whole conception of painting was, in the most honourable sense, highly literary, and he has always made a particular appeal to literary men. Evelyn more than once records his admiration for his pictures.[57] In the 'Parallel of Poetry and Painting' prefixed to his translation of du Fresnoy Dryden praises 'the famous picture of Poussin which represents the

Institution of the Blessed Sacrament', with the comment: 'Such are the subjects of noble pictures; and such are only to be undertaken by noble hands'.[58] In 1736 we find Pope, who was something of a painter himself, recommending 'that admirable piece for Expression, the Death of Germanicus by Poussin', as a model to his friend Ralph Allen.[59] In the same year James Thomson, another great admirer of Poussin, describes in *Liberty*

> . . . how painting, courted long,
> With Poussin came—ancient design, that lifts
> A fairer front and looks another soul.   (v. 500–2)

A little later Richard West tells Gray that he admires Shakespeare's 'old expressions' and believes that archaisms 'add a certain grace' to a poem, 'in the same manner as Poussin gave a beauty to his pictures by his knowledge in the antient proportions'.[60] Gray himself probably remembered 'The Shepherds of Arcady' as he wrote the conclusion of the *Elegy in a Country Church-Yard*.[61] There was therefore nothing new in the admiration for Poussin felt by Keats and his friends. What was new was the nature of the imaginative response which Poussin now evoked. Since it was the ambition of Keats to 'naturalize' himself in Grecian fable, Poussin was for him the perfect guide. In the fresh Ovidian beauty of Poussin's recreation of the ancient world Keats found something that spoke directly to his own imagination. I shall suggest in a later chapter that one of the principal prototypes for Keats's image of Apollo—who is ubiquitous in this first volume—may well have been Poussin's fine painting, 'The Inspiration of the Poet' (Plate XXIV).[62]

It has already become apparent that Keats's interest in painting and sculpture sharpened his own powers of observation and helped him to maintain that balance between the introvert and extrovert which is so triumphantly evident in his mature poetry. This can already be seen in 'Sleep and Poetry':

> A pigeon tumbling in clear summer air;
> A laughing school-boy, without grief or care,
> Riding the springy branches of an elm.

'When we have had continually before us the great works of Art to impregnate our minds with kindred ideas', Reynolds had pointed out in his Sixth Discourse, we are then, and not till then, fit to produce something of the same species. We behold all about us with the eyes of those penetrating observers whose works we contemplate; and our minds, accustomed to think the thoughts of the noblest and brightest intellects, are prepared for the discovery and selection of all that is great and noble in nature.[63]

Keats's study of the visual arts taught him how to paint pictures of his own. By allowing his imagination to work in the way in which a painter's works, he could produce a passage of which we cannot say whether it is based on a particular work of art or not. What could be more visual, for example, than the sestet of the sonnet 'On First Looking into Chapman's Homer'?—

> Then felt I like some watcher of the skies
> When a new planet swims into his ken;
> Or like stout Cortez when with eagle eyes
>   He star'd at the Pacific—and all his men
> Look'd at each other with a wild surmise—
>   Silent, upon a peak in Darien.

At first sight one would say that a picture must lie behind these last four lines, and some picture may yet turn up. But Cortez did not—after all—discover the Pacific, and two plausible prose sources have been suggested, the one a note in *The Excursion*, a poem which Keats is known to have admired, and the other the description of Balboa's discovery of the Pacific in Robertson's *History of America*.[64] It seems more likely that Keats, as Leigh Hunt implies, has designed his own 'heroic painting'.[65] As he did so, perhaps he remembered Fuseli's insistence on the importance of placing the principal figure in a proper and impressive attitude. 'It is not by the accumulation of infernal or magic machinery . . . that Macbeth can be made an object of terror', he remarked in his fourth lecture:

To render him so you must place him on a ridge, his down-dashed eye absorbed by the murky abyss; surround the horrid vision with darkness, exclude its limits, and shear its light to glimpses.

This art of giving to the principal figure the command of the horizon, is perhaps the only principle by which modern art might have gained an advantage over that of the ancients, and improved the dignity of composition. . . .[66]

In his notes on Milton we find Keats commenting on 'what may be called his *stationing or statuary*. He is not content with simple description, he must station. . . . So we see Adam *"Fair indeed, and tall—under a plantane"*—and so we see Satan *"disfigured— on the Assyrian mount"*.'[67] And so—we may add—we see Cortez —'*stout Cortez*'—

> Silent, upon a peak in Darien.

VIII

'THE REALM OF FLORA': *ENDYMION*

I have heard Hunt say and may be asked—why endeavour
after a long Poem? To which I should answer—Do not the
Lovers of Poetry like to have a little Region to wander in
where they may pick and choose, and in which the images are
so numerous that many are forgotten and found new in a
second Reading: which may be food for a Week's stroll in
the Summer?

KEATS to Benjamin Bailey[1]

KEATS was in the habit of thinking of Poetry as a continent or
a world, ruled over by the various great poets as the feudal de-
pendants of Apollo. The most memorable expression of the
thought is to be found in the opening lines of the sonnet from
which I have just been quoting:

> Much have I travell'd in the realms of gold,
> And many goodly states and kingdoms seen;
> Round many western islands have I been
> Which bards in fealty to Apollo hold.

One reason why he was so impatient of criticisms of *Endymion*—
in spite of his realization that it was full of faults—was that it
represented his great attempt to escape to a land of heart's
desire, the territory he had already described as 'The realm of
Flora and old Pan': the other was his conviction that only by
passing through this country had he any chance of reaching the
more serious territory of poetry that lay beyond it. In *Endymion* we catch sight of the charioteer on one or two occasions,
but the main inspiration of the poem is Keats's passionate nostalgia for a pagan world that corresponds to nothing in human
history but answers a deep craving of the human imagination.

Endymion is described on its title-page as 'A Poetic Romance',
and the meaning of this is underlined by one of the rhetorical
questions at the beginning of 'Sleep and Poetry': 'What is . . .

> More full of visions than a high romance?'

To create a poem that is 'full of visions' and to evoke again 'the
spell of Loneliness that hung about Endymion'[2] Keats summons

to his aid all the delights that he had so often discussed with Hunt and his other friends, and above all the beauty revealed to him by the work of great poets and painters.

While he was writing the poem Keats summarized the story of Endymion for the benefit of his sister Fanny, in one of his letters:

> Many Years ago there was a young handsome Shepherd who fed his flocks on a Mountain's Side called Latmus—he was a very contemplative sort of a Person and lived solitry among the trees and Plains little thinking—that such a beautiful Creature as the Moon was growing mad in Love with him—However so it was; and when he was asleep on the Grass, she used to come down from heaven and admire him excessively for a long time; and at last could not refrain from carying him away in her arms to the top of that high Mountain Latmus while he was a dreaming. (i. 154)

His fondness for this myth had already been evident in his first volume. There is a most interesting letter from Haydon to Wordsworth, written on the last day of 1816, which mentions that Keats 'is now writing a longer sort of poem, of "Diana and Endymion", to publish with his smaller productions'.[3] One reason for the lack of structure in the poem which comes first in the volume of 1817 is that Keats decided greatly to expand his 'Endymion' and to publish it separately, so that the poem which we have now to call 'I stood tip-toe' is in fact a fragment. It seems likely that some passages of *Endymion*—such as the celebrated opening lines—may have originated in the earlier poem, while it is noticeable that the myth of Endymion remains very prominent in 'I stood tip-toe'. Discussing the origin of mythology, in a passage in that poem which is reminiscent of *The Excursion*, Keats asks:

> . . . what has made the sage or poet write
> But the fair paradise of Nature's light? (125–6)

He goes on to mention the myths of Cupid and Psyche, Pan and Syrinx, Echo and Narcissus, and Cynthia and Endymion. We notice at once that each of these stories, which remained associated in Keats's mind for the remainder of his life, can be used to describe the origin of poetry; and that each of them has been a favourite with painters.

In 'I stood tip-toe' Keats praises the moon as the

> Closer of lovely eyes to lovely dreams,
> Lover of loneliness, and wandering, (120–1)

and as the 'Maker of sweet poets'; and of all the myths that he evokes it is that of Endymion that he describes as the 'sweetest of all songs',

> Coming ever to bless
> The wanderer by moonlight, to him bringing
> Shapes from the invisible world, unearthly singing
> From out the middle air. (184–7)

Here it is clear that Endymion is the Poet and Cynthia (who was born at the same birth as Apollo, as Keats knew from Lemprière) his Muse. The next paragraph of the poem throws a great deal of light on *Endymion*:

> He was a Poet, sure a lover too,
> Who stood on Latmus' top, what time there blew
> Soft breezes from the myrtle vale below;
> And brought in faintness solemn, sweet, and slow
> A hymn from Dian's temple; while upswelling,
> The incense went to her own starry dwelling.
> But though her face was clear as infant's eyes,
> Though she stood smiling o'er the sacrifice,
> The Poet wept at her so piteous fate,
> Wept that such beauty should be desolate:
> So in fine wrath some golden sounds he won,
> And gave meek Cynthia her Endymion. (193–204)

Here Keats is remembering that Diana is the goddess of chastity as well as of the moon. In *Polymetis* Spence tells us that Diana 'generally appears with a lunar crown, or cresent, on her forehead', in a chariot drawn by two horses. He also gives an account of the 'different offices' of the goddess and points out that it was the lunar Diana 'who was fabled to fall in love with Endymion; and if we consider the occasion of her love for him, according to the accounts the antients give of that fable, it may appear perhaps to have been only a philosophical amour, or what we call Platonic love: and so may not interfere with this goddess's general character of chastity'.[4] Keats will have nothing to do with this idea of 'a philosophical amour'. His Cynthia is not a virgin: on the contrary he proceeds to describe some of the wonders that took place on the bridal-night of the two lovers, concluding:

Cynthia! I cannot tell the greater blisses,
That follow'd thine, and thy dear shepherd's kisses:
Was there a Poet born?—but now no more,
My wand'ring spirit must no further soar.[5]   (239–42)

I do not intend to discuss the allegory of *Endymion* in any detail,
but there can be no doubt that at one level it portrays the poet's
quest for inspiration as an aspect of the soul's search for beauty.
Every poet may be described, in Ronsard's words, as '[Un]
Second Endymion, amoureux de la Lune'.[6]

Like the other 'beautiful Tales which have come down from
the ancient times of that beautiful Greece',[7] the story of Diana and
Endymion has always appealed to painters. Spence mentions that
'the story is very common, in particular on old Sarcophagus's;
and we see her on them, descending to a shepherd asleep, with
a veil over her head'.[8] The engraving in *Polymetis* (Plate XV)
may have been one of the earliest pictures of the myth that
Keats saw. With this representation, with its blowing scarf and
its stylized stars, we may compare lines 578–82 of Book I:

> ... Methought I lay
> Watching the zenith, where the milky way
> Among the stars in virgin splendour pours;
> And travelling my eye, until the doors
> Of heaven appear'd to open for my flight. . . .

Two of Tassie's gems show Endymion asleep, and in one of
these Diana is flying down towards him (Plate IX a), just as
Keats describes the story in his letter to his sister. Of the many
variations on this same theme a number must have been
available to Keats. He is not likely to have been greatly struck
by Verrio's ceiling at Hampton Court,[9] because the scene is
so crowded that Diana and Endymion do not immediately
strike the eye; while Benjamin West's 'Diana and Endymion'
was never one of his better-known paintings. But there are three
paintings which may well have been known to Keats in prints:
that by Annibale Carracci, a painter high in reputation in
his circle: that by Rubens, now in the National Gallery, in which
a very bodily Diana is rushing into the arms of a very bodily
Endymion: and that by Anne-Louis Girodet de Roucy (or de
Trioson), in which a strong beam of moonlight falls on the face
of a beautiful naked Endymion, watched by a descending Cupid.[10]

xv. Diana and Endymion (from Spence's *Polymetis*)

XVI. ZUCCARELLI: Diana appearing to Endymion

'Many Years ago there was a young handsome Shepherd who fed his flocks on a Mountain's side called Latmus . . . .'

Other representations of the myth which are likely to have been familiar to Keats are the painting by Zuccarelli in the Royal Collection (Plate XVI)[11] and Canova's sculptural treatment of the subject, which was more than once referred to in the *Annals of the Fine Arts*. One interpretation of the story that would have delighted him cannot (it seems) have been available: Poussin's eloquent painting, in which the young shepherd is on one knee, gazing into the face of Diana, while her horses are driven away through the sky.[12] Yet when Keats sat down to write his poem, we can be certain that the myth of Diana and Endymion had already a lively visual reality in his mind.

In creating a setting for the story Keats was equally indebted to paintings and prints. It has sometimes been suggested that the poetry of Keats is part of a 'return to Nature' in the sense that the scenes which he describes are truthful accounts of the real countryside of England; but *Endymion* lends little support to such a view. Keats seems to have begun the poem at Carisbrooke in the Isle of Wight: other parts of Book I appear to have been written in Hampshire and Kent, Book III in Oxford, and most of the remainder of the poem in London.[13] The world of the poem is none of these places, however, but the classical Arcadia as it had been re-created by poets and painters.

In answer to Leigh Hunt's criticism that the conversation between Endymion and Peona 'is unnatural & too high-flown for . . . Brother & Sister', Keats pointed out that 'they are both overshadowed by a Supernatural Power, & of force could not speak like Franchesca in the Rimini'.[14] If a critic had objected to the scenery in which the poem is set as 'unnatural', Keats could have made precisely the same reply. To have set a story about supernatural beings on Hampstead Heath would have been to make the mistake that Reynolds had censured in Richard Wilson, that of 'introducing gods and goddesses, ideal beings, into scenes which were by no means prepared to receive such personages'. 'His landscapes'—Reynolds had continued—

were in reality too near common nature to admit supernatural objects. In consequence of this mistake, in a very admirable picture of a storm, . . . many figures are introduced in the fore-ground, some in apparent distress, and some struck dead, as a spectator would naturally suppose, by the lightning; had not the painter injudiciously (as I think) rather chosen that their death should be imputed to a little Apollo, who appears in the sky, with his bent bow, and that those figures should be considered as the children of Niobe.[15]

In such a painting the artist should 'adapt the character of the landscape . . . to the historical or poetical representation'. The ideal is a painter who

sends the imagination back into antiquity; and, like the Poet, . . . makes the elements sympathise with his subject: whether the clouds roll in volumes like those of Titian or Salvator Rosa,—or, like those of Claude, are gilded with the setting sun; whether the mountains have sudden and bold projections, or are gently sloped; whether the branches of his trees shoot out abruptly in right angles from their trunks, or follow each other with only a gentle inclination. All these circumstances contribute to the general character of the work . . . .[16]

The setting of the opening scene is vividly realized. We see a forest on the side of Mount Latmos:

> . . . Paths there were many,
> Winding through palmy fern, and rushes fenny,
> And ivy banks; all leading pleasantly
> To a wide lawn, whence one could only see
> Stems thronging all around between the swell
> Of turf and slanting branches: who could tell
> The freshness of the space of heaven above,
> Edg'd round with dark tree tops? through which a dove
> Would often beat its wings, and often too
> A little cloud would move across the blue.   (79–88)

Here Keats, as Reynolds had said of Claude, 'conducts us to the tranquillity of Arcadian scenes and fairy land'.[17] And in the lines that follow we find just what we would expect to find in one of Claude's paintings:

> Full in the middle of this pleasantness
> There stood a marble altar, with a tress
> Of flowers budded newly; and the dew
> Had taken fairy phantasies to strew
> Daisies upon the sacred sward last eve,
> And so the dawned light in pomp receive.
> For 'twas the morn: Apollo's upward fire
> Made every eastern cloud a silvery pyre.

To these lines we might well apply Leigh Hunt's description of a passage in *The Faerie Queene*:

Character, Select Southern Elegance, with an intimation of fine Architecture; Painter, Claude.[18]

A few lines later, with the rush of children on to the scene, a particular picture may have been in Keats's mind:

> Now while the silent workings of the dawn
> Were busiest, into that self-same lawn
> All suddenly, with joyful cries, there sped
> A troop of little children garlanded;
> Who gathering round the altar, seemed to pry
> Earnestly round as wishing to espy
> Some folk of holiday. (107–13)

As he wrote these lines Keats probably remembered a print of Titian's 'The Worship of Venus', of Rubens's 'Sacrifice to Venus' (based on Titian's painting), or of Rubens's 'The Feast of Venus'.[19] In each of these paintings a crowd of *putti* come rushing in to surround an altar surmounted by a statue of Venus. But it is clear that a number of different influences, visual and literary, are co-operating at this point. As we have already seen, the image of an altar approached by a number of classical figures came early to Keats, and remained in his imagination, developing and increasing in significance, throughout his poetic career. This is the picture that we see in the succeeding lines:

> . . . there glimmered light
> Fair faces and a rush of garments white,
> Plainer and plainer shewing, till at last
> Into the widest alley they all past,
> Making directly for the woodland altar. (123–7)

This passage is followed by a description of a procession in honour of Pan which Keats clearly regarded as a set-piece, as he invokes the aid of a Muse:

> O kindly muse! let not my weak tongue faulter
> In telling of this goodly company,
> Of their old piety, and of their glee.

The procession must be quoted *in extenso*:

> Leading the way, young damsels danced along,
> Bearing the burden of a shepherd song;

Each having a white wicker over brimm'd
With April's tender younglings: next, well trimm'd,
A crowd of shepherds with as sunburnt looks
As may be read of in Arcadian books;
Such as sat listening round Apollo's pipe,
When the great deity, for earth too ripe,
Let his divinity o'er-flowing die
In music, through the vales of Thessaly:
Some idly trailed their sheep-hooks on the ground,
And some kept up a shrilly mellow sound
With ebon-tipped flutes: close after these,
Now coming from beneath the forest trees,
A venerable priest full soberly,
Begirt with ministring looks: alway his eye
Stedfast upon the matted turf he kept,
And after him his sacred vestments swept.
From his right hand there swung a vase, milk-white,
Of mingled wine, out-sparkling generous light;
And in his left he held a basket full
Of all sweet herbs that searching eye could cull:
Wild thyme, and valley-lillies whiter still
Than Leda's love, and cresses from the rill.
His aged head, crowned with beechen wreath,
Seem'd like a poll of ivy in the teeth
Of winter hoar. Then came another crowd
Of shepherds, lifting in due time aloud
Their share of the ditty. After them appear'd,
Up-followed by a multitude that rear'd
Their voices to the clouds, a fair wrought car
Easily rolling so as scarce to mar
The freedom of three steeds of dapple brown:
Who stood therein did seem of great renown
Among the throng. His youth was fully blown,
Shewing like Ganymede to manhood grown;
And, for those simple times, his garments were
A chieftain king's: beneath his breast, half bare,
Was hung a silver bugle, and between
His nervy knees there lay a boar-spear keen. (135–74)

A procession could hardly be described in words with a more powerfully visual effect: Keats could not have written more explicitly if (like a poet of the seventeenth century) he had set out to provide 'Instructions to a Painter'. In these lines accounts of pagan festivals which he had read in books are brought to life with the help of images remembered from paintings and prints. The immediate suggestion is of a Triumph. In Poussin's 'The Triumph of Flora', for example (Plate X), 'young damsels dance along', at least one of them with a basket of 'April's tender younglings', while the centre of the picture is the 'fair wrought car' containing the goddess. The 'venerable priest' may be seen on many Greek vases and in many paintings. We are once again in the country of the mind of Poussin and Claude. It is less important to speculate about the particular paintings which may have suggested details in this description than to recognize the fascination which such processions had for Keats. The passage points back to the 'crowd of nymphs soft voic'd and young, and gay' in the dedicatory sonnet of 1817 and to the fane

> Of liny marble, and thereto a train
> Of nymphs approaching fairly o'er the sward

in 'Sleep and Poetry', and forward to the 'Titian colours touch'd into real life' in the epistle 'To J. H. Reynolds, Esq.' and the 'leaf-fring'd legend' in the 'Ode on a Grecian Urn', in which (as in *Endymion*) we find a 'mysterious priest' following more slowly after the dancing maidens. It is illuminating to juxtapose such descriptions with a passage from one of Diderot's essays on painting quoted by a writer in the *Annals of the Fine Arts*. Diderot is writing about the effect of Catholic religious processions:

> Even I at times catch their enthusiasm! I cannot behold that slowly moving train of priests in their sacerdotal habits, those young Acolytes strewing flowers; I cannot hear the grave pathetic song chaunted by the priests, and chorused by the infinite voices of the multitude, without my bowels yearning, and my eyes filling with tears.[20]

Although the mood of the procession in *Endymion* is very different, Keats has the same yearning for the sense of community in worship which inspired Diderot's observation. It is significant that the lines introducing the procession link 'piety' and 'glee' and so remind us of Keats's phrase about the Greeks and their 'Religion of Joy'.[21]

As we read on we come on one or two references to sculpture, as when the heroes of Thermopylae are said to be 'not yet dead,

> But in old marbles ever beautiful'.

It is interesting to recall that Keats had first seen the Elgin Marbles only a few weeks before he began *Endymion*. In one of the sonnets that he wrote on the occasion he apologizes to Haydon for the fact that he cannot speak

> Definitively on these mighty things.

Something like that, perhaps, he was to do later, when he wrote the 'Ode on a Grecian Urn'. As he wrote *Endymion*, his imagination was only beginning to be stirred by the eloquent forms of the Parthenon Frieze, but already we notice that Keats was fascinated—as Thomson had been[22]—by the way in which human life appears as if frozen by the miracle of sculpture. At one point Endymion is described as being

> as dead-still as a marble man,
> Frozen in that old tale Arabian,   (405–6)

where the allusion is to the *Arabian Nights*[23] but the image of a sculptural form is also in the poet's mind. On several occasions we may apply to passages in *Endymion* an observation of Sir Anthony Blunt's on Poussin that 'the figures have that frozen appearance which is often to be seen in marble figures of dancers, as if they had been turned to stone in the middle of their action'.[24] It is not surprising that Keats was fascinated by the story of Niobe, the boastful mother whose children were destroyed by Apollo and Diana, and who was herself turned to stone. At line 337 he describes

> . . . the trembling knee
> And frantic gape of lonely Niobe,
> Poor, lonely Niobe! when her lovely young
> Were dead and gone, and her caressing tongue
> Lay a lost thing upon her paly lip,
> And very, very deadliness did nip
> Her motherly cheeks.

The main source of these lines is certainly Book IV of the *Metamorphoses*,[25] but a passage in a letter supports the view that visual representations of the story were also important to Keats. 'Every time I see him and mention you,' he wrote to Bailey of John Hamilton Reynolds on the 29th of October 1817 in a letter in which he copied out a passage from *Endymion*, 'he puts his hand to his head and looks like a son of Niobe's.' Prints of the sculptural representations of Niobe and her children in the Villa of the Medici at Rome were well known at this time. Spence discusses 'the manner of ranging the figures', which was very much in dispute.[26] The subject of Niobe had also been handled by several painters: there is a picture at Dulwich attributed to N. and G. Poussin, while Richard Wilson more than once illustrated the story.[27] And so the 'attitude' of the grief-stricken Niobe found its way into one of Keats's poems, and the attitude of one of her sons into one of his letters.

A little later we encounter a reference to the story of Diana and Actaeon which makes it clear that Keats was aware of the tragic overtones of Titian's great painting, though he does not mention them in 'Sleep and Poetry':

> . . . Haply, thou hast seen
> Her naked limbs among the alders green;
> And that, alas! is death   (512–14)

There is also the following landscape:

> This river does not see the naked sky,
> Till it begins to progress silverly
> Around the western border of the wood,
> Whence, from a certain spot, its winding flood
> Seems at the distance like a crescent moon   (540–4)

—a description which is overtly pictorial, since Keats comments that the sun is unwilling to leave

> So dear a picture of his sovereign power.

When Endymion tries to describe to his sister

> The loveliest moon, that ever silver'd o'er
> A shell for Neptune's goblet

he tells Peona of Diana's 'golden hair' and goes on to compare her to Venus:

> . . . Ah! see her hovering feet,
> More bluely vein'd, more soft, more whitely sweet
> Than those of sea-born Venus, when she rose
> From out her cradle shell. The wind out-blows
> Her scarf into a fluttering pavilion;
> 'Tis blue, and over-spangled with a million
> Of little eyes, as though thou wert to shed,
> Over the darkest, lushest blue-bell bed,
> Handfuls of daisies.   (624–32)

The whole passage is remarkably reminiscent of Botticelli's 'Birth of Venus', with its unforgettable portrayal of Venus standing on a huge shell, her spangled robe blown by the wind and held by her attendant Flora. But 'The Birth of Venus' was unknown in England at this time: it remained in a private collection outside Florence, and had never been engraved.[28] And in any case a careful reading makes it clear that whereas the first three and a half lines describe a Venus Anadyomene, the remaining lines return to Diana and describe her with certain of her usual attributes. Montfaucon points out that Diana is often found 'with an Horned-Moon upon her Head, and even sometimes without it, but cover'd with a large Veil. In one of our Figures this Veil is spangled all over with Stars.'[29] The Diana in his illustration is in the same iconographical tradition as Plate XV. Diana's scarf has become very like a 'pavilion'. As it represents the sky, it is natural to imagine it as blue; while it is easy to understand the process by which the stars have become 'a million Of little eyes'.

Another highly visual passage is the description of the changed face of nature as it appears to Endymion in his unhappiness:

> . . . All the pleasant hues
> Of heaven and earth had faded: deepest shades
> Were deepest dungeons; heaths and sunny glades
> Were full of pestilent light; our taintless rills
> Seem'd sooty, and o'er-spread with upturn'd gills
> Of dying fish; the vermeil rose had blown
> In frightful scarlet, and its thorns out-grown
> Like spiked aloe. (691–8)

A scene for Salvator Rosa: one is reminded of Leigh Hunt's description of Spenser's 'Cave of Despair', which he assigned to Salvator as a congenial subject:

Character, Savage and Forlorn Scenery, occupied by Squalid Misery.[30]

At line 862 we find another landscape waiting for its painter:

> Beyond the matron-temple of Latona,
> Which we should see but for these darkening boughs,
> Lies a deep hollow, from whose ragged brows
> Bushes and trees do lean all round athwart,
> And meet so nearly, that with wings outraught,
> And spreaded tail, a vulture could not glide

Past them, but he must brush on every side.
Some moulder'd steps lead into this cool cell,
Far as the slabbed margin of a well,
Whose patient level peeps its crystal eye
Right upward, through the bushes, to the sky.

When, a few lines later, Endymion sees

The same bright face I tasted in my sleep,
Smiling in the clear well,

we are reminded fleetingly of the story of Echo and Narcissus:
we shall see in a moment that a picture of this myth was very
prominent in Keats's mind as he wrote *Endymion*.

As we begin to read Book II we move from one gallery of
Keats's 'Musée Imaginaire' into another. Soon we come on lines
that are hardly characteristic of Keats but which are certainly
a reminder that we are reading the work of a major poet:

And like a new-born spirit did he pass
Through the green evening quiet in the sun.

The passage continues in a way that may remind us of a Claude
—a painter suggested not least by the unexpected 'bark' that
Keats introduces into his scene:

O'er many a heath, through many a woodland dun,
Through buried paths, where sleepy twilight dreams
The summer time away. One track unseams
A wooded cleft, and, far away, the blue
Of ocean fades upon him; then, anew,
He sinks adown a solitary glen,
Where there was never sound of mortal men,
Saving, perhaps, some snow-light cadences
Melting to silence, when upon the breeze
Some holy bark let forth an anthem sweet,
To cheer itself to Delphi.   (72–82)

The description of Endymion's amazement, a hundred lines later,
is reminiscent of that of Niobe in Book I:

. . . At this with madden'd stare,
And lifted hands, and trembling lips he stood;
Like old Deucalion mountain'd o'er the flood,
Or blind Orion hungry for the morn.

Highly visual as it is in effect, the image of Deucalion is probably of purely literary origin;[31] but that of Orion is likely to owe
something to Poussin, as de Sélincourt suggests.[32] In his 'Landscape with Orion' we see the huge figure of Orion, watched by
Diana from the heavens and guided by the dwarfed figure of her
emissary on his shoulders, stretching out his left hand and strid-
ing with a tentative eagerness in the direction of the rising sun.
This painting, which is now in America, belonged to several
English owners, among them Sir Joshua Reynolds. It was
well known as a print: Hazlitt was to write on it in his essay 'On
a Landscape of Nicolas Poussin' in *Table-Talk*, and it is significant that he there uses Keats's line as his motto.

Shortly after this we find Endymion wandering in a sort of
subterranean British Museum:

> . . . He went
> Into a marble gallery, passing through
> A mimic temple, so complete and true
> In sacred custom, that he well nigh fear'd
> To search it inwards; whence far off appear'd,
> Through a long pillar'd vista, a fair shrine,
> And, just beyond, on light tiptoe divine,
> A quiver'd Dian. Stepping awfully,
> The youth approach'd; oft turning his veil'd eye
> Down sidelong aisles, and into niches old.   (255-64)

There is nothing specific about that, but at line 392 we do find a
passage inspired by a particular painting:

> For on a silken couch of rosy pride,
> In midst of all, there lay a sleeping youth
> Of fondest beauty; fonder, in fair sooth,
> Than sighs could fathom, or contentment reach:
> And coverlids gold-tinted like the peach,
> Or ripe October's faded marigolds,
> Fell sleek about him in a thousand folds—
> Not hiding up an Apollonian curve
> Of neck and shoulder, nor the tenting swerve
> Of knee from knee, nor ankles pointing light;
> But rather, giving them to the filled sight
> Officiously. Sideway his face repos'd
> On one white arm, and tenderly unclos'd,
> By tenderest pressure, a faint damask mouth
> To slumbery pout; just as the morning south

XVII. POUSSIN: Echo and Narcissus

For on a silken couch of rosy pride,
In midst of all, there lay a sleeping youth
Of fondest beauty . . . .

> Disparts a dew-lipp'd rose. Above his head,
> Four lily stalks did their white honours wed
> To make a coronal; and round him grew
> All tendrils green, of every bloom and hue.

The visual quality of this description of Adonis during his winter sleep suggests that Keats had an original in his mind's eye. Wainewright asserted that the passage illustrates 'the precious Florentine gem' which represents the Hermaphrodite,[33] but there can be no doubt that Keats was remembering rather a print of Poussin's 'Echo and Narcissus' (Plate XVII). In the 'harmonious rhythms' of this painting, its 'extreme refinement' in the rendering of Narcissus' body, its 'eloquent contours and its subtle modelling'[34] we find the inspiration of Keats's Adonis. We have only to glance at the Poussin to see the 'Apollonian[35] curve Of neck and shoulder', the 'tenting swerve Of knee from knee', and the 'ankles pointing light'. The face of Narcissus is very much as Keats describes that of Adonis, with a 'slumbery pout'; while the 'four lilly stalks' making a crown above his head are clearly visible. Although Keats cannot have seen the original painting, something of the rich colouring must have been described to him by someone who had, as he describes it accurately enough. In general he follows the painting rather closely, although his background of 'tendrils green' is less elaborate. Instead of the nymph Echo and a single Cupid he has a number of 'serene Cupids watching silently'. Once again the inspiration which Poussin found in the *Metamorphoses* has enabled Keats to find a living image for a figure from classical mythology.

The description of Venus and Adonis a hundred lines later is also highly pictorial:

> . . . when lo! the wreathed green
> Disparted, and far upward could be seen
> Blue heaven, and a silver car, air-borne,
> Whose silent wheels, fresh wet from clouds of morn,
> Spun off a drizzling dew,—which falling chill
> On soft Adonis' shoulders, made him still
> Nestle and turn uneasily about.
> Soon were the white doves plain, with necks stretch'd out,
> And silken traces tighten'd in descent;
> And soon, returning from love's banishment,
> Queen Venus leaning downward open arm'd. (516–26)

One notices the similarity between this portrayal of Venus coming
to Adonis and the image of Diana approaching Endymion which
was so vivid in Keats's mind when he wrote the poem.

Near the beginning of Book III we find a passage in a very
different tone: Keats is addressing the moon:

> . . . The sleeping kine,
> Couched in thy brightness, dream of fields divine:
> Innumerable mountains rise, and rise,
> Ambitious for the hallowing of thine eyes;
> And yet thy benediction passeth not
> One obscure hiding-place, one little spot
> Where pleasure may be sent.   (57–63)

The first two lines, in particular, are in the very spirit of Samuel
Palmer; but precocious as he was—he exhibited at both the Royal
Academy and the British Institution in 1819, when he was only
fourteen—his 'visionary' paintings seem not to have begun until
a few years later, and there is little possibility that Keats could
have been influenced by him.[36] Nor can Keats have known anything of Edward Calvert's.[37] It may just be a coincidence that he
wrote these lines in the very year in which John Linnell met Blake,
yet the picture of the 'sleeping kine' is so strongly suggestive
of Blake and his circle that one is left wondering, against all
the probabilities, whether Keats may have seen some sketch that
was later (perhaps) to contribute an idea to Blake's strangely
evocative wood-engravings for Thornton's *Virgil*.[38]

Other passages in this Book remind us of Keats's interest in
painting and sculpture. In the course of his description of the
objects found on the bottom of the sea he mentions

> . . . sculptures rude
> In ponderous stone, developing the mood
> Of ancient Nox.   (131–3)

Lemprière would have told him that Nox was 'one of the most
ancient deities among the heathens', but the words 'developing
the mood' sound as if they might be art-critic's jargon.[39] When
Keats goes on to describe Glaucus at line 192, he has various
classical authorities to follow,[40] but he is also dealing with a
figure who had frequently been painted. Plate XVIII shows
Salvator Rosa's engraving of 'Glaucus and Scylla', which was

XVIII. SALVATOR ROSA: Glaucus and Scylla

XIX. POUSSIN: The Indian Triumph of Bacchus

And as I sat, over the light blue hills
There came a noise of revellers: the rills
Into the wide stream came of purple hue—
'Twas Bacchus and his crew! . . .
Onward the tiger and the leopard pants,
With Asian elephants.

well known at this time. Keats would also be familiar with
pictures illustrating the scene in which Circe transforms men
into animals, which he describes at line 497. When he wrote
lines 862–5—

> And then, behold! large Neptune on his throne
> Of emerald deep: yet not exalt alone;
> At his right hand stood winged Love, and on
> His left sat smiling Beauty's paragon

—he may well have remembered the portrayal of Neptune and
Venus in Tooke's *Pantheon* and Poussin's 'The Triumph of
Neptune and Amphitrite' as well as the section 'Of the Deities
of the Waters' in Spence's *Polymetis*. Such images no doubt
helped to inspire the Hymn to Neptune which follows.

The Triumph of Bacchus in Book IV is the only passage in
Keats that we know to have been related to a particular painting
by one of his friends. Severn tells us that it was inspired by
Titian's 'Bacchus and Ariadne', while Monckton Milnes went so
far as to describe Keats's lines as 'in fact the Bacchus and Ariadne
of Titian . . . translated into verse'.[41] We notice that the Indian
maiden who sings the song 'O Sorrow' and then goes on to
describe the arrival of Bacchus and his revellers is in the same
situation as Ariadne in Titian's portrayal of the story. In Keats's
poem the Indian maiden turns out to be Cynthia, and we are
presented with yet another account of the ending of loneliness
through love which is one of the main themes of the romance.
There can be no doubt that Titian's painting, which Keats had
already referred to in 'Sleep and Poetry', was in his mind as he
wrote the passage, but the correspondence is not so close as
Milnes's statement might seem to suggest. The painting shows
'young Bacchus' and his 'car', it shows his 'merry damsels' and
his 'jolly Satyrs'; but he is leaping from the car, not standing in
it, and we see no 'Silenus on his ass', no elephants and other
eastern animals accompanying the leopards which are so clearly
portrayed. It seems highly probable that Keats was also familiar
with some 'Indian Triumph of Bacchus', something in the same
iconographical tradition as the Poussin drawing at Windsor[42]
(Plate XIX). But the Titian was certainly in his mind, and it is
interesting to note how he caught at the sweeping movement
implicit in the dynamics of Titian's design—the godlike leap

which carries Bacchus towards Ariadne as a natural incident in his irresistible progress—and used a poet's prerogative to translate it into narrative.

Lemprière tells us of Endymion that 'it is said that he required of Jupiter to grant to him to be always young, and to sleep as much as he would; whence came the proverb of *Endymionis somnum dormire*, to express a long sleep'.[43] The poem *Endymion* is a young man's dream, and we notice that the elements of the dream derive more often from Keats's reading and from his knowledge of pictures than from first-hand experience. The critic who singled out passages which reminded him of Salvator Rosa, Claude, Poussin, and Titian was not merely being ingenious.[44] Some of the most satisfactory parts of the poem are those in which the yearnings of Keats's imagination have found some sort of 'objective correlative' in images created by painters enamoured (like himself) of 'the beautiful mythology of Greece'.

IX

SATURN AND THE TITANS

The thirst of reign and sweetness of a crown,
That caused the eldest son of heavenly Ops
To thrust his doting father from his chair,
And place himself in the imperial heaven,
Mov'd me to manage arms against thy state.
What better precedent than mighty Jove?
Nature, that fram'd us of four elements
Warring within our breasts for regiment,
Doth teach us all to have aspiring minds.

Tamburlaine the Great, Part I, II. vii.

It [*Hyperion*] is that in poetry which the Elgin and Egyptian
Marbles are in Sculpture.

RICHARD WOODHOUSE

It is always astonishing to remember that Keats began *Hyperion* within a few months of finishing *Endymion*.[1] When we pass from the one poem to the other we pass from the world of minor verse to that of major poetry, from a 'Poetic Romance' set in the Realm of Flora and old Pan to an epic fragment describing the end of the Golden Age. We pass, too, from one visual world to another, from a world of Arcadian landscapes and classical forms that is often on the point of dissolving into incoherence or commonplace prettiness, to a world dominated by great statuesque forms set against a sublime and superhuman background. We pass from a visual world inspired by paintings and prints to a visual world more often inspired by great sculptural masses and by the mountains and forests of Scotland. To create this new world of the eye Keats had now further resources to call on,

> . . . what I had seen
> Of grey Cathedrals, buttress'd walls, rent towers,
> The superannuations of sunk realms,
> Or Nature's Rocks toil'd hard in waves and winds,

as he was later to write in *The Fall of Hyperion*.

Keats was quite deliberate in his creation of this new visual world. As early as January 1818 we find him writing to Haydon about the proposal for an illustration to *Endymion*, in a passage that has already been quoted:

> It would be as well to wait for a choice out of *Hyperion*—when that Poem is done there will be a wide range for you—in Endymion I think you may have many bits of the deep and sentimental cast—the nature of *Hyperion* will lead me to treat it in a more naked and grecian Manner.
>
> (i. 207)

'A more naked and grecian Manner' is as clear a pointer to the verbal sculpture of *Hyperion* as we could well demand, and in the opening lines we are reminded of sculptural forms as forcibly as we are of Milton:

> Deep in the shady sadness of a vale
> Far sunken from the healthy breath of morn,
> Far from the fiery noon, and eve's one star,
> Sat gray-hair'd Saturn, quiet as a stone,
> Still as the silence round about his lair;
> Forest on forest hung above his head
> Like cloud on cloud. No stir of air was there,
> Not so much life as on a summer's day
> Robs not one light seed from the feather'd grass,
> But where the dead leaf fell, there did it rest.
> A stream went voiceless by, still deadened more
> By reason of his fallen divinity
> Spreading a shade: the Naiad 'mid her reeds
> Press'd her cold finger closer to her lips.[2]

'There is always a great charm in the openings of great Poems', Keats noted in a copy of *Paradise Lost*, while he went on to annotate lines 318–21 as follows:

> There is a cool pleasure in the very sound of vale. The English word is of the happiest chance. Milton has put vales in heaven and hell with the very utter affection and yearning of a great Poet. It is a sort of Delphic Abstraction—a beautiful thing made more beautiful by being reflected and put in a Mist.[3]

It is clear that he was annotating Milton with a view to *Hyperion*, a fact which is equally evident in his note to *Paradise Lost*, vii. 420–3, where—in another passage cited in an earlier chapter—he draws attention to

what may be called his [Milton's] *stationing or statuary*. He is not content with simple description, he must station,—thus here we not only see how the Birds *'with clang despised the ground'*, but we see them *'under a cloud in prospect'*. So we see Adam *'Fair indeed, and tall—under a plantane'*—and so we see Satan *'disfigured—on the Assyrian Mount'*.[4]

'No sooner am I alone', he wrote to George Keats and his wife on the 24th of October 1818, 'than shapes of epic greatness are stationed around me', and as we read on we find that few figures in poetry have ever been more superbly 'stationed' than Saturn, or more perfectly described:

> . . . Upon the sodden ground
> His old right hand lay nerveless, listless, dead,
> Unsceptred; and his realmless eyes were closed;
> While his bow'd head seem'd list'ning to the Earth,
> His ancient mother, for some comfort yet.

These lines could only have been written by a man deeply interested in the visual arts, and it is of sculpture that we are reminded rather than of painting. As at the beginning of *The Eve of St. Agnes* we notice that everything is silent, as it is colourless and chill. There Keats refers to the effigies in cathedrals:[5] here he is equally explicit, describing the unmoving Saturn and Thea

> . . . postured motionless,
> Like natural sculpture in cathedral cavern;
> The frozen God still couchant on the earth,
> And the sad Goddess weeping at his feet.

It is not surprising that critics have often compared these figures to the Elgin Marbles, and there can be little doubt that Keats remembered these great fragments (seen, perhaps, by candle-light) as he wrote the opening of his poem. Yet there is no Saturn in the Parthenon frieze, and the only figure that has been suggested as a model for Keats, that usually described as the Dionysus, bears little resemblance to Keats's figure (Plate I): it represents a powerful young god reclining; his head is not 'bow'd', and it is clear that his right hand was not 'nerveless, listless, dead', but held upwards.[6]

Nor does Saturn correspond to the description in 'Edward Baldwin's' *Pantheon*:

Saturn is represented by [Greek] sculptors under the figure of a very old man, with a long beard, and bearing a scythe in his hand . . . . his appearance is similar to that, under which you see Time painted in Gay's Fables and other common books: they may indeed be considered as the same deity, the Greek names for each differing only in a single letter; Κρόνος being Greek for Saturn, and Χρόνος for Time. It is in the sense of Time that the circumstance in the history of Saturn has sometimes been explained, that he is the devourer of his children.[7]

But if we inquire a little further into the iconography of Saturn we find that it is possible that Keats may have known of another mode of representing him. As the authors of *Saturn and Melancholy* have pointed out, 'ancient portraits of Saturn . . . fall into two classes, both of which show the god as an old man and endow him with the attributes of a sickle and a cloak pulled over his head'; but whereas the first shows him as a bust, or as a standing figure, the second 'shows him in the attitude of a thinker, seated, with his head on his hand'.[8] An example of this portrayal is to be found on the tomb of Cornutus in the Vatican, on which

Saturn . . . appears sadly reflecting, like Attis on other tombs. His right hand does not hold the sickle upright . . ., but lets it rest wearily upon his knee. His head is bent and rests upon his arm. For Cornutus . . . Saturn was symbolic of the sad tranquillity of death.[9]

Yet none of the representations of Saturn illustrated in *Saturn and Melancholy* is at all close to Keats,[10] and as one reads the description in *Hyperion* with more attention one finds reason to doubt whether Keats was in fact following any single original. Until line 87 there is no ambiguity about the posture of Saturn: he is sitting with his head bowed and his eyes closed, his right hand lying on the ground. But then he is described as 'couchant on the earth'. This use of a heraldic word is not only interesting in itself: it also raises uncertainties about Saturn's exact posture, as 'couchant' practically always means lying down.[11] In *The Fall of Hyperion* Keats revised the passage:

> Long, long, those two were postured motionless,
> Like sculpture builded up upon the grave
> Of their own power. A long awful time
> I look'd upon them; still they were the same;
> The frozen God still bending to the Earth,
> And the sad Goddess weeping at his feet.   (i. 382–7)

'Couchant' has gone, whether because Keats considered it too literary a word or because he realized that it was inconsistent with the description of Saturn's position which he had already given. It seems likely (in any event) that a number of passages of literature and a number of visual images all contributed to Keats's description. One of them may even have been a tombstone, for the posture of Saturn and Thea is reminiscent more than anything else of a sculptural group on a funeral monument — a fact which makes it interesting to note that Keats refers to a cathedral both in the passage itself and in the description of Fingal's cave in the letter which lies behind this part of the poem. Some forgotten portrayal of a mourning father and daughter may well have helped to inspire the passage—a father with head bowed and eyes closed in sorrow, a daughter whose long hair lies unregarded by her father's feet.

What makes the suggestion surprising and almost shocking is the difference of scale. All but the most elaborate tombs have figures of less than life size, but Saturn and his daughter are giant forms:

> She was a Goddess of the infant world;
> By her in stature the tall Amazon
> Had stood a pigmy's height: she would have ta'en
> Achilles by the hair and bent his neck;
> Or with a finger stay'd Ixion's wheel.   (i. 26–30)

The size of Saturn and Thea differs as dramatically from that of the figures on most tombstones as it does from that of the Elgin Marbles themselves.

These classical images demand a moment's attention. Why should Achilles be used as the embodiment of power at this point, rather than any other ancient hero? It is interesting to notice that Haydon was almost obsessively interested in Achilles. On the 7th of March 1812 he wrote in his Diary that he had been

in a torrent of enthusiasm, after [lying awake] in bed till three in the morning, about Achilles. The subject rushed into my head, in all its vigour. I was in doubt which to choose, Solomon or him. For a moment nothing would bear comparison.[12]

On another occasion Haydon refers to the 'terrific arm' of Achilles, 'his gigantic breast, his mighty limbs, [and] his heroic neck',[13] while a third passage harks back to the strength of a heroic neck:

The people of this country are little better than children in matters of art. So unused are they to see grand forms of Heroes, so unprepared are they for great Art, that if a neck be full & vigourous like a pillar, 'too thick' echoes through the Gallery, and down go all their cravats that they may feel their own skinny, meagre miserable necks.[14]

It was no doubt partly because he had heard Haydon holding forth on the subject of Achilles and his neck that Keats wrote that Thea

> . . . would have ta'en
> Achilles by the hair and bent his neck.

It is also worth remembering that there is a most striking visual representation of this sort of action in one of the fragments of the Elgin Marbles. A figure from the South Metope represents a Centaur wounded by a Lapith, who holds it back from flight by bending its neck backwards with a powerful arm (Plate XX). I have already quoted the passage in which Haydon praises this 'divine form', of which he made a careful drawing.[15] The remarkable muscular power of the reference to Ixion may also owe something to Haydon, and to the visual arts in general.[16] Haydon sketched this subject at least once, and thought of incorporating it in a painting which was never undertaken; while it also occurred to him that 'Ixion's wheel stopped' would figure well in the background of a painting of 'Orpheus suspending hell' with the music of his lyre.[17] Keats may also have remembered an anecdote of the archeologist Belzoni which is mentioned in the *Quarterly Review* for July 1818. The writer is describing a large treadmill water-wheel:

> At the second or third turn the Arabs became giddy and jumped out; the wheel, wanting its counterpoise, flew back, and the Irish servant, in attempting to escape, broke his thigh, and must have been killed, had not Belzoni caught hold of the circumference of the wheel, and, by his extraordinary strength, stopped its motion.   (xix. 423)

Here we have not only a wheel, but a wheel on or in which—as with Ixion—a man is suffering physical agony.

Keats rejects these classical comparisons in favour of an Egyptian image:

> Her face was large as that of Memphian sphinx,
> Pedestal'd haply in a palace court,
> When sages look'd to Egypt for their lore.

It is a perfectly understandable transition. 'As the candle gloomed across and struck against backs, legs, & columns',

xx. The Elgin Marbles: Lapith and Centaur

'*Does Mr Knight remember that divine form in a metope, grappling a Centaur by the throat, and heaving up his chest, and drawing in his breast, preparing to annihilate his enemy . . .?*'

XXI. Statue of Ramesses II ('The Young Memnon')

'In the morning Severn & I took a turn round the Museum, There is a Sphinx there of a giant size, & most voluptuous Egyptian expression.'

Haydon wrote in his Diary on the 8th of February 1811, 'I was peculiarly impressed with the feeling of being among the ruins of two mighty People[s]—Egyptians and Grecians'. Here Haydon is referring to Lord Elgin's collection while it was still in its shed at Park Lane, but the arrangement of the antiquities in the British Museum, in Keats's day as in ours, similarly juxtaposed Greek and Egyptian exhibits. As Helen Darbishire remarked, when Keats 'moved across from the Elgin Marbles, as we still do to-day, to contemplate the colossal Egyptian sculptures, he felt, we must suppose, the strange thrill that the stupidest sight-seer cannot miss in turning from the radiant humanity of the Greeks to the almost pre-human grandeur of the darker, older race'.[18] It was fortunate for the imagination of Keats that the Museum had so rich a collection of *Egyptiana*. 'How very magnificent the collection of sculpture is at this Museum!', a writer in the *Annals of the Fine Arts* commented in this same year, 'especially of Egyptian'.[19] The writer may well have been Haydon, who liked to look back on his friendship with Belzoni, the great excavator;[20] and we notice that the same page of the *Quarterly Review* which contains the opening paragraph of the notorious review of *Endymion* also contains the conclusion of an article describing 'the ruins of the most stupendous and magnificent temples in the world', in which the reviewer comments that 'from the exertions of such a man, the British Museum is likely to become the first repository in the world for Egyptian art and antiquities'.[21] Elsewhere Haydon emphasized the importance of the Egyptian discoveries for painters:[22] for Keats they were no less important. As Helen Darbishire pointed out:

To Keats Egypt brought a new world of plastic forms at a moment of special need. When he began to brood over the subject of *Hyperion*, his mind, we may imagine, instinctively groped for images to fit his vast conceptions of the early gods. Greek art might supply images for Apollo with his golden lyre or Neptune in his chariot, but how convey the larger majesty of Hyperion, 'Giant of the Sun', or of Thea or of Saturn? The colossal sculpture and architecture of Egypt met his need and passed into his poem.[23]

It is tempting to associate this 'Memphian sphinx' in *Hyperion* with the sphinx that Keats says that he saw in the Museum about the beginning of March 1819:

In the morning Severn & I took a turn round the Museum, There

is a Sphinx there of a ~~great~~ giant size, & most voluptuous Egyptian
expression, I had not seen it before. (ii. 68)

If the image of the 'Memphian sphinx' was suggested by something that Keats saw in the Museum at the beginning of March,
then we have further evidence for dating the composition of part
of the poem later than has been usual. Unfortunately, the matter
remains obscure. There is no 'giant Sphinx' in the Museum today and no record of there having been such a thing there in the
year 1819.[24] For lack of a better explanation one can only fall
back on the hypothesis that Keats is here using the word 'Sphinx'
inaccurately, and is in fact referring to the giant head and
shoulders of Ramesses II (Plate XXI), which was then known as
the 'young Memnon'. This great head, 'the wonder of travellers',
as Haydon called it,[25] was perhaps the most notable of all Belzoni's discoveries, and its recent arrival at the Museum had been
noticed prominently in the *Annals of the Fine Arts*. In the issue
dated 1st June 1818, a contributor writes that 'the celebrated
head of Memnon, from Thebes, and other relics of antiquity . . .
are nearly all delivered at the British Museum. We have seen
them.' Six months later we are told that 'these sculptured fragments continue to interest the public in a considerable degree';
while in the issue for March 1819 we hear that 'the Memnon's
head is erected at the British Museum, and has an imposing air.
The mouth is singularly beautiful in expression.'[26] The expression of the 'Memnon' attracted particular notice: de Quincey
was later to write of 'that sublime head which wears upon its lips
a smile co-extensive with all time and all space, an Æonian
smile of gracious love and Panlike mystery, the most diffusive
and pathetically divine that the hand of man has created'.[27]

If the head of the 'Memnon' was what was in Keats's mind
when he wrote about the 'Memphian sphinx', then the following
lines from the description of Hyperion might appear to be closely
associated with the passage quoted above on p. 166.

> Golden his hair of short Numidian curl,
> Regal his shape majestic, a vast shade
> In midst of his own brightness, like the bulk
> Of Memnon's image at the set of sun
> To one who travels from the dusking East:
> Sighs, too, as mournful as that Memnon's harp
> He utter'd. (ii. 371–7)

But although the suggestion of great size is reminiscent of the description of Thea, in fact it is not the 'Memnon' in the British Museum that is supposed to have given forth spontaneous music, but one of the two colossi of Memnon which still stand by the site of the mortuary temple of Amenophis III. The tradition is recorded by Strabo,[28] and is certain to have been known to Keats from more than one source. In Baldwin's *Pantheon*, for example, he could have read how 'an exquisite statue' had been erected in memory of Memnon, near the Egyptian Thebes, and how, 'as he was the son of Aurora, this statue had the peculiar property of uttering a melodious sound every morning when touched by the first beams of the day; and every night at sunset, it gave another sound, low and mournful, as lamenting the departure of the day'.[29] We know that Leigh Hunt once mentioned the tradition to Keats, in connexion with a poem he was writing:

One day [Keats] came to me full of the finest idea that poet ever had [Severn records,] which he said Leigh Hunt was then writing— It was a comparison of Nature's effects striking on an elegant mind to Memnon's image music at the suns rays—I told him he would find it in Akenside (a Poet he so hated that he would not look in him) & I quoted the whole passage to his great surprise, tho he declared that Hunt would do it a great deal better & that he would not tell him of Akenside.[30]

Keats seems to have been referring to a brief passage in Hunt's poem, 'Power and Gentleness', which was published in 1819:

> And him, great Memnon, that long sitting by
> In seeming idleness, with stony eye,
> Sang at the morning's touch, like poetry.

Whether or not Keats had read the passage in *The Pleasures of Imagination* before Severn's outburst, he heard it then:

> For as old Memnon's image, long renown'd
> By fabling Nilus, to the quivering touch
> Of Titan's ray, with each repulsive string
> Consenting, sounded through the warbling air
> Unbidden strains; even so did nature's hand
> To certain species of external things,
> Attune the finer organs of the mind. (i. 109–15)

Probably Keats had also read of the statute of Memnon's in Darwin's poem, *The Botanic Garden*:

> So to the sacred Sun in MEMNON's fane,
> Spontaneous concords quired the matin strain;
> —Touch'd by his orient beam, responsive rings
> The living lyre, and vibrates all it's strings;
> Accordant aisles the tender notes prolong,
> And holy echoes swell the adoring song.[31]

In a characteristic note on the subject Darwin discusses the phenomenon and quotes from Savary's *Travels*. We find Memnon's image again in Hayley's *Essay on Sculpture*:

> But quick as Memnon's statue felt the day,
> And spoke responsive to the rising day . . .
> Still, like the statue sever'd on the ground,
> Though weaker, still its wonted voice is found:
> Warm'd by that light they love, the very fragments sound.[32]

The image was something of a commonplace in the minor poetry of the eighteenth century, but Keats uses it with unusual success. Since Hyperion is the God of the Sun who is destined to be overthrown, the comparison of him to the ruined image of Memnon, near a temple sacred to the sun, is extremely apt; while the comparison of his sighs to the sound of Memnon's harp has an obvious appropriateness.

In his description of Hyperion's palace Keats also makes use of Egyptian images:

> . . . His palace bright
> Bastion'd with pyramids of glowing gold,
> And touch'd with shade of bronzed obelisks,
> Glar'd a blood-red through all its thousand courts,
> Arches, and domes, and fiery galleries;
> And all its curtains of Aurorian clouds
> Flush'd angerly.   (i. 176–82)

The inspiration of 'Bastion'd with pyramids' and 'bronzed obelisks' is clearly Egyptian: Helen Darbishire suggested that 'the whole scale of the multiform building with its thousand courts, its innumerable halls and galleries, its temple within temple, bears more likeness to what we know of the great Egyptian labyrinth than to any other building Keats might have seen or read of'.[33] The fact that the Egyptologist Pauw believed the 'the obelisks and pyramids [are] temples raised to the god of day, because one of their faces is turned to the east',[34] is consonant with Keats's subject. But the sources of this description must have been various. Keats was certainly remembering one of the passages in *Paradise Lost* which he had annotated, the description of Pandemonium in Book I,[35] and when we reach lines 217–24 we find images which are remote from anything Egyptian:

> . . . On he flared,
> From stately nave to nave, from vault to vault,
> Through bowers of fragrant and enwreathed light,
> And diamond-paved lustrous long arcades,
> Until he reach'd the great main cupola;
> There standing fierce beneath, he stampt his foot,
> And from the basements deep to the high towers
> Jarr'd his own golden region.

It is difficult to read such Miltonic passages without being reminded of a painter six years older than Keats who was soon to illustrate *Paradise Lost*. As we read the description of Hyperion's palace, we find imagery in many ways similar to that of Martin's 'The Fall of Babylon' (Plate XXII), and if Martin's painting was one of Keats's sources we have another piece of evidence pointing to a slightly later date for the composition of the poem.

'The Fall of Babylon' was completed by February 1819 and exhibited at the British Institution early that month.[36] It created something of a sensation. 'The exhibition at the Gallery this year contains nothing very striking', wrote a contributor to the *Annals of the Fine Arts*, 'with the exception of *Martin's* grand composition of the fall of Babylon . . ., the finest poetical landscape of the day.'[37] *The Examiner* devoted two and a half columns to praise of the picture:

The spectators crowd around it, some with silence, some with exclamatory admiration; sometimes very near to look at the numerous small objects that cannot be distinguished at a distance, sometimes further off to feast upon the grandeur of the whole; leaving it, but still thrilling with the strange and felicitous expression, coming back to look at it again, after having looked at most of the other pictures with an absent mind, like a lover who is but half attentive to other women in a delicious reverie on the superior charms of her who has the keeping of his heart. So exuberant is this noble work in matter for gazing and description that a very extended criticism ought to be written upon it to do it justice.[38]

Martin's vast view of a luxurious city is very much in the spirit of Hyperion's palace with its thousand courts: one of the most prominent architectural features of the picture is a huge pyramidal block, while the strange and hectic sky corresponds very well to Keats's

> . . . curtains of Aurorian clouds
> Flush'd angerly.

This makes it interesting that in a passage in a letter written on the last day of 1818 Keats wrote as follows:

> We with our bodily eyes see but the fashion and Manners of one country for one age—and then we die—Now to me manners and customs long since passed whether among the Babylonians or the Bactrians are as real, or even more real than those among which I now live—My thoughts have turned lately this way.   (ii. 18)

We know that Keats visited the British Institution in 1818 and 1820.[39] It seems probable that he did so early in 1819, as well, at the very time when he was working on *Hyperion*, and that he there saw Martin's celebrated painting. Even Haydon was often impressed by Martin, in spite of himself: 'that fellow should have wings!' he wrote in his Diary on one occasion. 'He is an extraordinary fellow in his way.'[40] A few years later Bulwer Lytton was to over-praise Martin in absurd terms which yet give us an excellent idea of the power which his contemporaries felt him to possess:

> I hasten to Martin,—the greatest, the most lofty, the most permanent, the most original genius of his age. . . . He has looked upon 'the ebon throne of Eld', and imbued a mind destined to reproduce what it surveyed, with
>> 'A mighty darkness
>> Filling the Seat of Power—as rays of gloom
>> Dart round.'
> Vastness is his sphere. . . . Alone and guideless, he has penetrated the remotest caverns of the past, and gazed on the primæval shapes of the gone world.[41]

We are again reminded of Martin when we read the descrip-

XXII. JOHN MARTIN: The Fall of Babylon

...His palace bright
Bastion'd with pyramids of glowing gold,
And touch'd with shade of bronzed obelisks,
Glar'd a blood-red through all its thousand courts ...

XXIII. JOHN MARTIN: Sadak in Search of the Waters of Oblivion

. . . The solid roar
Of thunderous waterfalls and torrents hoarse,
Pouring a constant bulk, uncertain where.
Crag jutting forth to crag, and rocks that seem'd
Ever as if just rising from a sleep,
Forehead to forehead held their monstrous horns.

tion of 'that sad place Where Cybele and the bruised Titans mourn'd':

> It was a den where no insulting light
> Could glimmer on their tears; where their own groans
> They felt, but heard not, for the solid roar
> Of thunderous waterfalls and torrents hoarse,
> Pouring a constant bulk, uncertain where.
> Crag jutting forth to crag, and rocks that seem'd
> Ever as if just rising from a sleep,
> Forehead to forehead held their monstrous horns;
> And thus in thousand hugest phantasies
> Made a fit roofing to this nest of woe.
> Instead of thrones, hard flint they sat upon,
> Couches of rugged stone, and slaty ridge
> Stubborn'd with iron.   (ii. 5–17)

This is strikingly reminiscent of one of Martin's earliest success-ful paintings, 'Sadak in Search of the Waters of Oblivion', shown at the Royal Academy in 1812 (Plate XXIII).[42] It is a picture which was much discussed: Keats is almost certain to have heard of it, and may well have seen the original or perhaps an early engraving. In Martin's scene of terrifying despair—which is very much in the spirit of Keats's description of the Titans—we notice particularly the great crags which

> Forehead to forehead h[o]ld their monstrous horns,

the great waterfall, and the overwhelming general impression of barren rock and jagged stone.

There are other passages in *Hyperion* which were probably influenced by the visual arts. The convulsion of Hyperion after his speech to his companions is bound to remind us of a cele-brated work of sculpture:

> At this, through all his bulk an agony
> Crept gradual, from the feet unto the crown,
> Like a lithe serpent vast and muscular
> Making slow way, with head and neck convuls'd
> From over-strained might.   (i. 259–63)

Keats must have been very familiar with engravings and repro-ductions of the Laocoon, which was frequently mentioned by Haydon, Hazlitt, and his other friends. Hazlitt, who was more interested in painting than in sculpture, frequently remembered his first sight of the Laocoon in the Louvre, while in his review of A. W. Schlegel's *Lectures on Dramatic Literature* he praises Schlegel's parallel between Greek art and Greek literature:

> Our author is right in affirming, that the true way to understand the plays of Sophocles and Æschylus, is to study them before the groupes of the Niobe or the Laocoon. If we can succeed in explaining this analogy, we shall have solved nearly the whole difficulty. For it is certain, that there are exactly the same powers of mind displayed in the poetry of the Greeks as in their statues. Their poetry is exactly what their sculptors might have written. Both are exquisite imitations of nature; the one in marble, the other in words.[43]

The description of Neptune in the second Book probably owes something to visual representations:

> Have ye beheld the young God of the Seas,
> My dispossessor? Have ye seen his face?
> Have ye beheld his chariot, foam'd along
> By noble winged creatures he hath made?
> I saw him on the calmed waters scud,
> With such a glow of beauty in his eyes,
> That it enforc'd me to bid sad farewell
> To all my empire.   (ii. 232–9)

The description of the fallen Titans reminds us of Giulio Romano's frescoes in the Sala dei Giganti, and occasionally of Michelangelo, as surely as it does of Dante (with Flaxman's illustrations) and of Milton. Images from these and other works of literature, painting, and sculpture, must all have contributed to the huge forms and the awe-inspiring setting of the poem.

But, of course, the primary inspiration for the descriptions of scenery in *Hyperion* was Keats's northern journey, undertaken to fill his mind with sublime imagery. There is a clear example of his drawing on a reminiscence of the Lake District in the description of the Titans near the beginning of Book II:

> Scarce images of life, one here, one there,
> Lay vast and edgeways; like a dismal cirque
> Of Druid stones, upon a forlorn moor,
> When the chill rain begins at shut of eve,
> In dull November, and their chancel vault,
> The Heaven itself, is blinded throughout night.
> Each one kept shroud, nor to his neighbour gave
> Or word, or look, or action of despair.   (ii. 33–40)

This may be set beside the letter in which Keats describes how he and Brown had set out

to see the Druid temple. We had a fag up hill . . ., which was rendered void, by the gratification of seeing those aged stones, on a gentle rise in the midst of Mountains, which at that time darkened all round.

(i. 306)

In another letter (already quoted in Chapter VI) we find Keats describing Fingal's Cave and peopling it with the characters of *Hyperion*:

Suppose now the Giants who rebelled against Jove had taken a whole Mass of black Columns and bound them together like bunches of matches—and then with immense Axes had made a cavern in the body of these columns . . .—such is fingal's Cave. (i. 348)

Keats identifies the Giants and the Titans.[44] His association of these figures from Greek mythology with Fingal's Cave may well have been encouraged by knowing that 'the Fingalian race were to the Scots, as Mr. Pinkerton well observes, what the Titanic were to the Greeks'.[45] Keats wrote his lines 'Not Aladdin magian' on the subject of Staffa; but the more important influence of the scene was to make itself evident in *Hyperion*, in the description of Saturn and Thea,

Like natural sculpture in cathedral cavern.

But we must turn now to Hyperion's successor, Apollo.

X

APOLLO

Any one, who has been much used to see collections of antient
statues, may remember that the first and chief thing by which
he used to distinguish an Apollo, . . . was the beauty of his face.

Polymetis

. . . For 'tis the eternal law
That first in beauty should be first in might.

Hyperion

Ce qui avait manqué au noble dieu du jour . . . voudrais-tu
le savoir? C'est la peine, la douleur, la mort, c'est le bûcher,
mon fils! Apollon, qui n'est que lumière, n'a pu descendre au
royaume sombre.

MICHELET[1]

I F we wish to understand the significance of Apollo to Keats—
and this is essential if we are concerned with speculation about
the meaning of *Hyperion* and about the reasons which may have
led Keats to redraft part of it and then abandon the poem altogether—we must look back for a moment to the earlier poems
and the letters. As we do so, we shall find that Apollo is not only
the hero of *Hyperion*—as Keats makes clear in his letter to
Haydon[2]—but also in a sense the hero of all his poetry and of
his entire poetic career.

Apollo is already a power to be reckoned with in the first
poem in the volume of 1817, where Keats refers to the poets
of the new age:

> Open afresh your round of starry folds,
> Ye ardent marigolds!
> Dry up the moisture from your golden lids,
> For great Apollo bids
> That in these days your praises should be sung
> On many harps, which he has lately strung;
> And when again your dewiness he kisses,
> Tell him, I have you in my world of blisses:
> So haply when I rove in some far vale,
> His mighty voice may come upon the gale.   (47–56)

Here we notice right away that Keats knows Apollo to be the
God of Poetry and the God of the Sun as well. Later in the same

poem there occurs the reference, already mentioned,[3] to a sculptural representation of Apollo:

> Stepping like Homer at the trumpet's call,
> Or young Apollo on the pedestal.

The reference to 'stepping' suggests that Keats had in mind the Apollo Belvedere, in which Apollo has just discharged an arrow and has the air of stepping forwards. The remarkable thing is that, of all the references to Apollo in the writings of Keats, this is one of only two that recall the Apollo Belvedere.[4] The explanation of this fact is probably to be found in the opinions of his friends.

In the eighteenth century no work of sculpture was more celebrated. There is an excellent full-page engraving of this statue in *Polymetis*, and in his discussion of whether this is 'the noblest of all the antient statues, that remain to us', we find that Spence is inclined to answer affirmatively:

> The air of the Apollo Belvedere, gives us an idea of something above human; more strongly, than any figure among the great numbers that remain to us. . . . As [its] excellence . . . consists in the expression of something divine . . ., this statue may, perhaps justly enough, claim the preference, even in this distinguished class of the best remains of all antiquity.[5]

Winckelmann had no doubt that the Apollo Belvedere was the most sublime of all the surviving works of ancient sculpture, while Reynolds also praises the Apollo in the highest terms.[6] But by the beginning of the following century a reaction begins to be noticeable. Although Haydon made the most elaborate measurements of the Apollo in his pursuit of the perfect proportions of the human form, he tried to persuade Canova that it was overrated.[7] 'I should be happy if I could produce such a figure as the Apollo', he once wrote in his Diary, 'but I should be much happier to produce the Theseus, the Lapitha, the Monte Cavallo figure, or the Elgin Woman. . . . The Apollo is a fine production, but these are finer—ten thousand times finer.'[8] Once he went so far as to write of 'the hard, marbly, puffed figure of the Apollo': on another occasion he gave his view more pointedly by saying that 'the Torso & the Apollo are Marbles, Statues; the Theseus, the Lapithae, & the Neptune living Gods.'[9] It is remarkable what a focus of discussion the Apollo Belvedere

became. Flaxman expressed more than one view on the subject:
on one occasion, according to Haydon, he 'told Hamilton . . .
that the Apollo in comparison with the Theseus was a dancing
master'.[10] Hazlitt, who (like Haydon) had seen the original in
the Louvre, was sometimes highly critical of the Apollo Belvedere: in his *Notes of a Journey through France and Italy* he was to
describe it as 'a coxcomb'.[11] Keats must have heard a great deal
of talk about the statue, and may well have been led by the
ambivalent views of his friends to concentrate on other images
of the God.

Other references in the early poems make it clear how often
Apollo was in Keats's mind. In the epistle 'To George Felton
Mathew' he remarks that his friend has been brought up

> Close to the source, bright, pure, and undefil'd,
> Whence gush the streams of song,

and expresses surprise that Mathew has never described

> How, from a flower, into a fish of gold
> Apollo chang'd thee:

a reminder of his constant reading of the *Metamorphoses*. In a
playfully gallant sonnet 'To G[eorgiana] A[ugusta] W[ylie]'
Keats professes that he can no more tell at what time or in what
mood she is 'most lovely' than he can say

> . . . which Grace more neatly
> Trips it before Apollo than the rest

—so referring to a subject that has frequently been painted.[12] In
the epistle 'To my Brother George' he tells him that in moments
of depression he has sometimes feared

> That I should never hear Apollo's song,
> Though feathery clouds were floating all along
> The purple west, and, two bright streaks between,
> The golden lyre itself were dimly seen.   (9–12)

In a characteristic vision of the Feast of the Gods Keats insists
that 'no mortal eye' can see the flowers in Elysium,

> And 'tis right just, for well Apollo knows
> 'Twould make the Poet quarrel with the rose. (45–46)

In 'Sleep and Poetry' Keats prays

> that I may die a death
> Of luxury, and my young spirit follow

> The morning sun-beams to the great Apollo
> Like a fresh sacrifice.   (58–61)

As I have pointed out in Chapter VII, Apollo is undoubtedly the
charioteer in the central vision of the poem. It is in the thought
of Apollo and his chariot and of 'the strange Journey it went'
that Keats seeks for support and inspiration. He looks back with
contempt to the eighteenth-century 'schism',

> Nurtured by foppery and barbarism,
> [Which] made great Apollo blush for this his land,

but takes comfort in the thought that now "tis a fairer season'.
In the epistle to Charles Cowden Clarke Keats writes of

> The wrong'd Libertas,—who has told you stories
> Of laurel chaplets, and Apollo's glories.

Apollo was one of Leigh Hunt's family circle, domesticated,
tamed, and vulgarized.[13] A handful of sonnets and an account of
a curious incident that took place one day in 1817 survive as
evidence of this. One evening in the early spring (as it seems)
Keats and Hunt were drinking wine when 'the whim seized them
to crown themselves, after the fashion of the elder poets, with
a wreath of laurel':

> While they were attired, two acquaintances of Mr Hunt called upon
> him:—Just before their entrance Hunt removed the crown from his
> own brows, and suggested to Keats that he might as well do the same.
> K. however, in the enthusiasm of the moment, vowed that he would
> not for any human being and he accordingly wore it without any
> explanation thro' the visit.
> He mentioned the circ.ce afterd to one or two of his friends express-
> ing his sense how foolish he had been; and his intention of recording
> it, by apologetic verses suited to the occasion.—He produced shortly
> afterd the following fragment of an Ode to Apollo.[14]

On this or some similar occasion Keats wrote a sonnet 'On Receiving a Laurel Crown from Leigh Hunt' which begins with the
words 'Minutes are flying swiftly' and expresses regret that he
cannot find his way 'into a delphic Labyrinth' on the spur of
the moment.[15] In another sonnet, addressed 'To the Ladies
who saw me Crown'd', Keats acknowledges that 'a Wreath
from the bay tree' is to him the loveliest thing on earth. The
'Hymn to Apollo' (referred to above as an Ode) is a poor piece

of verse in which Keats addresses 'Delphic Apollo' and wonders
why the god has not been provoked by his assumption of the
laurel crown into permitting Jupiter to crush him with his
thunder. The opening lines show that Keats was aware of
Apollo's characteristic attributes:

> God of the golden bow,
>   And of the golden lyre,[16]
> And of the golden hair,
>   And of the golden fire,
>   Charioteer
> Of the patient year.

Keats feigns that Apollo has intervened on his behalf, with his
'soft lute', and so prevented Jupiter from crushing him with his
thunderbolt. This makes it clear that Keats not only considered
himself a dependant of Apollo's, but a favoured dependant. This
view was supported by Leigh Hunt, who had introduced Keats's
sonnet on 'The Flour and the Lefe' in *The Champion* with a
description of Keats as

> . . . the youngest he
> That sits in the shadow of Apollo's tree,

and who now told him that he could see 'a flowering laurel' on
his brow.[17]

It is important to notice that Keats refers to his wearing of the
laurel crown as blasphemy against Apollo, and that in a letter to
George written about this time he recurs to this incident yet
again:

> I put on no Laurels till I shall have finished Endymion, and I hope
> Apollo is not angered at my having made a Mockery at him at
> Hunt's.   (i. 170)

As at least one critic has seen,[18] this whole affair mattered to
Keats much more deeply than it would to another man. To
Keats Apollo was more than a figure of speech or a literary
allusion: he was becoming something very close to the God of
his adoration. His consciousness of being under the care of
Apollo comes out clearly in a letter to Reynolds written on the
19th of February 1818:

> Now it is more noble to sit like Jove than to fly like Mercury—let
> us not therefore go hurrying about and collecting honey-bee like,

XXIV. POUSSIN: The Inspiration of the Poet

To see the laurel wreath, on high suspended,
That is to crown our name when life is ended.

buzzing here and there impatiently from a knowledge of what is to be arrived at: but let us open our leaves like a flower and be passive and receptive—budding patiently under the eye of Apollo.   (i. 232)

As the visual suggestion of this last passage reminds us, Keats must have been familiar with a great many pictures of Apollo, from that in Baldwin's *Pantheon* onwards.[19] But the painting which expresses Keats's relationship to Apollo most perfectly is undoubtedly Poussin's 'The Inspiration of the Poet' (Plate XXIV). This picture, now in Louvre, was in England in Keats's day.[20] In it we see Apollo seated, with his lyre, giving inspiration to a poet, while Calliope, the Muse of epic poetry, stands by his side. It shows the 'golden pen' and 'tablet whiter than a star' to which Keats refers in his sonnet 'On Leaving Some Friends at an Early Hour', as well as the 'laurel-wreath on high suspended' which is mentioned in 'Sleep and Poetry', the laurel-wreath

> That is to crown our name when life is ended.[21]

It is one of Poussin's finest paintings, a work—as Sir Anthony Blunt puts it—'d'un classicisme . . . pur' which has affinities with Poussin's 'Parnassus' and 'The Realm of Flora'. Its colouring recalls Veronese and the Titian of 'Sacred and Profane Love'. As for the figure of Apollo itself, as Blunt points out

> Si Poussin à cette époque admirait surtout la couleur vénitienne, il ne négligeait ni Raphaël ni l'art antique. L'Apollon combine des traits empruntés au compartiment de la voûte de la Stanza della Segnatura où est peint *Apollon et Marsyas* avec ceux qu'on trouve dans la figure d'Apollon à la Salle de Psyché, à la Farnésine. La composition du tableau rappelle le bas-relief de la Villa Albani, représentant *Hercule au jardin des Hespérides*.[22]

This same painting which may well (I conjecture) have been often in Keats's mind, suggests an explanation of a rather surprising image in his sonnet on the sonnet. Here, about the time when he was devising a new stanza to use in his Odes, Keats regrets that the English language must be 'chain'd' by 'dull rhymes', and suggests that a better stanza-form than that of the sonnet must be sought for:

> Let us find out, if we must be constrain'd,
> Sandals more interwoven and complete
> To fit the naked foot of poesy.

When one realizes that Keats had only to think of Poetry to think of Apollo, and see him vividly present in his mind's eye, it becomes much less surprising that he should think of the sonnet as a pair of sandals for the God of Poetry. Apollo was in fact the Patron of sandal-makers, and we notice that in 'The Inspiration of the Poet' and in most other portrayals of the god, Apollo is shown wearing an elaborate pair of sandals which are usually made of gold.

Of the many other references to Apollo in Keats's minor poems and in *Endymion*, only a few demand our attention before we turn to *Hyperion*. The early 'Ode to Apollo' celebrates Homer, Virgil, Milton, Shakespeare, and other great poets, and concludes:

> But when *Thou* joinest with the Nine,
> And all the powers of song combine,
>   We listen here on earth:
> The dying tones that fill the air,
> And charm the ear of evening fair,
> From thee, great God of Bards, receive their heavenly birth.

A light-hearted song written early in 1818 emphasizes the visual quality of Keats's imagination, as well as his devotion to Apollo. In it he abjures wine, proclaiming that:

> My bowl is the sky,
> And I drink at my eye,
> Till I feel in the brain
> A Delphian pain.

In lines which may be part of the same song his soul flies up to Apollo,

> God of the Meridian,
> And of the East and West,

until he is in danger of going mad. He prays for 'staid Philosophy' to enable him to see Apollo's bowers 'more unalarm'd'. In 'Apollo to the Graces'[23] the God himself speaks and tells the Muses that

> My Steeds are all pawing on the thresholds of Morn.

One of the most revealing evocations of the chariot of Apollo occurs in 'Otho the Great', where Ludolph in his love-madness refuses to listen to a suggestion which has been made to him:

> Though bright Apollo's car stood burning here,
> And he put out an arm to bid me mount,
> His touch an immortality, not I!   (III. ii. 41–43)

In an acrostic to his sister Keats tells her to

> ... sue the fair Apollo and he will
> Rouse from his heavy slumber and instill
> Great love in me for thee and Poesy;

while in the passage about 'The Enchanted Castle' in the epistle 'To J. H. Reynolds, Esq.', Keats wishes he had Apollo's 'sacred word' to enable him

> To shew this Castle in fair dreaming wise
> Unto my friend, where sick and ill he lies.

But, as he reflects in the sonnet to Spenser, it is impossible

> For an inhabitant of wintry earth
> To rise like Phœbus with a golden quell[24]
> Fire-wing'd and make a morning in his mirth.

For mortal men 'toil' is the condition of Apollo's favour.
  In 'I stood tip-toe' Keats had described how

> Phoebus awhile delayed his mighty wheels

on the bridal-night of Endymion and Cynthia. As Cynthia (or Diana) was the sister of Apollo it is not surprising that *Endymion* contains numerous references to Apollo—indeed, Keats could not have written a long poem at this point without mentioning Apollo's name frequently. There are several references to Apollo as the God of the Sun, as when Endymion describes

> ... his most kingly hour,
> When he doth tighten up the golden reins,
> And paces leisurely down amber plains
> His snorting four.   (i. 549–52)

But once again it is of Apollo's power as the God of Poetry that Keats is most keenly aware, as when he describes shepherds

> Such as sat listening round Apollo's pipe,
> When the great deity, for earth too ripe,
> Let his divinity o'er-flowing die
> In music, through the vales of Thessaly: (i. 141–4)

a description which is unusual because it attributes a 'pipe' to Apollo instead of a lyre or a lute.[25] At line 789 we are told that

> Ghosts of melodious prophecyings rave
> Round every spot where trod Apollo's foot,

and that people who are aware of this are on the way to 'the chief intensity'. In the second Book Keats writes that

> . . . the count
> Of mighty Poets is made up; the scroll
> Is folded by the Muses; the bright roll
> Is in Apollo's hand.   (ii. 723–6)

In Book III we hear how Neptune's 'bright team'

> Gulphs in the morning light, and scuds along
> To bring [him] nearer to that golden song
> Apollo singeth, while his chariot
> Waits at the doors of heaven.   (iii. 956–9)

In Book IV the Muses are described as 'Apollo's garland',[26] and Endymion declares that he will

> [Kneel] to god Phœbus, for a golden lyre.   (iv. 702)

Most interestingly of all, we soon find Keats addressing Endymion and declaring:

> Thy lute-voic'd brother will I sing ere long.   (iv. 774)

Here Keats is certainly referring to Apollo. Presumably he is making him a sort of brother-in-law of Endymion because he is the brother of Cynthia. In any event it is fitting that the last of the numerous references to Apollo in *Endymion* should announce in so many words that he is to be the hero of Keats's next poem.[27]

In *Hyperion* the first that we hear of the god who haunted Keats is that Clymene has heard a 'golden melody' that has deeply moved her, and a voice crying

> . . . Apollo! young Apollo!
> The morning-bright Apollo! young Apollo! (ii. 293–4)

This makes it clear to her that Hyperion and his generation are doomed. Apollo himself does not make his appearance until Book III. Then we are told that we are to leave the Titans and hear instead of the 'solitary sorrow' of Apollo. The Delphic harp and the Dorian flute are invoked:

For lo! 'tis for the Father of all verse.
Flush every thing that hath a vermeil hue,
Let the rose glow intense and warm the air,
And let the clouds of even and of morn
Float in voluptuous fleeces o'er the hills;
Let the red wine within the goblet boil,
Cold as a bubbling well; let faint-lipp'd shells,
On sands, or in great deeps, vermilion turn
Through all their labyrinths; and let the maid
Blush keenly, as with some warm kiss surpris'd.

(iii. 13–22)

Many readers must have been disconcerted by these lines, which
have a hectic quality much less impressive than the opening of
Book I. W. J. Bate, for example, remarks that 'the imagery,
frequently the idiom, even the conception of Apollo himself,
begin to remind us disturbingly of *Endymion*'.[28] My immediate
concern is to point out that one reason for the marked change of
style is that sculptural forms are giving way to imagery from
painting. Just as the cold sculptural forms which suggest sterility
at the beginning of *The Eve of St. Agnes* are succeeded by richness
and colour as Madeline makes her appearance, so the arrival of the
triumphant new generation of deities in *Hyperion* is heralded by
a burst of colour. Keats is once again writing 'Instructions to a
Painter'.

Who is the painter to be, and what is he to do? It is clear that
he must be a Venetian. A line that has already been quoted,

Some Titian colours touch'd into real life,

gives the effect that is required, and it is tempting to suppose that
the maid who is to

Blush keenly, as with some warm kiss surpris'd,

may have been suggested by Titian's 'Bacchus and Ariadne'. The
description of Apollo here reminds us of Bacchus in that painting,
and one remembers that Bacchus–Apollo figures exist, one being
the work of Poussin.[29] Yet it is hard to believe that any one
painting lies behind the description, and if we turn to Spence's
Polymetis we find there a full description of Apollo and of 'his
golden tresses famed'. It is interesting to notice that Spence
quotes a passage from Tibullus, 'the rather, because I suspect it
contains several strokes taken from some very celebrated

pictures'.[30] This passage shows that Keats's insistence on different shades of red in his description of Apollo was thoroughly orthodox:

> candor erat qualem praefert Latonia Luna,
> et color in niveo corpore purpureus,
> ut iuveni primum virgo deducta marito
> inficitur teneras ore rubente genas.[31]

But we notice particularly the emphasis that Spence lays on the eyes of Apollo:

There is one thing . . . which seems peculiar to Apollo; and of which we might have had as strong an idea from the painters of old, as we have of his fine hair from the statuaries, had the works of the former been so durable as those of the latter. All one can say of it now is, that there was probably, in the old pictures of Apollo, a certain brightness beaming from his eyes; and, perhaps, diffused all over his face; in the same manner, as the body of the principal figure is all luminous and resplendent, in the famous nativity by Correggio; or the transfiguration, by Raphael. What made me first suspect this, was the antient poets speaking so often of the brightness of Apollo's face, and the beaming splendour of his eyes. . . . Apollo was usually represented with a particular flow of light beaming from his eyes.[32]

Elsewhere[33] Spence quotes from the *Metamorphoses*, iv. 192–3:

> . . . quid nunc, Hyperione nate,
> forma colorque tibi radiataque lumina prosunt?

Such passages must have been in Keats's mind when he described the 'gloomless' eyes of Apollo and wrote lines 120–3 of Book III:

> . . . Thus the God,
> While his enkindled eyes, with level glance
> Beneath his white soft temples, stedfast kept
> Trembling with light upon Mnemosyne.

These are fine lines, but what we lack in the description of Apollo is any definite posture or attitude. Whereas Saturn has been 'stationed' perfectly at the beginning of the poem, all that we hear of Apollo, when he is introduced, is that

> [He] in the morning twilight wandered forth
> Beside the osiers of a rivulet,
> Full ankle-deep in lilies of the vale.   (iii. 33–35)

As he stands weeping in this vaguely described setting, 'an awful

Goddess' approaches him, much as Diana approaches the kneeling Endymion in Poussin's 'Diana and Endymion'.

This goddess of 'antique mien and robed form' is Mnemosyne, the mother of the Muses. She tells him that she is

> . . . an ancient Power
> Who hath forsaken old and sacred thrones
> For prophecies of thee, and for the sake
> Of loveliness new born.   (iii. 76–79)

As he gazes at her Apollo finds that he can read

> A wondrous lesson in [her] silent face:
> Knowledge enormous makes a God of me.
> Names, deeds, gray legends, dire events, rebellions,
> Majesties, sovran voices, agonies,
> Creations and destroyings, all at once
> Pour into the wide hollows of my brain,
> And deify me, as if some blithe wine
> Or bright elixir peerless I had drunk,
> And so become immortal.   (iii. 112–20)

There follows the apotheosis of Apollo:

> Soon wild commotions shook him, and made flush
> All the immortal fairness of his limbs;
> Most like the struggle at the gate of death;
> Or liker still to one who should take leave
> Of pale immortal death, and with a pang
> As hot as death's is chill, with fierce convulse
> Die into life: so young Apollo anguish'd:
> His very hair, his golden tresses famed
> Kept undulation round his eager neck.
> During the pain Mnemosyne upheld
> Her arms as one who prophesied.—At length
> Apollo shriek'd;—and lo! from all his limbs
> Celestial * * * * [34]

It is inevitable that we should wonder how *Hyperion* would
have continued. The only firm information that we have is Woodhouse's statement that the poem

would have treated of the dethronement of Hyperion, the former god of
the Sun, by Apollo—and incidentally of those of Oceanus by Neptune,
of Saturn by Jupiter, etc., and of the war of the Giants for Saturn's re-
establishment—with other events, of which we have but very dark hints

in the mythological poets of Greece and Rome. In fact, the incidents would have been pure creations of the poet's brain.[35]

Since Keats seems to have modified his plan after he had given Woodhouse this outline of the poem,[36] that does not take us very far; but it is clear that one of the major problems facing him was that of investing Apollo with the profound significance required of the protagonist of an epic poem.

As the language of Greek mythology came as easily to Keats as to the painters of the Renaissance, it is worth quoting Jean Seznec's account of the enigmatic appearance of Apollo in the Stanza della Segnatura, the astonishing room in the Vatican which was so enigmatically painted by Raphael:

> Apollo appears three times. His statue and a statue of Minerva adorn the Portico of Athens, where thoughtful groups, dominated by the lofty figures of Aristotle and Plato, give us one more illustration of the series of Liberal Arts, handmaidens of Philosophy. In the vault, witnessing the torture of Marsyas, Apollo symbolizes the victory of the mind over the dark world of matter. Last of all, in the fresco above the window, he is shown surrounded by Muses, playing his viol on the bank of the Castalian spring—the poets ascending the slope toward him, at the call of his song.[37]

Seznec goes on to discuss the significance of these portrayals of Apollo and to reject the suggestion that Apollo is 'the center about which these ideal spheres gravitate . . . the incarnation of pagan art and reason':

> No; there is no doubt that Apollo is not the principal theme nor the chief organizing force of the whole composition; he is not its soul. For it gives expression to a hierarchy of which he is not the summit. Plato, in the *School of Athens*, points upward at the sky, and the whole movement of the fresco centers in this culminating gesture . . . .[38]

Pico della Mirandola said that Christ was the only true Apollo, while in the painting of the Italian Renaissance, as Seznec remarks, Christ often inherited the iconography as well as many of the attributes of the classical Apollo.[39] But Keats is not writing in the Christian tradition. In *Hyperion* it is clear that Apollo was in fact to be 'the principal theme [and] the chief organizing force of the whole composition'. He *was* to be its soul. It is therefore worth considering whether Keats intended to make Apollo more than just the God of the Sun and of Poetry. We may remember

Seznec's observation on the place of Apollo in the encyclopaedic tradition of the fifteenth century:

Not only does he conduct the choir of the Muses, who set in motion the Planets . . ., but he himself has his abode in the midst of the Planets 'like the Dorian mode amid the strings of the lyre'.

In medio residens complectitur omnia Phoebus.

He is thus both the origin and the center of the Universal Harmony.[40]

In the work of the German humanist Conrad Celtes, as Edgar Wind points out, we find an attempt to illustrate the Orphic theology in which 'in the place of God the Father blessing Christ, we see Jupiter hovering over his son Apollo'.[41] If *Hyperion* had been completed—if (one is tempted to say) it could have been completed—it is at least conceivable that it would have developed into a pagan theodicy in which Apollo would have emerged as an almost Christ-like figure, like Prometheus in *Prometheus Unbound.*

But this is merely speculation, and against it there stand two significant facts. The first is that none of the earlier references to Apollo in Keats makes him more than the God of the Sun and the God of Poetry. These are two great roles, but they would hardly be enough for the central figure in an epic of comprehensive significance. Nowhere (we notice) does Keats by this point in time hint at Apollo's other role as the God of Healing (of which he must have been well aware). The other fact is simply that Keats gave up the poem. I am inclined to agree with Miss Ward's conjecture that Keats came to see that 'the conflict between his first optimistic theme and his increasingly tragic view of the individual's destiny could no longer be resolved in the character of Apollo'.[42] Even Leigh Hunt complained that 'Apollo, when he is superseding his divine predecessor, and undergoing his transformation into a Divus Major, suffers a little too exquisitely among his lilies'.[43] And while this may be partly due to an inadequacy of poetic technique, it is certainly also due to an inadequacy about the conception of Apollo. Keats may even have sensed something of the limitations in Apollo that Haydon had noted in his Diary, probably after one of his early conversations with Keats:

No man feels more acutely than myself the poetical beauties of the Pagan mythology. Apollo, with his fresh cheek & God like beauty, rising like a gossamer from out a laurel grove, heated with love, after having panted on the bosom of some wandering nymph, is rich, beaming, rapturous! But these are beauties fit for those who live in perpetual enjoyment of immortality, without a care or a grief, or a want. But what consolation to the poor, what relief to the widow & the orphan, to the sick, or the oppressed? Could the minds of such beings turn for assistance to a thoughtless & beautiful youth, warm with love & wine, just rising from having debauched a girl? Christianity is a religion adapted to give relief to the wretched & hope to the good, and Christ having suffered is a bond of sympathy between Man & his Saviour that nothing in any other religion before or after affords.[44]

Although Keats had no intention of embracing Christianity, he may well have felt that in his portrayal of Apollo he was in danger of turning back towards the Realm of Flora and old Pan. That was not the country towards which Apollo himself had seemed to be beckoning him. And so he laid *Hyperion* aside for a while, before returning to it in a brief and desperate attempt to 'devote himself rather to the ardours than the pleasures of Song'.[45]

XI

THREE LOVE STORIES

> Most artists at this time could create with equal ease in either style, and all critics could praise equally the Grecian or the medieval, for either could be made to accord with modern tastes.
>
> JOHN STEEGMAN[1]

'I n my next Packet . . . I shall send you . . . St Agnes eve, and if I should have finished it a little thing called the "eve of St Mark" you see what fine mother Radcliff names I have.' So Keats wrote to George and his wife in February 1819,[2] and these two poems, with the slightly later lyric, 'La Belle Dame sans Merci', serve to remind us of an important fact about Keats. There were two worlds of the imagination that spoke to his heart and feelings: the world of classical antiquity, as re-created by the 'neo-classical' painters: and the world of the Middle Ages, as re-created by the antiquaries and romance-writers of the eighteenth century. If Claude and Poussin had painted medieval subjects, instead of classical, Keats would no doubt have followed their example. One of the many reasons for being glad that this did not happen is the fact that Keats, in turning away from medievalism, escaped from Chatterton as a poetic influence.

If it had not been for the 'medieval' enthusiasm of the period, however, we would have been without one of the most delightful poems in the English language. *The Eve of St. Agnes* is the work of a man who had read *The Faerie Queene* and *Romeo and Juliet*, Milton's minor poems and Browne's *Britannia's Pastorals*, *The Anatomy of Melancholy* and *The Castle of Indolence*, the romances of Mrs. Radcliffe and the skilful medieval fabrications of Thomas Chatterton. Above all it is the work of a man who was profoundly moved by the beauty of our ancient cathedral cities, and particularly by that of Chichester. Just as Goethe's imagination had been stirred by the sight of Strassburg Minster and Blake's 'fervent love of Gothic' had been kindled by Westminster Abbey and its tombs, so Keats was stimulated by the atmosphere of Chichester to write his most successful narrative poem.

Keats had always been conscious of the charm of medieval buildings. In lines already quoted from the 'Specimen of an Induction' in his first volume he had asked rhetorically:

> . . . How shall I
> Revive the dying tones of minstrelsy,
> Which linger yet about lone gothic arches?

It is not surprising that the resultant poem should be so markedly visual in its effect, 'rather a picture than a story', as Leigh Hunt remarked in his review.[3] This feature of the poem is evident from the opening stanza onwards:

> St. Agnes' Eve—Ah, bitter chill it was!
> The owl, for all his feathers, was a-cold;
> The hare limp'd trembling through the frozen grass,
> And silent was the flock in woolly fold:
> Numb were the Beadsman's fingers, while he told
> His rosary, and while his frosted breath,
> Like pious incense from a censer old,
> Seem'd taking flight for heaven, without a death,
> Past the sweet Virgin's picture, while his prayer he saith.

We notice that the cold is accompanied by numbness and silence: the muttering of the beadsman's prayer is the only sound that is mentioned. Nothing could be more appropriate than the reference to 'the sculptur'd dead' as we hear how the old man, 'meagre, barefoot, wan', returns 'along the chapel aisle by slow degrees':

> The sculptur'd dead, on each side, seem to freeze,
> Emprison'd in black, purgatorial rails:
> Knights, ladies, praying in dumb orat'ries,
> He passeth by; and his weak spirit fails
> To think how they may ache in icy hoods and mails.

'The germ of this thought, or something like it, is in Dante', Hunt commented, 'where he speaks of the figures that perform the part of sustaining columns in architecture. . . . Most wintry as well as penitential is the word "aching" in "icy hoods and mails"; and most felicitous the introduction of the Catholic idea in the word "purgatorial".'[4] But Keats's reading here is merely reinforcing the striking visual effect of the monuments that he had seen in Winchester, Chichester, and elsewhere. He is remembering such things as the fine medieval railings which surrounded the shrine of St. Richard, in the retrochoir in Chichester Cathedral.[5] Keats could not have found a visual image more appropriate to the effect that he wished to obtain. As Haydon wrote in the *Annals of the Fine Arts* during the summer of this same year:

> Many of the old Gothic monumental figures, with both their hands across their breasts, and lying on their backs, are infinitely more sublime than all the works of John di Bologna, Baccio Bandinelli, with the rest of Michelangelo's imitators, or his own twisted male figures at the Medici tombs. There is in this immoveable stillness a look as if the figures were above the troubles of life, and saw through the imbecility of appetite or passion.[6]

Hazlitt was later to comment that 'sculpture, though not proper to express health or life or motion, accords admirably with the repose of the tomb',[7] and that is how Keats uses it here. We are about to hear a story of 'breathing human passion';[8] but first, as a contrast, we are shown the lifeless memorials of men and women who lived and died many centuries ago. The forms of the angels, high in the cornices, form a silent chorus to the action, a fitting link between the effigies on the tombs and the youthful revellers who soon come bursting on the scene, accompanied by the rich sound of music:

> The carved angels, ever eager-eyed,
> Star'd, where upon their heads the cornice rests,
> With hair blown back, and arms put cross-wise on their breasts.

Here, as de Sélincourt pointed out, 'the very architecture seems to be taking a silent part in the action. Such passages illustrate the manner in which the art of Keats at times approximates to the art of painting.'[9]

The most celebrated visual imagery in the whole poem occurs in stanza xxiv:

> A casement high and triple-arch'd there was,
> All garlanded with carven imag'ries
> Of fruits, and flowers, and bunches of knot-grass,
> And diamonded with panes of quaint device,
> Innumerable of stains and splendid dyes,

> As are the tiger-moth's deep-damask'd wings;
> And in the midst, 'mong thousand heraldries,
> And twilight saints, and dim emblazonings,
> A shielded scutcheon blush'd with blood of queens and kings.

In his brilliant study, *John Keats: The Living Year*, Mr. Robert Gittings has suggested that this description is based on the windows in Stansted Chapel, which Keats visited on the 25th of January 1819.[10] I am inclined to think that Keats was drawing on his memories of various stained-glass windows, and that one cannot point to any particular window as the original of the description. What is certain is that no other poet has succeeded so well in finding words with which to express the characteristic richness and mystery of painted glass. It is a perfect background for Madeline herself:

> Full on this casement shone the wintry moon,
> And threw warm gules on Madeline's fair breast,
> As down she knelt for heaven's grace and boon;
> Rose-bloom fell on her hands, together prest,
> And on her silver cross soft amethyst,
> And on her hair a glory, like a saint.

This picture is bound to remind us of the kneeling figure of an adoring saint in a religious painting. Her head is surrounded by the 'glory' or halo of a saint, while the mention of wings assimilates her to an angel.

It is characteristic of Keats that a number of literary reminiscences also contributed to this strikingly visual passage. Mr. E. C. Pettet has suggested that Keats remembered *The Lay of the Last Minstrel* as he wrote these stanzas,[11] while a forgotten poem published in 1815 and dedicated to Scott also contains a number of passages that remind us fleetingly both of *The Eve of St. Agnes* and of 'The Eve of St. Mark'. This is *The Fair Isabel of Cotehele, A Cornish Romance*, written by Richard Polwhele and published by the same James Cawthorn whom Keats and Brown had to dinner one day in 1819.[12] Canto I, section xiv, is particularly relevant:

> Thro' diamond panes of storied glass
> Scarce could the light of morning pass.
> Yet 'twas enough, through each dim pane,
> The room with richer tints to stain;
> Colouring, upon the shrine below,

The crucifix with finer glow,
And from its polish'd brilliance raying,
And on the Virgin's image playing,
But, where an amber radiance fell,
Illumining fair ISABEL!
No muse, in sooth, could paint it true—
So soft it was, and sombrous too!

The halo round Madeline's head probably derives from a Hazlitt lecture. In the seventh of his *Lectures on the English Comic
Writers* Hazlitt had contrasted Hogarth's characters from
common life with the 'patriarchs and apostles, prophets and
founders of religion, saints and martyrs [and] angels' painted
by Raphael, saying of the latter:

The light which they have kindled in the world, is reflected back
upon their faces: the awe and homage which has been paid to them, is
seated upon their brow, *and encircles them like a glory.* All those who
come before them, are conscious of a superior presence.[13]

We know that Keats borrowed a manuscript of Hazlitt's lectures
shortly before he wrote *The Eve of St. Agnes*, for on the 2nd of
January we find him quoting with approval from the sixth
lecture. It is appropriate that a phrase of Hazlitt's about Raphael, 'who lifted the human form half way to heaven',[14] should
have contributed to one of the greatest passages of verbal
painting in the poetry of Keats. Yet it is not merely verbal
painting: the glowing colour at this point is not only decorative:
it also symbolizes the sexual excitement of the lovers and contrasts brilliantly with the colourlessness and cold at the beginning of the poem.[15]

The element of the local and visual in the inspiration of 'The
Eve of Saint Mark' was explicitly acknowledged by Keats, who
described it as 'a Poem . . . quite in the spirit of Town quietude'
and told George and his wife that he thought it would give them
'the sensation of walking about an old county Town in a coolish
evening'.[16] The opening lines make it clear what he meant:

Upon a Sabbath-day it fell;
Twice holy was the Sabbath-bell,
That call'd the folk to evening prayer;
The city streets were clean and fair
From wholesome drench of April rains;

.   .   .   .   .

Twice holy was the sabbath-bell:
The silent streets were crowded well
With staid and pious companies,
Warm from their fire-side orat'ries;
And moving, with demurest air,
To even-song, and vesper prayer.
Each arched porch, and entry low,
Was fill'd with patient folk and slow,
With whispers hush, and shuffling feet,
While play'd the organ loud and sweet.

As Keats himself commented, as he introduced the poem, 'The great beauty of Poetry is, that it makes every thing every place interesting—The palatine venice and the abbotine Winchester are equally interesting.' It is easy to see why this poem, with its picture of Bertha reading an old missal, her eyes 'dazed with saintly imag'ries', and its descriptions of the decorated screen beside her and of her shadow on the wall, should have made such an appeal to the Pre-Raphaelites.[17] The visual quality of the poem even comes out strongly in the description of the footnotes in the book that Bertha is reading:

Sometimes the learned eremite,
With golden star, or dagger bright,
Referr'd to pious poesies
Written in smallest crow-quill size
Beneath the text;

while Mr. Gittings[18] has convincingly traced the strange jumble of pictures in the book to the east windows of Stansted Chapel, in which Keats saw most of the images which he describes—

. . . a thousand things,—
The stars of Heaven, and angels' wings,
Martyrs in a fiery blaze,
Azure saints in silver rays,
Aaron's breastplate, and the seven
Candlesticks John saw in Heaven,
The winged Lion of Saint Mark,
And the Covenantal Ark,
With its many mysteries,
Cherubim and golden mice.

*   *   *   *   *   *

In *The Eve of St. Agnes* and 'The Eve of Saint Mark' we see the

'Gothic', medieval, Chattertonian aspect of Keats's imagination. In *Lamia*, a third love story which he wrote during the summer of 1819, the inspiration is again predominantly classical. Keats found the story in Burton, who took it from the *Life of Apollonius* by Philostratus. As we read this poem we find ourselves once more in the world of Greek romance, the world of *Daphnis and Chloe* and *The Golden Ass*, the world that gave Psyche to the painters of the Renaissance and so provided Keats with the subject for the first of the Odes which he had written during the spring of the same year.

At the beginning of the Tale we are transported to the Golden Age, in lines which remind us that Keats had been studying the versification of John Dryden:

> Upon a time, before the faery broods
> Drove Nymph and Satyr from the prosperous woods,
> Before King Oberon's bright diadem,
> Sceptre, and mantle, clasp'd with dewy gem,
> Frighted away the Dryads and the Fauns
> From rushes green, and brakes, and cowslip'd lawns,
> The ever-smitten Hermes empty left
> His golden throne, bent warm on amorous theft.

This is the mood of a Bacchanal. Keats may be remembering the portrayal of Hermes (or Mercury) on the ceiling of the Farnesina, where the amorous god is surrounded by rich fruit and flowers and by nymphs, and seems to be flying straight towards the spectator; but the description is not detailed enough to make any specific identification convincing. The same is true of the lines in which the spirit of Lamia wanders about,

> Whether to faint Elysium, or where
> Down through tress-lifting waves the Nereids fair
> Wind into Thetis' bower by many a pearly stair;
> Or where God Bacchus drains his cups divine,
> Stretch'd out, at ease, beneath a glutinous pine;
> Or where in Pluto's gardens palatine
> Mulciber's columns gleam in far piazzian line. (i. 206–12)

A more precise visual reminiscence occurs a few lines later, when we hear how

> She saw the young Corinthian Lycius
> Charioting foremost in the envious race,
> Like a young Jove with calm uneager face.[19]

That last line could only have been written by a man who was
remembering pictures of Jupiter. We are reminded of a sentence
already quoted from a letter Keats wrote to John Hamilton
Reynolds the previous year: 'Now it is more noble to sit like
Jove than to fly like Mercury.'[20] In paintings Jove is commonly
shown sitting at his ease, 'with calm uneager face', while Mercury flies round the world to do his bidding.

As Lamia awaits Lycius we have a scene very much in the
spirit of Claude Lorrain:

> . . . Freshly blew
> The eastern soft wind, and his galley now
> Grated the quaystones with her brazen prow
> In port Cenchreas, from Egina isle
> Fresh anchor'd; whither he had been awhile
> To sacrifice to Jove, whose temple there
> Waits with high marble doors for blood and incense rare.
>
> (i. 222–8)

The description of Lycius, a few lines later, is also highly visual
in its effect:

> Till she saw him, as once she pass'd him by,
> Where 'gainst a column he leant thoughtfully
> At Venus' temple porch, 'mid baskets heap'd
> Of amorous herbs and flowers, newly reap'd
> Late on that eve, as 'twas the night before
> The Adonian feast.   (i. 315–20)

The poem as a whole is an extraordinary mixture of good and
bad, high accomplishment and utter tastelessness. After the
Huntian observation that 'There is not such a treat among them
all . . . As a real woman'—for example—we come on the
brilliant description of Corinth:

> Men, women, rich and poor, in the cool hours,
> Shuffled their sandals o'er the pavement white,
> Companion'd or alone; while many a light
> Flared, here and there, from wealthy festivals,
> And threw their moving shadows on the walls,
> Or found them cluster'd in the corniced shade
> Of some arch'd temple door, or dusky colonnade.
>
> (i. 355–61)

Many of the more successful passages describe scenes which

Keats can never have seen. An example is the passage about the
lovers in Part II:

> . . . Side by side
> They were enthroned, in the even tide,
> Upon a couch, near to a curtaining
> Whose airy texture, from a golden string,
> Floated into the room, and let appear
> Unveil'd the summer heaven, blue and clear,
> Betwixt two marble shafts.   (ii. 16–22)

That reads like a description of a painting—perhaps something
in the mood of Giulio Romano's 'Cupid and Psyche' (Plate
XXV). It is true that there is no 'curtaining' in Giulio's
picture, but we notice that this is a detail that would never have
occurred to a poet who was unacquainted with painting, and that
Keats was aware that one of the functions of such a curtain in
the composition of a picture is to point up the colours which
the painter has used.

The description of Lycius a little later is almost certainly
indebted to sculpture:

> Fine was [his] mitigated fury, like
> Apollo's presence when in act to strike
> The serpent.   (ii. 78–80)

The serpent which Apollo 'struck' was Python, sent by Jove to
persecute Latona; and he struck it, not with his hand, but with
an arrow. There can be little doubt that Keats is here referring
to the Apollo Belvedere, which was so often discussed at this
time. While the statue shows Apollo just after he has fired the
arrow, Keats describes him the moment before he releases it.
The immediately preceding lines—

> His passion, cruel grown, took on a hue
> Fierce and sanguineous as 'twas possible
> In one whose brow had no dark veins to swell

—may be compared with a passage in Milman's *The Belvidere
Apollo* in which he describes the young god 'in settled majesty
of proud disdain':

> All, all divine—no struggling muscle glows
> Through heaving vein no mantling life-blood flows,
> But animate with deity alone,

In deathless glory lives the breathing stone.
Bright kindling with a conqueror's stern delight,
His keen eye tracks the arrow's fateful flight:
Burns his indignant cheek with vengeful fire,
And his lip quivers with insulting ire.

The last passage in *Lamia* which demands our attention is the
description of the interior of the banqueting room that comes
magically into existence for the wedding of Lycius and Lamia:

Of wealthy lustre was the banquet-room,
Fill'd with pervading brilliance and perfume:
Before each lucid pannel fuming stood
A censer fed with myrrh and spiced wood,
Each by a sacred tripod held aloft,
Whose slender feet wide-swerv'd upon the soft
Wool-woofed carpets: fifty wreaths of smoke
From fifty censers their light voyage took
To the high roof, still mimick'd as they rose
Along the mirror'd walls by twin-clouds odorous.
Twelve sphered tables, by silk seats insphered,
High as the level of a man's breast rear'd
On libbard's paws, upheld the heavy gold
Of cups and goblets, and the store thrice told
Of Ceres' horn.   (ii. 173–87)

The architecture of the banqueting hall may be Gothic in
inspiration, but the interior is thoroughly 'Regency'. As Mario
Praz once pointed out,

The classicism of Keats is . . . a Regency classicism, that is to say
the resultant of a mixture of disparate elements which miraculously
blend together better than the components of Piranesi's chimneys or
of Regency furniture.[21]

Lamia is not a wholly successful poem, nor a wholly serious one;
yet it is illuminating to recognize in it the same blending of
disparate elements, the same Regency neo-classicism, that had
already produced the 'Ode to Psyche' and the 'Ode on a Grecian
Urn'.

XII

AN ACT OF PAGAN WORSHIP: THE 'ODE TO PSYCHE'

Proclus in his *Scholia* on Plato's *Cratylus*, describes the world united in Apollo and the Muses; in Apollo, as conducting intellectual and musical harmony; in the Muses, as giving harmony to the soul. . . . Still more beautiful was that fabulous device of Cupid and Psyche, by which this union was shadowed forth; for though it was a prototype of the marriage rites in its first sense, yet, agreeably to the double, or as Lord Bacon calls it, the germinant, sense in these matters, it seems to have been designed also to unfold by a more recondite sense, all that is agreeable and lovely, all that is intellectual and sublime, by a mystical, divine union in the soul of man.

The Reflector[1]

CRITICS have never felt at their ease with the 'Ode to Psyche'. It was the first of the mature Odes to be written, and Keats himself tells us that it was 'the first and the only' poem with which he had 'taken even moderate pains';[2] yet there is something artificial and *voulu* about it, and there remains the problem of what exactly it is about. In this chapter I shall try to do something to place the poem in its mythographical tradition, and also attempt to show its significance as the last of Keats's pagan hymns[3] as well as the first of the Odes that were to be printed in 1820. Written as it was

> . . . in these days so far retir'd
> From happy pieties,

the 'Ode to 'Psyche' reaches back to the nostalgia of

> Glory and loveliness have passed away,

but also forwards, however tentatively, to the poems that Keats was never to write: the poems in which he aspired to become 'a miserable and mighty Poet of the human Heart'.[4]

Already in 'I stood tip-toe' we find that the story of Cupid and Psyche made a deep appeal to Keats:

So felt he, who first told, how Psyche went
On the smooth wind to realms of wonderment;
What Psyche felt, and Love, when their full lips
First touch'd; what amorous, and fondling nips
They gave each other's cheeks; with all their sighs,
And how they kist each other's tremulous eyes:
The silver lamp,—the ravishment,—the wonder—
The darkness,—loneliness,—the fearful thunder;
Their woes gone by, and both to heaven upflown,
To bow for gratitude before Jove's throne.   (141–50)

He must already have met it in a number of different places. Few passages of poetry delighted him more than the Garden of Adonis in *The Faerie Queene*, and there the fable of Cupid and Psyche occurs prominently. Keats also knew the lines at the end of *Comus* in which it is proclaimed that from the marriage of Cupid and Psyche:

Two blissful twins are to be born,
Youth and Joy; so *Jove* hath sworn.

The story is prominent in the minor poetry of the later eighteenth century. In *The Botanic Garden*, for example, Erasmus Darwin describes how Hymen

Joins the fond pair, indulgent to their vows,
And hides with mystic veil their blushing brows.
Round their fair forms their mingling arms they fling,
Meet with warm lip, and clasp with rustling wing.—
—Hence plastic Nature, as Oblivion whelms
Her fading forms, repeoples all her realms;
Soft Joys disport on purple plumes unfurl'd,
And Love and Beauty rule the willing world.   (iv. 55–62)

Keats must have read some of Darwin's verse, and although he had a low opinion of it[5] it is worth noticing that the lines just quoted were given in the prose version of the story of Cupid and Psyche that appeared in *The Champion* on the 29th of January 1815.[6] If Keats looked into *The Temple of Nature*, another of Darwin's poems, he will have found a further version of the story.[7] Mrs. Tighe's *Psyche*, which we know to have delighted him early in his career, clearly remained in his memory to contribute more than one echo to the Ode.[8] But of course, as Keats knew, 'he, who first told' the story was Apuleius:

You must recollect that Psyche was not embodied as a goddess before the time of Apuleius the Platonist who lived after the Augustan age, and consequently the Goddess was never worshipped or sacrificed to with any of the ancient fervour—and perhaps never thought of in the old religion—I am more orthodox than to let a hethen Goddess be so neglected.   (ii. 106)

The Golden Ass was a favourite book with Keats and his friends. In one of the essays in his *Table-Talk* Hazlitt gives us a glimpse of the sort of conversation in which Keats must sometimes have taken part:

W—, M—, and myself were all that remained one evening. We had sat together several hours without being tired of one another's company. . . . W— then spoke of Lucius Apuleius and his Golden Ass, which contains the story of Cupid and Psyche, with other matter rich and rare, and went on to the romance of Heliodorus, Theagenes and Chariclea. This, as he affirmed, opens with a pastoral landscape equal to Claude, and in it the presiding deities of Love and Wine appear in all their pristine strength, youth and grace, crowned and worshipped as of yore. The night waned, but our glasses brightened, enriched with the pearls of Grecian story. Our cup-bearer slept in a corner of the room, like another Endymion, in the pale ray of an half-extinguished lamp.[9]

In this revealing passage we notice not only the enthusiasm for Greek mythology that was characteristic of Keats and his circle, but also the natural association of literature and painting which is the clue to so much in his poetry.

    The antecedents of the 'Ode to Psyche' are the very early 'Ode to Apollo', which is like a painting of Parnassus come to life;[10] the Hymns to Pan, Neptune, and Diana in *Endymion*;[11] the single stanza of the 'Ode to May', in which Keats asks if he may sing to Maia

As thou wast hymned on the shores of Baiæ,

and looks back nostalgically to the song of the ancient poets,

Rich in the simple worship of a day;[12]

and the sonnet 'To Sleep', which occurs in the same letter as the Ode itself, and which is in fact a Hymn to Sleep.[13] The 'Hymn to Pan' is particularly revealing. At first the 'satyr king' is adored as a nature-god, but at line 288 he is suddenly invested with a much profounder significance:

Dread opener of the mysterious doors
Leading to universal knowledge—see,
Great son of Dryope,
The many that are come to pay their vows
With leaves about their brows!

Be still the unimaginable lodge
For solitary thinkings; such as dodge
Conception to the very bourne of heaven,
Then leave the naked brain: be still the leaven,
That spreading in this dull and clodded earth
Gives it a touch ethereal—a new birth:
Be still a symbol of immensity . . . .

We will not understand the 'Ode to Psyche' unless we recognize that it is essentially a pagan act of worship. Keats himself
draws attention to this when he proclaims that he is 'more
orthodox than to let a hethen Goddess be so neglected'. Wordsworth's comment on the Hymn to Pan—'a very pretty piece of
Paganism'[14]—is no less applicable to this later poem. Whereas
Milton wrote Odes 'On the Morning of Christ's Nativity', 'The
Passion', and 'Upon the Circumcision', Keats wrote Hymns to
Pan, Neptune, and Diana and Odes to Apollo, Maia, and Psyche.

But why to Psyche? Was it only because she had been 'neglected' that Keats decided to become her 'priest'? If we wish to
answer these questions, we must consider for a moment some of
the allegorical interpretations of the fable of Cupid and Psyche.

Perhaps the most influential of all was that of Philippus
Beroaldus, first published in 1500. According to this, the story
describes what happens when the human Soul, child of God and
of Matter, sets herself up as superior to Venus, goddess of Love.
As a punishment, Venus entangles her with Desire. Urged on by
her wicked sisters, Flesh and Free Will, the Soul betrays Desire
and wounds him. She is consequently expelled from his house,
scourged by Consuetudo (Custom) and Tristities (Sadness),
and subjected to a series of ordeals by Earth, Fire, Water, and
Air. In each case she has to be saved from the element that is
testing her by one of the other elements: for example she is
saved from Earth by the intervention of Fire.[15] In the end Desire
intervenes to rescue the Soul from the consequences of her errors
and has her immortalized in the presence of all the gods. Desire
and the Soul are then married, at a great wedding feast, in order

to chain the wayward activities of Desire. Voluptas, the child
born from their union, is the *summum bonum* of the philosophers.

   Thomas Taylor the Platonist, whose translation of *The Fable
of Cupid and Psyche* was published in 1795 and may well have
been known to Keats, gives a rather different interpretation of
the story. I quote from his introduction:

   When Psyche is represented as descending from the summit of a lofty
mountain into a beautiful valley, this signifies the descent of the soul
from the intelligible world into a mundane condition of being, but yet
without abandoning its establishment in the Heavens.... This invisible
husband proves afterwards to be Love; that is to say, the soul, while
established in the Heavens, is united with pure *desire* ... or, in other
words, is not fascinated with outward form. But in this beautiful
palace she is attacked by the machinations of her two sisters, who
endeavour to persuade her to explore the form of her unknown husband. The sisters ... signify imagination and nature; just in the same
manner as reason is signified by Psyche. Their stratagems at length
take effect, and Psyche beholds and falls in love with Love; that is to
say, the rational part through the incentives of phantasy and the
vegetable power, becomes united with impure or terrene desire; for
vision is symbolical of union between the perceiver and thing perceived. In consequence ... Cupid, or *pure desire*, flies away, and Psyche,
or soul, is precipitated to earth. ... After this commence the wander-
ings of Psyche, or soul, in search of Love. ... The difficult tasks which
Psyche is obliged to execute ... are images of the mighty toils and
anxious cares which the soul must necessarily endure after her lapse,
in order to atone for her guilt, and recover her ancient residence in the
intelligible world. In accomplishing the last of these labours she is
represented as forced to descend even to the dark regions of Hades;
by which it is evident that Psyche is the image of a soul that descends
to the very extremity of things, or that makes the most extended
progression before it returns. ... Cupid, however, or pure desire, at
length recovering his pristine vigor, rouses Psyche, or soul, from
her deadly lethargy. ... She ascends to her native heaven, becomes
lawfully united with Cupid, ... [and] lives the life of the immortals;
and the natural result of this union with pure desire is pleasure or
delight.[16]

Perhaps it is not altogether absurd to juxtapose Beroaldus's
view that the ordeals suffered by Psyche to regain Amor are to be
understood as stages in a mystical initiation, or the elaborate
interpretation of Thomas Taylor, with a famous passage which
occurs in the same letter as the 'Ode to Psyche' itself:

The common cognomen of this world among the misguided and superstitious is 'a vale of tears' from which we are to be redeemed by a certain arbitrary interposition of God and taken to Heaven—What a little circumscribed straightened notion! Call the world if you Please 'The vale of Soul-making' Then you will find out the use of the world. . . . I say '*Soul making*' Soul as distinguished from an Intelligence— There may be intelligences or sparks of the divinity in millions—but they are not Souls till they acquire identities, till each one is personally itself. . . . This . . . I think . . . a grander system of salvation than the [Christian] religion—or rather it is a system of Spirit-creation. . . . I can scarcely express what I but dimly perceive . . . that you may judge the more clearly I will put it in the most homely form possible—I will call the *world* a School instituted for the purpose of teaching little children to read—I will call the *human heart* the *horn Book* used in that School— and I will call the *Child able to read, the Soul* made from that *school* and its *hornbook*. Do you not see how necessary a World of Pains and troubles is to school an Intelligence and make it a soul? (ii. 101–2)

But the transition to the poem is less easily made.

The first thing that strikes one, on setting the 'Ode to Psyche' against the background of the story and its interpreters, is that whatever significance Keats saw in the fable he here concerns himself only with the happy ending. He describes Cupid and Psyche,

Their woes gone by, and both to heaven upflown,[17]

and there we do not see them 'bow[ing] for gratitude before Jove's throne', but in the present enjoyment of their love. Keats makes no reference at all to Psyche's initial offence in wishing to see her lover or to the ordeals to which she was subjected. He describes Cupid and Psyche in a setting which owes a good deal to *The Faerie Queene* as well as to *The Golden Ass*, reminding us particularly of Spenser's description of the scene in the Garden of Adonis:

And his true loue faire *Psyche* with him playes,
Faire *Psyche* to him lately reconcyld,
After long troubles and vnmeet vpbrayes,
With which his mother Venus her reuyld,
And eke himselfe her cruelly exyld:
But now in stedfast loue and happy state
She with him liues, and hath him borne a chyld,
Pleasure, that doth both gods and men aggrate,
Pleasure, the daughter of *Cupid* and *Psyche* late.   (III. vi. 50)

'Pleasure', the last word in the story as it had been told by Apuleius himself:

> Jupiter . . . toke a potte of immortalitie, and said: Holde Psyches and drinke to the ende thou maist be immortall, and that Cupide may be thine everlastinge husbande. By and by the great bankette and marriage feast was sumptuously prepared, Cupide satte downe with his deere spouse betweene his armes. . . . Their drinke was Nectar the wine of the goddes, Vulcanus prepared supper, the howers decked up the house with Roses and other sweete smelles, the Graces threwe about baulme, the Muses sange with sweete harmony, Apollo tuned pleasauntly to the Harpe, Venus daunsed finely: Satirus and Paniscus plaide on their pipes: and thus Psiches was married to Cupide, and after she was delivered of a childe, whom we call Pleasure.[18]

'To expound the theory of divine Voluptas', as Wind remarks, 'there was no want of Neoplatonic witnesses',[19] yet there seems to be little point in searching the pages of 'Orpheus', Hermias, Proclus, Iamblichus, Dionysius the Areopagite, and Plotinus in search of a key to Keats. One is tempted, instead, to fall back on Erasmus Darwin, to whom Cupid and Psyche are simply love-deities. When Hymen leads them to the altar:

> 'Behold he cries, Earth! Ocean! Air above,,
> 'And hail the DEITIES OF SEXUAL LOVE!
> 'All forms of Life shall this fond Pair delight,
> 'And sex to sex the willing world unite.[20]

Images which occur in letters written soon after the Ode remind us that it was the work of a man who was deeply in love with Fanny Brawne, and with Love itself. On the 25th of July 1819, Keats tells Fanny Brawne that he will 'imagine you Venus tonight and pray, pray to your star like a Hethen'. On the 6th of August he parodies the Anglican litany when he tells her that they 'might spend a pleasant Year at Berne or Zurich—if it should please Venus to hear my "Beseech thee to hear us O Goddess" '. In October he tells her that he 'could be martyr'd for my Religion—Love is my religion. . . . My Creed is Love and you are its only tenet.' In a later letter of uncertain date he thanks Fanny Brawne for avoiding social life for his sake and says: 'I could build an Altar to you for it.'[21] It is difficult not to conclude that Fanny Brawne served (at least) as a sort of model for Psyche, and one is reminded of Raphael's manner of painting the fable, as described by Leigh Hunt:

He was so fond of La bella Fornarina that . . . when he painted the story of Cupid and Psyche on the walls of the Chigi palace, he was . . . perpetually going away and staying with his fair friend. . . . [So] Chigi at last prevailed on him to let him shut them both up together in the rooms that were to be adorned. They were so; and Cupid and Psyche were painted, as it were, at the light of her eyes.[22]

Whatever else it is, the 'Ode to Psyche' is a poem about love.

But it is also, at least potentially, something more. As we have already seen, the myths in which Keats was most deeply interested tended to be those which can be used to describe the origin of poetry. Keats probably knew the remark of Agathon in *The Symposium* that Eros is not only a poet himself but also 'the source of poetry in others',[23] and he certainly knew Hunt's masque, *The Descent of Liberty*, in which Poetry is addressed in these words:

> O best Enchantress, unconfined,
> Full of all the Mighty Mind,—
> Lustrous forehead laurel-leaved,
> Whom Psyche of her love conceived
> In the voiceful, golden house,
> When first he came mysterious,
> O spare us from addressing thee,
> All accomplished POETRY. . . .[24]

He must also have been acquainted with the view expressed in the epigraph to this chapter, by which the fable of Cupid and Psyche is taken to unfold 'all that is agreeable and lovely, all that is intellectual and sublime, by a mystical, divine union in the soul of man'. Although the Ode is not a profound enough poem to render a full investigation of the significance of Psyche to Keats either fruitful or possible, it seems clear that something of these interpretations of the myth has helped to colour his conception. It is not a Neoplatonic poem, but suggestions of Neoplatonism hang about it. We notice (for example) that the temple which Keats is going to build for Psyche is to be

> In some untrodden region of my *mind*,
> Where branched *thoughts*, new grown with pleasant pain,
> Instead of pines shall murmur in the wind.

He continues:

> A rosy sanctuary will I dress
> With the wreath'd trellis of a working *brain*,

> With buds, and bells, and stars without a name,
> With all the gardener *Fancy* e'er could *feign*,
> Who breeding flowers, will never breed the same.[25]

Throughout this description of the Garden of Delight that he
will build for Psyche there is a remarkable insistence on the
mind and its powers:

> And there shall be for thee all soft delight
> That shadowy *thought* can win.

This is the Realm of Flora with a difference. The flowers, the
trees and the other delights in this pleasaunce are the creation of
the Mind and the Imagination, as is appropriate when the
goddess to be honoured is the Human Soul itself.

As Thomas Taylor pointed out, in dedicating his translation
of *The Fable of Cupid and Psyche* 'To the President [Benjamin
West], Council, and Members of the Royal Academy', the story
'has been a favorite subject of the most eminent artists, ancient
and modern'. Ancient representations of Cupid and Psyche were
well known to Keats and his contemporaries. In a note to the
relevant passage from *The Botanic Garden*, for example,
Erasmus Darwin had written as follows:

> Described from an antient gem on a fine onyx in possession of the
> Duke of Marlborough, of which there is a beautiful print in Bryant's
> Mythol[ogy], Vol. II, p. 392. And from another antient gem of Cupid
> and Psyche embracing, of which there is a print in Spence's Polymetis,
> p. 82.[26]

No fewer than twenty of Tassie's gems portray Cupid and
Psyche, and certain of these are of classical origin. But just as
the story of Psyche as a goddess began with Apuleius, so its
most remarkable chapters were written in the Renaissance by
painters.[27] This makes particularly interesting the highly visual
description near the beginning of the Ode. As usual in the
Odes, the poet is in a trance-like state:

> I wander'd in a forest thoughtlessly,
>   And, on the sudden, fainting with surprise,
> Saw two fair creatures, couched side by side
>   In deepest grass, beneath the whisp'ring roof
> Of leaves and trembled blossoms, where there ran
>   A brooklet, scarce espied:

'Mid hush'd, cool-rooted flowers, fragrant-eyed,
  Blue, silver-white, and budded Tyrian,
They lay calm-breathing on the bedded grass;
  Their arms embraced, and their pinions too;
  Their lips touch'd not, but had not bid adieu,
As if disjoined by soft-handed slumber,
And ready still past kisses to outnumber
  At tender eye-dawn of aurorean love:
    The winged boy I knew;
But who wast thou, O happy, happy dove?
    His Psyche true!

It would be hard to find a passage that more aptly illustrates the force of Leigh Hunt's protest that

to say . . . that the poet does not include the painter in his more visible creations, is to deprive him of half his privileges. . . . Thousands of images start out of the *canvass* of his pages to laugh at the assertion.[28]

The reminder in Hunt's next sentence that 'the great Italian painters' derived 'half of the most bodily details of their subjects' from the poets is no less appropriate. In the 'Ode to Psyche' Keats found his inspiration in a passage of literature which had already had a memorable influence on the visual arts. The words of Apuleius and the images created by painters to illustrate his story were equally present in Keats's mind as he wrote.

The greatest of these paintings are the series by Raphael and his associates on the ceiling of the Farnesina Palace in Rome. Hazlitt once wrote that 'in the story of Cupid and Psyche' Raphael 'even surpassed himself in a certain swelling and voluptuous grace, as if beauty grew and ripened under his touch, and the very genius of ancient fable hovered over his enamoured pencil'.[29] 'If any thing could have raised my idea of Raphael higher', he wrote on another occasion, 'it would have been some of these frescoes. I would mention the group of the Graces in particular; they are true Goddesses. The fine flowing outline of the limbs, the variety of attitudes, the unconscious grace, the charming unaffected glow of the expression, are inimitable. Raphael never perhaps escaped so completely from the trammels of his first manner, as in this noble series of designs.'[30] Although both passages were written after the death of Keats, they may serve as a reminder of the enthusiastic admiration for Raphael among his friends. He must have known engravings of these

XXV. GIULIO ROMANO: Cupid and Psyche

XXVI. GIORDANO: The Worship of Psyche

O latest born and loveliest vision far
Of all Olympus' faded hierarchy!

XXVII. CANOVA: Cupid and Psyche

What Psyche felt, and Love, when their full lips
First touch'd.

xxviii. 'The group of Cupid and Psyche kissing.'

frescoes, and although Raphael has nothing corresponding to the central group in the Ode the voluptuous quality of his painting may well have influenced the poem. The gloriously rich borders of flowers and fruit with which Raphael's Cupid and Psyche are surrounded may have combined with the descriptions in Apuleius, Spenser and Mrs. Tighe to inspire the

> . . . cool-rooted flowers, fragrant-eyed,
> Blue, silver-white, and budded Tyrian

which we find in the Ode.[31] The other most famous series of paintings of this subject, that by Raphael's pupil Giulio Romano in the Sala di Psiche in the Palazzo del Te in Rome, is also very likely to have been known to Keats in engravings. At the right-hand extremity of 'The Marriage Feast of Cupid and Psyche' we find a highly erotic portrayal of the lovers on a couch in the open air, with fauns preparing to sacrifice a goat in the background (Plate XXV). This is one of the 'voluptuous reveries which enchant the palace', as Fuseli said in his second lecture.[32] Other series clearly deriving from Raphael's are to be found in the Castel Sant'Angelo in Rome and the Palazzo Doria in Genoa. A list of all the painters who have been inspired by the story of Cupid and Psyche would contain many dozens of names. A series of particular interest to us is that by Luca Giordano in London, which Keats could well have seen.[33] One of these paintings (Plate XXVI) shows Psyche being worshipped in a manner that seems to parody pictures of the Adoration of the Virgin Mary and which certainly recalls the 'Ode to Psyche'. 'Cupid and Psyche' was also a favourite subject with Salvator Rosa, and it was attempted by men of such varied manners and abilities as Reynolds, West, Richard Westall, Etty, David, and François Gérard. Fuseli's 'Eros and Dione', one of the plates in Darwin's *The Temple of Nature*, is in the same tradition. Canova, the sculptor whose taste has such a kinship with that of Keats, executed more than one 'Cupid and Psyche', as a writer recorded in the *Annals of the Fine Arts* for the 1st of June 1818.[34] A reproduction of one of these is given in Plate XXVII.

Knowledge of the iconographical tradition reveals the fact that Keats is on the whole 'orthodox' in his description of Cupid and Psyche, whatever he may be in his religion. In his poem, as one would expect, Cupid is given wings (the Greek word ψυχή means 'butterfly' as well as 'soul')—also described as 'pinions' and 'lucent fans'.[35] Why Keats should call Psyche a 'dove' is less clear. Doves traditionally draw the chariot of Venus,[36] while Cupid is often accompanied by a dove (as in Mrs. Tighe's poem);[37] perhaps Keats was chiefly concerned to find a rhyme for 'love'. About the torch at the end of the poem there is no problem:

> A bright torch, and a casement ope at night,
> To let the warm Love in!

Bate has suggested a reminiscence of the words of Apuleius, when he describes how Psyche was left abandoned on the rocks to await her unknown lover: 'The Torches . . . were put out.'[38] But as Cupid is conventionally portrayed with a torch, this is unnecessarily far-fetched. In *Polymetis* Spence describes a mischievous Cupid 'as intent to burn one with the torch he holds in his hand'.[39] Keats tells Psyche that he will leave out a torch for Cupid because it is the emblem of ardour, and also simply to guide Cupid to her temple.

But while the 'Ode to Psyche' has an obvious genealogy, literary and pictorial, there does not appear to be any one painting which supplies all the details for Keats's description of Cupid and Psyche,

> . . . couched side by side
> In deepest grass.

Such a painting may well have eluded my search—the work, perhaps, of one of the host of minor painters who streamed along in the wake of Raphael, or even of some minor or minimus English painter who exhibited at the Royal Academy or the British Institution. But on the whole it seems unlikely, and one revealing detail supports this view. Line 14,

> Blue, silver-white, and budded Tyrian,

reads differently in the letter:

> Blue, freckle-pink, and budded syrian.[40]

If Keats had been describing a painting he would not have been very likely to hesitate between 'freckle-pink' and 'silver-white', or between 'syrian' (a word with no colour significance) and 'Tyrian' (which means purple). Such a revision would not be surprising if he had been thinking of a print, but a print is less likely to disappear than a painting. It seems probable that Keats has here composed and painted his own picture, taking hints—as a good poet or painter will usually do—from any predecessor whose work appealed to him.

It remains a striking fact that a story which has inspired so many painters should lie behind the first of the Odes, and it is illuminating to compare Keats's attitude to the love of Cupid and Psyche with that of Wordsworth, if Haydon gives a fair account of the latter:

> Once I was walking with Wordsworth in Pall Mall, & we ran in to Christie's, where there was . . . in the corner . . . the group of Cupid & Psyche kissing (Plate XXVIII). After looking some time, he turned round to me with an expression I shall never forget, & said, 'The Dev-ils'.[41]

Along with his comment on the Hymn to Pan, this anecdote gives us a glimpse of the imaginative gulf which lies between these two poets. The visual representations of Cupid and Psyche helped to bring the fable to life in the imagination of Keats, and he was as attracted by the pagan delight in the senses which inspired them as Wordsworth appears to have been repelled. The 'Ode to Psyche' is the affirmation of a young man who had begun to hate parsons,[42] a defiant celebration of the 'happy pieties' which had for too long been banished by the 'melancholy round' of the church bells and the 'dreadful cares' of institutional Christianity.[43]

XIII

THE 'ODE ON A GRECIAN URN'

Painting can only make use of a single instant of the action, and must therefore choose the one which is most pregnant, and from which what precedes and what follows can be most easily gathered.   LESSING

The great principle of composition in Painting is to represent the event, doing and not done. . . . The moment a thing is done in Painting half the interest is gone; our power of exciting attention depends . . . upon the suspense we keep the mind in, regarding the past and the future.   HAYDON[1]

THE 'Ode on a Grecian Urn' is the most memorable outcome of the debate about the relations between Poetry and the Visual Arts which was pursued so vigorously at this time. But for this debate Keats would hardly have called the Urn a 'Cold Pastoral', while the third and fourth lines of the poem,

> Sylvan historian, who canst thus express
> A flowery tale more sweetly than our rhyme,

also have their background in this same controversy. Every reader of the Ode notices the emphasis that Keats throws on the silence of the Urn, with the words 'quietness', 'silence', 'unheard melodies', 'soft pipes', 'ditties of no tone', 'silent', and 'silent form'.[2] It is illuminating to set this feature of the poem against the famous observation attributed to Simonides, that a poem is a speaking picture, a picture a silent poem: an observation which was quoted time and time again by men like Spence and Caylus, and attacked by Lessing.[3] Haydon often referred to the saying, and in his Diary we find him describing one of his own paintings as 'silently speaking, full of beauty . . ., above . . . the passions & follies of the World, too elevated to speak'.[4] Nothing could be more appropriate than the fact that the Ode was first published in the *Annals of the Fine Arts*.[5]

As I have mentioned in Chapter III, one has only to turn over the pages of the *Annals* to be reminded how common a practice it was to write a poem inspired by a particular work of art. The habit was not confined to Keats and his circle. As it happens, there could be no more vivid illustration of the fashion than the subjects set for Prize Poems at Oxford at this time.[6] In 1806 the subject was 'A Recommendation of the Study of the Remains of Ancient Grecian and Roman Architecture, Sculpture, and Painting', while from 1810 to 1820 the subject every year was a work of classical art or architecture, as follows:

The Statue of the Dying Gladiator, The Parthenon, The Belvidere Apollo, The Pantheon, Niobe, The Temple of Theseus, The Horses of Lysippus, The Farnese Hercules, The Coliseum, The Iphigenia of Timanthes, The Temple of Diana at Ephesus.

As if to emphasize the background of the poems, George Robert Chinnery's lines on 'The Statue of the Dying Gladiator', which were successful in 1810, have footnotes referring to Winckelmann, the Abbé Bracci, C. P. Landon, Montfaucon, and 'the French Encyclopædia'. Richard Burdon's lines on the Parthenon, the following year, particularly mention the frieze—that is, the Elgin Marbles:

> In slow procession move around the frieze
> Virgins, and youths, and guardian deities.

I have already quoted from a poem which won a prize in 1812, Milman's 'Belvidere Apollo'. Alexander Macdonnell's verses on 'The Horses of Lysippus' contain a Keats-like reference to 'Titian's colours'. It is curious to notice that the poem which won the prize in 1819, the year when Keats wrote his Ode, was soon to be illustrated by an engraving of a Greek vase:[7] this poem, 'The Iphigenia of Timanthes' by H. J. Urquhart, opens with the following lines:

> While the rapt world with ceaseless wonder views
> The rescu'd works of Sculpture's Attic muse,
> Those forms by fabling bards on Ida seen,
> The heavenly Archer, and the Paphian Queen . . . .

No product of the 'Attic muse' made a deeper appeal at this time than the vases and urns which had been so assiduously collected in the previous century. William Hayley, who is in many ways typical of the age, referred in his *Essay on Sculpture* to the Greek genius, which

> Form'd the fine vase Oblivion's power to foil.[8]

Many of the books of antiquities published in the eighteenth century contain illustrations of vases and urns—books like Montfaucon's *Antiquité expliquée*, Spence's *Polymetis*, and Caylus's *Recueil d'Antiquités égyptiennes, étrusques, grecques et romaines.* The two huge folios of Millin's *Peintures de Vases antiques*, with Cléner's coloured engravings, appeared in 1808 and 1810.[9] There is no reason to suppose that Keats would have regarded such works as dry and uninteresting: on the contrary the list of his books compiled by Charles Brown[10] contains Potter's *Antiquities of Greece*, Lemprière's *Classical Dictionary*, and Baldwin's *Pantheon*,[11] as well as a few classical texts and one or two classical books which can no longer be identified with certainty, such as a certain *Description des Antiques*. And, of course, Keats had the run of the libraries of a number of friends, including Charles Dilke, whom he reports, in February 1819, to be deep 'in greek histories and antiquities'.[12]

Another book with illustrations which Keats may well have seen is Kirk's *Outlines from the Figures and Compositions upon the Greek, Roman, and Etruscan Vases of the late Sir William Hamilton; with Engraved Borders*, of which a second edition appeared in 1814—a book of particular interest because both the title and the introduction draw attention to the ornamentation on the vases: 'Nothing can exceed the different borders, in simplicity, in variety, in elegance, in richness, or in beauty, and all modern ornaments seem to sink in the comparison.'[13] When Keats refers to the fact that the Urn is 'leaf-fring'd', therefore, he is remembering a feature of these works which was frequently admired.

In the 'Ode on Indolence' Keats describes himself contemplating three personages 'like figures on a marble urn', and puzzled by their significance:

> And they were strange to me, as may betide
> With vases, to one deep in Phidian lore.

It is clear that a vase or an urn was sometimes the 'shape of beauty' that helped him to escape from mundane reality and disturbing thoughts. Haydon records in his Diary for the 17th of December 1824 that he has 'passed an hour in the evening devouring on [*sic*] two or three of my Elgin fragments, the solace of my melancholy fits'. We may similarly imagine Keats, a few years earlier, studying a Greek urn 'with mute thought'

(to borrow another phrase of Haydon's)[14]—whether in the
British Museum or (with the aid of a book of engravings) in
the home of one of his friends. He must have known the Portland Vase well, for example, a work whose significance was frequently debated at this time, and which Erasmus Darwin refers
to in *The Botanic Garden*:

> Or bid Mortality rejoice and mourn
> O'er the fine forms on PORTLAND's mystic urn.[15]

The interest shown in the Portland Vase is indicated by the fact
that *The Botanic Garden* contains no fewer than four engravings
of it, possibly the work of Blake.[16] Haydon was so struck by
the Vase that he was soon to introduce some figures from it into
'The Raising of Lazarus'—'against all common sense', as he commented, 'but it is picturesque, & will afford food for critics'.[17]

Whereas there have been few critics to concern themselves
with Haydon's methods of composition, those of Keats have
provided 'food for critics' ever since his death. This makes it
worth noticing that the 'Ode on a Grecian Urn', like Haydon's
'The Raising of Lazarus', is eclectic in its inspiration[18]—as may
be verified by a brief consideration of the evidence provided by
the poem itself. The last stanza makes it clear that the Urn is
made of marble:

> O Attic shape . . . with brede
> Of marble men and maidens overwrought.

This bears out Leigh Hunt's description of the Ode as a poem
'on a sculptured vase'.[19] It is possible that Keats is imagining
something like the Portland Vase, which is made of very dark
glass, with the figures and their surroundings standing out in
relief in milky white. But the more obvious supposition is that
he is thinking of one of the large neo-Attic urns made in Rome
between *c.* 50 B.C. and *c.* A.D. 50. These urns, which were intended either as funerary caskets or as purely decorative objects,
are much larger and much less common than the black-figured
and red-figured vases of the classical age.[20] Some of them are of
great beauty, and the figures portrayed on them have that air of
having been magically arrested at one moment in time, as if
frozen, that we know to have appealed to Keats.[21] A fine example
is the Townley Vase (Plate XXIX), which reached the British
Museum in 1805, and which Keats must often have seen in

Room 11, where it was placed next to the statue of Venus which now stands outside the Director's Office. Keats was no doubt struck by the grace and gaiety of the figures on the Townley Vase, but a glance makes it clear that there is no close correspondence between this scene and those described in the Ode. Another fine vase that was certainly known to Keats was the Vase of Sosibios, of which we have a tracing or drawing said to have been made by Keats himself (Plate XXX).[22] This vase was in the Louvre, as it is today; but engravings of it were certainly available. It portrays some sort of religious procession, and we notice particularly the youth with pipes (only partly visible in the sketch) and the elaborate bands of leaves round the neck and handles. But it has nothing of the Bacchic excitement of the Ode, nor does it show a heifer 'lowing at the skies'. There is another vase in the Louvre, the Borghese Vase (Plate XXXI), which is much closer to the Ode both in detail and in spirit. Except a tree, all the chief features of the first three stanzas are to be found on it, and the particularly fine band of leaf-decoration along the top might have suggested the description 'leaf-fring'd'. It is a scene of Bacchic abandon, in which the 'bold Lover' and his 'maiden loth' are particularly clear, and pipes and timbrels are also in evidence. Piranesi's book of engravings of *Vasi, candelabri,* and other works of art—the same collection that contains the print that seems to have helped to suggest the 'Ode on Indolence'—includes two illustrations of this vase, one of them outstandingly fine.[23]

Yet the Borghese Vase does not provide a source for the fourth stanza:

> Who are these coming to the sacrifice?
>   To what green altar, O mysterious priest,
> Lead'st thou that heifer lowing at the skies,
>   And all her silken flanks with garlands drest?
> What little town by river or sea shore,
>   Or mountain-built with peaceful citadel,
>   Is emptied of this folk, this pious morn?
> And, little town, thy streets for evermore
>   Will silent be; and not a soul to tell
>   Why thou art desolate, can e'er return.

No stanza in English poetry has a greater suggestive power. One reason for this is the very vagueness of the picture portrayed. There is one vivid detail—the heifer lowing at the skies[24]

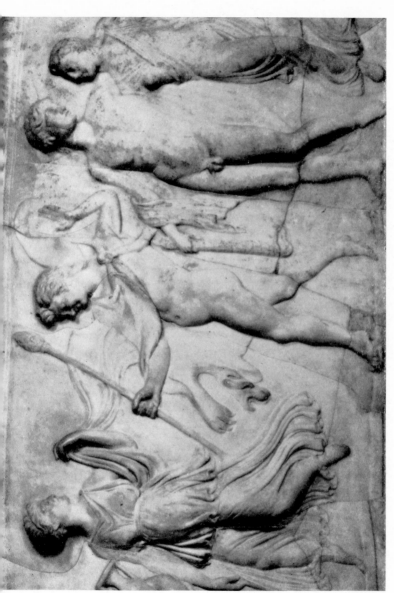

XXIX. The Townley Vase

What men or gods are these? What maidens loth?
What mad pursuit? What struggle to escape?
What pipes and timbrels? What wild ecstasy?

By John Keats.

xxx. The Sosibios Vase: Drawing attributed to Keats

O Attic shape! Fair attitude! with brede
Of marble men and maidens overwrought.

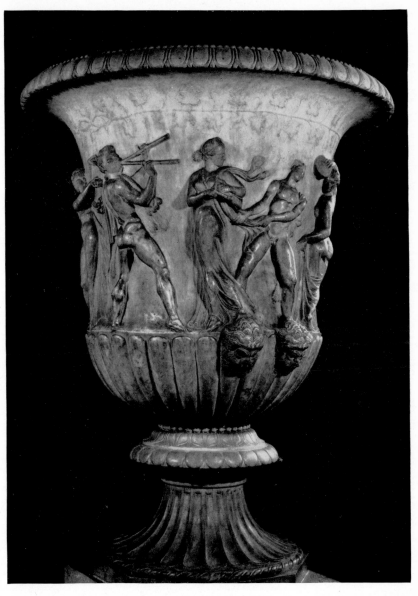

XXXI. The Borghese Vase

Bold Lover, never, never canst thou kiss,
Though winning near the goal—yet, do not grieve;
She cannot fade, though thou hast not thy bliss,
For ever wilt thou love, and she be fair!

xxxii. The Holland House Urn

—and beyond that almost everything is indefinite. The heifer is led by a mysterious priest—itself an unlikely fact: the animal to be sacrificed is usually led by the *victimarius*, with his axe, while the priest waits at the altar. Other people accompany the procession, but the poet does not know what 'little town' they come from or what its situation may be.

The only urn portraying a sacrifice of this sort that seems to have been mentioned in connexion with the Ode is the ornate urn which stood in Holland House and which was included in Piranesi's collection of engravings (Plate XXXII). This shows a *suovetaurilia*—the sacrifice of a pig, a sheep, and a bull—and includes a man playing a pipe, at least two trees, and swathes of leaves and fruit. The great objections to the suggestion are the fact that the bull is not lowing and the fact that nothing could be less mysterious or imaginative than this vase. Whereas the Townley Vase and the Borghese Vase are objects of great beauty, this is over-elaborate and banal.

There is no need, in any case, to invoke the Holland House urn. Unless some other urn or similar work of art turns up which contains both the scenes described in the Ode,[25] we can say with some confidence that the main inspiration of stanza iv was one of the great fragments of the Elgin Marbles: the heifer led to sacrifice from the South Frieze. As may be seen from the illustration (Plate XXXIII), the heifer looks as if it might well be lowing, while the battered condition of the man leading it would justify both the word 'mysterious' and the supposition that he is a priest rather than a *victimarius*. The finely chiselled robes of the men may have suggested the 'silken garlands'. Above all, the vagueness and the evocative power of Keats's lines match the eloquent suggestiveness of the Parthenon sculptures. Nothing could be more in keeping than the poet's speculations about the unseen altar to which the heifer is being led and the little town from which the other figures in the Panathenaic procession have come.

While the heifer was almost certainly suggested by the Elgin Marbles, the atmosphere of the stanza surely owes a great deal to the paintings of Claude Lorrain. The elegiac tone of Keats's lines is profoundly in sympathy with the serene nostalgia of Claude's religious processions. A particularly fine example of a little town 'mountain-built with peaceful citadel' may be found

in his 'View of Delphi with a Procession'. Plate XXXIV shows
a well-known engraving of the preliminary drawing for this
painting. Two other works by Claude, his 'Landscape with the
Father of Psyche sacrificing at the Milesian Temple of Apollo'
(Plate XXXV: exhibited at the British Institution in 1816) and
his 'Landscape with Bacchus at the Palace of the Dead Staphylus'
(Plate XXXVI), are equally characteristic examples of what a
writer in the *Annals* was to call 'the grand quiescence of Claude'[26]
—a quality which Keats recaptures in these evocative lines. We
may also be reminded of Poussin. A mountain-citadel may be
seen in his 'Autumn' (Plate XXXIX), while the general contrast
between the Bacchic stanzas in the Ode and the religious procession in the fourth stanza is reminiscent of the contrast
between the early and later work of the painter who influenced
Keats so deeply.

This religious procession, which so unforgettably intrudes
into the poem, takes us very close to the heart of the imagination
of Keats. Processions of this sort are prominent in painting, and
they are described in great detail by such scholars as Montfaucon, Spence, and Caylus: in the *Annals* we find two long
quotations from accounts in Potter's *Antiquities*.[27] Processions[28]
already appear in Keats in the dedicatory sonnet and 'Sleep and
Poetry' in the volume of 1817. More than one may be found in
Endymion, and it is a striking fact that 'a venerable priest'
follows the music-making young revellers in the procession in
honour of Pan, as he does in this Ode. But the most revealing
procession of all is that in the epistle 'To J. H. Reynolds, Esq.',
written just after Keats had completed *Endymion*. Keats is
listing a number of agreeable subjects of contemplation, and
then a pagan sacrifice is mentioned with an abruptness that
reminds us of the 'Ode to a Grecian Urn':

> . . . flowers bursting out with lusty pride;
> And young Æolian harps personified,
> Some Titian colours touch'd into real life.—
> The sacrifice goes on; the pontiff knife
> Gleams in the sun, the milk-white heifer lows,
> The pipes go shrilly, the libation flows:
> A white sail shews above the green-head cliff
> Moves round the point, and throws her anchor stiff.
> The Mariners join hymn with those on land.

xxxiii. The Elgin Marbles: South Frieze

Who are these coming to the sacrifice?
To what green altar, O mysterious priest,
Lead'st thou that heifer lowing at the skies?

XXXIV. CLAUDE: View of Delphi with a Procession

What little town by river or sea shore,
Or mountain-built with peaceful citadel,
Is emptied of this folk, this pious morn?

XXXV. CLAUDE: 'The grand quiescence of Claude': Landscape with the Father of Psyche sacrificing at the Milesian Temple of Apollo

XXXVI. CLAUDE: Landscape with Bacchus at the Palace of the dead Staphylus

. . . There rose to view a fane
Of liny marble, and thereto a train
Of nymphs approaching fairly o'er the sward.

We notice the association of flowers, Titian, and the sacrifice. The 'milk-white heifer' may be from the Elgin Marbles: it is certainly most unlikely that Keats is here describing any particular painting: but the fact that he goes on in the very next line to those I have quoted to name Claude's 'Enchanted Castle' strongly suggests that Claude was one of the sources of these 'imageries'. We are in the country of the imagination into which Keats so often found his way as he gazed at a Claude painting or engraving. Diderot once wrote that the conceptions of Homer and Virgil ferment in the imagination of artists:[29] in the same way the conceptions of Titian, Poussin, and Claude fermented in the imagination of John Keats.

If the 'Ode on a Grecian Urn' is not a direct description of any particular Greek urn, this need not be surprising: in the light of Keats's general practice, indeed, it would be surprising if it were. Even when his debt to a work of art is undeniable, he is almost certain to introduce details which are not to be found in his original, and as a rule he uses a painting or a work of sculpture as a springboard for his own imagination. I have already shown how in a passage undoubtedly inspired by 'The Realm of Flora' he goes on to describe a scene which is not to be found in Poussin's painting. The same thing happens in the epistle 'To J. H. Reynolds, Esq.,' where no one could possibly have identified the picture that Keats had in mind if he had not identified it himself, and where the 'golden galley' in the background corresponds to nothing in 'The Enchanted Castle' at all, but derives from other paintings of Claude's. And so in the Ode, where his imagination is delighting in the realm created by Greek art and by 'neo-classicism', we find him moving naturally on from a Bacchic thiasos to a sacrificial procession.[30]

In being eclectic int his way the Ode resembles the Parthenon frieze itself, which represents 'an idealized rendering of the procession at the Great Panathenaea'.[31] It also resembles a great many paintings. Reynolds censured 'the Dutch school' and even 'Rubens himself' for keeping too faithfully to 'a representation of an individual spot' in their landscapes, and pointed out that

Claude Lorrain, on the contrary, was convinced, that taking nature as he found it seldom produced beauty. His pictures are a composition of the various draughts which he had previously made from various beautiful scenes and prospects.[32]

Richard Wilson followed his master Claude in this as in so much else. Turner did the same. As Cosmo Monkhouse pointed out,

Turner's drawings were recklessly unfaithful to the actual appearance of the places they were supposed to represent. . . . In his picture of *Kilchurn Castle* we find that he has not only completely changed the character of the country (river, mountain, foreground, background, and all), but has built out of his own imagination a castle quite different from the real one.[33]

Wordsworth approved of a similar practice in the higher kinds of poetry. Writing to the Bishop of Lincoln about an unnamed critic or aesthetic theorist, he remarked that he

confounds *imagery* and *imagination*. Sensible objects really existing, and felt to exist, are *imagery*; and they may form the materials of a descriptive poem, when objects are delineated as they are. Imagination is a subjective term: it deals with objects not as they are, but as they appear to the mind of the poet. The imagination is that intellectual lens through the medium of which the poetical observer sees the objects of his observation, modified both in form and colour; or it is that inventive dresser of dramatic *tableaux*, by which the persons of the play are invested with new drapery, or placed in new attitudes; or it is that chemical faculty by which elements of the most different nature and distant origin are blended together into one harmonious and homogeneous whole.[34]

Fortunately enough there is a clear example of this sort of imaginative treatment of an original in one of the better of Wordsworth's numerous sonnets on particular works of art:

UPON THE SIGHT OF A BEAUTIFUL PICTURE
Painted by Sir G. H. Beaumont, Bart.

Praised be the Art whose subtle power could stay
Yon cloud, and fix it in that glorious shape;
Nor would permit the thin smoke to *escape*,
Nor those bright sunbeams to forsake the day;
Which stopped that band of travellers on their way,
Ere they were lost within the shady wood;
And showed the Bark upon the glassy flood
For ever anchored in her sheltering bay.
Soul-soothing Art! whom Morning, Noontide, Even,
Do serve with all their changeful pageantry;

> Thou, with ambition modest yet sublime,
> Here, for the sight of *mortal* man, hast given
> To one brief moment caught from fleeting time
> The appropriate calm of blest *eternity*.   (My italics.)

'The images of the smoke and the Travellers are taken from your Picture', Wordsworth wrote to Beaumont; 'the rest were added, in order to place the thought in a clear point of view, and for the sake of variety.'[35] It seems highly probable that the 'Ode on a Grecian Urn'—like a painting of Claude's—is a 'composition of . . . various draughts' and that Keats, like a painter, or like Wordsworth, took certain images from one particular source and added others and so 'built out of his imagination [an urn] quite different from the real one' with which he may have begun.

It was perhaps because he sensed that there was no obvious connexion between the first three stanzas and stanza four that Keats decided to add a final stanza 'in order' (like Wordsworth) 'to place the thought in a clear point of view'.[36] As a number of the earlier poems inspired by works of art include a moral of some sort, a contemporary reader would not have been surprised to find a moral at the end of the Ode.[37] The daring decision was to make the Urn speak. It is true that this was not quite without precedent, whether or not Keats was aware of the fact. Schiller's lines, 'The Antique Statue to the Northern Wanderer', are supposed to be spoken by the statue itself—though this is an epigram of no account beside the great Ode.[38] In an earlier poem of Keats's own, in a passage obviously inspired by painting, we find another analogue:

> There must be too a ruin dark, and gloomy,
> To say 'joy not too much in all that's bloomy'.[39]

The inept wording should not prevent us from noticing the parallel. If Keats knew the introduction to Henry Moses's *Collection of Antique Vases*, he will have read there that inscriptions 'are often found' on painted vases, and that they sometimes contain 'a moral sentiment'.[40] And so Keats decided to give his Urn 'a moral sentiment' and to make this sentiment an affirmation of the profound significance of Beauty (a subject to which he recurred frequently in his letters about this time). Perhaps he remembered a remark that Reynolds had made in his Fourth Discourse, when he was arguing that beauty is more important to a painter than the literal truth. 'A painter', Reynolds had said, 'must compensate the natural deficiencies of his art. He has but one sentence to utter, but one moment to exhibit.'[41] It is certain that no painter has ever immortalized 'one moment' more memorably than Keats did in the 'Ode on a Grecian Urn': what is perhaps less certain is that he was well advised to make his 'one sentence' explicit in words.[42]

XIV

MONETA

Juno was called . . . Moneta . . . because she gives wholesome
counsel to those who consult her.   Tooke's *Pantheon*[1]

On the 21st of September 1819 Keats told Reynolds that he had
'given up Hyperion':

> There were too many Miltonic inversions in it—Miltonic verse
> cannot be written but in an artful or rather artist's humour. I wish to
> give myself up to other sensations.

Since Keats transcribed three passages from *The Fall of Hyperion*
in a letter written to Woodhouse the same day,[2] it is clear that
he was not merely abandoning the earlier form of the poem: the
text that was to be published in 1820 as 'Hyperion A Fragment'.
The obvious interpretation of the letter is that he had abandoned
the whole project. Against this there is the statement by Charles
Brown, in sentences of his *Life of John Keats* which seem to
refer to October:

> A comic faery poem . . ., *The Cap and Bells*, . . . occupied his morn-
> ings pleasantly . . . In the evenings, at his own desire, he was alone in
> a separate sitting-room, deeply engaged in remodelling his poem of
> 'Hyperion' into a 'Vision'.[3]

If Brown's memory is to be trusted, Keats did not finally give
up his attempt to recast the poem on the 21st of September. It
would follow that some part of *The Fall of Hyperion* was written
later than the Ode to Autumn, which Keats copied into his letter
to Woodhouse on that day. All that we know for certain is that
Keats tried to recast *Hyperion* during the summer or early
autumn, and abandoned the attempt in September or shortly
afterwards.

While it is certain that dissatisfaction with the style of the
poem was a principal reason for Keats's abandonment of it, it is
hard to believe that it was the only reason. I have argued above
that Keats may well have been in doubt about the adequacy of

Apollo as a protagonist. The 'sort of induction' that stands at the beginning of *The Fall*[4] makes it clear that he had a further reason for uncertainty: he did not know—only time would tell —whether he was a 'Poet' or a 'Fanatic'. He had objected, in a letter, to Wordsworth's attempt to impose 'the whims of an Egotist' on the world in the form of a highly idiosyncratic 'Philosophy':[5] how could he be sure that this was not what he himself would be doing in a poem with a philosophical significance like *Hyperion*? We are reminded of Haydon's disapproving comment:

> One day he was full of an epic Poem! another, epic poems were splendid impositions on the world! & never for two days did he know his own intentions.[6]

The hesitation that seemed so culpable to Haydon may appear to us in a more creditable light: perhaps Keats reflected that no great epic poem had ever been written by a young man.[7]

In the absence of further evidence a number of the questions raised by *The Fall of Hyperion* are likely to remain unanswered. Fortunately, our primary concern is with the visual aspect of the 'Dream', the nature of the shapes and forms that the dreamer sees in his vision. We notice at once that while the visual imagery is extremely striking it is much harder to trace to specific sources than the imagery in Keats's earlier poems.

The visual quality of the poem becomes evident at the end of the induction:

> Whether the dream now purposed to rehearse
> Be Poet's or Fanatic's will be known
> When this warm scribe my hand is in the grave.

The last line is arresting simply because Keats is looking at his own hand with an unusual detachment. We are reminded of the curiously vivid fragment which Keats jotted down on a spare piece of paper about the same time:

> This living hand, now warm and capable
> Of earnest grasping . . .

It is worth remembering that artists often draw their own hands. On the 3rd of July 1808, for example, Haydon had sketched his own hand, and added the date.[8]

When Keats begins to describe his vision, he starts by using
a curious sort of poetic shorthand, describing how he stood

> In neighbourhood of fountains, by the noise
> Soft-showering in mine ears; and, by the touch
> Of scent, not far from roses.   (i. 22–24)

In the following lines we find ourselves looking at the remains
of a feast:

> . . . Turning round,
> I saw an arbour with a drooping roof
> Of trellis vines, and bells, and larger blooms,
> Like floral censers swinging light in air;
> Before its wreathed doorway, on a mound
> Of moss, was spread a feast of summer fruits,
> Which nearer seen, seem'd refuse of a meal
> By Angel tasted, or our Mother Eve;
> For empty shells were scattered on the grass,
> And grape stalks but half bare, and remnants more,
> Sweet smelling, whose pure kinds I could not know.
> Still was more plenty than the fabled horn
> Thrice emptied could pour forth, at banqueting
> For Proserpine return'd to her own fields,
> Where the white heifers low.   (i. 24–38)

Here Keats is obviously remembering the feast described in
Paradise Lost, Book V: that he is also thinking in sharply visual
terms is emphasized by the sudden word 'white' in the last line,
with its characteristic reference to lowing heifers. The same
quality shows itself again a few lines later, when Keats describes
himself as sinking down

> Like a Silenus on an antique vase.   (Plate XXXVII)

We are not told what feast it is that has taken place, but it seems
a reasonable conjecture that it has been a Feast of the Gods, a
celebration by the new generation of deities of their victory over
their predecessors. Visually, it is as if we had come on the scene
of the wedding-feast of Cupid and Psyche, as painted by Giulio
Romano, a few moments after the end of the festivities.

From this garden of delights the dreamer is transported to a
very different scene. Now

> . . . the fair trees were gone,
> The mossy mound and arbour were no more.

Instead he finds himself in an immense temple which is awe-
inspiring rather than delightful:

> I look'd around upon the carved sides
> Of an old sanctuary with roof august,
> Builded so high, it seem'd that filmed clouds
> Might spread beneath as o'er the stars of heaven;
> So old the place was, I remembered none
> The like upon the earth: what I had seen
> Of grey Cathedrals, buttress'd walls, rent towers,
> The superannuations of sunk realms,
> Or Nature's Rocks toil'd hard in waves and winds,
> Seem'd but the faulture of decrepit things
> To that eternal domed monument.   (i. 61–71)

Here Keats makes it clear that this Miltonic or Martinesque
edifice derives from visual memories from various sources,
and we can hardly doubt that images from his northern tour
have combined with images from paintings and perhaps from
the engravings of ancient temples in books of classical and
Egyptian antiquities. Livingston Lowes[9] suggested a Biblical
source for the lines that follow:

> Upon the marble at my feet there lay
> Store of strange vessels, and large draperies,
> Which needs had been of dyed asbestos wove,
> Or in that place the moth could not corrupt,
> So white the linen; so, in some, distinct
> Ran imageries from a sombre loom.
> All in a mingled heap confus'd there lay
> Robes, golden tongs, censer, and chafing dish,
> Girdles, and chains, and holy jewelries.   (i. 72–80)

We can hardly doubt that illustrated books of antiquities and
frequent visits to the British Museum also contributed to the
passage.

It is of such visits that we are reminded when we read the
description of

> An Image, huge of feature as a cloud,
> At level of whose feet an altar slept

a few lines later. Moneta tells the dreamer that the image
represents Saturn, and shows him a vision in which he sees
Saturn himself sitting in silence,

> Deep in the shady sadness of a vale.

XXXVII. The Borghese Vase

The cloudy swoon came on, and down I sunk
Like a Silenus on an antique vase.

This is not the place for a detailed comparison between the corresponding passages in the two versions of the poem, but one or two of the revisions are relevant to the subject of this study. As soon as we reach the description of Saturn with which *Hyperion* had opened—which happens at line 294 of *The Fall*— we find that the rewriting involves the omission of lines 4–7:

> Sat gray-hair'd Saturn, quiet as a stone,
> Still as the silence round about his lair;
> Forest on forest hung above his head
> Like cloud on cloud.

Otherwise the initial description of Saturn is extremely close to that in *Hyperion*. In the description of Thea, however, the image of the Amazon who could have bent the neck of Achilles or 'stay'd Ixion's wheel' is omitted, as is that of the Memphian sphinx. The lines that follow are also cut—

> But oh! how unlike marble was that face:
> How beautiful, if sorrow had not made
> Sorrow more beautiful than Beauty's self

—but we notice that Keats is still thinking in terms of sculpture:

> I mark'd the goddess in fair statuary
> Surpassing wan Moneta by the head,
> And in her sorrow nearer woman's tears.   (i. 336–8)

A similar analogy is suggested by the reference to 'the three fixed shapes Ponderous' at lines 391–2. Another new line with a visual background occurs in the description of the effect of Saturn's speech:

> . . . Thus he spake, and sent
> Strange musings to the solitary Pan.   (i. 410–11)

I cannot be the only reader who has wondered why Pan should suddenly appear on the scene: he does so (I think) because Pan is so often to be found in the background of landscape-paintings. It may be Pan in person, as it were, or a 'term' of Pan—a bust on a pillar of the sort that we see in Poussin's 'The Realm of Flora' and in many other paintings.

But by far the most striking feature of *The Fall of Hyperion* is the description of Moneta.[10] In *Hyperion* the goddess who speaks is called Mnemosyne, and she addresses Apollo. In *The Fall* she is usually called Moneta, and she addresses the dreamer. Moneta is simply the Latin translation of the Greek word Μνημοσύνη, and refers (like that) to the Mother of the Muses. It seems likely that one reason for the change is that Mnemosyne is rather a cumbersome word if it is frequently repeated: a word of three syllables fits more readily into English verse than a word of four syllables. It is probable that Keats liked the admonitory overtones of the Latin form—possible also that he remembered the sentence from Tooke's *Pantheon* that stands at the head of the present chapter, though that relates to Moneta as an attributive adjective for Juno, and therefore refers to a different use of the same name. What is certain is that there is no change in the identity or significance of the goddess: on two occassions, indeed, the name Mnemosyne is retained.[11]

In *Hyperion* there is no elaborate description of Mnemosyne. Of 'antique mien and robed form', she is clearly to be envisaged as a classical goddess, with long vestments and 'ample skirts'. Apollo also says that he has seen her before, or dreamed of her:

> Goddess! I have beheld those eyes before,
> And their eternal calm, and all that face,
> Or I have dream'd.   (iii. 59–61)

In *The Fall* the description is slightly more detailed:

> Then the tall shade, in drooping linens veil'd,
> Spake out, so much more earnest, that her breath
> Stirr'd the thin folds of gauze that drooping hung
> About a golden censer from her hand
> Pendent.[12]   (i. 216–20)

But the important thing is that Keats now makes of the description of Moneta's face a passage of great poetry:

> But yet I had a terror of her robes,
> And chiefly of the veils, that from her brow
> Hung pale, and curtain'd her in mysteries
> That made my heart too small to hold its blood.
> This saw that Goddess, and with sacred hand
> Parted the veils. Then saw I a wan face,
> Not pin'd by human sorrows, but bright blanch'd
> By an immortal sickness which kills not;
> It works a constant change, which happy death
> Can put no end to; deathwards progressing
> To no death was that visage; it had pass'd
> The lily and the snow; and beyond these

I must not think now, though I saw that face—
But for her eyes I should have fled away.
They held me back, with a benignant light,
Soft-mitigated by divinest lids
Half-closed, and visionless entire they seem'd
Of all external things—they saw me not,
But in blank splendor beam'd like the mild moon,
Who comforts those she sees not, who knows not
What eyes are upward cast.   (i. 251–71)

These lines are so moving that one can well understand how Miss Ward is tempted to look for a psychological explanation. Her suggestion that Keats may have been remembering the body of his mother (who died when he was fourteen), laid out in its grave clothes, may contain part of the truth.[13] The lines immediately before the passage just quoted may be taken to support the suggestion—

As near as an immortal's sphered words
Could to a mother's soften, were these last

—although Keats may simply be referring to the fact that Moneta is the Mother of the Muses. Another image that certainly contributed to the passage is that of the moon, which Keats explicitly mentions. We are here presented with another—incomparably greater—portrayal of Endymion gazing at Diana in her clouded heaven. Earlier in the poetry of Keats this image is poetical and appropriate: here it has become so moving and so pregnant with meaning that we are tempted to call the passage religious—though there is nothing that is Christian about it. It is difficult to see how Keats could have made Apollo as powerful a symbol as he here makes Moneta.

XV

'TO AUTUMN'

The history of Constable's development is the history of the sharpening of the eye's focus upon nature, the history of the emancipation of English art from the Claude-glass and from Sir George Beaumont's brown tree.

JONATHAN MAYNE[1]

'How beautiful the season is now', Keats wrote to Reynolds from Winchester on the 21st of September 1819, in a letter which has already been quoted: '—How fine the air. A temperate sharpness about it. Really, without joking, chaste weather— Dian skies—I never lik'd stubble fields so much as now—Aye better than the chilly green of the spring. Somehow a stubble plain looks warm—in the same way that some pictures look warm—this struck me so much in my sunday's walk that I composed upon it.' The reference to 'Dian skies' reminds us that Keats never ceased to associate classical mythology with the scenes of external nature; but the explicit reference to painting is even more interesting and makes it clear that the sense of warm fruition so brilliantly created by the poem owes something to the visual arts. It is not surprising that 'To Autumn' has more than once been compared to the work of individual painters. The poem could not have been written before the development of English landscape painting in the later eighteenth century.[2]

The season of autumn had always meant a great deal to Keats. The references to it in *Endymion* provide a useful background to the Ode.[3] Near the beginning Keats expresses the hope that he will be finishing the poem when autumn comes,

> With universal tinge of sober gold.

Endymion lies down to rest on leaves which have been dried

> . . . on the cooler side of sheaves
> When last the sun his autumn tresses shook,
> And the tann'd harvesters rich armfuls took.

The 'autumn mists' at the end of Book I point forward to the Ode. In Book II we hear of

> The creeper, mellowing for an autumn blush,

while in Book IV there is a characteristic reference to 'golden store In Autumn's sickle' and another to 'the flowers of autumn'. Even more striking is the occurrence of Autumn in a typical list of delights in an early sonnet. Keats is writing about the encouraging anticipations of Spring that one may sense even in January, when 'after dark vapours have oppress'd our plains' there comes a day 'Born of the gentle South' which fills our minds with 'the calmest thoughts', thoughts

> ... of leaves
> Budding,—fruit ripening in stillness,—autumn suns
> Smiling at eve upon the quiet sheaves.

In 'Apollo to the Graces' the god asks 'which of the fairest three' will ride with him

> Across the gold Autumn's whole Kingdoms of Corn.

In *Otho the Great* Albert says that the Emperor has been

> More generous to me than autumn's sun
> To ripening harvests. (iv. i. 166–7)

The references to autumn in 'Fancy', one of the lighter poems printed between the two groups of Odes in 1820, are similar in tone: first we hear of 'Autumn's red-lipp'd fruitage'

> Blushing through the mist and dew;

then of

> All the heaped Autumn's wealth;

and finally of

> Acorns ripe down-pattering,
> While the autumn breezes sing.

As he wrote the Ode Keats may well have remembered a line from Chatterton, whom he always associated with autumn—

> Whanne Autumpne blake and sonne-brente doe appere

—as well as a line from one of Shakespeare's sonnets which he once quoted in a letter:

> And Summer's green all girded up in sheaves.[4]

It is clear that he regarded autumn as the season of harvest and achievement, disregarding its other role as the herald of winter and of death. There could hardly be a greater contrast than that between the Ode to Autumn and Shelley's 'Ode to the West Wind', in which the clouds are blown across the sky and the dead leaves are like 'Pestilence-stricken multitudes'.

To remember Shelley is to realize in how different a spirit 'To Autumn' could have been written. All the other Odes of Keats could well be annotated from *The Anatomy of Melancholy* (which was one of Keats's favourite books), and Burton is one of many writers who hold that 'Of seasons of the year, the autumn is most melancholy'.[5] In *The Seasons* Autumn is apostrophized as the time 'Of Philosophic Melancholy'.[6] Gray once described his *Elegy* as 'a few autumnal Verses' written 'dureing the Fall of the Leaf'.[7] Whether it was written in the Virgilian mood of Gray's *Elegy* or in the warning voice of Lawrence's 'The Ship of Death', a melancholy poem on autumn would concentrate on the falling leaves and the approaching winter:

> Now it is autumn and the falling fruit
> And the long journey towards oblivion.

There was in fact every reason for Keats to 'build [his] ship of death': by the time when he wrote the poem he knew that this might be the last autumn that he would ever see. Five months later we find him writing to James Rice:

> How astonishingly does the chance of leaving the world impress a sense of its natural beauties on us. Like poor Falstaff, though I do not babble, I think of green fields. I muse with the greatest affection on every flower I have known from my infancy. . . . I have seen foreign flowers in hothouses of the most beautiful nature, but I do not care a straw for them. The simple flowers of our spring are what I want to see again. (ii. 260)

Yet the remarkable thing is that Keats does not allow melancholy to cloud the poem. There are no dead leaves in the Ode, and there is no cold autumnal wind. Keats also avoids all personal applications. The comparison between the seasons of the year and those of a man's life is of course a poetic commonplace, and it is the theme of one of the sonnets of Keats, in which he refers to the autumn of human life as a quiet time when a man is contented to look

On mists in idleness—to let fair things
Pass by unheeded as a threshold brook.[8]

In another sonnet, 'When I have fears that I may cease to be',
Keats makes a movingly personal application of the same image,
fearing that he may die before 'high-piled' books

Hold like rich garners the full-ripen'd grain.

The remarkable thing is that no hint of this sort is to be found
in the Ode, which contains no reference to his fear that he might
die long before his own life reached its autumn. This is not a
poem about Keats: it is a poem about Autumn.

It consists of only three stanzas. The first describes the fruit-
fulness of Autumn with emphasis on its beneficent activity—the
verbs 'load', 'bend', 'fill', 'swell', 'plump', 'set budding', and
'o'erbrimmed' being of central importance. The second offers a
number of alternative personifications of the season—three of
them being markedly inactive. The third concentrates on the
sounds of autumn, its 'music'.[9] It is the second stanza that is
most relevant to our inquiry.

The seasons have been personified by writers and painters
from the earliest times. When in the fourth Book of *Endymion*
Keats refers to

... the Seasons four,—
Green-kyrtled Spring, flush Summer, golden store
In Autumn's sickle, Winter frosty-hoar,
Join[ing] dance with shadowy Hours,   (421–4)

it becomes evident that he was aware of a general iconographical
tradition, and it is possible that he was remembering Poussin's
'Dance to the Music of Time', in which the four Seasons are
holding hands and dancing to music provided by Father Time,
while the Hours dance round Apollo's chariot in the sky above.[10]
But instead of providing one elaborate personification in the
Ode, as Spenser would have done, Keats avails himself of the
poet's privilege of offering the reader alternative images, one
after the other:

Who hath not seen thee oft amid thy store?
Sometimes whoever seeks abroad may find
Thee sitting careless on a granary floor,
Thy hair soft-lifted by the winnowing wind;

Or on a half-reap'd furrow sound asleep,
　　Drows'd with the fume of poppies, while thy hook
　　　Spares the next swath and all its twined flowers:
And sometimes like a gleaner thou dost keep
　　Steady thy laden head across a brook;
　　Or by a cyder-press, with patient look,
　　　Thou watchest the last oozings hours by hours.

We are here presented with something of a paradox: English
and natural as the poem is in its effect, it is difficult to believe
that all these images are the result of first-hand observation of
English life, and about each of them there is even a slight suggestion of the classical figure of Ceres.

Whether or not Keats was conscious of the fact, it seems
likely that the first image was inspired by the story of Cupid and
Psyche. The first of the tasks imposed on Psyche by the angry
Venus was to separate 'a great quantitie of wheate, barley, mill,
popy seede, peason, lintels, and beanes . . . mingled . . . al
together on a heape'.[11] Thinking the task impossible, we are told,
Psyche 'went not about to dissever the graine . . . but . . . satte
still and saide nothing'; but fortunately for her the ants came
and separated the grain for her. Keats's description of Autumn
'sitting careless on a granary floor' is strikingly realized in one
of Giulio Romano's paintings in the 'Sala di Psiche' (Plate
XXXVIII). In this picture Psyche's hair does seem to be 'soft
lifted' by the wind, and it is a natural transition of thought to
imagine the wind as winnowing the grain to assist the ants.
Keats's portrayal of Autumn seated among the grain has also
something in common with such paintings as that by an associate
of Tintoretto, in the National Gallery of Scotland, or the figure
of 'Ceres' in a landscape by Vouet in the National Gallery in
London.[12]

The second image, which describes Autumn

　　. . . on a half-reap'd furrow sound asleep,
　　Drows'd with the fume of poppies, while [her] hook
　　Spares the next swath and all its twined flowers,

also seems at least in part to be literary or artistic in its inspiration. Poppies do not (after all) have a soporific smell, so that
anyone whom Keats had seen asleep during harvesting had not
been sent to sleep by poppies but more likely by work and sun—
helped, perhaps, by cider or beer. The poppies may have been

XXXVIII. GIULIO ROMANO: Psyche asleep among the Grain

Sometimes whoever seeks abroad may find
Thee sitting careless on a granary floor,
Thy hair soft-lifted by the winnowing wind.

XXXIX. POUSSIN: Autumn, or The Grapes of the Promised Land

And sometimes like a gleaner thou dost keep
Steady thy laden head across a brook.

XL. POUSSIN: Summer, or Ruth and Boaz

Perhaps the self-same song that found a path
Through the sad heart of Ruth, when, sick for home,
She stood in tears amid the alien corn.

XLI. GEORGE WRIGHT and E. MALPAS: Spring

suggested by Apuleius, and they have, of course, a strong literary association with soporifics, but their main reason for being there is no doubt that they are associated with Ceres.[13] A representation of harvesters resting during the heat of the day is a common feature of pictures of Autumn. In an edition of *The Seasons* published in 1807, for example, with engravings by Bartolozzi and P. W. Tomkins after pictures by William Hamilton, the print at the beginning of Autumn portrays a boy-reaper asleep beside sheaves of grain, a rake, a basket, and a barrel. It is called the 'Reaper's Repose'.[14]

The third image almost certainly has a classical ancestry, and an interesting one. The figure of a girl with a basket on her head is a favourite motif in the painters whom Keats admired most passionately, and is finely introduced into one picture of Poussin's in particular. Late in his career Poussin executed four paintings called after the seasons, each of them also illustrating a passage from the Bible. On one side of his 'Autumn, or The Grapes of the Promised Land', we see a clear representation of a girl carrying a basket (Plate XXXIX). As Poussin seldom painted a figure without studying ancient sculpture and coins, we may be certain that this girl is descended from the Canephoroe, the maidens who were consecrated to Ceres, the goddess (as Lemprière reminds us) 'of corn and of harvests'.[15] In Poussin's painting (we notice) it is primarily the fulfilment of autumn that is insisted on, though there are also omens of approaching winter. It seems likely that Keats was remembering a print of 'Autumn', or some similar work of art, when he wrote his second stanza. It is also possible that he was influenced by 'Summer, or Ruth and Boaz' (Plate XL), with its memorable portrayal of Ruth,

> . . . when, sick for home,
> She stood in tears amid the alien corn.[16]

The English quality of the poem—in spite of these classical reminiscences—comes out very clearly in the last of the four images:

> Or by a cyder-press, with patient look,
> Thou watchest the last oozings hours by hours.

In the prominence which it gives to the grape-harvest Poussin's 'Autumn' is typical of representations of the season. The figure

of Bacchus is also frequently portrayed, as in the fine plaque by
Massimiliano Soldani in the Royal Collection. There is no Bacchus in the Ode, however, and only a suggestion of Ceres; while
instead of the grape-harvest it is the cider-harvest which is
referred to. It seems apposite to quote from a book that we know
Keats to have possessed, Aikin's *Natural History of the Year*.[17]
The epigraph of the section on September comes from a poem
which I have not identified:

> Now soften'd suns a mellow lustre shed,
> The laden orchards glow with tempting red;
> On hazel boughs the clusters hang embrown'd . . . .

'This is, in general, a very pleasant month', Aikin writes, 'the dis-
tinguishing softness and serenity of autumn prevailing through
great part of it'. Soon we come on a passage from Thomson's
Autumn about the twittering of swallows, followed by a reference to the cider-harvest:

> [The apples] are now gathered for our English vintage, the *cider-
> making*, which in some counties, particularly Worcestershire, Somer-
> setshire, and Devonshire, is a busy and important employment.[18]

The image of Autumn 'by a cyder-press' is characteristically
English. It may well remind us of Edward Calvert's memorable
engraving, 'The Cyder Feast', executed less than a decade later.

These four brief personifications of Autumn are much more
skilful than the personification in the 'Ode to Psyche', and this
is one great reason for the lack of contrivedness that is so note-
worthy in the later poem. Like Psyche, Autumn might be said to
have been neglected in antiquity: Keats comes near to alluding
to this at the beginning of the last stanza:

> Where are the songs of Spring? Ay, where are they?
> Think not of them, thou hast thy music too.

But there is no defiant paganism in this poem, no 'Dian skies'
(as in the letter), no dryads. Keats does not proclaim that he is
going to write about Autumn, still less that he is going to
become her priest and build her an altar: he simply writes the
poem. It is a development towards the truth of nature that is
analogous to Constable's emancipation 'from the Claude-glass
and from Sir George Beaumont's brown tree'.

One has only to read the poem without the middle stanza to
realize how essential the four images of autumn are to the

structure of the Ode. The main effect is that the poem becomes unacceptably static: nothing happens. It is true that three of the four images of Autumn are completely inactive: the important thing is that in the second stanza we—the readers—begin to move. It is we who 'seek abroad' and find the four figures: first we find Autumn 'sitting careless on a granary floor': then we move to the harvest field, where we see one gleaner asleep, and another carrying her load across a brook: and finally we move to a cider-press. This is the way in which one's eye moves as one examines a landscape-painting: the design of the picture guides the eye from one part to another in such a manner that one becomes aware of the unity of the scene depicted.

It is illuminating to recall for a moment some of the illustrated editions of *The Seasons* with which Keats must certainly have been familiar. 'For more than one hundred and fifty years', as Ralph Cohen has recently reminded us, Thomson's was 'the most illustrated poem in the English language',[19] while Constable and Turner were only the most illustrious of a host of nineteenth-century painters who were in the habit of taking subjects from *The Seasons* for independent landscape-paintings.[20] As Cohen has pointed out, 'the engravings to *The Seasons* were marked, from the very beginning, by conflicting allegorical and naturalistic tendencies'.[21] In particular we notice that some of the illustrators —such as William Kent, whose illustrations were engraved by Nicolas Tardieu for the edition of 1730—portray mythological or allegorical characters above the clouds[22] and human beings on the earth below: while other illustrators (probably the majority) confine themselves to depicting human beings engaged in the activities appropriate to the season. Formally the 'Ode to Autumn' is comparable with the first type of illustration —indeed if the personifications are strictly regarded as such, it might be argued that there are no human beings in the poem at all; but in effect the poem is much closer to the second type of illustration, because the effect of the four figures in the second stanza is that of human beings in a landscape. I am not suggesting that any particular illustration is a source for the poem, but simply that the general mode of proceeding in the Ode is analogous to what we find in many of these illustrations. In the illustration to *Spring* engraved by E. Malpas from the original by George Wright, for example (Plate XLI), we see one man ploughing in the foreground, another sowing a little further away, a shepherd and shepherdess with their sheep on a little hill, a fisherman, a boat on a river, clouds blown across the sky by the wind, a rainbow, and a flock of birds high in the air beyond a large tree in the middle distance.[23]

It is obvious that 'To Autumn' could easily be made into a 'picture in writing' of the sort that Leigh Hunt was to propose a few years later.[24] In the sky we would see barred clouds throwing a warm light on the stubble-plains below (the effect that Keats notices in his letter from Winchester), swallows gathering in the air, a little river winding its way across the landscape, and a 'hilly bourn' to one side of the picture, with lambs gambolling and bleating. Elsewhere in the picture there would be a woman sleeping on a granary floor, seen through an open door, a reaper asleep, a girl crossing the brook with a basket on her head, and a patient figure watching by a cider-press; as well as cottages, with vines and apple-trees, nut-trees, and autumnal flowers. The only difficulty would be to determine the precise time of day. It has sometimes been maintained that Keats moves from morning to evening in the course of the poem, but all that is certain is that the first and second stanzas appear to describe morning or the heat of the day, and that by the third stanza it is evening. Unlike a painter, a poet is not confined to one moment of time, and Keats has availed himself of the advantage inherent in his medium.

As it happens, there was one poem well known in Keats's day which is a description of a landscape painting. This was *The Picture; Verses . . . suggested by A Magnificent Landscape of Rubens*, by William Lisle Bowles. Rubens's landscape is also autumnal, but it is Flemish, and the time of day that is represented is the morning. Bowles's poem is too long and too dull for an attempt at a detailed comparison with 'To Autumn' to serve any useful purpose, but one or two sentences may be quoted from John Landseer's prose description of the same picture. The distortion due to selection is unimportant, as I am concerned merely with an analogy: I am not suggesting that either the poem or the painting was in the mind of Keats as he wrote his Ode:

The season represented, is that which succeeds the harvest. . . . On the immediate fore-ground, the fowler . . . is . . . creeping under the concealing shadow of an old weather-torn tree-stump, which is festooned with the mandrake-vine . . . and fringed with bramble. . . . A little way beyond, a Flemish waggon and horses are fording a rivulet. . . . Beyond the vine-mantled and dark brown tree-stump, a rivulet is seen winding round a rocky knoll, from which a group of tall trees . . . rise high in the landscape. . . . Though the country represented is flat, the scene is extensive; the artist having taken a somewhat elevated station for his view: in consequence the spectator's eye is taught to wander to a considerable distance. . . . The whole forms an apparent, if not a real, portrait of a real scene. . . . The sun has manifested sufficient power to have dispelled the morning mists which so frequently shroud these low and flat meadow-lands; and . . . the clouds are breaking, if not into splendour, into fleecy forms, dappled colours, and cheerful promise.[25]

'The spectator's eye is taught to wander to a considerable distance': it is illuminating to remember Landseer's remark not only as we read the second stanza of the poem, but also as we read the third stanza, on which a recent critic (unconcerned with the possibilities of pictorial influence) has commented as follows:

The five sounds lead us away from the farm-scenes of the previous stanza, as we cross the harvested fields to the river bank, listen to the sheep on the hillside beyond, and then finally glance upwards into the skies where the swallows are gathering for their flight to warmer lands. Life, Keats tells us in this last detail, goes on elsewhere, and will return to the land which now seems bereft. It is a large and almost empty scene from which we are gently withdrawn as the visual details lead our attention out of the land and into the skies. The sense of perspective, or depth, is a remarkable achievement, which depends partly on the way in which our mind's eye moves across the expanse of the fields to the clouds on the horizon, and partly on the details of sound.[26]

Landseer sums up by saying that Rubens 'appears . . . to have promised himself to produce an interesting picture of such a *cheerful* tone and character, as, while it did honour to the land of his birth, might harmonize with human feelings . . . on a fine autumnal morning'.[27] Keats's evocation of Autumn, too, is 'of a *cheerful* tone and character', though the word is too simple for the complex objectivity of his re-creation, with the hint of transitoriness at the end which gives frame and definition to his landscape and saves it from any danger of over-luxuriance or sentimentality. It is an extraordinary fact that this poem, the work of a man who was deeply apprehensive about his own future, is yet written in 'a more peac[e]able and healthy spirit'[28] than the poetry that he had written when his hopes for the future had still been high.

'To Autumn' is so flawless a poem that critics have sometimes been tempted to read more into it than is really there. I agree with Dr. Leavis that Middleton Murry went too far when he described the poem as 'the perfect and unforced utterance of the truth contained in the magic words: "Ripeness is all" '.[29] It must particularly be noticed that whereas in *The Picture* Bowles draws a moral, or a series of morals, from the landscape which he is regarding, in the Ode to Autumn Keats does no such thing. No doubt it is for this reason that some critics have preferred the poem to the 'Ode on a Grecian Urn', with its greater imaginative resonance. The Ode to Autumn, like Constable's 'Dedham Vale', or 'The Hay Wain', means what it is.

* * * * * *

The end of a poet's study of the Sister Art of Painting is not to enable him to describe a particular painting in his verse. It is to sharpen his perceptions, and so increase the range and power of his descriptions of the visible universe. And not only of the universe as it actually is—if the paradox may be permitted—but of the universe as it ought to be: the mind's images which represent the soul's imaginings. In one of his letters to Haydon Keats writes of 'looking upon the Sun the Moon the Stars, the Earth and its contents as materials to form greater things—that is to say ethereal things'.[30] It is the same thought that Marvell expressed in 'The Garden':

> Mean while the Mind, from pleasure less,
> Withdraws into its happiness:
> The Mind, that Ocean where each kind
> Does streight its own resemblance find;
> Yet it creates, transcending these,
> Far other Worlds, and other Seas;
> Annihilating all that's made
> To a green Thought in a green Shade.

'You speak of Lord Byron and me', Keats wrote in another letter. 'There is this great difference between us. He describes what he sees—I describe what I imagine—Mine is the hardest task.'[31] Here he seems to be echoing a remark in one of Haydon's Diaries: 'It is comparatively easy painting what you see—the great effort is painting what you imagine.'[32] A man of creative genius, whether he is a painter or a poet, will be able to describe what he imagines in such a way as to produce a memorable visual image only if he can first describe what he sees. The one is the discipline or induction to the other. The face of Moneta (for example) is not a face that Keats ever saw. It is a face that he imagined. That he was able to give his imagining such an unforgettable form was the final result of the lifetime of thought and vision comprised in the few brief years of his adult existence.

THE 'ODE ON INDOLENCE'

I T is inevitable that the 'Ode on Indolence' should be regarded as a sort of postscript to the 'Ode on a Grecian Urn'. Whatever its place in the sequence of composition, it is clearly an inferior poem, characterized by repetitions of word and image from other poems which give it the air of being the work of some gifted imitator of Keats. Yet in fact it is the work of the poet himself, and this makes it interesting to inquire whether the poetic procedure in this Ode tends to confirm that which has been tentatively ascribed to the 'Ode on a Grecian Urn'.

Keats describes the mood in which the poem originated. On the 18th of March 1819 he got a black eye, playing cricket. The next day he wrote to George and his wife in America:

This morning I am in a sort of temper indolent and supremely careless: I long after a stanza or two of Thompson's Castle of indolence—My passions are all asleep from my having slumbered till nearly eleven and weakened the animal fibre all over me to a delightful sensation about three degrees on this side of faintness—if I had teeth of pearl and the breath of lillies I should call it langour—but as I am (especially as I have a black eye) I must call it Laziness—In this state of effeminacy the fibres of the brain are relaxed in common with the rest of the body, and to such a happy degree that pleasure has no show of enticement and pain no unbearable frown. Neither Poetry, nor Ambition, nor Love have any alertness of countenance as they pass by me: they seem rather like three figures on a greek vase—a Man and two women—whom no one but myself could distinguish in their disguisement. This is the only happiness; and is a rare instance of advantage in the body overpowering the Mind.   (ii. 78–79)

Here is the first stanza of the poem:

> One morn before me were three figures seen,
>   With bowed necks, and joined hands, side-faced;
> And one behind the other stepp'd serene,
>   In placid sandals, and in white robes graced;
> They pass'd, like figures on a marble urn,
>   When shifted round to see the other side;

> They came again; as when the urn once more
> Is shifted round, the first seen shades return;
> And they were strange to me, as may betide
> With vases, to one deep in Phidian lore.

We notice that whereas in the letter Poetry, Ambition, and Love are 'a Man and two women' (it is probable that Poetry is the man, and that this is because Keats instinctively personified it as Apollo), in the poem we are told that Love and Poesy are maidens, while there is no reason to suppose that the third figure (Ambition) is a man. Here are the relevant lines:

> The first was a fair Maid, and Love her name;
> The second was Ambition, pale of cheek,
> And ever watchful with fatigued eye;
> The last, whom I love more, the more of blame
> Is heap'd upon her, maiden most unmeek,—
> I knew to be my demon Poesy.

The reference to the 'skirts' of the three figures strengthens the impression that they are all women.

The conception of the young poet in 'the flowery grass' looking at the three mysterious figures in long robes and sandals as they move past him is thoroughly 'neo-classical' in the art-historian's sense of the term.[1] As Sidney Colvin pointed out, the most likely visual source for the poem seems to be a vase of the type illustrated in Plate XLII, from Piranesi's *Vasi e candelabri*.[2] This sculptured urn or vase portrays a bearded man, with a staff, leading two young women. The second woman holds the wrist of the first. Their feet appear to be bare, not sandalled. As the engraving is uncoloured, and shows a marble urn, it is natural to think of the robes as white. The figures are 'side-faced', though their heads are not bowed. Their robes are finely depicted, and the procession (rather surprisingly described in Piranesi[3] as showing 'Sacerdoti, e Sacerdotesse che danzano in onor di Bacco') has a mysterious air.

Although the urn is not a close parallel to the scene described in the Ode, two facts suggest that time spent in looking for a closer parallel would be time wasted. The first is the obvious discrepancy between the description in the letter (which would presumably be closer to the actual Urn) and that in the poem itself. The second is the fact that Keats manifestly describes the three figures as doing something which no figures on an urn can do—

> A third time pass'd they by, and, passing, turn'd
> Each one the face a moment whiles to me.

We are reminded of the charioteer talking 'to the trees and mountains' in 'Sleep and Poetry'. He does no such thing in 'The Realm of Flora', which is the main source of the passage. It is the imagination of Keats that makes him do so.

As in 'Sleep and Poetry' Keats completely reinterprets the allegory of Poussin's painting, so in the 'Ode on Indolence' he gives an allegorical significance to a scene of whose original meaning he is ignorant:

> And they were strange to me, as may betide
> With vases, to one deep in Phidian lore.

In the letter he puts this in another way: no one but himself (he says) 'could distinguish [the three figures] in their disguisement'. The parallel with the 'Ode on a Grecian Urn', where Keats makes the Urn the bearer of a message to mankind, is sufficiently obvious. In each case he is using his visual source as a springboard for the imagination, and not as an original that must be followed with pedantic accurancy.[4]

XLII. Greek Vase

'Neither Poetry, nor Ambition, nor Love have any alertness of countenance as they pass by me: they seem rather like three figures on a greek vase—a Man and two women—whom no one but myself could distinguish in their disguisement.'

NOTES

INTRODUCTION

1. *The Letters of John Keats 1814–1821*, edited by Hyder Edward Rollins, 1958, i. 175. Subsequent references are to this edition.

2. *John Keats*, by Amy Lowell, 2 vols., 1925; *Keats and Shakespeare: A Study of Keats' Poetic Life from 1816 to 1820*, by John Middleton Murry, 1925; *Keats*, by H. W. Garrod, 1926; *The Evolution of Keats's Poetry*, by Claude Lee Finney, Cambridge, Mass., 2 vols., 1936. *Keats' Craftsmanship*, by M. R. Ridley, 1933, also has very little to say on this subject, as does the recent admirable study by Walter Jackson Bate (*John Keats*, 1963). E. C. Pettet (*On the Poetry of Keats*, 1957) and Aileen Ward (*John Keats: The Making of a Poet*, 1963) touch on the matter. In *John Keats: The Living Year*, 1954, and *The Mask of Keats: A Study of Problems*, 1956, Mr. Robert Gittings is more interested in other visual influences on the poet's work.

3. Particularly in Sidney Colvin's book, *John Keats: His Life and Poetry: His Friends Critics and After-Fame*, 1917. It was only after I had begun my work that I found that Colvin—who was Keeper of Prints at the British Museum—had pointed out that 'a whole treatise' might be written on Keats's debt to the visual arts. The comments Colvin does allow himself are exceptionally shrewd and well informed.

Of living critics, Edmund Blunden has been the most constantly aware of this aspect of Keats's genius, but he has never investigated the matter in great detail. *English Bards and Grecian Marbles: The Relationship between Sculpture and Poetry especially in the romantic period*, by Stephen A. Larrabee, New York, 1943, throws some light on one aspect of the matter, as do the articles by D. S. Bland (notably 'Poussin and English Literature', *The Cambridge Journal*, vi (1952–3), 102–22; cf. *Modern Language Review*, 1955, 502–4).

4. 'I am no Prophet, nor the Son of a Prophet; But considering the Necessary Connection of Causes and Events, and upon seeing some Links of that Fatal Chain, I will venture to pronounce (as exceeding Probable) That if ever the Ancient Great, and Beautiful Taste in Painting revives it will be in England': *An Essay on the Theory of Painting*, 1715, 211.

5. Quoted in *The Life, Studies, and Works of Benjamin West*, by John Galt, 1820, ii. 140–1.

6. *Annals of the Fine Arts*, vol. iii (1818), 609. Hazlitt writes in 1821 that 'the study of the fine arts . . . came into fashion about forty years ago': *The Complete Works of William Hazlitt*, edited by P. P. Howe, 1930–4, xix. 53 (the passage reappears in the essay on Crabbe in *The Spirit of the Age*).

7. The Louvre collection became known as the Musée Napoléon in 1803. For a historical account see *Trophy of Conquest: The Musee Napoleon and the Creation of the Louvre*, by Cecil Gould, 1965.

8. *The Complete Works*, viii. 15–16.

9. Ibid. x. 107.

10. The work appeared in two volumes in 1824.

11. *Rhymes on Art*, 2nd ed., 1805, xi, xvii.

12. Buchanan's *Memoirs of Painting*, i. 9.

13. Vol. iv (1819), p. v.

14. 'Some years ago', wrote a contributor to the *Annals* in the winter of 1819–20, 'when the art was in its dim dawn, . . . old pictures were cloistered up from public gaze and the desiring eye of the painter, as though they had been forbidden ware, and only at a sale could they creep out into any thing like general investigation; . . . it is upon conveying the memory back to those days that one feels a delight and a touch of gratitude at witnessing the happy change which has taken place in this respect. The most splendid collections of old original pictures of consummate excellence are now annually displayed before the public': vol. iv. 563–4.

15. An account of the founding of the British Institution may be found in William T. Whitley's *Art in England 1800–1820*, 1928. The first of the regular exhibitions of old masters took place in 1813 and was confined to the work of Sir Joshua Reynolds. A useful (though occasionally inaccurate) condensation of the early annual catalogues was published in 1824: *An Account of all the Pictures exhibited in the . . . British Institution, from 1813 to 1823.*

16. See Chapter VI below.

17. The formation of a National Gallery had been frequently suggested from the later eighteenth century onwards, and sometimes opposed (as it was by Constable). It was due to Wordsworth's friend Sir George Beaumont that it finally became a reality. The Angerstein pictures were purchased in 1824, to form the foundation of the national collection.

18. Of course this statement requires some qualification. Whitley quotes a reminiscence of the public days at Grosvenor House and Bridgewater House by Mrs Jameson: 'We can all remember the loiterers and loungers, the vulgar starers, the gaping idlers we used to meet there—people who instead of moving amid these wonders and beauties "all silent and divine", with reverence and gratitude, strutted about as if they had the right to be there, talking, flirting, peeping and prying, lifting up the covers of chairs to examine the furniture, touching the ornaments—and even the pictures!' (*Art in England 1800–1820*, 110).

19. See *Engravings of . . . The Marquis of Stafford's Collection of Pictures . . . with Remarks on Each Picture*, by William Young Ottley, 4 vols., 1818; *A Catalogue of Pictures by British Artists, in the possession of Sir John Fleming Leicester, . . . by John Young . . . Keeper of the British Institution*, 1821; *A Catalogue of the Celebrated Collection of Pictures of the late John Julius Angerstein*, by John Young, 1823 (the text is given in French as well as English); and the ten volumes of the *Galerie du Musée de France, publiée*

par Filhol, graveur, Paris, 1814 (an eleventh volume was published in 1828). For *Les Monuments antiques du Musée Napoléon* see page 284, n. 22 below.

20. *Imagination and Fancy*, by Leigh Hunt, with an Introduction by Edmund Gosse, n.d., 101–2. There is an excellent introduction to 'English Painting from Blake to Byron', by Geoffrey Grigson, in *From Blake to Byron*, edited by B. Ford, 1957 (*The Pelican Guide to English Literature*, vol. 5).

CHAPTER I: LEIGH HUNT

1. *The Autobiography of Leigh Hunt*, edited by J. E. Morpurgo, 1949, 417.

2. Ibid. 438.

3. *The Pantheon, Representing the Fabulous Histories of the Heathen Gods, and Most Illustrious Heroes . . .*, by Andrew Tooke, first appeared in 1698, and was frequently reprinted, into the nineteenth century. Different editions have different 'Copper Cuts': those Hunt describes are to be found in the edition of 1774, and no doubt in some subsequent editions. By the 33rd edition, in 1810, they had been replaced by others. 'A slight cymar' comes from the description of Venus in Dryden's 'Cymon and Iphigenia', line 100.

4. *Autobiography*, 76.

5. Ibid. 67.

6. Ibid. 414.

7. *The Indicator*, i. 1822, 115–16 (no. xv, 19 Jan. 1820).

8. Ibid. 278 (no. xxxv, 7 June 1820).

9. *Autobiography*, 87.

10. Ibid.

11. *The Indicator*, i. 278.

12. *Autobiography*, 87–88.

13. Ibid. According to Galt, 'Angelica and Medora' was the subject of the first painting which West executed in England: it was exhibited at the Spring Gardens Exhibition in 1764. *The Life of Benjamin West*, ii. 6.

14. *The Indicator*, i. 286 (no. xxxvi, 14 June 1820).

15. The passage is quoted in the second appendix of Edmund Blunden's *Leigh Hunt: A Biography*, 1930, 361.

16. *Annals of the Fine Arts*, iii, no. 10 (Sept. 1818), p. 499.

17. See Edmund Blunden, *Leigh Hunt's 'Examiner' Examined*, 1928, 9–10.

18. *On the Judgment of Connoisseurs*, 1816, reprinted in *The Autobiography and Memoirs of Benjamin Robert Haydon*, with an introduction by Aldous Huxley, 1926, i. 237.

19. *The Reflector, A Quarterly Magazine*, 1811, p. 125.

20. *The Reflector*, pp. 207–8.

21. *Autobiography and Memoirs*, i. 122.

22. *The Reflector*, pp. 208–9.

23. Ibid. 220–1.

24. 'Omnes artes, quæ ad humanitatem pertinent, habent quoddam commune vinculum; & quasi cognatione quadam inter se continentur.' *Oratio pro Archia Poeta, sub initio*.

25. *The Reflector*, pp. 346–7.

26. *The Indicator*, i. 399 (no. 1 [50], 20 Sept. 1820).

27. i. 10 (no. ii, 20 Oct. 1819).

28. i. 271 (no. xxxiv, 31 May 1820).

29. i. 277 (no. xxxv, 7 June 1820).

30. See below, Chapter VII.

31. Sonnet, 'After dark vapours', dated 31 Jan. 1817; printed in *The Examiner*, 23 Feb. 1817.

32. *The Diary of Benjamin Robert Haydon*, edited by Willard Bissell Pope, Cambridge, Mass., i (1960), 465.

33. Ibid. ii. 423.

34. There is a particularly interesting passage in the issue of *Leigh Hunt's London Journal* for 28 May 1834:

> He that would run the whole round of the spirit of Heathenism to perfection, must become intimate with the poetry of Milton and Spenser; of Ovid, Homer, Theocritus, and the Greek tragedians; with the novels of Wieland, the sculptures of Phidias and others, and the pictures of Raphael, and the Caraccis, and Nicholas Poussin. But *a single page of Spenser or one morning at the Angerstein Gallery*, will make him better acquainted with it, than a dozen such folios as Spence's Polymetis, or all the mythologists and book-poets who have attempted to draw Greek inspiration from a Latin fount. (p. 66, Hunt's italics.)

35. *Leigh Hunt: A Biography*, 97.

36. *The Diary*, ii. 63.

37. *Autobiography*, 257; *The Story of Rimini, A Poem*, 1816, p. xiii.

38. Sonnet to Hampstead ('They tell me, when my tongue grows warm on thee'), last line.

39. *Leigh Hunt: A Biography*, 133.

40. *Autobiography*, 258.

41. I quote from *Leigh Hunt's Literary Criticism*, edited by L. H. and C. W. Houtchens, 1956, 420–45. Since I follow the sequence of Hunt's article, individual references are unnecessary. In the quotations from Spenser I preserve Hunt's italics and make no attempt to correct the text.

42. *Imagination and Fancy*, 113.

43. Ibid. 128.

44. Ibid. 121.

45. Ibid. 117.

46. Ibid. 125.

47. Ibid. 126.

48. Haydon, *Autobiography and Memoirs*, i. 255.

49. *Letters*, i. 414; cf. page 252, n. 43 below.

50. The markings are recorded by Amy Lowell, ii. 545–74.

51. *Leigh Hunt's Literary Criticism*, 437.

52. Ibid.

53. *The Keepsake*, 1828, 240: reprinted in *Essays (Selected) by Leigh Hunt*, with an introduction by J. B. Priestley (Everyman's Library), 1929, 216.

54. *Leigh Hunt's Literary Criticism*, 445.

55. 103.

CHAPTER II: HAYDON

1. *Diary*, i. 430.

2. *The Letters of John Keats*, i. 416.

3. *Autobiography*, i. 126.

4. *The Life and Death of Benjamin Robert Haydon*, by Eric George, 1948, 119.

5. *Diary*, i, p. xii.

6. *Annals of the Fine Arts*, v. 367 and 371.

7. *Letters*, i. 114. Keats had in fact met Haydon before this, as Rollins points out in a footnote.

8. Ibid. 117.

9. *Diary*, ii. 107.

10. *Letters*, i. 122.

11. The 'Epic' on which Haydon was engaged at this time was 'Christ's Triumphal Entry into Jerusalem' (Plate II). Keats may possibly be suggesting that *Endymion*, like Haydon's earlier 'Dentatus', was its creator's first attempt on a large scale.

12. *Diary*, iii. 575.

13. *Autobiography*, i. 41.

14. 'Once being at dinner at Sir Joshua's, in company with many painters, in the course of conversation Richardson's Treatise on Painting happened to be mentioned, "Ah!" said Johnson, "I remember, when I was at college, I by chance found that book on my stairs: I took it up with me to my chamber, and read it through, and truly I did not think it possible to say so much upon the art"': *The Life of Sir Joshua Reynolds*, by James Northcote, 1818, i. 235–6.

15. *The Works of Sir Joshua Reynolds*, edited by Edmond Malone, 2nd ed., 1798, i. 86. (I have also consulted R. Wark's edition of *The Discourses*, California, 1959.)

16. Jonathan Richardson, quoted by Eric George, op. cit. 154.

17. *Memoirs of the Life of John Constable*, by C. R. Leslie, 1951 (The Phaidon Press), 173.

18. *Annals of the Fine Arts*, i. 160.

19. *Autobiography*, i. 160–1. A number of poets addressed poems to Haydon: many of them are listed on pages 306–7 of *The Life and Death of Benjamin Robert Haydon*.

20. *Autobiography*, i. 156.

21. Ibid. i. 255.

22. *Diary*, iii. 104.

23. *Autobiography*, i. 115.

24. *Letters*, i. 258.

25. *Diary*, ii. 316–17.

26. *Autobiography*, i. 145; cf. *Diary*, i. 252.

27. *Essays and Criticisms by Thomas Griffiths Wainewright*, collected by W. Carew Hazlitt, 1880, 117–18.

28. *Autobiography*, i. 64–65.

29. Ibid. 66.

30. Ibid. 67.

31. *Annals*, v. 349–50.

32. *Autobiography*, i. 69.

33. Ibid. 107–8.

34. Ibid. 207.

35. *English Bards, and Scotch Reviewers*, 1027–1032.

36. *Autobiography*, i. 207.

37. 'Lord Elgin and his Collection', a book-length article by A. H. smith, based on the Elgin family archives, in *The Journal of Hellenic Studies*, xxxvi (1916), 163–372.

38. There is no lack of farcical footnotes, such as that provided by a 'foppish acquaintance' of Keats who 'joined him one afternoon in front of the marbles, viewed them condescendingly through an eye-glass, and, having obtruded his company and his vapid remarks for an unwelcome length of time, ended by saying, "Yes, I believe, Mr. Keats, we may admire these works safely"'. *The Life and Letters of Joseph Severn*, by William Sharp, 1892, 32.

39. *Autobiography*, i. 235.

40. Ibid. i. 236.

41. *Letters*, i. 122 n.

42. *Autobiography*, i. 251.

43. *Life, Letters, and Literary Remains, of John Keats*, 1848, i. 28. Cf. *Letters*, i. 414. In 1638 Milton told his friend Diodati that he was 'letting his wings grow and beginning to fly': *Private Correspondence and Academic Exercises*, ed. P. B. and E. M. W. Tillyard, 1932, 14.

44. *Autobiography*, i. 269–71. Cf. *Diary*, ii. 173–6. Haydon introduced the head of Keats into the picture, as marked in Plate II.

45. Adam Smith's *The Theory of Moral Sentiments* had reached a sixth edition by 1790. The other books referred to are *A Visit to Paris in 1814* (1815) and *Paris Revisited, in 1815, By Way of Brussels* (1816), both by John Scott; *Essays on Song-Writing; with a Collection of . . . English Songs* (1772 and subsequent editions), by John Aikin; *A Classical Tour through Italy*, by J. C. Eustace, 1813; *Letters from England: by Don Manuel Alvarez Esprielle. Translated from the Spanish*, 1807 (in fact the work of Southey); and perhaps John Pinkerton's *History of Scotland*, 2 vols., 1797.

46. Those which require annotation are *The Works of A. R. Mengs . . . Translated from the Italian, published by J. N. d'Azara*, 2 vols., 1796; *Memoirs of the Life of Nicholas Poussin*, by Maria Graham (afterwards Lady Maria Callcott), 1820; *Narrative of the Operations and Recent Discoveries within the Pyramids, Temples, Tombs, and Excavations, in Egypt and Nubia*, by Giovanni Battista Belzoni, 1820; and *Reflections on the Painting and Sculpture of the Greeks, . . . Translated from The German Original of the Abbé Winkelmann . . . by Henry Fusseli*, 1765.

47. *Autobiography*, i. 13–14. For Bell and his pupils see, for example, Haydon's *Diary*, i. 413.

48. *The Life and Death of Benjamin Robert Haydon*, 12.

49. 'Not having seen Michel Angelo's original works, I am not able to judge of his principles but from prints': *Diary*, ii. 47. 'The absence of books of reference & Prints is a bitter pang': ibid. 502.

50. *Autobiography*, i. 293.

51. In 1813, when he was in great financial trouble, Haydon began to sell some of his most prized possessions. 'At last collecting my prints after Sir Joshua I wrote to Colnaghi; he came and seeing my picture "The Judgment of Solomon" refused to buy, but offered the loan of £10': *Autobiography*, i. 162.

52. According to Whitley's *Art in England 1800–1820*, pp. 256, 275, and 288, 'The Miraculous Draught of Fishes' and 'St. Paul Preaching at Athens' were exhibited in 1816, to be followed by 'The Blinding of Elymas' and 'The Death of Ananias' in 1817, and 'The Healing of the Lame Man at the Beautiful Gate of the Temple' and 'Christ's Charge to St. Peter' in 1818. It was on the last day of 1818 that Keats wrote that he was beginning to understand the Cartoons. See above, pp. 97–98.

53. *Autobiography*, i. 99.

54. Ibid. 18.

55. *Annals of the Fine Arts*, iii. 632.

56. *Autobiography*, i. 106–7.

57. *Annals of the Fine Arts*, iii. 565. Few details of the casts sold in 1823 are given in the Sale Catalogue, but it is worth noticing that they also included 'The Gladiator' (no. 192), a 'Cast of Torso and pedestal' (no.

194), and a Silenus and a Venus 'presented by his excellency the president of the Royal Academy, Petersburgh, to Mr. Haydon' (nos. 181 and 211).

58. *Autobiography*, i. 162; *The Life and Death of Benjamin Robert Haydon*, 136.

59. Cf. *John Keats*, by Amy Lowell, 1925, i. 593–6. For Wainewright's ideal room see *Essays and Criticisms*, pp. 25, 139 ff., 209, and 219.

60. This is the opinion of Miss Ward, op. cit. 151, and of Walter Jackson Bate, op. cit. 302 n.

61. Cf. *Poetics: Or, A Series of Poems, and Disquisitions on Poetry*, by George Dyer, 1812, ii. 172: 'None but artists can judge by what magical interminglings and workings on rough gross materials, by what gradual operations and technicisms of advance, a painting or piece of sculpture is wrought out to its utmost perfection, so as to look like nature.'

62. *The Works of Sir Joshua Reynolds*, i. 46.

63. *Letters*, i. 264.

64. Ibid. i. 169.

65. Cf. *Letters*, i. 210.

66. *Letters*, ii. 230.

67. Ibid. 241.

68. Ibid. 244.

69. Robert Gittings calls it a 'parody' of Wordsworth and thinks that it was written in April 1819: *John Keats: The Living Year*, 110–12. It was on the 11th of that month that Keats had met Coleridge and accompanied him at 'his alderman after dinner pace for near two miles'. *Letters*, ii. 88.

70. *Letters*, ii. 280.

71. *Autobiography*, i. 282. The story of Keats and Charles Cripps, though too long to insert in the chapter, deserves summarizing here, as evidence that Haydon considered Keats competent to help him with a promising young artist. When Keats was in Oxford in September 1817, Haydon wrote to him as follows:

> Will you oblige me by going to Magdalen College, and ask for the Porter—and will you enquire of him about a Young Man who was copying when I was at Oxford the Altar piece there by Moralez.—I am anxious to know about that Young Man, the copy promised something—will you if you can see the Young Man, and ascertain what his wishes in Art are—if he has *ambition*, if he seems to possess *power*—if he wishes to *be great*—all of which you can soon see—In these cases should any friend be disposed to assist him up to London & to support him for a Year I'll train him in the Art, with no other remuneration but the pleasure of seeing him advance—I'll put him in the right way, and do every thing to advance him. . . . Do oblige me by exerting Yourself. (*Letters*, i. 161.)

The name of the young man was Charles Cripps. On the 28th of September Keats told Haydon that, with the help of Bailey, it would be possible for Cripps to get to London:

I have a great Idea that he will be a tolerable neat brush. 'T is perhaps the finest thing that will befal him this many a year: for he is just of an age to get grounded in bad habits from which you will pluck him. He brought a Copy of Mary Queen of Scotts. it appears to me that he has coppied the bad style of the painting as well as couloured the eyebals yellow like the original. He has also the fault that you pointed out to me in Hazlitt—on the constringing and diffusing of substance. However I really believe that he will take fire at the sight of your Picture—and set about things. If he can get ready in time to return to Town with me which will be in a few days—I will bring him to you.   (i. 167.)

The subsequent history of young Cripps may be followed in the letters. Keats went to considerable trouble to help him, but Haydon behaved capriciously. On the last day of the year Haydon wrote in his *Diary* (ii. 177):

> Of young Bewick I have the greatest hopes. . . . I have another in training I picked up at Oxford last summer, & I think he will shine also. May every year add to the hopes & prospects of my glorious Country in Art, and may I be spared while my life is valuable . . . .

On the 23rd of January the following year Keats wrote that 'Cripps is improving very fast—I have the greater hopes of him because he is so slow in devellopment—a Man of great executive Powers at 20—with a look and a speech almost stupid is sure to do something'. Unfortunately Cripps did not become a notable painter.

On 'Haydon and his School' see F. Cummings in the *Journal of the Warburg Institute*, 1963, 367–80. Cf. also his 'Phidias in Bloomsbury', *Burlington Magazine*, 1964, 323–8.

CHAPTER III: ANNALS OF THE FINE ARTS

1. *Autobiography*, i. 249.

2. *Annals of the Fine Arts*, ii. 521–2.

3. iii. 276.

4. iii. 288.

5. i. 270.

6. *Annals of the Fine Arts*, iii, no. 10; *The Works of Hazlitt*, xviii. 51; *The Champion*, 30 Oct. and 6 Nov. 1814.

7. iv. 406–16 and v. 84.

8. v. 309.

9. iii. 109.

10. On Hope see *Le Crépuscule néo-classique: Thomas Hope*, by Sándor Baumgarten, Paris, 1958.

11. *Annals of the Fine Arts*, ii. 413 and iii. 260.

12. Contributors to the *Annals* often italicized the second 'e', to draw attention to the bad French.

13. ii. 535 and iii. 649.

14. iv. 562.

15. *Autobiography*, i. 248–9.

16. Ibid. 124.

17. See pages 97–98 below.

18. iii. 245 (quoting *Endymion*, i. 137–8).

19. iv. 559.

20. iii. 88.

21. v. 128.

22. v. 334.

23. *Autobiography*, i. 249.

24. i. 113.

25. i. 162.

26. ii. 52.

27. iv. 243.

28. *The Works of Sir Joshua Reynolds*, ed. Malone, i. 190–1.

29. i. 52.

30. i. 53.

31. ii. 66–67.

32. ii. 561. The second sonnet is quoted above, on pp. 222–3.

33. iv. 162. The sonnet is signed 'P. R.' Wainewright rightly attributes it to B. W. Procter (*Essays and Criticisms*, 231).

34. It was probably this meeting in print that led Procter to send Keats his *Dramatic Scenes* and *A Sicilian Story*. Earlier he had given Hunt a copy of the former book for Keats, but Hunt had forgotten to pass it on. In June 1820 Procter sent Keats a copy of *Marcian Colonna*, remarking in the covering note: 'I am looking forward with some impatience to the publication of your book.' *The Letters of John Keats*, edited by Maurice Buxton Forman, 3rd ed., 1947, 470. Keats responded with a copy of his volume of 1820.

CHAPTER IV: HAZLITT

1. *The Complete Works*, viii. 7.

2. *Letters*, ii. 71–76.

3. Ibid. 24 and n.

4. *The Complete Works*, xi. 269.

5. *The Life of William Hazlitt*, by P. P. Howe, new edition, 1947, 6.

6. 'So stands the statue that enchants the world' (the Medici Venus) is from Thomson's *Summer* (line 1347). It is a favourite quotation of Hazlitt's. The other quotations in his passage are from Wordsworth's sonnet, 'The world is too much with us' (adapted), and from *Comus*, 251–2.

7. *Complete Works*, x. 107. The next quotation is from viii. 353.

8. *The Life*, 58.

9. Ibid.

10. Ibid. 58–59.

11. Ibid. 60.

12. Ibid. 59.

13. Ibid. 60.

14. *Collected Letters of Samuel Taylor Coleridge*, edited by Earl Leslie Griggs, ii. (1956), 990.

15. *The Life*, 71–72. Hazlitt was dissatisfied with the portrait, and destroyed it before he had completed it.

16. Ibid. 95.

17. *Diary*, ii. 65.

18. *The Complete Works*, xi. 317.

19. Above, p. 60. The collection formed by the Regent Orleans was sold by Philippe Égalité at the French Revolution. The Italian and French pictures were brought to London and purchased jointly by the Duke of Bridgewater, the Earl of Gower (later Marquis of Stafford), and the Earl of Carlisle. Having chosen the paintings that they wished to keep for themselves, they exhibited the collection for public sale in Pall Mall from the 26th of December 1798 to the end of August 1799.

20. *The Complete Works*, x. 9.

21. *The Life*, 114–15.

22. Ibid. 82.

23. *The Complete Works*, viii. 201. See p. 203 above.

24. Ibid. xviii. 7 n.

25. Ibid. viii. 74. The quotation is from *Tristram Shandy*, iii. ch. 12, where Sterne is in fact satirizing the jargon of connoisseurs. 'Corregiescity' is his coinage.

26. Ibid. x. 226.

27. See Plate XL.

28. *Endymion*, ii. 198.

29. *The Complete Works*, v. 98. There are two paintings by Poussin with this title, nos. 19 and 99 in the Catalogue of the Louvre *Exposition Nicolas Poussin*, 1960 (2nd ed., corrected 1962). The earlier is in England at Cjatsworth; the later is in the Louvre.

30. Ibid. v. 102. Cf. iv. 19 and iv. 368.

31. Ibid. viii. 9–10.

CHAPTER V: THE REST OF 'OUR SET'

1. *Poetios: Or, A Series of Poems, and Disquisitions on Poetry*, 2 vols., 1812, ii. 178.

2. *Letters*, i. 113–14.

3. 'Oxford in the Vacation', first sentence.

4. *Letters*, ii. 37.

5. Ibid. ii. 7.

6. Ibid. i. 203.

7. Ibid. i. 214.

8. Ibid. ii. 77–78.

9. *The Keats Circle*, edited by Hyder Edward Rollins, 2nd ed., 2 vols., Cambridge, Mass., 1965, i, p. lxi. On Brown I have also consulted *The Everlasting Spell: A Story of Keats and his Friends*, by Joanna Richardson, 1963.

10. This drawing is reproduced in the books by Aileen Ward and Walter Jackson Bate, and in several earlier studies.

11. *The Plymouth and Devonport Weekly Journal*, 1, 8, 15, and 22 Oct. 1840. Reprinted in *Letters*, i. 421–42, to which I give references.

12. See above, p. 100.

13. *Some Letters & Miscellanea of Charles Brown*, edited by Maurice Buxton Forman, 1937, 41–42.

14. Ibid. 87–89.

15. Ibid. 92–93.

16. *The Life and Letters of Joseph Severn*, by William Sharp, 1892, 19. The next ten references are all to Sharp's book.

17. 27.

18. 27–28.

19. 28.

20. 28.

21. 29.

22. 29.

23. 31.

24. 32.

25. 221–2.

26. 226.

27. *Janus Weathercock: The Life of Thomas Griffiths Wainewright*, by Jonathan Curling, 1938, 44–45.

28. Ibid. 53.

29. *Essays and Criticisms*, 305.

30. He compares the lines 'O, for a draught of vintage!' (from the 'Ode to a Nightingale') to Stothard's 'glowing design of *The Vintage*' (*Essays*, 158–9): remarks that stanzas xxxii–xxxvi of *The Eve of St. Agnes* 'harmonize sweetly' with the 'sentimental' manner of Correggio (*Essays*, 174–5): and makes the interesting claim that the description of the sleeping youth in *Endymion*, ii. 392 ff., 'illustrate[s] the precious

Florentine gem' representing a Hermaphrodite figure (*Essays*, 290–1). Cf. pp. 156–7, above.

In another essay (*Essays*, 47 n.) Wainewright describes a print by Giulio Bonasoni and comments: 'We think we know one bard, an ardent admirer of nature, animate and inanimate, yet no lover of underbred, colloquial, city vulgarisms; in short, a *genuine* descendant from the Elizabethan stock, who will thank us, for introducing this elegant stranger to him, (if indeed they are not already acquainted). Should our choice gain the mede of *his* approbation, we should not heed a jot the blind gabbling of a million of cold-matter-of-fact critics, or soi-disant artists . . .'. This passage almost certainly refers to Keats, and leaves open the possibility that Keats and Wainewright may have met.

31. 'The wily eyes of Gioconda' seems a phrase worth rescuing (*Essays*, 275).

32. *Essays*, 314–15. The next eight references are to this book.

33. 202–3.

34. 32.

35. 40.

36. 198.

37. 254.

38. 172.

39. 183.

40. 199.

41. *The Complete Works of William Hazlitt*, x. 8.

42. *Essays*, 186.

43. Ibid. 58–59.

44. Ibid. 210–11; cf. 56.

CHAPTER VI: THE LETTERS

1. *Letters*, i. 235–6. As Rollins notes, Keats mistakenly attributed 'Uriel' to 'Leslie', a pupil of Allston's.

2. Ibid. ii. 83. 'Bewick' was not Thomas Bewick the wood-engraver, but William Bewick the painter. According to Thomas Landseer's *Life and Letters of William Bewick* ([1871], ii. 169 ff.), all the visitors, including Keats, were introduced to Sir John Leicester. *Letters*, ii. 83 n. 4.

3. He was also a publisher. His publications included Brown's *Narensky: or, The Road to Yaroslaf*, 1814, and Richard Polwhele's *The Fair Isabel of Cotehele, A Cornish Romance*, 1815 (see above, pp. 194–5).

4. Cf. p. 228 above. For the possible influence of the 'Sphinx' on *Hyperion* see pp. 166 ff. above. 'Egyptiana' were very much in fashion at this time. Thomas Hope, for example, was as interested in Egyptian antiquities as in Grecian. One of Keats's letters to Haydon has the valediction, 'Your's like a Pyramid'. *Letters*, i. 149.

5. The triptych is illustrated in *St Cross Hospital Near Winchester: Its History and Buildings* by William Thorn Warren (Winchester and London, 1899). Warren comments, 'This Triptych is considered by some good judges to be the work of Jan de Mabuse, a Flemish painter, famous for the beauty of expression and finish which his portraits possess.' Mr. Peter Guy points out that in B. B. Woodward's *History of Winchester*, p. 230 n. 3, it is stated that this 'is an early painting but is not by Albert Dürer'. This explicit denial seems to suggest that this painting, strange as it must seem, was at one time attributed to Dürer.

6. An engraving by Pierre Lombart (or Lombard) is often found.

7. 'When that aged Tamer Kewthon sold a Certain Camel Called Peter to the Overseer of the Babel Skyworks, he thus spake, adjusting his Cravat round the tip of his Chin—My dear Ten Storyupinair—this here Beast though I say it as shouldn't say't not only has the Power of subsisting 40 day and 40 Nights without fire and Candle but he can sing . . . .' *Letters*, i. 150. In *Publications of the Modern Language Association of America*, 1936, li. 1109 ff., Lowes showed that this passage was suggested by an engraving in the *Universal Family Bible*, 1773, a book Keats is known to have possessed.

8. *Letters*, ii. 137. This statue, which is now in the Vatican, is reproduced in Montfaucon's *Antiquity Explained*, i (1721), between pages 98 and 99.

9. 'Attitude is every thing' would be a characteristic remark on Fuseli's part, though I have not found it in his Royal Academy lectures. Keats is making fun of his name (fusil = musket)—and also of the awkward and apparently contorted positions of many of his figures.

10. T. S. R. Boase, *English Art 1800–1870*, 1959, 5. Boase writes that, beside West, 'poor Haydon . . . was always to remain an envious incompetent' (p. 4).

11. Ibid. 5.

12. *Annals*, iii. 510.

13. *Childe Harold's Pilgrimage to the Dead Sea: Death on the Pale Horse: and Other Poems*, 1818 (anonymous).

14. *The Complete Works*, xviii. 138.

15. *Annals*, iii. 81; ii. 524.

16. 'Never was there a more exquisite creature painted', Haydon wrote of the girl with the basket on her head at the left-hand side of Raphael's 'The Healing of the Lame Man at the Beautiful Gate of the Temple' (*Diary*, i. 232: see Plate VI above). 'It is impossible to look at her without . . . longing to press such an innocent creature to your bosom, and yet tremble for fear of offending her by such a conception.' Cf. i. 363. For a characteristic use of 'intense' and 'intensity' see *Diary*, ii. 10.

17. *Annals*, iv. 559.

18. *Autobiography*, i. 256.

19. *Annals*, iii. 601.

20. Ibid. iv. 560.

21. *John Keats*, 1917, 325.

22. This has been accepted without question by Finney, Rollins (in his edition of the *Letters* at ii. 19 n. 4), and other writers on Keats.

23. As Gittings points out in *John Keats: The Living Year*, 56, Leigh Hunt was later to write enthusiastically about these frescoes in his *Autobiography*. In a passage first printed in *The Liberal* in 1822 he describes the paintings as being 'like a dream of humanity during the twilight of creation' (*Autobiography*, 341).

24. See *A Victorian Romantic: Dante Gabriel Rossetti*, by Oswald Doughty, 1949, 68–69, and 'Alt-Italienische Gemälde als Quellen zum *Faust*' in *Faust. Kunst-historische Aufsätze von Georg Dehio* (München/Berlin, 1914).

25. A note in the copy of the Catalogue in the Print Room of the British Museum gives the price.

26. 'On A Dream' ('As Hermes once . . .'), 10–14.

27. Presumably 'Credulity, Superstition and Fanaticism'.

28. *The Works*, i. 172.

29. Op. cit. 237, 400.

30. *Diary*, ii. 286.

31. *The Letters of Percy Bysshe Shelley*, edited by F. L. Jones, 1964, ii. 276–7.

32. See above, p. 41.

33. *Essays and Criticisms*, 296.

34. Ibid. 296–300.

35. *The Faerie Queene*, ii. xii (The Bower of Bliss).

36. The subject has often been painted. The painting formerly attributed to Rubens, but now thought to be the work of a pupil or imitator, is reproduced as plate 2 in the Phaidon Press edition of Burckhardt's *Recollections of Rubens*. In this, the dead body of Leander is being conveyed over the waves by nereids.

37. Finney, op. cit. i. 192; cf. 'Christmas Day 1818' by Aileen Ward, *Keats-Shelley Journal* (New York), x (Winter 1961), 24 n.

38. *Letters*, ii. 201.

39. Ibid. i. 115.

40. Ibid. i. 125.

41. *The Keats Circle*, ii. 212.

42. *The Autobiography of Leigh Hunt*, 276. My italics.

43. *Letters*, i. 331.

44. Ibid. i. 305.

45. Ibid. i. 302. Gilpin uses the same word, though as a noun, writing of the moment 'before the whole burst of that magnificent scene was presented' in his description of Windermere. *Observations, on Several Parts of England, particularly the Mountains and Lakes of Cumberland and Westmoreland*, 3rd ed., 1808, i. 142.

46. 'I hope I shall never marry. Though the most beautiful Creature were waiting for me at the end of a Journey or a Walk; though the carpet were of Silk, the Curtains of the morning Clouds; the chairs and Sofa stuffed with Cygnet's down; the food Manna, the Wine beyond Claret, the Window opening on Winander mere, I should not feel—or rather my Happiness would not be so fine, as my Solitude is sublime.' *Letters*, i. 403.

47. Ibid. ii. 20.

48. Ibid. i. 307–8. For Keats's admiration of the bare-foot girls see i. 318 and 439. 'We were not bound on a journey of discovery into "the busy haunts of men",' Brown wrote in his 'Walks in the North'. 'Not that cities, their rise, progress, and increasing prosperity, or the reverse . . . were objects of indifference; but attention to them, and a love of the beauty and sublimity of nature are so widely distinct in character as not to be harmonized together. Besides, large towns rarely lay in our route.' *Letters*, i. 422.

49. *Observations, relative chiefly to Picturesque Beauty . . .; particularly the High-Lands of Scotland*, 1789, 2 vols.; and the book already cited in note 44 above.

50. Gilpin particularly praises the Lodore waterfall: *Observations, on . . . Cumberland and Westmoreland*, i. 199–200.

51. See above, pp. 174–5.

52. *Letters*, i. 318. Brown observes that it was a scene 'that *even* Keats confessed to be equal and similar to the best parts of *his favourite* Devon'. (*Letters*, i. 439. My italics.)

53. i. 309.

54. i. 301.

55. ii. 198.

56. i. 242.

57. i. 307.

58. i. 342.

59. i. 360.

60. ii. 52.

61. ii. 130.

62. i. 388.

63. *An Epistle to Dr. Arbuthnot*, lines 340–1.

CHAPTER VII: *POEMS*, 1817

1. *Diary*, ii. 176 (from the description of 'the immortal dinner').

2. Sir Benjamin Ward Richardson, *The Asclepiad*, April 1884 (see Finney, op. cit. i. 88). Colvin silently merges Richardson's reminiscences with those of Henry Stephens (*John Keats*, 30–32).

3. See the official catalogue of the *Exposition Nicolas Poussin* at the Louvre in 1960, pp. 68–69. (The catalogue is the work of Sir Anthony Blunt.) I

have also consulted throughout Denis Mahon's *Poussiniana: Afterthoughts arising from the Exhibition* (Éditions de la Gazette des Beaux-Arts, 1962), and Walter Friedlaender's *Nicolas Poussin: A New Approach*, 1966.

4. W. B. Yeats, *Autobiographies*, 1955, 115–16.

5. For a discussion of this tendency in German poetry see *Aesthetic Paganism in German Literature from Winckelmann to the Death of Goethe*, by Henry Hatfield, Cambridge, Massachusetts, 1964. Cf. E. M. Butler, *The Tyranny of Greece over Germany*, 1935.

6. *The Life and Letters of Joseph Severn* by William Sharp, 29.

7. *Life of John Keats* by Charles Armitage Brown, edited by D. H. Bodurtha and W. B. Pope, 1937, 42.

8. See below, pp. 282–3.

9. *The Works*, i. 81.

10. Quoted by Hatfield, 102.

11. *The Complete Works*, xix. 13 and iv. 115.

12. *The Keats Circle*, ii. 276.

13. A 'Bacchanalian Dance' by Poussin was exhibited at the British Institution in 1816. It later became part of the Angerstein Collection.

14. Lines 407 ff.

15. See *Claude Lorrain: The Paintings* by Marcel Röthlisberger, 2 vols., 1961, i. 222–3. As Röthlisberger points out, the sleeping water nymph in the foreground is reminiscent of antique sculpture, cf. Titian and of. Poussin.

16. *A Descriptive, Explanatory, and Critical Catalogue* . . ., 1834, 359–67.

16b. Many readers and commentators have of course noticed the references here: see, for example, *Mythology and the Romantic Tradition in English Poetry* by Douglas Bush (Cambridge, Mass., 1937), 86 n. Larrabee seems to refer to an illustrated edition of Lemprière, which is unknown to me (op. cit. 210).

17. I owe the reference to Hatfield, 62.

18. Cf. *Endymion*, iii. 790–5.

19. *Annals of the Fine Arts*, iv. 566. The author, who signed himself 'Echion', was Edward Chatfield (see *DNB*), a pupil of Haydon's.

20. iii. 15.

21. *Letters*, i. 131.

22. *The Works*, ii. 137–8.

23. Poussin's copy of 'The Feast of the Gods' is in the National Gallery of Scotland.—A passage illustrating the importance to Keats of what one might call 'Feast of the Gods imagery' occurs in a letter written early in 1819:

> I like Claret whenever I can have Claret I must drink it.—'t is the only palate affair that I am at all sensual in. . . . If you could make some wine like Claret to drink on summer evenings in an arbour! . . . It fills . . . one's mouth with a gushing freshness—then goes down cool and fever-

less . . . and the more ethereal Part of it mounts into the brain . . . [and] walks like Aladin about his own enchanted palace so gently that you do not feel his step—Other wines of a heavy and spirituous nature transform a Man to a Silenus; this makes him a Hermes—and gives a Woman the soul and imortality of Ariadne for whom Bacchus always kept a good cellar of claret (*Letters*, ii. 64).

Within a few weeks Keats would be writing the 'Ode to a Nightingale'.

24. *The Poems of John Keats*, edited by E. de Sélincourt, 3rd ed., 1912, 538.

25. *Letters*, i. 263.

26. Keats wrote 'postern grate': I adopt the emendation of Monckton Milnes.

27. Cf. 'To Hope':

> When by my solitary hearth I sit,
> And hateful thoughts enwrap my soul in gloom;
> When no fair dreams before my 'mind's eye' flit,
> And the bare heath of life presents no bloom.

28. Röthlisberger, i. 384–7.—Colvin (op. cit., p. 265) and de Sélincourt (ed. cit., p. 475) maintain that the 'magic casements' passage in the 'Ode to a Nightingale' was inspired by this picture. This must remain a conjecture.

29. *The Farington Diary by Joseph Farington, R.A.*, edited by James Greig, vi (1926), 51.

30. Pages 67–68 above.

31. *The Complete Works*, xviii. 66.

32. Page 110 above.

33. *The Complete Works*, x. 13.

34. Röthlisberger, ii, plate 301.

35. Ibid. ii. 142.

36. *The Works*, i. 274.

37. *The Farington Diary*, iv. (1924), 115.

38. *The Complete Works*, x. 72. John Landseer describes this painting and Titian's other *poesie* as 'Lyric Odes': *Catalogue*, 136.

39. Page 159 above.

40. *The Complete Works*, xi. 92.

41. 'Epistle to J. H. Reynolds, Esq.', 19. For the fact that the 'Bacchus and Ariadne' was exhibited in 1816 see Whitley, op. cit. 254.

42. Later Keats was to complain that Hunt made 'fine things petty and beautiful things hateful—Through him I am indifferent to Mozart, I care not for White busts . . .' (*Letters*, ii. 11).

43. Röthlisberger, ii, plate 207: not the painting for which Plate XXXIV above represents a drawing.

44. See above, pp. 149 ff. and 220.

45. *Titian's Diana & Actaeon* by E. K. Waterhouse (Charlton Lecture on Art, 1951), 1952, 17–18.

46. v. 349.

47. *The Complete Works*, x. 32.

48. Ibid. iv. 72 ('On Beauty').

49. *The Poems*, edited by E. de Sélincourt, 410.

50. *Polymetis*, 250–1.

51. *John Keats*, i. 223.

52. The verses are signed 'L. Verduc'.

53. *The Complete Works of John Keats*, edited by H. Buxton Forman (1901, reprinted 1929), iii. 256–7.

54. *Essays and Criticisms*, 199.

55. *The Works*, ii. 166.

56. Ibid. i. 136–9.

57. See particularly the references on pp. 65 and 785 of *The Diary of John Evelyn*, edited by E. S. de Beer, 1959 (Oxford Standard Authors).

58. *Of Dramatic Poesy and other Critical Essays*, edited by George Watson, ii. 189.

59. *The Correspondence of Alexander Pope*, edited by George Sherburn, 1956, iv. 20.

60. *Correspondence of Thomas Gray*, edited by Paget Toynbee and Leonard Whibley, 1935, i. 195.

61. See Jean H. Hagstrum, *The Sister Arts*, Chicago, 1958, 296–301.

62. See above, p. 181.

63. *The Works*, i. 158.

64. *The Poems*, edited by E. de Sélincourt, 563; *John Keats*, by Amy Lowell, i. 181–3.

65. 'The men of Cortez staring at each other, and the eagle eyes of their leader looking out upon the Pacific, have been thought too violent a picture for the dignity of the occasion; but it is a case that requires the exception. Cortez's "eagle eyes" are a piece of historical painting, as the reader may see by Titian's portrait of him. The last line . . . makes the mountain a part of the spectacle, and supports the emotion of the rest of the sonnet upon a basis of gigantic tranquillity.' *Lord Byron and Some of his Contemporaries*, 2nd ed., 1828, i. 412. The reference to Titian is of little importance, as the portrait of Cortez is simply a head and shoulders; but Hunt's use of the terms 'picture' and 'a piece of historical painting' is of some interest.

66. *Lectures on Painting by the Royal Academicians: Barry, Opie, and Fuseli*, edited by Ralph N. Wornum, 1848, 454.

67. *The Complete Works*, edited by H. Buxton Forman, iii. 264–5.

CHAPTER VIII: *ENDYMION*

1. *Letters*, i. 170.

2. *The Poetical Works*, edited by H. W. Garrod, 2nd ed., 1958, xciv (from the rejected Preface). I am indebted to the authorities of the Pierpont

Morgan Library for a photograph of this part of the Preface which makes it
virtually certain that the word is 'Loneliness' (as Buxton Forman read it)
and not 'loveliness' (as Woodhouse and Garrod believed). As Loneliness
is one of the main themes of *Endymion*, the point is of some importance.

3. *Benjamin Robert Haydon: Correspondence and Table-Talk. With a Memoir
by his Son. F. W. Haydon*, 1876, 2 vols., ii. 30.

4. *Polymetis*, 184.

5. Cf. the sonnet 'To My Brother George', lines 10–12:

> Cynthia is from her silken curtains peeping
> So scantly, that it seems her bridal night,
> And she her half-discover'd revels keeping,

and *Endymion*, iv. 563–6:

> Who, who from Dian's feast would be away?
> For all the golden bowers of the day
> Are empty left? Who, who away would be
> From Cynthia's wedding and festivity?

6. From the first poem in *Le Bocage royal*: Pléiade edition, i. 792.

7. *Letters*, i. 154.

8. *Polymetis*, 184.

9. In the State Bedroom of William III.

10. Annibale Carracci's 'Diana and Endymion' is in the Farnese Gallery
in Rome. (See *The Farnese Gallery* by J. R. Martin, Princeton, 1965,
plate 44.) Rubens's 'Diana and Endymion' is reproduced on p. 313 of the
volume of *National Gallery Illustrations* devoted to *Continental Schools
(excluding Italian)*, 1937. The painting by de Trioson may be found as
plate 31 in the *Galerie du Musée de France*, 1828, vol. xi. It has recently
been reproduced in *Apollo* (November 1965), as an illustration to M. A.
Goldberg's article 'John Keats and the Elgin Marbles'.

It is interesting to notice that Wordsworth later wrote a sonnet on a
painting of Diana and Endymion (attributed to Lucca Giordano) which
was given him by his eldest son. He describes

> The fair Endymion couched on Latmos-hill;
> And Dian gazing on the Shepherd's face
> In rapture,—yet suspending her embrace;

and remembers how when he himself was a boy Cynthia would turn to him

> A face of love which he in love would greet.

11. This painting is No. 679 in Michael Levey's *The Later Italian Pictures
in the Collection of Her Majesty the Queen*, Phaidon Press, 1964. According
to Levey, the picture was engraved by Wagner at Venice as being in the
collection of Joseph Smith. It was bought by George III in 1762 and
placed in the Gallery at Kew. It was removed to Windsor in 1828.

12. As Sir Anthony Blunt points out (*Exposition Nicolas Poussin*, p. 65),
the portrayal of Diana in this painting recalls that of the Muse in the
Louvre 'Inspiration of the Poet': an interesting fact to students of Keats.
Cf. p. 181 above.

13. *The Poetical Works*, lxxxix–xcii.

14. *Letters*, i. 213–14.

15. *The Works*, ii. 165–6.

16. Ibid. ii. 129.

17. Ibid. ii. 128.

18. *Imagination and Fancy*, 126.

19. Titian's 'The Worship of Venus' is reproduced as plate 41 in Hans Tietze's *Titian* (Phaidon Press, 1950); the paintings by Rubens may be found in the Phaidon edition of Burckhardt's *Recollections of Rubens*, plates 81 and 100. Wainewright recommends the 'splendid and somewhat scarce print by Bolswert' of Rubens's 'Garden of Love', *Essays and Criticisms*, 32.

20. *Annals of the Fine Arts*, v. 273 n.

21. *The Life and Letters of Joseph Severn*, 29.

22. For example, see *Summer*, 1344–7:

> . . . With wild surprise,
> As if to marble struck, devoid of sense,
> A stupid moment motionless she stood:
> So stands the statue that enchants the world.

Cf. also *Endymion*, ii. 200 and 210.

23. The Eldest Lady's Story in 'The Porter and the Three Ladies of Bagdad'.

24. *Art and Architecture in France 1500 to 1700* (The Pelican History of Art), 1953, 186.

25. Lines 165 ff.

26. *Polymetis*, 98–99.

27. A Niobe by Wilson belonging to Sir George Beaumont was exhibited at the British Institution in 1814. Another was in the Stafford Gallery (*Engravings of . . . the Marquis of Stafford's Gallery*, iv, near the end). For a discussion of these paintings and of engravings from them see *Richard Wilson* by W. G. Constable, 1953, pp. 160–2 and plates 18–21*b*. There are further references to Niobes by Wilson in *Annals of the Fine Arts*, ii. 90 and 541.

'Niobe' was the subject set for an Oxford Prize Poem in 1814, when J. L. Adolphus was successful with a poem which alludes to ancient sculptural representations of the story.

In 1818 it is mentioned in the *Annals of the Fine Arts* (iii. 528) that casts of the famous Italian group of Niobe and her Children are to be sent to England in gratitude for casts of the Elgin Marbles. At iv. 151 we hear that '*The group of Niobe and her children* is put up in the riding room at Carlton-house. They are exceedingly beautiful, but of a more artificial and academical style than the Elgin marbles: every thing is as it were in an attitude; the heads and limbs look conscious of their own grace. . . . The heads are well known for their pathetic beauty.'

28. 'Botticelli and Nineteenth-Century England', by Michael Levey, *Journal of the Warburg and Courtauld Institutes*, 1960, xxiii. 292.

29. *Antiquity Explained, And Represented in Sculptures by the Learned Father Montfaucon, Translated into English by David Humphreys, M.A.* i. (1721), 94, and plate 45, fig. 6. Cf. Supplementary Volume (1725), 59.

30. *Imagination and Fancy*, 123.

31. *Metamorphoses*, i. 318. Keats uses the word 'mountain'd' again in *Hyperion*, ii. 123. *OED* gives one or two similar usages, notably one from Feltham's *Resolves*.

32. *The Poems*, 431.

33. *Essays and Criticisms*, 290 n.—Bailey remarks that this 'sleeping Adonis' is 'another Titianlike picture' (*The Keats Circle*, ii. 253).

34. Denis Mahon, *Poussiniana*, 27.

35. Keats uses the word again in one of his notes on *Paradise Lost*, where he writes that 'The management of this Poem is Apollonian'. *The Complete Works*, edited by H. Buxton Forman, iii. 262.

36. See *Samuel Palmer: The Visionary Years*, 1947, by Geoffrey Grigson, and *Paintings and Drawings by Samuel Palmer in the Ashmolean Museum Oxford*, n.d.

37. See *A Memoir of Edward Calvert Artist by his Third Son* [Samuel Calvert], 1893, and Raymond Lister's *Edward Calvert*, 1962.

38. Published in 1821.

39. It is possible that Keats knew of the Italian poem on Michelangelo's 'Night', of which a translation was published in the *Annals of the Fine Arts* in 1819:

> Night's marble figure, stranger, which you see
> Recline with so much grace and majesty. . . .   (iv. 69)

40. Notably *Metamorphoses*, xiii. 905 ff.

41. 'He had an ample capacity for Painting & Music', Severn wrote, '& applied them largely to his Poetry, I could point out many passages taken from the one & the other — Titians picture of Bacchus & Ariadne is the original of the scene in the Endymion.' *The Keats Circle*, ii. 133. Bailey remarks that 'the artistic painting of Bacchus, . . . seems to have been copied from a well known picture of Titian, of which, the Original is in the National Gallery', ibid. 284. Monckton Milnes refers to the picture (*Life, Letters, and Literary Remains*, ii. 69).

42. See *The French Drawings in the Collection of His Majesty the King at Windsor Castle* by Anthony Blunt, 1945.

43. Cf. Montfaucon's summary of Apollodorus: 'Some say he [Endymion] was the Son of *Jupiter*: He was so beautiful that the Moon fell in Love with him; and *Jupiter* giving him his choice of having whatever he liked best, he chose to sleep always, and continue immortal without ever waking.' *Antiquity Explained*, Supplementary Volume, 118–19. A few sentences before, Montfaucon remarks that 'according to the Notions of some of the

Greeks, *Sleep* was a Friend to the Muses; and therefore in a *Musæum* at *Træzena*, there was an Altar on which they sacrificed to the Muses, and to *Sleep*. The reason of the Muses being thus in company with *Sleep*, is easily guessed. A Student, and Follower of the Muses, who tires his Spirit and Imagination, hath need of Repose and Rest, in order to quiet his Mind, and to recover new Strength, for pursuing his Studies.' Cf. the note on a plate representing 'Le Sommeil' in *Les Monumen[t]s Antiques du Musée Napoléon, dessinés et gravés par Thomas Piroli . . . publiés par F. et P. Piranesi* (1804–6): 'On s'étonnera peut-être du rapport que les Anciens établissaient entre les Muses et le Sommeil, mais les poètes et tous ceux qui connaissent les moments propices où l'imagination se développe n'en seront point surpris.' Cf. the title of Keats's poem 'Sleep and Poetry'.

44. *The London Magazine*, April 1820, 385–6.

CHAPTER IX: SATURN & THE TITANS

1. Almost the only evidence about the composition of *Hyperion* is in the letters, and some of the references are far from clear. On the 23rd of January 1818 Keats told Haydon that he was going to write a poem on Hyperion (i. 207). Before they left for America in June George and his wife probably knew of this intention (ii. 12). On the 20th of September, while he was nursing Tom, Keats told Dilke that he had been 'obliged to write, and plunge into abstract images' (i. 369)—almost certainly a reference to the poem. On the 27th of October, in a letter to Woodhouse, Keats implies that he has been 'cogitating on the Characters of saturn and Ops' (= Cybele: i. 387). On the 18th of December he wrote to America:

I think you knew before you left England that my next subject would be 'the fall of Hyperion' I went on with it a little last night—but it will take some time to get into the vein again. I will not give you any extracts because I wish the whole to make an impression. (ii. 12)

On the last day of the year he describes his 'large poem' as 'scarce begun' (ii. 18). A few days later he is still at work on the poem (ii. 21). On the 14th of February he tells George and his wife that he has 'not gone on with Hyperion—for to tell the truth I have not been in great cue for writing lately' (ii. 62); and adds—'I must wait for the spring to rouse me up a little'. On the 8th of March he tells Haydon that he has been 'in a sort of qui bono temper, not exactly on the road to an epic poem' (ii. 42). On the 15th of April he is 'still at a stand in versifying' (ii. 84).

On the 20th of April 1819 Woodhouse made a copy from Keats's manuscript, and noted that the latter had been 'written in 1818/9' (Finney, op. cit. ii. 489). Woodhouse also wrote the following note in his interleaved and annotated copy of *Endymion*, dating it 'April. 1819':

K. lent me the fragment here alluded to for perusal. It contains 2 books & ½—(ab^t 900 lines in all). He said he was dissatisfied with what he had done of it; and should not complete it. (Finney, 490)

On the 14th of August Keats told Bailey that he had recently 'been writing parts of my Hyperion' (ii. 139). It has been reasonably conjectured, therefore, that what Keats was doing in August was beginning work on the version that we call *The Fall of Hyperion*.

On these few facts and conjectures one has to construct a chronology that seems to fit in with what is known of Keats's poetic career as a whole. This has been done by a number of accurate scholars, most recently by Miss Ward and Professor Bate. The most I would claim is that it appears to be possible that the description of Hyperion's palace was written after the opening of the British Institute Exhibition in February 1819, when Martin's painting, 'The Fall of Babylon', was displayed. (There is the further possibility that Keats saw the picture before it was publicly exhibited.) It is also tempting to suppose that the description of Thea's face was added after Keats had seen the 'Head of Memnon' in the British Museum. Rollins seems to be relying to some extent on conjecture when he dates the relevant passage in the letter 'about March 3 or 4' (ii. 67 n. 5). It is also of interest that lines 31–36 are detachable: in *The Fall of Hyperion* they do in fact disappear, along with the classical images; eight new lines (331–8) are there inserted between line 25 ('With reverence, though to one who knew it not') and line 37 ('There was a listening fear in her regard').

2. The figure of Saturn had appealed to the imagination of Keats as early as the time when he wrote *Endymion*, ii. 993–4 (by the end of August 1817, if we follow Garrod's dating: *Poetical Works*, xci):

> I roam in pleasant darkness, more unseen
> Than Saturn in his exile.

At iii. 129 'Saturn's vintage' is used to signify great antiquity, and at iv. 956–7 we hear of 'old Saturnus' forelock' and of 'his head Shook with eternal palsy'.

With the opening lines of *Hyperion* we may perhaps compare the fifth stanza of Thomson's *Castle of Indolence*, a poem to which Keats refers in a letter (see p. 244 above).

3. *The Complete Works*, iii. 258.

4. Ibid. 264–5.

5. See pp. 192–3 above.

6. There is striking evidence of the importance of the Elgin Marbles to Keats in a sentence in his article on Kean in *Richard Duke of York*: 'We see nothing of Talbot, and missing him is like walking among the Elgin Marbles and seeing an empty place where the Theseus had reclined' (*The Complete Works*, iii. 237).—It will be evident that I disagree with Larrabee's view that Saturn is 'very much like the Elgin Theseus' (op. cit. 217).

7. *The Pantheon*, 4th ed., 1814, 33. See pp. 282–3 below.

8. *Saturn and Melancholy: Studies in the History of Natural Philosophy Religion and Art* by Raymond Klibansky, Erwin Panofsky, and Fritz Saxl, 1964, 196–7.

9. Ibid. Klibansky illustrates the tomb of Cornutus in his plate 13. Cf. his plate 56.

10. See also the discussion of portrayals of Saturn in *The Survival of the Pagan Gods* by Jean Seznec, 1953 (Bollingen Series xxxviii: Pantheon Books, New York).

11. I find that the ambiguity about the posture of Saturn has been noticed by Newell F. Ford in his brief article: 'Keats's Saturn: Person or Statue?', *Modern Language Quarterly*, 1953, xiv. 253–7.

12. *Diary*, i. 226.

13. Ibid. i. 198.

14. Ibid. i. 279. There is a Haydon drawing of Achilles, with a very powerful neck, in the Print Room of the British Museum (1881.7.9.484).

15. Page 36 above. The drawing is reproduced as plate ii in volume i of Huxley's edition of the *Autobiography*.

16. There is an interestingly apposite note in Hayley's *Essay on Sculpture*: 'In contemplating the Farnesian Hercules, I believe many spectators feel an involuntary mechanical impulse to muscular exertion' (edition of 1800, p. 293).

17. *Diary*, i. [162]; i. 92; i. 181.

18. 'Keats and Egypt', *The Review of English Studies*, iii, No. 9, Jan. 1927, 10. I have also consulted 'Egypt and *Hyperion*', by Barbara Garlitz, *Philological Quarterly* (Iowa), xxxiv, 1955, 189–96.

19. *Annals*, iv. 151.

20. 'What pleasures have I enjoyed in that study!', Haydon wrote in his *Diary* towards the end of 1823. 'In it have talked & walked Scott, Wordsworth, Keats, Procter, Belzoni, Campbell, Cuvier, Lamb, Knowles, Hazlitt, Wilkie, and other Spirits of the Time': ii. 442.

21. *Quarterly Review* (Apr. 1818) xix. 204.

22. The passage occurs in his description of his visit to Paris in 1814: 'Spent the day [June the 28th] at the private library of the Institute, copying the dresses of the Ancient Egyptians, from the great Work published by Napoleon [E. F. Jomard's *Description de l'Égypte*]; exceedingly useful. The French expedition to Egypt has been proved a great delight to the learned, by the exposition of several cities, which no single Traveller could explore before. The consequence to us Painters is a complete series of the costumes, features, & manners of the inhabitants, copied from their temples, still perfect & uninjured. They are worth the sacrifice they have made.' *Diary*, i. 375.

23. *The Review of English Studies*, iii, p. 2.

24. I am grateful to Dr. Donald Strong and Dr. A. F. Shore for their help on this point. The Museum has a number of small sphinxes, but these are obviously irrelevant. Dr. Shore points out that 'in Guides printed in 1819 and 1820 a royal head, no. 97 (at present exhibited in Bay 25 of the Egyptian Sculpture Gallery), was referred to as the head of a sphinx'. But

as it is only a little more than life-size, Keats would hardly have described it as 'great' or 'giant'.

As I point out in Note 1, pp. 269–270 above, the lines describing the 'Memphian sphinx' are detachable, and could have been added after the composition of the first draft of the opening passage.

25. *Diary*, ii. 492.

26. *Annals of the Fine Arts*, iii. 323–4 and 589, iv. 151.

27. *The Collected Writings of Thomas de Quincey*, edited by David Masson, 1889, i. 41 n.

28. *The Geography*, xvii. i. 46.

29. *The Pantheon*, 269.

30. *The Keats Circle*, ii. 133.

31. *The Botanic Garden: A Poem, in Two Parts*, 1791, p. 18 of the text and p. 17 of the Notes.

32. Page 7.

33. *The Review of English Studies*, iii. 6.

34. *The Quarterly Review*, July 1818, xix. 407.

35.
> Anon out of the earth a Fabrick huge
> Rose like an Exhalation, with the sound
> Of Dulcet Symphonies and voices sweet:
> Built like a Temple, where *Pilasters* round
> Were set, and Doric pillars overlaid
> With Gold'n Architrave; nor did there want
> Cornice or Freeze, with bossy Sculptures grav'n;
> The Roof was fretted Gold. Not *Babilon*,
> Nor great *Alcairo* such magnificence
> Equald in all thir glories, to inshrine
> Belus or Serapis thir Gods, or seat
> Thir Kings, when *Ægypt* with *Assyria* strove
> In wealth and luxurie.   (i. 710–22.)

'What creates the intense pleasure of not knowing?', Keats asks in his note on this passage. 'A sense of independence, of power, from the fancy's creating a world of its own by the sense of probabilities . . . .' *The Complete Works*, edited by H. Buxton Forman, iii. 260–1.

36. *John Martin, 1789–1854: His Life and Works*, by Thomas Balston, 1947, 48; *Art in England 1800–1820*, by William T. Whitley, 1928, 298. According to Whitley the Exhibition opened 'early in February'.—I find that Edmund Blunden has anticipated me in suggesting that Martin influenced *Hyperion*, although he does not specify individual paintings: see his lecture 'Romantic Poetry and the Fine Arts', *Proceedings of the British Academy*, 1942, 101–18.

37. iv. 121.

38. Quoted by Balston, 48.

39. See above, pp. 92–93.

40. *Diary*, iii. 11, 45. One of Haydon's comments on Martin is shrewd, and helps to account for the fact that literary people had a particular tendency to overrate him: 'Martin & Danby are men of extraordinary imaginations, but infants in *painting*. These Pictures always seem to Artists as if a child of extraordinary fancy had taken up a brush to express its inventions. The Public, who are no judges of the Art, as an *Art*, over praise their inventions, & the Artists, who are always professional, see only the errors of the brush': *Diary*, iii. 276.

41. *England and the English* by Edward Lytton Bulwer, 1833, ii. 211–12. Heine's description of Martin and Berlioz is of interest:

> Leurs œuvres... ne rappellent ni la Grèce païenne ni le catholique moyen âge, mais elles nous reportent plus haut dans la période de l'architecture assyrio-babylonio-égyptienne, de ces poèmes de pierre qui nous retracent le drame pyramidal de la passion de l'humanité, le mystère éternel du monde. (*Lutèce*, edition of 1863, 387–8: quoted by Jean Seznec in *John Martin en France*, London, 1964, 33.)

For a wide-ranging survey of the development of interest in the East see *La Renaissance orientale*, by Raymond Schwab, Paris, 1950.

42. Balston, 32–35.

43. *The Complete Works*, 62; cf. vi. 349.

44. Unlike 'Baldwin': 'As under the reign of Saturn there was a rebellion of the Titans, so under the reign of Jupiter happened the war of the Giants': *The Pantheon*, 1814, 69.

45. *Poetics* by George Dyer, 1812, i. 17 n.

CHAPTER X: APOLLO

1. *Polymetis*, 83; *Hyperion*, ii. 228–9; *Bible de l'Humanité*, Paris, 1854, 221.

2. *Letters*, i. 207.

3. See p. 123 above.

4. For the other see p. 199 above. Cf. p. 40 above.

5. *Polymetis*, plate xi, and p. 83.

6. *The Works*, ii. 19–21. When Benjamin West visited Italy the Italians were particularly eager to see how he would react to the Belvedere Apollo. 'The Italians concluding that, as he was an American, he must, of course, have received the education of a savage, became curious to witness the effect which the works of Art in the Belvidere and Vatican would produce on him. . . . It was agreed that the Apollo should be first submitted to his view, because it was the most perfect work among all the ornaments of Rome, and, consequently, the best calculated to produce that effect which the company were anxious to witness. The statue [was] then enclosed with doors. . . . When the keeper threw open the doors, the Artist . . . exclaimed, "My God, how like it is to a young Mohawk warrior". The Italians . . . were excessively mortified to find that the god of their idolatry was compared to a savage.' *The Life*, by John Galt, i. 104–6.

7. *Diary*, i. 481.

8. Ibid. 117.

9. Ibid. 247 and 487.

10. Ibid. ii. 15.

11. *The Complete Works*, x. 222.

12. In Poussin's 'A Dance to the Music of Time' in the Wallace Collection, for example, we see the Hours dancing in the foreground, and above the Muses dancing round Apollo's chariot high among the clouds. Cf. p. 291 n. 10 below.

13. In 'The Cap and the Bells' Keats makes 'Hum' say:

> If ever you have leisure, sire, you shall
> See scraps of mine will make it worth your while,
> Tit-bits for Phœbus! (lxiii)

The dreadful phrase 'tit-bits for Phœbus' satirizes Hunt's over-familiarity with Apollo.—The fullest discussion of 'The Cap and the Bells' may be found in *The Mask of Keats: A Study of Problems* by Robert Gittings, 1956, chap. 10.

14. *The Poetical Works*, edited by H. W. Garrod, 430 n–431 n.

15. The sestet of Hunt's sonnet, 'On Receiving a Crown of Ivy from the Same [John Keats]' describes the vision that followed the crowning:

> Tress-tossing girls, with smell of flowers and grapes
> Come dancing by, and downward piping cheeks,
> And up-thrown cymbals, and Silenus old
> Lumpishly borne, and many trampling shapes,—
> And lastly, with his bright eyes on her bent,
> Bacchus,—whose bride has of his hand fast hold.

16. Apollo's golden lyre was often in Keats's mind. That is how he comes to refer to it in a joking passage in a letter to Benjamin Bailey: 'I shall never be a Reasoner because I care not to be in the right.... —So you must not stare if in any future letter I endeavour to prove that Appollo as he had a cat gut string to his Lyre used a cats' paw as a Pecten....' *Letters*, i. 243.

17. *The Examiner*, 16 March 1817; and his sonnet 'To John Keats' ("Tis well you think me . . .'), last line.

18. Walter Jackson Bate, op. cit., particularly p. 138.

19. See pp. 282–3 below.

20. According to *Exposition Nicolas Poussin*, 46–47, Bryan sold the painting at Coxe's on 19 May 1798. It was bought for 100 gns., probably by Thomas Hope. By 1824 (Sir Anthony Blunt informs me) it was in the part of the Hope Collection which was in London (see *British Galleries of Painting and Sculpture* by C. M. Westmacott, 1824). According to the *Annals of the Fine Arts*, i. 370 ff., a painting with this title was to be found in the Dulwich Collection in 1817. This was no doubt Poussin's rather later

painting of the same name, which had been at Great Cumberland Lodge, Windsor, about 1803 (*Exposition*, 57). Hazlitt, in his *Sketches of The Principal Picture-Galleries in England* (1824), refers to 'Apollo giving a Poet a Cup of Water to drink' as being at Dulwich: *The Complete Works*, x. 24.

21. 'Sleep and Poetry', line 36.

22. *Exposition Nicolas Poussin*, 48.

23. This fragment is 'written to the tune of the air in "Don Giovanni"'. Apollo asks:

> Which of the fairest three
> Today will ride with me?

and each of them replies that she will.—In a reference to Wordsworth's *Peter Bell* Keats makes it clear that he shares J. H. Reynolds's 'fixed aversion to those three rhyming Graces Alice Fell, Susan Gale and Betty Foy; and now at length especially to Peter Bell—fit Apollo'. 'The more he may love the sad embroidery of the Excursion'—he remarks a line or two later—'the more he will hate the coarse Samplers of Betty Foy and Alice Fell': *Letters*, ii. 94.

24. 'Quell' as a noun also occurs in *Macbeth*, I. vii. 72, and *Endymion*, ii. 537, where Love has 'a sovereign quell . . . in his waving hands'.

25. Apollo almost always plays a stringed instrument. When he is portrayed with Marsyas, we notice that Marsyas commonly plays on pipes. The 'pipe' here is probably due merely to the exigency of the rhyme.

26. iv. 12.

27. Other references to Apollo in *Endymion* occur at ii. 362, and iii. 42, 463 and 786. There are two references in *Lamia*, which was written soon after Keats had abandoned his first attempt to write *Hyperion*. The first is quoted above on p. 199: the second is a clear reminiscence of *Hyperion*:

> Deaf to his throbbing throat's long, long melodious moan. (i. 75)

28. *John Keats*, 403.

29. *Exposition Nicolas Poussin*, plate 12 and pp. 51–52.

30. *Polymetis*, 84.

31. Tibullus, III. iv. 29–32: 'His radiance was such as the moon, daughter of Latona, spreads before her, and over his body's snow was a crimson flush, such as dyes the fair cheeks and blushing face of a maid when she is first escorted to her young husband's home.'

32. *Polymetis*, 85.

33. Ibid. 185 n. 26. 'What use to you now are your beautiful shape and colour and your radiant brightness, son of Hyperion?'

34. After the word 'Celestial' in the Woodhouse transcript there follow in pencil the words 'Glory dawn'd: he was a god!' *The Poetical Works*, edited by H. W. Garrod, 305 n.

Keats may have been remembering Dante's reminiscence of the story of Marsyas at the beginning of the *Paradiso*:

> . . . Do thou
> Enter into my bosom, and there breathe
> So, as when Marsyas by thy hand was dragged
> Forth from his limbs, unsheathed. O power divine!

As Wind comments:

To obtain the 'beloved laurel' of Apollo, the poet must pass through the agony of Marsyas. . . . The cruelty inflicted on Marsyas by Apollo . . . expresses the supreme sense of disproportion by which the god attacks the human frame, which is agonized as it succumbs to the divine ecstasy. . . . The words recall the Virgilian *numine afflatur* which is inscribed over Raphael's *Parnassus*. In Virgil those words—*adflata est numine*—express the frenzy of the Sibyl as she becomes possessed by the approaching god, whom she tries vainly to shake off from her anguished breast. . . . The torture of the mortal by the god who inspires him, was a central theme in the revival of ancient mysteries, its illustration in *Apollo and Marsyas* being only one of many variations. Its most elaborate development was in the story of Amor and Psyche, in which the ordeals suffered by Psyche to regain Amor were understood as stages of a mystical initiation (*Pagan Mysteries in the Renaissance*, 144–5).

35. *The Poems*, edited by de Sélincourt, 486.

36. Ibid. 486–9.

37. *The Survival of the Pagan Gods*, 144.

38. Ibid. 145.

39. Ibid. 76 n. 122.

40. Ibid. 142.

41. Op. cit. 48.

42. Op. cit. 313. Cf. the excellent discussion of *Hyperion* in *The Romantic Comedy* by D. G. James, 1948, 134–51. See also 'Keats, Milton, and *The Fall of Hyperion*' by S. M. Sperry, *Publications of the Modern Language Association of America*, lxxvii. 1 (March 1962), 77–84.

43. *Lord Byron and Some of his Contemporaries*, 2nd ed., 1828, i. 419.

44. *Diary*, ii. 67. The entry is dated November 5, 1816.

45. *The Complete Works of John Keats*, iii. 256: more fully quoted above on p. 138.

CHAPTER XI: THREE LOVE STORIES

1. *The Rule of Taste from George I to George IV*, 1936, 148.

2. *Letters*, ii. 62.

3. *The Indicator*, i. 343 (no. xliii, 2 August 1820).

4. Quoted by de Sélincourt in *The Poems of John Keats*, 465.

5. These railings are now in the Victoria and Albert Museum.

6. iv. 244.

7. *The Complete Works*, x. 164.

8. 'Ode on a Grecian Urn', 28.
9. *The Poems of John Keats*, 465.
10. Chapter 8.
11. *On the Poetry of Keats*, 1957, 18–29.
12. See above, p. 92.
13. *The Complete Works*, vi. 147. (My italics.)
14. Ibid. 149.
15. There is a passage in Haydon's *Diary* that seems reminiscent of *The Eve of St. Agnes*:

As I looked toward a solemn corner of the Abbey just illumined by a rich painted Window, 'casting a dim religious light' in which stood the altar, embrowned as it were in shadow—I felt a dreadful influence awe me, and as a misty beam of light streamed through the glittering glass and gave a solemnity to the solitude of the corner, as the organ was roaring and the angelic voices of the boys were chanting, [so] that one's sense was lost, in rapture; I fancied the spirit of God was reposing behind the Altar, and I thought I perceived its influence breathing, as it were, a purity around it. I had that sort of sensation as when in the dead of night, the whole house buried in sleep, you sit watching an innocent, beautiful & sleeping infant and listen to its little breathings, which is all that gives one an Idea of any thing living amidst the quiet and balmy repose that seems to hang over the World.   (i. 181)

The similarity may be fortuitous: or Haydon may have mentioned this experience in conversation: or Keats may even have dipped into the *Diary*. It is perhaps worth noticing that the passage about 'Ixion's wheel stopped', quoted above on p. 165, occurs in the immediately preceding entry. The passage quoted in this note is dated September 9, 1810.

16. *Letters*, ii. 201.
17. Rossetti considered the 'Eve of Saint Mark' as being, with 'La Belle Dame sans Merci', 'the chastest and choicest example of his maturing manner', and wrote that it 'shews astonishingly real mediaevalism for one not bred as an artist': D. G. Rossetti, *John Keats: Criticism and Comment* (letters to H. Buxton Forman, privately printed, 1919). The passage is quoted in *Keats and the Victorians: A Study of His Influence and Rise to Fame: 1821–1895* by George H. Ford, New Haven, 1944, 121–2. Holman Hunt exhibited his well-known picture, 'The Eve of St. Agnes', in 1848. Other Victorian paintings of subjects taken from Keats are listed on p. 181 of Ford's book.

Those seeking fuller documentation on this subject may refer to *Pre-Raphaelitism: A Bibliocritical Study*, by W. E. Fredeman, Cambridge, Mass., 1965.

18. *John Keats: The Living Year*, chap. 9.
19. The word 'uneager' seems to have appealed to Keats about this time. All MSS. of *The Eve of St. Agnes* give the first line of stanza viii as

She danc'd along with vague, uneager eyes.

(*The Poetical Works*, edited by H. W. Garrod, 239 n.)

In the printed version 'uneager' gives way to 'regardless'. The only other example of the word cited in the *OED* is in a poem by Keats's biographer: see *Memorials of Many Scenes* by R. M. Milnes, new ed., 1844, p. 186.

20. See above, p. 180.

21. I translate from 'Keats e lo stile Regency', by Mario Praz, *Il Tempo*, 17 Feb. 1954. I owe this reference to Professor Praz.

CHAPTER XII: 'ODE TO PSYCHE'

1. *The Reflector*, i. 346–7 (March 1811): the essay is reprinted in George Dyer's *Poetics*, 1812, ii. 1–26.

2. *Letters*, ii. 105.

3. If there is any real distinction between a 'hymn' and an 'ode', as Keats uses the terms.

4. *Letters*, ii. 115. Boiardo 'was a noble Poet of Romance; not a miserable and mighty Poet of the human Heart'.

5. *Letters*, i. 113.

6. I am indebted to Mr. Donald Low for this reference.

7. *The Temple of Nature; or, The Origin of Society: A Poem, with philosophical notes*, 1803, pp. 60–62; quoted in part on p. 207 above.

8. Cf. in particular *Psyche; or, The Legend of Love*, I. i:

> Fair Psyche through *untrodden* forests went
>
> .   .   .   .   .   .
>
> While *dear remembrance* bade her ever weep; (my italics)

and II. xli:

> No suppliant tears her vengeance shall abate
> Till thou hast raised an altar to her power,
> Where perfect happiness, in lonely state,
> Has fixed her temple in secluded bower,
> By foot impure of man untrodden to this hour!

as well as VI. liii:

> Thus, in her lover's circling arms embraced,
> The fainting Psyche's soul, by sudden flight,
> With his its subtlest essence interlaced.

Keats may also have remembered the 'flowery bank' in a 'woodland shade' where we discover Psyche at the beginning of Mrs. Tighe's poem, when he described the 'deepest grass' on which Cupid and Psyche are lying. The influence of Mrs. Tighe on Keats has often been pointed out. E. V. Weller grossly exaggerated it in *Keats and Mary Tighe*, New York, 1928.

9. *The Complete Works*, viii. 200–1. According to Hazlitt's son, 'W—' was Charles Jeremiah Wells, whom Keats knew.

10. In Raphael's 'Parnassus', in the Vatican, for example, we see Homer, Virgil, and Dante. The twelfth line of Keats's poem may have been suggested by a print of Poussin's 'Parnassus', in which Homer is kneeling in

front of Apollo, who is offering him a cup. Homer is smiling, and appears to be looking at the radiant god. Keats writes:

> But, what creates the most intense surprise,
> His soul looks out *through renovated eyes*. (My italics.)

11. *Endymion*, i. 232–, iii. 943– and iv. 563–.

12. See p. 18 above for Leigh Hunt's comment on Jupiter and Maia in Spenser.

13. Cf. n. 3 above. See my *English Literature 1815–1832*, 1963, 121 n. for an attempt to emphasize the close relationship between this sonnet and the Odes.

14. *The Life and Letters of Joseph Severn* by William Sharp, 33. Mrs. Moorman suggests that Wordsworth's comment, even if accurately reported, may not have been intended to be scornful: *William Wordsworth: A Biography: The Later Years*, 1965, 317–18.

15. If Keats knew of this interpretation of the part played by the elements in the fable, the knowledge may lie behind lines 36–39:

> O brightest! though too late for antique vows,
> Too, too late for the fond believing lyre,
> When holy were the haunted forest boughs,
> Holy the air, the water, and the fire.

16. Pages vi–xvi. It is interesting to notice that Taylor includes at the end of the book three Hymns of his own composition: to Venus, to Love, and to Neptune. In another of his books, *Sallust on the Gods and the World*, 1793, he includes, as well as translations of five Hymns by Proclus, five Hymns of his own composition: to Ceres, to Jupiter, to Minerva, to Vesta, and to Mercury. They are poor poems, and throw no light on the Hymns and Odes of Keats.

17. 'I stood tip-toe', line 149.

18. *The Golden Asse of Apuleius Done into English by William Adlington*, with an introduction by Thomas Seccombe, 1913, 137.

19. Op. cit. 62.

20. *The Temple of Nature*, p. 61.

21. *Letters*, ii. 133, 138, 223–4 and 278. Comparable images occur in several of the poems. In one of his sonnets to Haydon on the Elgin Marbles, for example, Keats praises Haydon for having seen the light 'Of their star in the East, and gone to worship them'. In his 'Lines on Seeing a Lock of Milton's Hair' Keats proclaims that he would like to

> . . . offer a burnt sacrifice of verse
> And melody

to the memory of Milton. In 'Sleep and Poetry' he says that he will hide 'In the very fane, the light of Poesy' (line 276). In the 'Ode on Melancholy' occur the more familiar lines:

> Ay, in the very temple of Delight
> Veil'd Melancholy has her sovran shrine.

In a letter to his sister, written very soon after the 'Ode to Psyche', Keats light-heartedly mentions, as one of a number of things that one can desire, 'a rocky basin to bathe in, a strawberry bed to say your prayers to Flora in' (*Letters*, ii. 56).

Similar images can occasionally be found in the writings of Keats's friends. Particularly striking, since Haydon was a devout Christian, is his description of how he once found himself praying to one of the fragments of the Elgin Marbles:

> As I looked at the Lapitha who grapples a Centaur [Plate XX], I dwelt on it with more intensity than ever. Its beauty, its divinity, came over my soul like the influence of an angelic spirit, & totally abstracted from the World and its affairs, I caught myself actually uttering a prayer to it! . . . All night its Divinity has beamed to my brain—never was I so impressed with its inspiration . . . (*Diary*, i. 479).

One is reminded of Goethe, who tells us that on Christmas Day, 1786, he offered his morning prayer to the colossal head of Jupiter. I owe the reference to Hatfield, op. cit. 102.

22. *The Indicator*, ii. 50 (22 Nov. 1820). An expert on Raphael tells me that Hunt took the anecdote from Vasari: that Vasari does not name 'sua Donna': and that one should not believe the story.

23. *The Symposium*, 196 E.

24. *The Descent of Liberty, A Mask; by Leigh Hunt, A New Edition*, 1816, 54–55.

25. The idea of the Fancy or Imagination as a gardener may come from Mrs. Tighe: cf. *Psyche*, last stanza:

> The page remains—but can the page restore
> The vanished bowers which Fancy taught to bloom?

C. W. Hagelman has related the end of Keats's poem to his study of the structure of the brain: *Keats–Shelley Journal* (New York), xi, Winter 1962, 73–82.

26. Note to iv. 48.

27. See F. A. Gruyer, *Raphael et l'Antiquité*, 2 vols., Paris (1864), ii. 169 ff.

28. *Imagination and Fancy*, 101.

29. *The Complete Works*, xvii. 149.

30. Ibid. x. 239.

31. These borders are not a background, in the usual sense. Indeed we find Leigh Hunt complaining of the 'singular absence of the love of rural nature' in Raphael, and commenting that 'a tree or so is an absolute godsend': *The Indicator*, 22 Nov. 1820.

32. *Lectures on Painting by the Royal Academicians: Barry, Opie, and Fuseli*, edited by Ralph N. Wornum, 1848, 390.

33. They are in the Royal Collection.

34. *Annals*, iii. 260 (a catalogue of Canova's works). When Severn

accompanied Keats to Italy he took with him a letter of introduction to Canova from Sir Thomas Lawrence.

35. In *Endymion*, i. 764–5, Keats refers to 'the fans Of careless butterflies'. Dryden also uses the word in the sense of 'wing'.

36. Cf. *Endymion*, iii. 21.

37. *Psyche*, iii. 21.

38. *John Keats*, 494–5.

39. *Polymetis*, 71.

40. *Letters*, ii. 106. It is difficult to imagine a picture in which 'Their arms embraced, *and their pinions too*' (line 16).

41. *Diary*, ii. 470 (cf. *Autobiography*, i. 351). The same story is elaborated in a letter to Miss Mitford. 'I dislike his selfish Quakerism, his affectation of superior virtue; his utter insensibility to the frailties—the beautiful frailties of passion. I was walking with him in Pall Mall; we darted into Christie's . . . . In the corner [there was] a beautiful copy of the "Cupid and Psyche" kissing. . . . You remember this exquisite group? . . . Wordsworth's face reddened, he showed his teeth, and then said in a loud voice, "THE DEV-V-V-VILS!" There's a mind! Ought not this exquisite group to have roused his "Shapes of Beauty", and have softened his heart as much as his old grey-mossed rocks, his withered thorn, and his dribbling mountain streams?'. Quoted by Eric George in *The Life and Death of . . . Haydon*, 138–9. George assumes that Haydon is referring to Canova's statue (Plate XXVII), but the reference may equally be to the celebrated ancient representation (Plate XXVIII).

42. *Letters*, ii. 63; cf. ii. 70. There are several other anti-clerical remarks in his letters about this time.

43. Sonnet 'Written in Disgust of Vulgar Superstition'.

CHAPTER XIII: 'ODE ON A GRECIAN URN'

1. *Laokoon and How the Ancients represented Death* by G. E. Lessing, 1914 (Bohn's Popular Library), 91–92; Haydon's *Diary*, ii. 215–16. Although the *Laokoon* was published in German in 1766, no English translation appeared until 1836. References to the book are not common at this period.

2. Cf. *Endymion*, iii. 32–33:

> And, silent as a consecrated urn,
> Hold sphery sessions for a season due.

3. Simonides's observation is quoted in the first number of the *Annals*, p. 8. Wordsworth often alludes to the remark: see an informative pamphlet, *Wordsworth's Interest in Painters and Pictures* by Martha Hale Shackford, Wellesley, Mass., 1945, 7. Miss Shackford points out that Wordsworth wrote poems on pictures by a dozen different painters (p. 73).

4. *Diary*, ii. 62 (25 Oct. 1816).

5. *Annals*, iv. 638–9 (no. 15, Jan. 1820).

6. I refer to *Oxford Prize Poems: Being A Collection of such English Poems as have at Various Times Obtained Prizes in the University of Oxford*, with illustrations, 8th ed., 1830.

7. The illustration first appears, without the text of the poem, in *Illustrations, historical and descriptive, of the Oxford Newdigate prize poems. With engravings* (Oxford, printed by W. Baxter, for R. Pearson, adjoining the town-hall. Sold also by Baldwin, Cradock, and Joy, Paternoster-Row, London. 1824). By about 1828 the *Illustrations* were bound up with the *Poems*.

8. *An Essay on Sculpture: In A Series of Epistles to John Flaxman, Esq., R.A.*, 1800, p. 86.

9. *Peintures de Vases antiques vulgairement appelés étrusques . . . gravées par A. Cléner accompagnées d'explications par A.-L. Millin*, 2 vols., Paris, 1808, 1810. The collection consists of painted vases only.

10. *The Keats Circle*, i. 253–60.

11. As Miss Ward emphasizes, it is a fact of some interest that Keats owned Baldwin's *Pantheon* (which was in fact the work of William Godwin). The full title of the first edition, which appeared in 1806, is *The Pantheon: or Ancient History of the Gods of Greece and Rome. For the Use of Schools, and young persons of both sexes. By Edward Baldwin*. The title-page also contains the following statement of purpose:

> The purpose of this book is to place the Heathen Mythology in two points of view: first, as it would have struck a Traveller in Greece, who wishe[d] to form a just conception of the Religion of the country, free from either favour or prejudice; secondly, regarding Mythology as the introduction and handmaid to the study of Poetry, the author has endeavoured to feel his subject in the spirit of a poet, and to communicate that feeling to others.

The Preface begins by stating that 'it is universally confessed that of all systems of mythology and religion, that of the Greeks is the most admirably adapted to the purposes of poetry'. Godwin attacks Tooke, whose work is said to be a mere translation of a French work by a Jesuit called Pomey. 'The author', Godwin observes of Pomey–Tooke, 'seems continually haunted by the fear that his pupil might prefer the religion of Jupiter to the religion of Christ.' 'It is the object of this volume to remedy' the shortcomings of Pomey–Tooke. 'As a collection of the most agreeable fables that ever were invented', the author continues, the study of ancient mythology 'is admirably calculated to awaken the imagination; imagination, which it cannot be too often repeated, is the great engine of morality.'

On the first page of the text itself we are told that 'one reason why the Gods of the Greeks are so interesting to us, is that the Greeks were the finest writers in the world; and they have said such fine things about their Gods, that nobody who is acquainted with their writings, can recollect these imaginary beings without emotions of pleasure.' On page 8 we read

that 'the language of the Greeks was the language of poetry: every thing
with them was alive: a man could not walk out in the fields, without being
in the presence of the Naiads, the Dryads, and the Fauns . . .' .

Here is Godwin's account of the story of Diana and Endymion:

Diana is said to have fallen in love . . ., though she were the Goddess of
Chastity; the object of her flame was Endymion, a shepherd of Caria:
she saw him naked on the top of mount Latmos, and thought she had
never beheld so beautiful a creature: as she was the most bashful and
modest of existing beings, she cast him into a deep sleep, that she might
kiss him unseen and undiscovered even by him she loved: every night
she visited the beautiful shepherd, whom Jupiter endowed with perpetual
youth, and every night she loved him better than the night before.

Godwin goes on to explain the story in a thoroughly conventional way:
'The meaning of the fable is, that Endymion was a great astronomer'
(p. 207).

On p. 37 we are told that 'the names of the Titans were Oceanus,
Cœus, Creus, Hyperion . . .'. On p. 48 we come on a passage that may
serve as a footnote on 'the true, the blushful Hippocrene':

Delphi . . . was sacred to the God Apollo: near to the town of Delphi
was the mountain Parnassus . .; at the foot of the mountain, and near
to the oracle, flowed the Castalian stream, the waters of which were
supposed to communicate inspiration . . . [and nearby] was the fountain
Hippocrene, on a spot which Pegasus . . . having struck with his hoof,
this fountain rushed out [Ovid, *Met.* v. 256], the waters of which were
violet-coloured, and are represented as endowed with voice and articu-
late sound.

All editions are dedicated to the Reverend Matthew Raine, D.D., Master
of the Charterhouse School. A note at the top of the title-page of the
second edition (1809) proclaims that the book has been 'Adopted in the
Charterhouse School', perhaps superseding Tooke. A third edition appeared in 1810, and a fourth in 1814. Some of the plates are changed between one edition and another: in the first and fourth editions, for example,
Venus is clothed: in the second and third she is naked.

12. *Letters,* ii. 64.

13. *Outlines,* 3. Since Keats uses the word 'leaf-fring'd', it is worth
remembering that when these urns and vases were engraved the band of
ornamental leaves often found round the handles was commonly made into
a rectangular border surrounding the whole design, as Kirk points out on
page ii of his introduction: 'The various beautiful borders which surround
these designs, were not so placed in the original vases, but served there,
merely to ornament the handles, and other parts; nor were the border and
figures, which are upon the same Plate in this work, always upon the
same vase.'

14. *Diary,* i. 461.

15. *The Botanic Garden,* 1791, 88.

16. These engravings are sometimes ascribed to Blake. In *Bibliotheca*

Bibliographici, 1964, Sir Geoffrey Keynes limits himself to saying (p. 70) that the four engravings of the Portland Vase are unsigned, whereas the other five engravings in vol. i are the work of Blake (one after Fuseli).

17. *Diary*, ii. 382.

18. This has been the conclusion of everyone who has looked into the matter: see (for example) *John Keats* by Sidney Colvin, 415–18, and *The Romantic Imagination* by C. M. Bowra, 2nd impression, 1957, 128 ff. Paul Wolters reached a generally similar conclusion in his article, 'Keats' Grecian Urn', *Archiv für das Studium der neueren Sprachen und Literaturen*, LXII. Jg., CXX. Band (der neueren Serie XX. Band), Braunschweig, 1908, 53–61.

19. *Lord Byron and Some of his Contemporaries*, 2nd ed., 1828, i. 434.

20. As these black-figured and red-figured vases (unlike the marble urns) often portray two scenes, it is tempting to consider the possibility that Keats was in fact thinking of one of them; and if what he had in mind was an engraving, the transmutation (conscious or unconscious) to marble would have been easily made. But two facts tell against this. One is simply that no painted vase with the two scenes in question has yet been adduced. The other is that it would have been unusual (at least) to call a painted vase an 'urn' at this time. The usual distinction is brought out in the introduction to Kirk's *Outlines*, where we are told that whereas the ashes of the lower classes 'were carried from the funeral pile and put into vases . . ., the higher classes had their ashes put into marble urns highly sculptured' (p. xi).

While painted vases were seldom called 'urns', marble urns were very often referred to as 'vases', as may be seen in the present chapter and in the Appendix. I owe this point to Professor R. M. Cook.

21. Cf. *Endymion*, i. 405–6 and ii. 200.

22. The copy by Keats, which is now in the Keats–Shelley Memorial House in Rome, is almost exactly the same size as the engraving in *Les Monumen[t]s antiques du Musée Napoléon, dessinés et gravés par Thomas Piroli, avec une explication par M.͏ʳ Louis Petit Radel, Publiés par F. et P. Piranesi*, vol. ii, Paris, 1804 (plate xxii). But although it has been described as a tracing, there are slight differences of detail between the two: for example the dancing maiden carries a tambourine in Piroli, but not in Keats. As Mr. Noel Machin has pointed out (*The Observer*, colour supplement, 28 Feb. 1965), this and other details in the Keats copy correspond fairly closely to plate 38 in *A Collection of Antique Vases* [1814] by Henry Moses. If Moses is the source, it cannot be a tracing, as his engraving is considerably smaller than the copy by Keats. It seems likely that what we have is either a tracing from some other engraving of the Sosibios Vase, or (more probably) a free-hand drawing by Keats.

Dilke appears to be our authority for attributing the copy to Keats.

23. There is a Wedgwood plaque, based on the Borghese Vase, in which the border of leaves goes round all four sides. It is possible that Keats saw this, and certain that he must have known some of the fine Wedgwood

copies of vases and other works of art produced at this time. I have looked, without success, for a Wedgwood Vase with the two scenes on it which Keats describes. The fact that the Wedgwood reproductions are valuable works of art in their own right is borne out by the fact that one of their copies of the Portland Vase was sold at Christie's in 1964 for 2,900 gns.

The possibility of a Wedgwood original for the Urn occurred to me independently of Dwight E. Robinson's interesting article, 'Ode on a "New Etruscan" Urn: A Reflection of Wedgwood Ware in the Poetic Imagery of John Keats' (Keats–Shelley Journal, New York, xii (Winter 1963), 11–35. I must record my disagreement with much in Dr. Robinson's article.

There was a display of vases from the Louvre in London in 1816. A writer in the Annals of the Fine Arts refers to this (i. 180–1), while a later writer mentions that he 'cannot forget the splendid marble vase' that he saw on that occasion (v. 418). It is tempting to wonder whether the Borghese Vase could have been among the exhibits, but Mme Adhémar tells me that the Louvre authorities have no record of such a loan (or indeed of any loan at this time), and that it is unlikely, as the Borghese Vase was not acquired until 'vers 1811–1815'.

24. There was something about the lowing of cattle that made a deep appeal to Keats. 'The effect of cattle lowing I never had so finely', he remarked in a letter from Scotland (Letters, i. 329), and see the passage quoted above on p. 220.

25. It is, of course, possible that Keats saw a book of engravings of vases or urns in which two with the scenes described in the Ode were given on the same page, or on facing pages. Plate 30 in the second volume of Montfaucon's Antiquity Explained (1721), for example, has seven horizontal rows of figures. The top and bottom rows are taken from the Borghese Vase, while the five rows between them contain figures from a long sacrificial procession. In one row we see a bull being led to sacrifice, while at least two of the others are markedly Bacchanalian in character. But the bull is not lowing, there is no close correspondence to the scenes which Keats describes, and the 'legend' is not 'leaf-fring'd'. (The view that Keats was remembering the 'heifer' in the Elgin Marbles is by no means a novel one.)

26. Annals, iv. 566. Colvin reproduces the 'Landscape with the Father of Psyche . . .' (as 'A Sacrifice to Apollo'), and mentions its importance (op. cit. 417). It was exhibited at the British Institution in 1816.

27. Annals, iv. 228–9, quoting The Antiquities of Greece, i, pp. 217 and 231, on sacrificial processions.

28. There is a reference to a sister of Sir Joshua Reynolds as being a great 'collector of processions' (i.e. pictures of processions) in a curious satirical poem on print-collecting published in 1814: Chalcographimania; or, the Portrait-Collector and Printseller's Chronicle, with Infatuations of every Description by Satiricus Sculptor (W. H. Ireland), 143.

29. See Jean Seznec, *Essais sur Diderot et l'Antiquité*, Oxford, 1957, 62.

30. See also the Appendix to the present study, on the 'Ode on Indolence'.

31. *An Historical Guide to The Sculptures of the Parthenon*, published by the Trustees of the British Museum, 1962, 22.

32. *The Works*, i. 105.

33. *The Earlier English Water-Colour Painters*, 1890, cited by Miss Shackford, p. 32.

34. Reminiscences by Christopher Wordsworth, Jr., in *The Prose Works of William Wordsworth*, edited by A. B. Grosart, 1876, iii. 464–5.

35. *The Letters of William and Dorothy Wordsworth: The Middle Years*, edited by Ernest de Sélincourt, 1937, ii. 468.

36. There is no evidence to indicate whether the poem was all written at one time. If it originally consisted of only the first three stanzas, it would have been the same length as the Ode to Autumn and the 'Ode on Melancholy' (as the latter was printed, without the rejected opening stanza). It is a striking fact that the conclusion would then have resembled that of the 'Ode to a Nightingale', if not also that of the 'Ode on Melancholy'. At the end of the 'Ode to a Nightingale' the song of the bird dies away in the distance and Keats feels cheated by the failure of his 'fancy':

> Was it a vision, or a waking dream?
> Fled is that music:—Do I wake or sleep?

Similarly the third stanza of the 'Ode on a Grecian Urn' ends with the poet claiming that the eternal passion of the lovers on the urn is

> All breathing human passion far above,
> That leaves a heart high-sorrowful and cloy'd,
> A burning forehead, and a parching tongue.

This is (after all) a very natural way to end a poem inspired by a work of art (or by the music of a bird's song). We find a similar ending in Southey's lines 'On a Landscape of Gaspar Poussin'. In a 'lonely hour' the painting has come to his rescue:

> . . . My willing soul
> All eager follows on thy faery flights,
> Fancy! best friend. . . .
> . . . Well it is sometimes
> That thy delusions should beguile the heart,
> Sick of reality.

So the poet willingly enters the world of the picture—only to feel a sense of anti-climax at the end:

> . . . Delightful thoughts
> That soothe the solitude of weary Hope,
> Yet leave her to reality awaked,
> Like the poor captive, from some fleeting dream
> Of friends and liberty and home restored,
> Startled, and listening as the midnight storm
> Beats hard and heavy through his dungeon bars.
>   (*The Poetical Works*, n.d., ii. 221–3)

37. A poem by William Lisle Bowles, for example, *The Picture*, describes Rubens's 'Landscape with Castle Steen' in Thomsonian blank verse, and contains a good deal of moralizing. He says that everything in this 'richest rural poem' is Subserving to one magical effect / Of truth and harmony.

The poem was well known at this time. See pp. 240–1 above.

38. I have not found a translation of the poem by this time, but Keats might easily have heard of it in conversation. It is hard to believe that his knowledge of Schiller was confined to *The Robbers* (which everyone knew) and *The Armenian; Or, The Ghost Seer*, to which he refers in a letter (*Letters*, ii. 173 and note).

39. Epistle 'To George Felton Mathew', 51–52.

40. *A Collection of Antique Vases*, 7.

41. *The Works*, i. 86. Quoted in *Annals*, i. 18.

42. There is no end to the parallels that have been cited, from Plato to Hazlitt, from Boileau's 'Rien n'est beau que le vrai' (*Épître*, IX, l. 43) to Shaftesbury's '*all* Beauty is TRUTH' (*Sensus Communis*, IV. iii). I have been particularly struck by a passage in J. G. Cooper's *Letters concerning Taste* (2nd ed., 1755, 7–8):

> The ALMIGHTY has . . . so *attun'd* our Minds to Truth, that all Beauty from without should make a responsive Harmony vibrate within. . . .
> *Truth* is the Cause of all Beauty;

—and by the way in which Akenside makes a sort of Trinity of Beauty, Truth and Goodness in more than one passage of *The Pleasures of Imagination*, notably at i. 372–5:

> . . . Thus was beauty sent from heaven,
> The lovely ministress of truth and good
> In this dark world: for truth and good are one,
> And beauty dwells in them, and they in her,
> With like participation

and at i. 414–7:

> . . . The eternal shrine,
> Where truth conspicuous with her sister-twins,
> The undivided partners of her sway,
> With good and beauty reigns.
>
> (Text 'As First Published')

See also ii. 66–67 and 97–99. Although Keats apparently told Severn that he hated Akenside (p. 169 above), it is clear that he had read him with some attention.

As Dr. E. L. Stahl pointed out in a letter to *The Times Literary Supplement* (19 March 1964), 'the relation between Beauty and Truth was widely discussed in the eighteenth century, not least in Germany', and it forms 'the central part of the argument in Schiller's long poem *Die Künstler* of 1789, in which he asserts that man *on earth* cannot apprehend truth except in its sensuous form, that is in the shape of beauty:

> Was wir als Schönheit hier empfunden,
> Wird einst als Wahrheit uns entgegengehn.'

Coleridge once wrote that beauty is 'the shorthand hieroglyphic of truth—the mediator between truth and feeling, the head and the heart, a silent communion of the Spirit with the Spirit in Nature'. But this passage was not published: it occurs in a note printed by J. H. Muirhead in *Coleridge as Philosopher*, 1930, 195. Such speculations were in the air at the time.

Whatever sources Keats may have had for the famous affirmation of his Urn, his letters make it clear that the conclusion of the Ode was inspired by his own persistent uncertainty about his capacity for philosophical speculation.

In November 1817, writing to Benjamin Bailey, Keats refers to 'the great Consolations of Religion and undepraved Sensations. of the Beautiful. the poetical in all things' (*Letters*, i. 179). A few days later he tells Bailey, a convinced Christian, that he himself is 'certain of nothing but of the holiness of the Heart's affections and the truth of Imagination', adding that 'What the imagination seizes as Beauty must be truth—whether it existed before or not.' He explains his meaning by saying that 'the Imagination may be compared to Adam's dream—he awoke and found it truth' (i. 184–5). He says that he is insisting on this point because he has 'never yet been able to perceive how any thing can be known for truth by consequitive reasoning'. He is defending his own, intuitive, method of speculation.

Towards the end of the same year Keats tells his brothers that 'the excellence of every Art is its intensity, capable of making all disagreeables evaporate, from their being in close relationship with Beauty & Truth' (i. 192). Contrasting himself with Dilke and Coleridge, he isolates '*Negative Capability*' as the great characteristic of a poet, who must be capable of 'remaining content with half knowledge'. 'With a great poet' —he adds—'the sense of Beauty overcomes every other consideration, or rather obliterates all consideration' (i. 194). Three months later, writing to Bailey again, he admits that he has not 'one Idea of the truth of any of my speculations', adding that he will 'never be a Reasoner' (i. 243).

We may compare with these passages the letter in which Keats tells John Taylor that he has 'been hovering for some time between an exquisite sense of the luxurious and a love for Philosophy'. He now continues: 'Were I calculated for the former I should be glad—but as I am not I shall turn all my soul to the latter' (i. 271). Here 'the luxurious' has an affinity with Beauty, and 'Philosophy' with Truth. This I would associate with his determination to write the most serious kind of poetry. In October 1818, in the same letter in which he refers to his 'mighty abstract Idea . . . of Beauty in all things', there is a key passage in which he says that if only his brothers could be fit and happy then he himself would be 'most enviable —with the yearning Passion I have for the beautiful, connected and made one with the ambition of my intellect' (i. 403–4). It was when he felt incapable of such a connexion that he doubted his own poetic powers.

A little later we find his sense of his own intellectual limitations recurring, when he says that he 'never can feel certain of any truth but from a clear perception of its beauty' (ii. 19). In March 1819 he remarks that poetry is 'not so fine a thing as philosophy', any more than 'an eagle is

. . . so fine a thing as a truth'. He is now striving to see the truth of Milton's lines in *Comus*:

How charming is divine Philosophy
Not harsh and crabbed as dull fools suppose
But musical as is Apollo's lute.   (ii. 81)

Truth is Beauty, in fact. Keats wanted to believe that—to reach some high ground of thought and insight from which the truth of the proposition would become evident to him.

It seems to me that the statement that 'Beauty is truth' represents something that Keats believed, while the statement that 'truth [is] beauty' represents something that he *wanted* to believe—but only occasionally managed to believe, much as if it were an article of religious faith.

CHAPTER XIV: MONETA

1. 33rd edition, 1810, 86. An alternative reason for the title is that Juno 'was believed to be the goddess of money'.

2. *Letters*, ii. 171–2. Reynolds was staying with Woodhouse in Bath, and Keats knew that the two letters would be read by both men: cf. ibid. 169.

3. *Life of John Keats* by Charles Armitage Brown, edited by D. H. Bodurtha and W. B. Pope, 1937, 62. Cf. *The Keats Circle*, ii. 72. Unfortunately Brown does not give a precise date.

4. Keats quotes ten and a half lines in the letter to Woodhouse, and comments: 'Here is what I had written for a sort of induction.' It seems clear that the 'induction' is the first paragraph of the poem only, consisting of eighteen lines in all. Some modern critics use the term to refer to a longer passage at the beginning of *The Fall*, with confusing results.

5. *Letters*, i. 223–4.

6. *Diary*, ii. 317.

7. *Hyperion* is clearly epic in its essential nature, even if we accept de Sélincourt's view (ed. cit. 487) that Keats soon modified his intention of writing a full-length epic.

8. *Diary*, i. [14]. When Benjamin West died, on the 10th of March 1820, a cast was made of his right hand, which was holding a pencil. As John Young commented in *A Catalogue of Pictures by British Artists, in the possession of Sir John Fleming Leicester* (1821, p. 18): 'Whatever may have been his thoughts at the awful moment of dissolution, it is evident, from the obvious action of the hand, that the disposition to express those thoughts by the pencil was his ruling passion.'

9. *Publications of the Modern Language Association of America*, li. (1936), p. 1109.

10. Whether or not the apotheosis of Apollo was to have been described in *The Fall*—and we must assume that it was—we note that in this version the dreamer himself suffers a torture in some ways analogous to that inflicted on Apollo in *Hyperion*. As he struggles to climb the great

flight of steps that leads up to the lofty altar he goes through the experience of dying before death.

Keats may here have been remembering a line in the *Fasti*: 'Qua fert sublimes alta Moneta gradus'—'Where high Moneta lifts her steps sublime' (i. 638).

11. *The Fall of Hyperion*, i. 331 and ii. 50.

12. In Schiller's poem, 'Das verschleierte Bild zu Sais' ('The Veiled Image at Saïs'), a young man is driven to Egypt by his passion for knowledge—

> Ein Jüngling, den des Wissens heißer Durst
> Nach Sais in Ägypten trieb. . . .

—There he finds a lonely temple in which there is a veiled image. He asks a priest what is behind the veil, and receives the reply: 'Die Wahrheit'. Although he is warned not to disturb the veil, which is of gauze, he draws near, only to feel a strange chill seizing on him as he is about to profane the sanctuary, and an unseen hand repulsing him:

> Er tritt hinan mit ungewissem Schritt—
> Schon will die freche Hand das Heilige berühren,
> Da zuckt es heiß und kühl durch sein Gebein
> Und stößt ihn weg mit unsichtbarem Arme.

We are not told what he sees when he draws the veil aside, but only that the priests find him next day lying senseless and pale by the pedestal of the statue of Isis. He knows no further happiness during the brief period of life that remains to him. The similarity to *The Fall of Hyperion* is striking.

13. Op. cit., p. 340.

CHAPTER XV: 'TO AUTUMN'

1. *Memoirs of the Life of John Constable*, by C. R. Leslie (Phaidon Press edition, 1951), editor's preface, p. ix.

2. 'The Greek poets, then, did not describe the scenery of nature in a picturesque manner, because they were not accustomed to see it with a painter's eye. Undoubtedly they were not blind to all the beauties of such scenes, but those beauties were not heightened to them, as they are to us, by comparison with painting—with those models of improved and selected nature which it is the business of the landscape painter to exhibit. They had no Thomsons, because they had no Claudes . . .'. Thomas Twining, *Aristotle's Treatise on Poetry, Translated* (1789), in *Eighteenth-Century Critical Essays*, edited by Scott Elledge, New York, 1961, ii. 1001.

Mr. D. S. Bland has written on the general affinity between the Ode to Autumn and Constable in two short articles: *Philological Quarterly*, xxxiii. 219–22, and *English*, viii. 75–78.

3. My references are to *Endymion*, i. 56, i. 439–41, i. 991, ii. 416, iv. 422–3, and iv. 814.

4. 'I always somehow associate Chatterton with autumn', Keats observes in a letter, just after writing the passage about 'To Autumn' quoted at

the beginning of this chapter, and just before telling Reynolds that he has given up *Hyperion* (*Letters*, ii. 167). The quotation from Chatterton is from *Ælla* (*The Works*, 1803, ii. 218): that from Shakespeare's twelfth sonnet occurs in an earlier letter to Reynolds (i. 189).

5. Part I, section i, member iii, subsection ii.

6. *Autumn*, line 1,005.

7. *Correspondence of Thomas Gray*, edited by Paget Toynbee and Leonard Whibley, 1935, i. 241.

8. 'Four seasons fill the measure of the year', lines 11–12.

9. The idea of the 'music' of a season is, of course, a commonplace. It is to be found in *The Seasons*, and also in *The Natural History of the Year* (see p. 292 n. 17 below), p. 153: 'Those sweet and mellow-toned songsters, the woodlark, thrush, and blackbird, commence at this time [September] their autumnal music.'

10. Poussin's painting, which is in the Wallace Collection, is reproduced and discussed in Denis Mahon's *Poussiniana*, 1962, and in Friedlaender, op. cit., p. 42. Cf. Claude's 'Landscape with Apollo and the Seasons dancing to the Music of Time' (Röthlisberger, fig. 328), and *Paradise Lost*, iv. 267.

11. *The Golden Asse*, ed. cit. 129.

12. It is now thought that the Edinburgh picture is more likely to represent Summer than Autumn. Such uncertainty is common, in the case of personifications of these two seasons. As it is a recent acquisition, the Vouet landscape is not included in the volume of *National Gallery Illustrations: Continental Schools* (*excluding Italian*) published in 1937. My search for an engraving of Giulio Romano's 'Psyche' has so far been unsuccessful.

13. 'Ceres was represented with a garland of ears of corn on her head, holding in one hand a lighted torch, and in the other a poppy, which was sacred to her.' Lemprière's *Classical Dictionary*, 1804, article on Ceres. Cf. Montfaucon's *Antiquity Explained*, 1721, i. 58 and ii. 47.

14. *The Seasons Illustrated with engravings by F. Bartolozzi and P. W. Tomkins . . . from original pictures . . . by William Hamilton R.A.*, 1807.

15. Cf. Montfaucon, i. 53: 'The *Canephora*, or Figure with a Basket on her Head, is one of those Virgins which are consecrated to *Ceres*, and called *Canephoræ*, because they carried Baskets of Fruits on their Heads.'

16. Arnold Davenport has argued that Keats remembered the Book of Ruth as he wrote the poem: 'A Note on "To Autumn"', in *John Keats: A Reassessment*, edited by Kenneth Muir, 1950. If there is anything in my suggestion, perhaps Keats thought of the young woman among the corn as Ruth (rather than the figure kneeling before Boaz).

In the case of this fine painting I have allowed myself to depart from my usual principle of reproducing works of art in the form in which they are most likely to have been known to Keats. The painting can have been known to him only in a print, such as that in vol. iv. of the *Galerie du Musée de France*, 1814 (no. 256).

17. *The Natural History of the Year. Being an Enlargement of Dr. Aikin's Calendar of Nature. By Arthur Aikin*, 4th edition, 1815. I quote from p. 135. An unspecified edition of the book occurs in Charles Brown's list of Keats's books: *The Keats Circle*, i. 254.

18. Aikin, 155.

19. *The Art of Discrimination: Thomson's 'The Seasons' and the Language of Criticism*, 1964, 250.

20. In the catalogue of the Royal Academy Exhibition of 1829, for example, Constable's 'Hadleigh Castle' was accompanied by the following lines from *Summer*:

> . . . The desert joys
> Wildly, through all his melancholy bounds,
> Rude ruins glitter; and the briny deep,
> Seen from some pointed promontory's top,
> Far to the blue horizon's utmost verge,
> Restless, reflects a floating gleam.

In his last lecture Constable 'quoted from Thomson's *Seasons* the sixteen introductory lines to the "Winter" as a beautiful instance of the poet identifying his own feelings with external nature'. *Memoirs of the Life of John Constable* by C. R. Leslie, 1951, 328. Cf. Geoffrey Grigson, op. cit., p. 263.

21. Cohen, 259–60.

22. This effect of clouds opening to reveal the gods and goddesses of classical antiquity was a favourite with Keats. Cf. pp. 126–7 above.

23. The edition is undated. Cohen dates it '1770?' (p. 266).

24. See p. 21 above.

25. *Catalogue of . . . Pictures contained in the National Gallery*, 1834, 240–4.

26. 'The Ode "To Autumn"' by B. C. Southam in the *Keats–Shelley Journal* (New York), vol. ix, part 2, Autumn 1960, 97.

27. Page 243 (Landseer's italics).

28. *Letters*, ii. 106.

29. *Keats and Shakespeare*, third impression, 1935, 189; *Revaluation*, 1936, 262–3.

30. *Letters*, i. 143.

31. Ibid. ii. 200.

32. *Diary*, i. 180.

APPENDIX

1. In a general way it may remind us of the Judgment of Paris, and of the Choice of Hercules. The latter is the subject of the only original poem in *Polymetis* (pp. 155–62), a composition in ten-line stanzas of which a line here and there may have appealed to Keats:

> For thou art only tir'd with indolence:
> Nor is thy sleep with toil and labour bought;
> Th'imperfect sleep, that lulls thy languid sense
> In dull oblivious interval of thought:
> That kindly steals th'inactive hours away
> From the long, lingring space, that lengthens out the day.
>
> (st. xvii)

As Spence remarks, 'choices' of this allegorical kind are frequent in classical literature (pp. 142–3).

We may also compare the design of the poem with that of an 'Intended Monument for Thomson' in Robert Heron's well-known edition of *The Seasons* (Perth, 1793). This shows the poet reclining on one elbow, watched by a Muse, on top of the tomb, which rests on a catafalque with sculptural representations of three female figures, hand-in-hand and classically dressed, who mourn the dead poet. Beside them we see an old man, Saturn or Time.

2. *John Keats*, by Sidney Colvin, pp. 414–15.

3. The vase is illustrated in a double-spread engraving in vol. i.

4. As Garrod points out in his edition (p. 447 n.), there is some uncertainty about the correct order of the stanzas of the Ode.

INDEX

As a rule, names occurring in the notes are listed in the index only if they do not also occur in the relevant passage of the book. The index excludes the Preface.

PRINTED IN GREAT BRITAIN
AT THE UNIVERSITY PRESS, OXFORD
BY VIVIAN RIDLER
PRINTER TO THE UNIVERSITY